IN SEARCH of LOST TIME

A LITERARY MEMOIR BY A VIETNAMESE AMERICAN SCHOLAR

Qui-Phiet Tran

Copyright © 2024 by Qui-Phiet Tran

ISBN: 978-1-950186-55-6

All rights reserved. No part of this publication may be reproduced or transmitted in any form or by any means, mechanical or electronic, including photocopying and recording, or by any information storage and retrieval system, without permission in writing from the author and/or publisher.

All permissions are held by the author, who releases the publisher from all liability. The content is the sole responsibility of the author, and he indemnifies the publisher from any legal claims.

Cover image: Dalat Pine Forest, by Xuan Hiep Vo

MANDORLA BOOKS
WWW.MANDORLABOOKS.COM

PRAISE FOR *IN SEARCH OF LOST TIME*

Qui-Phiet Tran has crafted an extraordinary memoir, weaving together memory and meditation, literature and lived experience, religion and reminiscence, into a rich tale that is at once authentically Vietnamese and profoundly American. Here is love and loss, family and fear, scenes of shocking violence and serene moments of solitude. Though it follows a general forward chronology, the narrative is connected more by memory than by time, so that something like a Van Gogh painting emerges, layers of text that create an impression of tremendous depth, each emotional and historical layer dependent on the layers beneath. I found this book deeply moving, and our world is enriched by its existence.

~Samuel Snoek-Brown, Ph.D.
Associate Professor of English at Pierce College and author of
Hagridden and *There Is No Other Way to Worship Them*

Through memory and imagination, Qui-Phiet Tran vividly recounts his quest to recapture a personal past that is rooted in his native land's tragic history. Marcel Proust and William Faulkner, Tran's literary mentors, would nod their approval.

~Chip Dameron, Ph.D.
Former Vice-President for Academic Affairs at
The University of Texas at Brownsville and author of
Waiting for an Etcher, *China Sketchbook*, and *Mornings with Dobie's Ghost*

Qui-Phiet Tran's book unsparingly touches many Vietnamese souls in exile. It shows that their past or home is not lost but lives on within themselves. As Tran puts it in the Epilogue, the past is "incarnate in the present." This alluring theme subtly echoes Proust and Faulkner, who have a profound influence on Tran's writing. I am in love with this fascinating memoir and feel the impetus to study these two giants in Western modern literature.

~Lê Thị Huệ, publisher and editor,
Gio-O Literary Journal, San Jose, California

To the memory of my father

TABLE OF CONTENTS

Preface i
Foreword iii
Prologue: My Years of Reading Proust and Faulkner v
Paradise Lost: Dalat 1
Displacement 13
Quảng Bình 18
Escape to Đồng Hới 26
Pangs of First Love 33
Huế 44
Dalat: Home Sweet Home 73
The Road of Life 79
Saigon 96
Of Hearth and Home 109
The Tết Offensive 116
Via Dolorosa 133
Via Dolorosa (Continued): America 139
University of Texas at Austin 142
America Day by Day 145
The Greatest Calamity 171
American Travelogue 182
"Solveig's Song" 198
My Father's Death 203
Ancestral Debt 208
Exile's Return (I) 223
In Search of Lost Time (I) 233

In Search of Lost Time (II)..250
Illness...264
Exile's Return (II): Vietnam Diary...268
In Search of Lost Time (III)...301
Paradise Regained: Dalat..311
Epilogue: Why I Write 327
Works Cited..332

PREFACE

The idea of writing this book was born after I was released from the hospital following an intensive cancer treatment. Later, it became a strong desire after I returned from my Fulbright teaching appointment at Vietnam National University where I had ample opportunity to search for my past. The more I became aware of my mortality, the more I felt the urgency of my project.

During my preparation of the memoir, I discovered that my book would not have enough room for all that I wanted to say. There is more to say about Vietnam than about America, where I spent more years of my life than in my native country. Though Vietnam was now a new country that I could hardly recognize, ironically, it appeared so familiar to me. I swam in a sea of memories, everything evoked a new aspect, a new meaning which I didn't see then.

That is the kind of memoir I have chosen for my project. I don't care much about recovering facts as about *remembering* them. Memories, when evoked, metastasize like wildfires. Proust's world, when remembered, gets so large that having written 4,000 pages about the search for lost time, he still wants to start over. What has Proust discovered that makes him so excited about rewriting his book? It is the depths within himself where his unfathomable past lies. The search for lost time never ends.

This memoir is not only my personal search for lost time but also a record of an unrecoverable lost world for many Vietnamese people in exile. Writing in my working language, I discover that the language of exile and sorrow is a universal language and it is appropriate for me to share my work with those whose native language is not Vietnamese.

This book is respectfully dedicated to the memory of two persons at the University of Huế who had helped me turn things around in my life and my academic career. Professor Lê Tuyên granted me asylum in his Faculty of Education upon my return from Saigon. Professor Lê Thanh Minh Châu, President of the University of Huế, not only sent me to the States for graduate study but also provided moral and material support for my family at home. Acknowledgment is due to the U.S. Fulbright Scholar Program, which granted me a teaching fellowship at Vietnam National University after my illness recovery. The appointment gave me plenty of free time to observe Vietnam and was crucial to my preparation for my book. I am also indebted to the ACLS (American Council of Learned Societies) for a grant to do research on Proust and Eudora Welty. My work was interrupted due to a tragedy in my family, but the Proust-related project which I have accomplished now, according to me, is more important and rewarding than the original one.

It is important for any publishing author to thank his or her editor. It has been a great pleasure to work with Jennifer Leigh Selig. Not only has she tried to keep my voice almost intact in my memoir, she has painstakingly gone over my inchoate writing and made it shine as much as it can.

I could not have thought about writing this book, let alone complete it, without my family. I thank my four precious sons, Quốc-Hưng, Gia-Thụy, Phúc-Long, and Phúc-Kiến, who diligently helped their mother take good care of their grandfather during my absence and who have shown their steadfast devotion to me and their mother since our reunification in the States. Next, my profound indebtedness and love go to my dear wife Võ Thị Ngân. She has always been by my side, making sure I am well attended to. Without her, I would not have been who I am today. The last person I pay tribute to is my late father, Mr. Trần Quí Bút, whose many sacrifices I could not appreciate well enough in words. To him I owed my life, my happiness, my security. I wrote this book because of him.

A word has to be said about the characters in my book. A memoirist is supposed to deal with real characters and to tell truths about them. While I sing the praises of my angels, I also refer to those who hurt me. Although most of them are dead now, I changed their identity to protect them. Because my characters are many, I could have missed doing this for some people. But in my thinking, all rancor, if any, is futile. The cruel world we lived in no longer exists.

My final acknowledgment is due to the authors whose work appears in my book. Because it is impossible for me to contact individual authors, I would like to ask them to accept this statement as an apology and a tribute to them for making their wartime writing part of the flowering of South Vietnamese literature in the 1960 through mid-1970s period.

Qui-Phiet Tran, Ph.D.
Professor Emeritus of English at Schreiner University in Kerrville, TX
Houston, TX / Garden Grove, CA
October 2024

FOREWORD

I admire and respect Qui-Phiet Tran. He has been a friend since the time we met at Rice University one summer many years ago. It was a rich literary conference on "William Faulkner and Modern Critical Theory," hosted by Professors Frank Lentricchia and Wesley Morris. Twelve of us had been selected for this NEH event that lasted for one week. Phiet and I often talked about the great value of Faulkner's worldview and his rich insights into history and myth.

I remember being favorably impressed by Phiet's grasp of the deep stories Faulkner expressed in his fiction and prose writing. Phiet's writing exploring Faulkner's regional southern world was equally enlightening and thought-provoking.

As a participant, he was not only passionate in expressing his point of view; he was respectful of others and listened with a gentle openness.

We remained in contact during his illustrious and successful tenure as a Professor of English at Schreiner University in Kerrville, Texas, not far from our home in New Braunfels, Texas.

His epic memoir stands as a testament to a life richly lived, with great mindfulness and exquisite soulfulness. In it he recounts, among other themes, his deep relationship with mentors Marcel Proust and William Faulkner.

In the final pages of his memoir and the Epilogue, "Why I Write," one discovers the healing qualities he gained from reading these writers, wherein he found "compatibility in the dark literary figures" they created, which helped alleviate the sorrows of exile when he returned to Vietnam in 1995.

He learned on this essential return to his origins that he was there to recover the ancestors, to give them a place in history: only by writing about his lost world, he knew, "will it be kept alive."

He grasps with elegant insightful writing, that "reading Proust makes me understand why even insignificant things have a mystery and a soul of their own...." And there, in his much-beloved home, he finds the model for his book: "It is simply exhuming the past to love and remember."

Readers of this rich literary memoir will be enchanted and transported by such a soul who believes that writing down the past, not just speaking about it, will ensure its survival. Such literary wisdom is Phiet's gift to us as we recollect our own mythic journey.

~Dennis Patrick Slattery, Ph.D.

Distinguished Professor Emeritus in Mythological Studies,
Pacifica Graduate Institute and author, most recently, of
The Fictions in Our Convictions: Essays on the Cultural Imagination

PROLOGUE

My Years of Reading Proust and Faulkner

By now anyone who wishes to write about time, memory, and the anguish of the soul, particularly obsession, should read Marcel Proust's *À la recherche du temps perdu* [*Remembrance of Things Past*]. I had read Proust's classic several years before I wrote my book. Phyllis Rose, in *The Year of Reading Proust,* says that she "began to see a grand historical theme for my novel 9on the Belle Époque) while I was reading Proust." Rose explains Proust's appeal as follows: "Proust seemed to have many things he wanted to say, or rather to explain, about human nature, and I wanted to hear" and "what I looked forward to most [when reading Proust] were revelations about myself." André Aciman also says in an interview: "To read Proust is to read oneself." Because I was writing a literary memoir/autobiographical novel about exile and home that had a lot to do with memory and time and mental anguish, I wanted to learn how to do it by reading Proust. Although reading Proust to understand myself is important, it is not as important as knowing the world in which I live and understanding what has preoccupied the human mind since time immemorial, that is, time and memory, and many other things related to human nature, the human mind, and the human world.

The first thing that intrigues me in Proust's novel is the relation of obsession and memory. Proust's character that best illustrates this theme is Albertine, Marcel's most mysterious girlfriend. Though Marcel's love of her was ambiguous and intermittent when she was living, she became a perpetual obsession with him after death. What makes men remember their dead lovers most, Proust says, is their "human bodies." "[B]ecause they contain thus within themselves the hours of the past," Proust explains, "*human bodies* have the power to hurt so terribly those who love them, because they contain the memories of so many joys and desires already effaced for them, but *still cruel for the lover who contemplates and prolongs in the dimension of Time the beloved body of which he is jealous, so jealous that he may even wish for its destruction"* (emphasis added). The quoted passage shows the formidable power of memory when it becomes permanent obsession. But contrary to Proust's description of the use of involuntary memory to evoke *moments bienheureux* (delightful moments) of the past earlier in the novel, in the remaining pages of *The Past Recaptured* he concentrates on the relation of memory and obsession. What torments Marcel is not his anguished remembrance of Albertine after her death but her "beloved body" that haunts him. What does her body have to make him so jealous after death? I think this has something to do with her freedom from him because her *"beloved body"* no longer belongs to him. Also, because time leaves Albertine's body after death, her memories are passed to her living lover for him to bear and to suffer alone.

The alluring image of Albertine and her band of young girls strolling on the Balbec beach in *À l'ombre des jeunes filles en fleurs* [*Within a Budding Grove*] resurfaces as a recurrent motif in my narrator's mind in his exile and even in old age: "Trang and the girls march hand in hand in the direction of my street. They walk and laugh and giggle along their way, their white dress and pants fluttering in the summer breeze like white butterflies. They flicker for a short while in my mind like the images on a magic lantern. They move with the lantern but are not progressing and go out of my mind as fast as they came." This is like the "avatars" Faulkner says Lena Grove moves through in *Light in August*, like "something moving forever but without progress across an urn." Because time is congealed or arrested, images of Trang and her band are not merging with conventional time but become a haunting presence due to their repeated recurrence. Perpetual remembering with time can become a cruel obsession that can be effaced only after death. Though my narrator is angry and jealous when seeing the photo of Trang and her husband on their altar, the sad look on her face, which has obsessed him since their permanent separation, releases in him a flood of sweet memories that tortures him with remorse for mistreating her spirit.

Time is another major theme of my memoir. Any writing about the search for lost time would be inadequate without our referring to Henri Bergson's and Marcel Proust's theory of memory and time. Because Bergson's philosophy is too important to state in a few lines here, I shall focus on what is relevant to time in literature. Bergson calls *durée* (real duration) the kind of time that can be resurrected by involuntary memory. This psychological time, made up of a succession of heterogeneous, interpenetrating states, can be resurrected only through intuition. Proust also wants to resurrect the past, but he is interested in trying to manipulate time, to be free from its contingency rather than studying its nature and function like Bergson. In his last novel *Le temps retrouvé* [*Time Regained*] Marcel, now an old man, says he wants to restore time to its former felicitous period, "to attain to what I had sometimes perceived in the course of my life, in *brief lightning flashes* ... at those moments of perception which had made me think life was worth living" (emphasis added). Proust turns Bergson's characterization of the *durée* as separate heterogenous states into brief lightning flashes that he calls *moments bienheureux* (delightful moments) when time is "restored to its pristine shape" by the stimulation of involuntary memory.

Howard Moss in *The Magic Lantern of Marcel Proust* identifies as many as eleven major reminiscences provoked by a variety of sensory stimuli. Two famous episodes are the madeleine dunked in tea, which restores Marcel's entire Combray, and his stumbling on two uneven paving stones in the courtyard of the Guermantes mansion, which brings back Marcel's remembrance of his Venice experience. But sound is the most evocative sensory stimulus because it strikes right at the chords of the human heart. It brings back the sufferings and the joys of Marcel's childhood. The tinkling of the bell at his garden gate announced the arrival of Swann, "the unconscious author of his sufferings" as the latter's stay would delay Marcel's mother to come to his room. The sound of the bell also excited him because it meant that Swann was leaving and that Marcel would see his mother soon. To young Marcel, the sound of the bell provoked nothing but a childish emotional reaction to an ordinary event in our eyes. But when the bell is heard again by old Marcel, it evokes a profound ontological and epistemological meaning: *"When the bell of the garden gate had pealed, I already existed and from that moment onwards ... there must have been no break in continuity, no single second at which I had ceased or rested from existing, from thinking, from being conscious of myself ...[that] I could retrace my steps to [that moment] by descending to a greater depth within myself"* (emphasis added). The continuous ringing of the bell within Marcel means that the past is not lost, the self is not changed, and time is free of its contingency because it flows but does not advance and change like chronological time.

Earlier in the novel Marcel's *moments bienheureux* were evoked through the stimulation of various senses such as tasting, smelling, and touching. Delightful sensations Marcel experienced included, to cite a few, "exquisite pleasure," "exaltation," "felicity," "ineffable vision," etc. Only when evoked by the sound of music or the peal of the bell are the resurrections of the past informed with a complex significant meaning. There is in Proust's novel an instance in which sound provokes pain and sorrow rather than delight. On hearing the little phrase from Vinteuil's septet after his breakup with Odette, Swann thought that she had returned. Her "apparition tore him with such anguish that his hand rose impulsively to his heart." The sound of music stimulates powerful emotions and vivid memories. Swann remembers every detail of "the time when I was happy, the time when I was loved." Music can trigger different emotional responses in different people. For Marcel, who is a writer, Vinteuil's septet stimulates in him aesthetic questions such as the nature and function of art; for Swann, who isn't an artist, the little phrase during his courtship of Odette was a metaphor for love, but after his discovery of Odette's betrayal, the same piece of music evokes a source of unbearable anguish and sorrow.

Like Proust, I use sound to evoke painful memories of the past. My protagonist's experience with the power of sound happens before his departure from his country and permanent separation from his sweetheart. "In the completely still, quiet, dark night I can hear the feeble monotonous cry of the crickets around my house. I can hear the dogs far away, their high-pitched uninterrupted howling sharp, piercing, and forlorn. In the night their sound drags out eternally, tearing your heart out. Suddenly, all the sounds related to home and my sweetheart vanish after the emission of the horn blasts of the ship." The Bergsonian *durée* that my hero enjoyed is interrupted and terminated by the deafening horn blasts of the ship waiting to take him and the refugees to the south.

On the eve of his journey to Dalat, his childhood hometown, to search for his past, my narrator visits a section of a busy street in Saigon at rush hour. Overwhelmed by traffic noises and the sound of light rain, he experiences for the first time a Proustian-like *moment bienheureux*. He writes in his journal: "I walk home, relishing the taps of the rain on my shoulders as well as the compressed buzz of the night traffic. The plangent din triggers an amalgam of things—sounds, images, impressions, feelings—coming en masse out of and from inside of me, nebulous, unorganized, robust, full, oppressive but ethereal and soothing." This rare *moment bienheureux* in my hero's search of lost time happens when there is a compression of the past and the present into a congealed *full* present. In *Time Regained* we have seen that this permanent present, which is hidden within Marcel, is awakened by the peal of his garden gate bell at his Combray childhood home.

Marcel's successful recovery of lost time at the end of *Time Regained* stimulates his desire to write a book about his search. But his euphoria vanishes when he thinks about the enormous demands of the project on him. Feeling "the approach of death" because of ill health and old age, Marcel asks with alarm: "Is there still time? Am I well enough?" In the last scene of the novel Proust pictures his protagonist walking on stilts, giddily below him, yet "within me, as though from a height, which was my own height, of my leagues, at the long series of the years." We suffer the tyranny of time and the confinement of space. This precarious Learian condition of old age is reminiscent of my hero in the last chapter of my memoir. When he tries to climb the hilltop near his childhood home and looks down below the city, he is overcome by "a sensation of dizziness, exhaustion, and fear." Like Marcel, he is afraid that he does not have enough time and health to complete his search, any more write a book about it in his lifetime.

The next writer who profoundly influences my writing is William Faulkner. For convenience's sake I shall focus on *The Sound and the Fury*, Faulkner's most important novel, that deals with obsession and time. In Faulkner's novel, Quentin's obsession with his sister Caddy, his family, and his past is so strong that he does not bother about what is going on, that is, the present or chronological time. He is already dead, and it *is* his obsession with the past, or the past itself, that kills him.

The past my hero is searching for does not always appear in its pristine shape. His unsatisfied longing, repressed for a long time, explodes into the present and becomes the present. One can see this, for example, when my narrator in a vision sees a reenactment of his sweetheart's summer promenade with her band of young girls on New Year's Day in the new land long after his departure from his home country. The vision comes effortlessly by itself, out of nowhere, not provoked by any sense stimulus as in Proust. This type of past, according to Jean Pouillon in his study of time in Faulkner, "is real because it is always there, and it is *the past that is the present*" (emphasis added).

The past evoked in the Proustian mode, one that consists of *moments bienheureux*, is not popular with modern writers. Following the Faulknerian tradition, writers who deal with the question of time and memory, usually in a historical context, explore a past that is dark, convoluted, and obsessional, a past that is spontaneously remembered, not evoked by the senses. In Claude Simon's *The Flanders Road,* for example, the dead characters reenact their continued heroic but unsuccessful resistance against their Nazi enemy. The past is not dead but lives in the mind of the survivor/narrator who retells their imagined exploits in a new light. Similarly, in my book, my narrator, in his imagined journey through Vietnam, revisits major historical events that shaped the destiny of his native country. The phantom combatants of the former South Vietnamese army are still obsessed with their heroic past before the fall of South Vietnam. Though they are dead and free of time, they are not free of the burden of memory. Every night, they assemble to perform their former military rituals—saluting the South Vietnamese flag, soundlessly singing the national anthem—on time, without fail, dedicatedly, and emotionally. Though entirely free of chronological time, they are subject to a past that Pouillon, in his Faulkner essay, calls "atemporal" time, i.e., one that they cannot abolish because it is their fate.

This "atemporal" obsessional past time is not conceivable without space as its background. My phantom characters gather in an unchanged location known as the Rù Rì Pass, which has witnessed so many tragic events in Vietnam's history, the most important of which was the defeat of the South Vietnamese army by the communist forces. The Russian theorist Mikhail Bakhtin developed a concept called the "chronotope" to denote the "intrinsic interconnectedness of temporal and spatial relationships in literature." In the chronotope, memory depends on space rather than on time because space, which undergoes no change or little change, vividly evokes memory. Because of the density of memory, time is "viscous and sticky" and "drags itself in space." Nowhere is this more visible than in war literature in which an obsessive past is remembered or evoked in an unchanged space. In Bảo Ninh's *Nỗi buồn chiến tranh* [*The Sorrow of War*], perhaps the best novel about the Vietnam War, the protagonist feels that he is "going back in time" and the past is "hanging heavy on him." Not only does the novel represent Pouillon's definition of a novel of fate in the Faulknerian tradition, but it also illustrates Bakhtin's concept of the chronotype by "materializing time in space." The novel is "thick and concrete rather than lengthening, thinning out, and progressing on a straightforward line like historical and biographical time."

***

The relation of time and space discussed above brings us back to the notion of "a place in Time" that Proust mentions at the end of *Time Regained*. Occupying a place in time simply means existing in space and time, but because of illness and "the approach of death," Proust's narrator fears he cannot "maintain my hold upon a past which already went down so far." Marcel's wish is to have enough strength to write about men who occupy "a very considerable place compared with the restricted one allotted to them in space…." According to Proust, these "giants" who occupy a place "prolonged past measure" can jump "into the years [and] touch epochs that are immensely apart." He is obviously referring to himself or to writers who deal with time and memory like him. It's amazing that Proust's 4,000-page novel is only an overture to this central project on time and memory that his narrator says he "should not fail" to do "if strength were granted me for long enough to accomplish my work." Though the search for the depths of time is the job of "giants," it takes place within "the dimension of Time." This means a writer is one who is as capable as a "giant" but as humble as a normal human who sees himself occupying a small place in time. Though Proust says his protagonist has regained time at the end of his search, he never lost it. His angst over time was caused by his overwhelming perception of the existential burden of human responsibility. "And I felt … a sense of weariness and almost of terror at the thought that *all this length of time had not only, without interruption,* been lived, experienced, secreted by me, that it was my life, was in fact me, but also that I was compelled so long as I was alive to keep it attached to me (emphasis added). By contrast, the dead South Vietnamese combatants on the Rù Rì Pass, after their imaginary reenacting of their routine game of history and time, are "pushed into the beginning of Time, the fathomless past, confounded with the nameless ancient warriors." This primordial time, in contrast to time regained by Proust after his search, is known in Maurice Blanchot's theory as time without time, time of the absence of time. According to Blanchot, this is the cause of "oubli, souvenir de l'immémoriel, sans mémoire" (oblivion, remembrance of the immemorial, without memory), quoted by Etienne Pinat in "La Question du Temps Chez Maurice Blanchot" ["The Question of Time in Maurice Blanchot"]. This is the fate of the South Vietnamese *soldiers* in my book for whom the bell never tolls. Even the dead are *not* free of the curse of memory and time.

***

In her memoir Phyliss Rose shares with us—and the authors interviewed in *The Literary Hub*—why the reading of Proust is so compelling—his revelation of human nature in his characters and in us. Rose also says why it is important to write to explain, like Proust, the laws that "govern [human] behavior."

Rose is indebted to Proust for learning to write her book by reading him. Though she once "really caught up in Proust," she says that "[it] never occurred to me to say 'Proust has done what I wanted to do.'" Resisting Proust's total influence, Roses states that she is "bound to the concrete," not to "the nocturnal muse" with "dreams" and "archetype" like Proust. By contrast, not only do I read like Proust and Faulkner, but I also think, feel, and write like them. Because I have my own personality and style, I see their profound influence on me as a confluence, an impetus that helps me unlock my creative potential and makes me become a better writer.

PARADISE LOST

Dalat

By the time I understood what an earthly paradise meant to me, it had long ended. Of my short but happy childhood I remember very little. The farthest my memory can reach back was when I was around eight. Caring much about the past, I had intended, when living at home with my late father, to ask him to tell me about the most momentous events that I had lived through as a child but was not aware of or remembered very dimly. But because I procrastinated and so much went on back then, I never availed myself of such an opportunity. When I became aware of the necessity to consult my father about my childhood, it was too late. He had died long before I could take my first trip home after my twenty-three years of living in the United States.

Being the first-born male child in a family haunted by the fear of generational extinction once my father—the only remaining clan member—was gone, I was the apple of my parents' eye. I remember when I was a little boy, my parents often told me that because I was always sick and thought not to live beyond my first year, they took me to Linh Sơn Buddhist Temple in Dalat and "sold" me to the Buddha. Once I became the Buddha's child, I would be protected from evil spirits that they thought were the cause of my sickness. In addition to entrusting me to the Buddha's care, my parents did everything they could think of to save my life. The iron chain I wore around my left ankle in a rare childhood photo was an extraordinary story of their utmost devotion to me. When all orthodox medical treatment had failed, my mother took me to her native An Lương Village in Bình Định Province to seek my grandfather's help. Counseled by a local necromancer, my grandfather surreptitiously removed a nail from a bridge and had a blacksmith make a talisman out of it for his daughter's baby. Mother had held the secret for over half a century, and only told me all about it in our reunion in 1999—the year I returned to Vietnam for a Fulbright lecture appointment. "*Tý Anh*," my ninety-year-old mother still called me by my childhood name which means "Little First-Born Male Child." "We owed your life to Grandpa," she was sobbing. "He stayed up all night on that night to watch the blacksmith. The forging had to be done continuously. Had it been interrupted due to the blacksmith's falling asleep or had the chain broken for some reason, your life would have ended."

My mother told me these two "cures"—being sold to the Buddha and wearing an iron protection band around my ankle as a token of being entrusted to supernatural beings—had healed me completely. Another photo shows my happy family when I was around two. Mother holds me in her arms with a big smile on her beautiful face; Father stands akimbo and erect, looking serious but obviously very proud probably because he was a *Quốc tử giám* (Imperial Academy) graduate. Next to him is my twelve-year-old half-brother, a schoolboy at Lycée Yersin (a French junior school in Dalat, my former hometown), in his school uniform. There is a scowl on my face, but I look chubby and healthy.

I do not recall how often my parents took me to Linh Sơn Temple, but my first visit to this place left an ineffable impression on my mind and later turned around my life. I remember after the noon prayer ceremony we sat down to eat lunch with the abbot. As I spilled some grains of rice from my bowl, the old monk picked them up and put them into his bowl. My father immediately gave me a lecture on what he called *"hạt ngọc của Trời"* (Heaven's pearls)— that is, rice grains. "Don't waste any of them, son," he said. "While you're blessed to have them for your nourishment, many children go hungry." Before our departure, while my parents were lingering in the temple to talk with the abbot, I sneaked out to explore its premises. As I was wandering around, I saw a giant tortoise resting at the foot of a miniature. There were some Chinese characters on its carapace. I heard that the late abbot was the author of the characters and the tortoise belonged to him. The animal disappeared after his death and was seen returning on every anniversary of his passing.

The abbot's symbolic gesture of atonement for my sin during the meal, my father's lecture on "waste not, want not," and my encounter with the mysterious tortoise were to lead me later to Oriental religions, particularly Taoism and Buddhism. Before this happened, however, I had developed an infatuation with a corrupt form of mysticism, being influenced by my reading of supernatural stories when I was in second grade. Our private library had a pretty good collection of fiction by authors of the Tự Lực Văn Đoàn (Independent Literary Group) founded and led by the two writers Khái Hưng and Nhất Linh and Chinese fantastic fiction such as *Phong Thần* [*Stories of Deities*]. I was so engrossed in accounts of men who could summon and enlist genii for their service that at night when everybody was asleep I would slip out and, turning in the direction of the dark, mysterious mountains in front of our house, would timidly recant what a character says in the novel, *"Hear ye, hear ye, the five gods of thunder above, please come down."* As you may guess, I performed the ceremony without my parents' knowledge. This was going on for a short while and finally ended because the genii did not answer my summons.

I grew up in a family considered "modern" by Vietnamese standards in the 1930s. My father graduated in 1904 from the last class of the Imperial Academy, a special higher educational institution for the children of the mandarinate at Vietnam's Royal Court in Huế. Though run by a Vietnamese staff, the school adopted a curriculum designed by the French Protectorate in Hanoi to train administrators for the Vietnamese government. Students received a heavy dose of French history, language, and culture. An orphan with an adventurous mind and a great love for the colonialists' culture and language, my father felt no obligation to live up to the expectations of his oldest brother, himself a *mandarin*. So, upon his graduation he packed up and went south to seek new opportunities rather than staying at home to wait for his appointment as a *tri huyện* (district chief). He ended up in Dalat, a resort city founded by the French, met a beautiful young widow with a three-year-old boy, who also left her home after her husband's death to come to the land of opportunities, married her without his brother's consent, and founded a private primary school with his new bride on its instruction staff.

As my parents were tied up all day at school and perhaps because of the impact of French culture they had been exposed to, they were relaxed on matters of child-rearing. I was often left alone doing things my way. I do not remember what my childhood was like, but two things I liked best were roaming in the woods with my playmates in our neighborhood and devouring novel after novel by authors like Khái Hưng and Nhất Linh. For lack of parental supervision and suitable reading material for children, my "food for thought" was books for adults. At eight my hero, for example, was the young female character Lan in Khái Hưng's *Hồn Bướm Mơ Tiên* [*A Butterfly's Fairy Dreams*], who runs away from home and chooses to become a nun rather than marrying a man her parents pick for her and she does not love. I liked the book because it is not only about tender feelings which suit my character, but also because it describes North Vietnam's charming countryside before the Indochina war. How wonderful to live in Vietnam back then! Life in the country was like an idyll—simple, serene, and carefree. Books about a heavenly past that's no more, about how it's remembered, also had a strong appeal to me. I had—and still have—numerous moments of *déjà vu*, which were perhaps echoes of my experience with literature rather than with my real life. Now and then I can still hear the voices of characters in books I read then. When academic or scholarly activities tire me out, I escape to my fictional little world to be with my favorite characters. To me, the literature I read in my childhood is best because it *is* intimately real. Its world *is* my world, my hero's life *is* my life, and I know it instinctively without recourse to the intellect. Even today if I open a book like *Hồn Bướm Mơ Tiên* and read a couple of pages from it, my childhood in Dalat becomes alive—so real, so close, so intimate. With no effort of visualization, I see again things that appear to me as in a pastoral—a moving love story taking place in North Vietnam's peaceful countryside and me, an eight-year-old child, who reads the novel and is impressed with their beautiful romance. I read the book with the same joy, melancholy, and anguish as when I read it as a young boy in my native city of Dalat. Books we read as children keep our paradise intact so we can go back and unearth it at our convenience.

I continued growing up in that world of heavenly sounds, voices, and images. After my father's school business failed because one of his close associates played dirty tricks on him, he went into semi-retirement and let my mother handle all the family business. Now that he had plenty of time for me and my brother, he proved himself such a wonderful parent. He would take us—my sister Như Cẩm, who was two years old and was too young to join us—to a restaurant, Linh Sơn Temple, or his friends' homes for a visit. A poet trained in the Sino-Vietnamese tradition, he composed poems in the T'ang fashion, very popular among Imperial Academy scholars, which he recited in a beautiful but sad voice while lulling us to sleep in his lap.

In June 1942 a tragedy occurred and marked a turn for the worse in my family. Như Cẩm, my father's only female child, took ill and died soon afterward. I remember vividly the scene of her last moments. Having just returned from an extended home visit, my father discovered that my sister was having a seizure and my mother wasn't around. A servant was sent out to a place my mother frequently visited, which was a gambling house, and she got home on time to witness my sister in her death's throes. My mother panicked, feverishly trying to shut all the windows, covering them with blankets to keep shafts of cold air from coming into my sister's room. But it was too late. Như Cẩm had her last convulsion, then her body went still. She died but it looked like she was asleep, her fever making her face rosy and more beautiful than ever. For the first time, I saw death and knew what it meant. It meant I was not going to see my beloved baby sister anymore. The sky came crashing on me.

Như Cẩm had been the apple of my father's eye. I had seen him light incense on our ancestors' altar after her birth to thank them for their blessing because, according to a *phong thủy* (*feng shui*) master's assessment, there would be a serious dearth of female heirs in our clan due to the dominance of the *yang* over the *yin* element in the astrological position of my grandfather's tomb. Như Cẩm's loss therefore was a blow to my father. It was also a blow to me. Not only had I been very close to her, but deep down in me there was a vague fear—which became clearer as I grew older—that as the clan's future head, I would have many difficulties in governing a pack of male relatives without a faithful female sibling's support.

My family did not know how to mourn my sister's death. A strict Confucianist, my father would repress his grief, and when he could not bear it any longer, he would transform it into lyrical poems which he recited in such a sad voice. My mother, by contrast, after burying Như Cẩm, went back to her favorite schedule, dividing her time between a horse carriage rental business and throwing her money away at a gambling house. At six my brother was too young to understand what it meant to have a tragedy in the family. I was the only one who was closest to Như Cẩm as I often held her in my arms and played with her. When she died, I didn't wail like my mother, nor did I try to swallow my sorrow like my father, but I stood still and let tears roll down my face. Later, I went out to the brook behind our house, found a secluded spot, sat down, and cried. I cried until I felt better, then wiped my tears and came back to the house. I did that often, even after things had returned to normal, because I did not want to show my sorrow in front of people.

My father, a gentle, soft-spoken man who had never raised his voice against any servant in our household, one day had a quarrel with my mother over my sister's death. I do not know if the tragedy was the cause of my parents' conflict that happened frequently afterward, but I do remember whenever they had a quarrel it was my mother who was most violent. One day I saw her bring down a cupboard full of valuable glassware. There was a loud noise and splinters of our whole fortune flew about, making everybody in the house cower with fright. After her temper was released, my mother disappeared for several days. My father would take care of us, especially my brother, bathing him and taking us to a restaurant to eat. I had never seen my father in such pitiful shape when we ate in the restaurant on that day. He was not eating at all but went on feeding my brother. Suddenly, he looked at me and ruefully said, "Ty Anh, Ba will be gone for a while. Can you take care of yourself and your brother for Ba?" "Yes, Ba," I said, wanting to cry. I wanted to say a lot more to him to make him feel better, but I didn't know how. Maybe in our family we children were not taught to express our feelings freely and naturally. Even my half-brother, then a high school student, never took time talking with us, playing with us, or telling my parents about school, but would go to his room and shut the door behind him when he got home. In short, in my family everyone lived his or her own life, minded his or her own business. Maybe that was why later, when the house broke down, sending everybody adrift everywhere, nobody, except my father, tried to regroup.

My father had been gone for a few weeks when one day coming home from school, I saw him lying on the sofa in the living room with my mother sitting by him. It was the first time since I had grown up that I saw them together. My mother told me my father was sick and needed to rest. But she did not tell me to go away. I felt a sudden urge to get close to him to hold his hand and say *"Oh, Ba"* to him but was held back by something. I just looked at him. Tears welled up in my eyes, but I did not know why I tried to swallow them rather than letting them burst out. Maybe it was my parents, and later it was our culture, that had taught kids like me not to cry, not to openly show our emotions, particularly our affection and love, even to our loved ones. My suppressed tears turned to a little sob, and I do not remember how long I stood in the living room. Instructed by my mother, I went upstairs and started feeling afraid that something might happen to my father, just as it had happened to Như Cầm. Barely turning eight, I did not know that everybody, particularly my father, would die someday. No one in our house used the word "death" to refer to what happened to my sister. It was a calamity, a great tragedy, only I did not know that it was also the inevitable truth in life.

My father was gravely ill. A doctor was sent for, but his condition did not improve. He ran a very high fever and slept all the time. When he awakened, he dismissed the doctor and prescribed his own medication. At the same time, my mother invited a monk from Linh Sơn Temple to come and pray for my father's recovery. As the monk performed his prayer rituals far into the night when I was sound asleep, I was exposed for the first time to a most blissful experience with sounds that was to influence later my search for the past. I awakened to the steady tick-tock of a wooden gong the monk used to measure his beautiful chant of the prayer. In the still night when the turmoil of the day ended and my full consciousness was suspended, I was adrift along that stream of heavenly sounds, completely washed of sorrow and worry.

My father got better a few days after his self-treatment. Just as his illness had brought my parents back together, his recovery made them even closer. But at this time my father made a decision that he might not have known would have an adverse effect on all of us. After the birth of our youngest brother, my father wanted to take all the family to his native village in Quảng Bình to be close to, as he said, our *"mồ mã ông bà"* (ancestors' tombs). According to his plans, my father would leave first with me and my younger brother, and my mother would stay on in Dalat to sell the property. As it turned out, my mother, who visited us later in our new ancestral home in Quảng Bình, did not like to live in a small rural village. So, after a short stay, she took my youngest brother back to Dalat. Assured by my mother's promise to sell our home in Dalat and to join us shortly, my father was hoping for our family reunion in the country he had left forty years earlier.

My brother and I stayed on with Father in Quảng Bình for another year. I was then nine and he was seven. This was the last and only time in my childhood, and in my entire life, I was most happy. No longer traveling to tend patients, Father stayed at home with us all the time. His return to his ancestral place was seen by his people as their great honor because their native son was a scholar. Naturally, the villagers gave me and my brother very special treatment because we were Father's children. For the first time, I was exposed to sounds and images that were to lay the foundation for my later quest for the past. I liked best the sounds of the country I heard at night in my sleep. Father hired a group of men and women to ram the building site of our ancestral home to secure a solid foundation for the construction. They worked late into the night after I had long been sent to bed. As if to make their job more fun and productive, they sang many love folksongs together. I was gently awakened from my sleep by waves of melodious sounds, only to be rocked to sleep again, except that this time, I was conscious of what was going on around me—the heavenly bliss of growing wings and floating in the sea of melody. It was the first time I was exposed to these sounds, but I found them very familiar, very dear and precious to me. I felt as though the peasants were my own people and they were singing for me that night. Father's village in my sleep was so peaceful, so pleasurable. I did not miss Dalat and my mother at all.

As my father's country is a region that receives more rain than sunshine, I came under the spell of another kind of sound—that of the rain falling on the roof and windowpanes of our ancestral home. Again, the felicitous sensation they provided was linked to night sleep and dreams. There were light taps on the windowpanes. I did not know when the rain stopped, but the taps were in sync with the twittering of crickets, and found an echo in my heart. Nature became livelier than ever during my sleep. Cuddling comfortably in my warm bed and being lulled by this melody of nature, I drifted off to sleep again, feeling vaguely that I was to carry these sounds everywhere and hear them again in my dreams in my later life.

But not all the sounds I heard during my stay in Quảng Bình were heavenly. Some nights I woke up to the rumble of distant thunder with eerie feelings of fear, anxiety, and sadness. I was too young to know what else thunder would presage except heavy rains, but in the depths of my unconscious there must be a connection between it and the story of my young uncle's drowning in a flood my father would often tell us, his warning us against getting close to deep waters, and my vague inkling of a certain misfortune that would soon befall our family.

As for images of the country, I was particularly drawn to the coleuses planted for ornament in front of our home. I was attracted to these plants almost instinctively the first time I saw them as if I had lost something precious for a long time and had just found it now. I missed them when I left home with my father on a long trip. They were no longer objects but became images of things from a distant past that were dear and close to me. I carried them within me everywhere as part of myself, vaguely knowing that I was going to lose them someday. During my short stay in our ancestral home before I was sent back to Dalat to live with my mother, in addition to my regular contact with the world around me, I had developed the habit of unconsciously evoking my memories of the coleuses and other ordinary things I had seen in the past. Ultimately, they would become objects of my search years later.

Could it be said that my anguish over the loss of paradise indicated my loss of innocence? I did not know what suffering meant because my childhood was a happy one until the war broke out and my family fell apart. But a keen consciousness of happiness felt too early by a child is also an abnormal sign, let alone his excessive preoccupation with the past. It indicated that I not only had lost my innocence, my childhood had ended, and I was on the threshold of an impending disaster, but I had a foreboding that my days ahead would not be the same. My presentiment turned out to be true. I returned to Dalat in March 1945 only to realize that my pristine, idyllic world was no more.

Back in Dalat, I was sent to a Vietnamese French elementary school, but my schooling was interrupted by the Japanese coup against the French colonial regime. The face of the city completely changed overnight. There was joy and excitement everywhere when those *"Tây mít"* (pot-belly Frenchmen) that we hated were rounded up and marched at the Asians' gunpoint. I heard adult people around me whisper about the Japanese soldier's so-called "legendary exploits"—that the long sword that the Japanese officer was carrying could become a radio receiver/transmitter by simply planting it on the ground, that though the Japanese foot soldier was short he was strong and full of stamina because the Japanese military ration was high in sugar content, that the Japanese soldier was invincible because he was tough, wily, highly disciplined, and so on. Everywhere everybody raved about the Japanese, Japanese was a required subject at school, and many Vietnamese were studying the language rather than French. To top it off, we received word from my father in Quảng Bình that he himself was dabbling in the new language, taking advantage of his excellent knowledge of Chinese linguistics. I never asked him why he was interested in Japanese, but I was sure seeking a chance to serve the new occupiers was not his motive (he could have landed a good job in the defunct French protectorate administration with his excellent French language skills). My guess was, like many Vietnamese intellectuals, my father might have fallen for the Japanese proposal for a Southeast Asia common welfare bloc whose membership would include Vietnam. He, for one, would be willing to serve his country in his capacity as a Japan scholar.

Our euphoria over the Japanese wore off shortly. There were rumors about atrocities committed by Japanese soldiers against my people. A blood-curdling story I heard concerned a Vietnamese woman brutally executed by the Japanese for allegedly selling them grains mixed with sawdust to feed their horses. They thrust the wriggling victim into their dead animal's belly, stitched it with barbed wires, then buried her alive with the beast before her family's eyes. The Japanese occupation was also the cause of the famine of 1945 which claimed more than one million lives in the north. The Japanese confiscated foodstuff from Vietnamese farmers to feed their troops and to use grains for fuel in lieu of coal to run their military trains. Frequent air strikes by the Allies prevented farmers from growing their crops, thus hastening the occurrence of the great famine. In the north, trees stood gaunt and bare because starved peasants had consumed all their foliage and barks. A report said that when there was nothing left to eat, some folks resorted to eating human flesh. I read in a memoir by a refugee writer from Hanoi that he had seen a dying woman, her baby no bigger than a kitten clinging to her body, sucking on her dry breast. In Quảng Bình, where my father and my brother lived, things were better because they could eat two small meals with one bowl of rice bran for supper.

School resumed, but classes were frequently interrupted by air raid sirens that sent us scampering to trenches in the playground for shelter. Those moments were scary, but they were perhaps the most pleasant and memorable ones in my childhood. Because my mother was concerned about my safety, she entrusted me to Ngành, one of my schoolmates and the daughter of a Chinese-Vietnamese couple who were renting a flat on our premises. Ngành was three or four years older than I and her class was next to mine. (According to custom, I called her *chị* because she was older than I.) Every time there was a siren, *chị* Ngành would rush over to fetch me and take me to the shelter, holding my hand in her warm, smooth hand. Because I did not have a sister and my mother was always aloof to me, I looked to *chị* Ngành for comfort because she was an older sister and mother figure to me. I wanted her to care for me more. I also wanted to tell her that I cared for her, too, but I was too timid to do so. I do not remember what she said to me when we both ran to the shelter, but what she said must have been very soothing because she was such a sweet girl.

The air sirens grew less frequent and finally ended. I was with Ngành less often until I did not see her anymore as her family moved out of their flat. I do not remember whether she came to say goodbye to me, or I was bold enough to go and find her. Though I liked her a lot, my mind was preoccupied with fun things for kids my age, such as trapping sparrows and catching crickets. But I began to miss Ngành a few days after she left. I went to her former place several times to look for her only to miss her more. When the war broke out and we left Dalat for good, so much happened that I had no time to think of her. In 1960 when I visited the Gia family in Dalat, they told me they had seen her and her family after the war but did not know their whereabouts. I thought about Ngành every now and then. It was she who acquainted me for the first time with tender feelings that you would call puppy love.

One day in July or August 1945, we were all bombarded with many breaking news stories: the Japanese had surrendered to the Allies, Vietnam became an independent country, and it was *Cụ Hồ* who made the proclamation in Hanoi. For the first time, I heard terms such as *Cụ Hồ* (Uncle Hồ), *Việt Minh*, *Thực dân Pháp* (French colonialists), *Phát xít Nhật* (Japanese fascists), as well as *độc lập* (independence), *tự do* (freedom), *hạnh phúc* (happiness), and the like. Though I was not old enough to fully understand those abstract words, I was electrified by the way in which Sang, my seventeen-year-old half-brother, and the adults in my family raved about those magical expressions and what was associated with them. Sang quit school to join the city paramilitary organization with his buddies and then enlisted himself in the *Vệ Quốc Quân* (Fatherland Protecting Army), the predecessor to the current People's Army. I saw him and many *các anh, các chị* (older brothers and sisters) my brother's age in a parade at a public *mít-tinh* (meeting), an Anglicized word used for the first time since Vietnam's independence. Adults exuberantly displayed patriotic feelings everywhere. We children were no exception. I recall us second and third graders joining older students in our school in chasing French kids and throwing rocks at them. At nine I already learned to hate the French and knew how to vent my outrage on the helpless French kids! We children lost our innocence so early because of our people's oppression. Our rage was formed during our reading of writers who depict the brutality of French colonialism against our people, was fueled by the Việt Minh propaganda, and blew up when ignited by incitement as happened today.

Patriotism ran high as we were told that the French were coming back to Indochina after Japan's surrender to the Allies. Dalat was a French resort city, so the return of the French was most likely. Trains bound for the front were full of troops. Seeing off those *anh chị* who gave up their education for their lofty cause moved me to tears and filled my heart with pride. They were so young and beautiful in their khaki uniform, and I was particularly impressed with the precision of their movements during a drill ceremony. There was an air of strong determination on everybody's face.

While endearing terms and associated concepts continued to hold us spellbound, words with unpleasant, shocking meanings began to circulate. Not only, for example, did I hear for the first time people say *"Việt gian"* (Việt traitor), but I saw his incarnate! One sunny morning during a meeting at the city stadium as the crowd went frenzied with speech after speech by members of the people's committee, rounds of applause, and patriotic music, there were shouts *"Việt gian! Việt gian!"* Seconds later, a man in his thirties wearing a white shirt and blue trousers, his face bleeding, was dragged to the front of the stadium. Someone in the podium stood up and gave a short speech denouncing the French and the *Việt gian* which he concluded by holding his fists high and shouting, "Down with French colonialists! Down with Việt traitor!" to which the crowd responded by roaring back "Down with! Down with!" Next, the man was tied to a pole, blindfolded, and immediately executed by a firing squad. Afterward, a soldier went to him and shot two to three times at his temple. I witnessed the execution of that *Việt gian* from start to finish because I was curious to see what a *Việt gian* looked like, and successfully managed to edge my way close to the scene. But curiosity was not my whole reason for trying to see the man, it was also my desire to see his execution. When the meeting was over and the crowd dispersed, I lingered with some onlookers for another while, my eyes riveted to the man's crumpled bloody body, curious and afraid. That first experience of mine with the killing of a human has haunted my mind ever since.

Rumor had it that the man had spied for the French and that a French flag was found in his house at his arrest. There was no way to confirm all this. Nor did the local government bother to prove that the executed person was a real *Việt gian*. But no other spy was executed in public in Dalat since then. Perhaps because the government had successfully consolidated its power, there was no need to whip up the public anymore.

In December 1946, news about the return of the French to Indochina after Japan's surrender to the Allies made us lose hope in our fragile newly regained independence. My mother panicked when our city was ordered to get ready for evacuation. My father was still stuck in Quảng Bình, and Sang, who was the only male adult in the family, had joined the army. On the appointed day my mother stuffed our horse carriage (since my father's return to his native hometown, renting out our carriage with driver and animal was our main livelihood) with food, clothes, and necessities. After the four of us—my mother, my youngest brother, our loyal maid, and I—had squeezed in, we joined a long caravan of refugees leaving our beloved city as fast as we could.

I do not remember much of that trek, except that our destination was Phan Rang, a small town on the coast about 120 kilometers from Dalat. I only have selective memories of major events in my life. The journey must have been long and exciting as the beauty of Dalat and its suburbs with its pine groves and wildflowers was breathtaking. As we left our hill country and hit the plains, the landscape turned flat and boring, and the heat was unbearable. That was the best I can recall of the evacuation, and today little of the flight comes to mind when I try to recover it. The uprooting was so sudden and brutal that it dulled my mind and blocked my perception of the new experience. It was unthinkable for a ten-year-old boy to realize that he was not to return to his hometown ever again.

DISPLACEMENT

We arrived in Phan Rang around noon. It was too hot for us who came from a mountain resort where the year-round temperature was around 70 degrees F. The wind blew strong in this small coastal town, bringing specks of sand to our eyes and fanning our faces like a flame. We stopped and unloaded our stuff at a house whose owner with whom my mother appeared to have more than a nodding acquaintance. That night all our family crammed in a creaky queen-sized bamboo bed.

A month after our coming to Phan Rang the government said that the French landing was a false alarm, so we were allowed to return home. While everyone was preparing to leave, my mother seemed to stay put. I knew nothing about her plans, but her failure to take us back to Dalat at this juncture did have an adverse impact on the rest of my life.

Sometime later, another event happened and hastened the course of my destiny. One afternoon when returning from an errand, I saw my father sitting in our shed and talking with my mother. He had traveled around seven hundred kilometers from Quảng Bình to search for us after hearing rumors about the landing of French troops on coastal provinces and about their massacre of civilians. I loved and missed him very much, so it was wonderful to see him again. As said before, I felt closer to my father than to my mother. Though during my father's absence my mother never scolded me and always left me alone, I found her aloof to me. When I was growing up, I never saw my mother care for me dearly. I was the first-born of my father and my mother, but Sang *was* my mother's own son, and in my mind, they *belonged* to each other. I felt that Sang never liked me because we did not have the same father. I did not like him either for the same reason and because he always remained distant from me and even talked back to my *own* father sometimes. I did not miss Sang at all when he left home to join the army.

I riveted my attention on the story of my father's dangerous journey that brought him here. In a petulant voice choked by emotion and with a strong accent because of his extended stay in a northern province, my father, who looked so thin in his white pajamas, told us that in Quảng Bình he had heard that many civilians had been killed in the fighting between the Việt Minh and the French, and that French troops had committed many atrocities in Dalat after their reoccupation of the city. He had taken my brother with him on a 400-kilometer trek from Đồng Hới to Quảng Ngãi where he found his nephew, the city's police chief. After he had entrusted my brother in his care, he continued his trip all the way to Dalat. Thanks to the tips provided by a former acquaintance, my father turned southward again and finally found us here in Phan Rang. I do not know what happened to our parents during my long-awaited reunion, but about a week later I was told to get ready to leave with my father. According to their plans, my father later told me, we would return to Quảng Bình first and wait for my mother to join us after she had sold the property. "Why don't you take Ty Anh with you first," my mother assured my nervous father. "We all will be with you no later than the year-end." Despite my mother's assurance, I saw that my father was not happy. I had an eerie feeling that it would be the last time we were together. I felt that my mother did not want to live with us in our small ancestral village in Quảng Bình, nor did she want to return to Dalat. Why my mother was willing to give up her home and business in Dalat to stay in this impoverished place was beyond me. Our parting was so sad. I wanted to go with my father, but I did not want to leave my little brother. But what brought me to tears was the moment when we were about to take off, my brother, who would not let my father touch him during his entire visit, started crying and would not let go of him.

We left early in the afternoon. After several hours of sitting in a horse carriage, we got off and began to travel on foot for a good while. We finally arrived at a stream where the road ended. My father seemed familiar with traveling in this area as he quickly took me downstream where there were two slender bamboo poles stretching across the roaring stream used as a makeshift bridge to get to another lane hidden somewhere. Because my father was very afraid of water (his older brother drowned in a flood while playing with his buddies), he was terribly shaking while crawling over the "bridge" with a heavy sack on his back and with his head constantly looking back to make sure I was still there. I was so scared because the bamboo poles crackled all the time and the water below looked very deep. But we finally made it to a tunnel to catch the train before dark. All around us was so quiet and dreary. Suddenly, I thought of my mother and my little brother and cried.

It took us several days to get to Bình Định, my mother's native province. Because the railroad system was heavily damaged by the Allies' air strikes, our train operated only on short schedules and on short distances. To avoid being spotted by French warplanes, most trains ran at night only. During the day, they were either hidden away in tunnels or covered with leaves on top if they had to run. Passengers seemed to live in darkness all the time as any light could trigger enemy air raids.

We got off at Bồng Sơn, the last existing railroad station under the government's control, and stopped by my uncle's house for a brief stay. Surprisingly, Sang was here. He threw his arms around me and held me up. He made me cry when he asked, "Do you miss *Má* (Mother), dear?" There was a tear in his eye, and he too missed Mother. For the first time I felt close to him. He also was very nice to my father, calling him *Papa* all the time. (A former French major at Lycée Yersin, he used the French expression to address my father.) My father looked very pleased.

The next day, we said goodbye to my uncle and left for Phú Mỹ, my grandparents' village. We were right on time for the family's commemoration of the anniversary of my grandmother's death, so everybody was happy to see us. For the first time I met in person the same uncles and aunts who told me they had witnessed my miraculous recovery ten years earlier. They were all delighted to see their favorite nephew again. Several kids my age or older also came to meet me. They were introduced to me as my cousins and assigned to play with me during my visit.

After my oldest uncle had performed the required rituals—lighting incense, whispering his prayers, and prostrating himself several times—before our ancestors' shrine, my father was invited to pay his respects to their spirits. Halfway through his performance, he suddenly broke down and sobbed like a child. This was the first time I saw my father cry. I thought he missed my grandmother, but one of my aunts came forward and comforted him. "Please don't worry," she said. "I'm sure once she [my mother] has sold the property, she will join you and the children in Quảng Bình." Why my father was so emotional was beyond my comprehension at that time. Perhaps visiting my grandparents' home reminded him of my mother and my youngest brother in Phan Rang, or perhaps in the back of his mind, our reunion was not a happy prospect for us because of the impending war. Suddenly, it occurred to me that this must have been related to my parents' little quarrel I had heard the night before our departure. My mother seemed to have told my father to forget about her. When my father was still living, it never occurred to me that I would be writing a memoir or an autobiographical novel someday, so asking him about an old story was out of the question. Even if there was such a need, I would not dare approach my father for help. Though he was an extremely devoted parent, due to his Confucian upbringing, rarely did he betray his innermost feelings in front of his children.

I had a great time visiting my mother's relatives and no longer felt homesick. Coming from a hilly region where farming did not exist, I had a lot of fun playing with my cousins. Never did I get tired of flying kites, going bird nesting, chasing baby ducks with them, or admiring boundless lush rice fields punctuated with immaculate white cranes. What I enjoyed most was seeing a play performed in the open by the soldiers for the villagers. They played French colonialists who oppressed our people but were kicked out of our country thanks to *Cụ Hồ*. I was immensely tickled by a soldier who played a "pot-bellied" French man. This colonialist and his band beat our peasants but were later arrested and put on trial when the Revolution became successful. I greatly admired our soldiers' acting skills and command of oral French. Like my brother Sang, they had attended French schools but gave up their education and joined the army to fight the enemy. The same patriotic fervor I had felt in Dalat when hearing *Cụ Hồ*'s proclamation of Vietnam's independence now returned to me. Suddenly, I did not want to play with my cousins anymore. I had lost my innocence for good.

After staying at my grandparents' home for about a week, we resumed our northbound trip. My father was anxious to see my brother who was staying with *anh* Kỳ in Quảng Ngải. (Kỳ was my cousin, but because in Vietnamese there is no specific word for the French term "cousin" and because he was the son of my father's oldest brother, the term for older brother, *anh*, is used to refer to him.) Besides, there were rumors that French troops were preparing to attack Đà Nẵng. If that happened, we would not be able to return to Quảng Bình. It took us several days to reach Quảng Ngãi and we arrived late in the evening. Upon entering my cousin's home, I saw his wife bathing my brother in a basin. Suddenly, I felt jealous of him. Ever since I can remember, except my father, no adults in the family had bothered to pay attention to my needs.

Shortly after our arrival, *anh* Kỳ came home. He was in his early forties and looked very dignified with a carbine flung across his shoulders. In the early post-revolution period, only high-level police and military officials could carry guns. *Anh* Kỳ greeted my father very respectfully, but I saw that my father was not happy to learn that his nephew was a police officer as he told me later that this career was unsuitable for the Trần clan which boasted of a long tradition of adhering to the Buddhist teaching of non-violence, non-coercion, and non-interference in others' lives. We were invited to sit down for dinner. My brother was spoon-fed by *anh* Kỳ's wife, though he was old enough to eat by himself. I was surprised that while my father was eating, my cousin stood waiting upon him. He addressed Father with respectful expressions such as "Yes, Sir" and "No, Sir."

I was flattered by *anh* Kỳ's special treatment of me and greatly impressed to see his gun hung on the wall. He was the only surviving son of Uncle Bảo, my father's oldest half-brother. My father used to tell me that Uncle Bảo was a brutal man. After the death of my grandparents, my father, who was then around thirteen, moved in to live with his brother. Instead of sending my father to school, Uncle Bảo made him care for his young children and tend buffaloes. He would also beat my father for no reason. My father, who always defended his relatives because he wanted to save face, blamed *feng shui* for his brother's insanity. The story went like this: though not an expert in this art, Uncle Bảo had my grandfather's bones exhumed and moved to an unpropitious location. The results: my father's older brother drowned in a flood when he was sixteen, my grandmother died soon afterward at age thirty-five, and my father's younger brother also died in the same year as my grandmother. At fifteen, my father ran away from Uncle Bảo's home, arrived in Huế 500 kilometers away, knocked at the door of one of my late grandfather's former students, and later was admitted to the Imperial Academy as the surviving son of the mentor of King Hiệp Hòa and King Kiến Phúc of the Nguyễn dynasty. (In our family shrine in Quảng Bình, I saw a gold-plated rod that my father said belonged to my grandfather. It was said that a king's master might resort to this special rod when his majesty had a discipline problem. The rod was displayed in his majesty's room as a symbol of his master's authority only. No teacher would dare inflict corporal punishment on his king student!)

That was the first and last time I saw *anh* Kỳ. We did not get news of him until 1954 after we had left Quảng Bình and resettled in Huế. And it was such bad news! According to my father's acquaintances, *anh* Kỳ was suspiciously killed in "an accident." His wife also died a few years later. They had a teenage son who lived with his relatives. In 1960 my father went to Quảng Ngãi to bring him to Huế to live with us. My father's warning to his nephew when he visited him in Quảng Ngãi about the danger of pursuing a career, which, in his view, would usually hurt innocent people, apparently came true.

QUẢNG BÌNH

With my brother joining us, we left Quảng Ngãi soon afterward on the last leg of our journey to Quảng Bình. Thanks to the good road condition, we made it home in one piece. We got off at Đồng Hới railroad station and took a rickshaw to Văn La, my father's village, about ten kilometers away. I settled in our new home with a heavy heart because I missed my old home in Dalat, my mother, and my little brother. Above all, I missed my wonderful old days in the Langbiang mountainous region. Suddenly, I felt depressed. Coming from a beautiful resort city, I did not like living in a small village. What my father had told me about Văn La when it was under Việt Minh control was still fresh in my mind. The village then was run by a people's revolutionary committee composed mainly of tenants and former servants of landowners. They were told by the Việt Minh to call their former masters *"đồng chí"* (comrades). My father and his old friend, a retired mandarin, were required to undergo marching drills and wear shorts when practicing. Those who had ties with the French system or the former royal court were singled out for harassment. To protect himself, my father destroyed his license to practice medicine because it was issued in French though he had hidden it on the roof when the Revolution first came. He was smart enough to keep his graduation diploma from the Imperial Academy which he believed should be fine because it was in Chinese and no one on the people's committee could understand its contents.

Now that the Việt Minh had gone, the villagers treated my father better. But my days and months in Văn La wore on, and I got more and more depressed. Life was getting harder for us because the war had just broken out and my father totally lost contact with my mother. We had to live within our means because my mother had stopped sending us money. Our servants had left us because we could not afford to keep them. Only my father's grandnephew, a man in his forties, stayed to cook for us and took care of me and my brother.

When it rains, it pours, as the saying goes. I contracted malaria one year after living in Văn La. Because my father was away tending his patients to make a living for us, I was left alone at home taking care of myself. The illness made me crave citrus fruits, which were plentiful in our backyard, and the more I ate them, the worse my condition grew. Its attack occurred every day during which I had to lie down in bed and cover myself with thick blankets and yet still shivered while outside the heat sizzled. For the first time, I regretted coming there to live with my father. It was unbearable for a child like me to care for himself when contracting that terrible disease. While living in Dalat with my parents before the war came and before my family was broken, I had never been left alone when I was sick.

My father got back right on time when I was gravely ill. Because he could not find quinine, which was standard Western medicine for malaria at that time, he treated me with herbs. It took me a long while to get cured, but my father said that my recovery was a miracle, not because of the curative power of the herbs.

One year after our arrival in Quảng Bình, the war spread to northern provinces. One afternoon in 1947, we were ordered by the Việt Minh, who had just returned to Văn La, to leave as quickly as possible because the French had landed in Đồng Hới and the government would strictly implement the so-called *"tiêu thổ kháng chiến"* (scorched-earth strategy) by burning all things to the ground. After my father had dismissed his loyal grandnephew, we fled to a neighboring village about 15 kilometers away. We stopped to rest at a relief shelter. That evening, each of us was given a bowl of vegetable congee for supper. Having walked all afternoon, my brother and I were famished and wolfed down our ration in seconds. Our eyes were glued on Father's bowl left intact. "Eat the soup for Ba, dears," he gently said, pouring his congee into our bowls. "Ba isn't hungry." I was on the brink of tears but went on to eat my portion. My brother was too young to understand our father's sacrifice. I cried all night that night.

We reached Trung Quán village, our destination, the next morning. The homeowner, a man in his early fifties, greeted us nicely, but not as warmly as *anh* Kỳ had welcomed us in Quảng Ngãi. He was a distant nephew of my father's. My hunch told me this wasn't going to be a good place for me and my brother, and it turned out to be true. The old man's children lacked manners. They did not call us "uncles" as required by custom. When they wanted us to come to them, they just rudely commanded, "Come here, kids." No sooner did my father leave us with his old nephew than he took off to neighboring villages to work as a roving physician. After a few days, he came back apparently with enough money to keep the family for a month. Around a fortnight after our arrival in Trung Quán, my father decided we could be on our own. By then, I had totally recovered from malaria and was able to cook and care for the family.

We now lived in a nice house that Father rented. I went to the village's open market which met every morning to buy necessary items, such as firewood, cooking oil, and fish sauce. Because we could not afford to buy meat and fish at the market regularly, we supplemented our diet with live crabs and small fish I caught in the rice field. I also went fishing and occasionally had a big catch. I prepared fish dishes when my father was away. Being a devout Buddhist, he would not allow me to kill live things for food.

My father used to go away to see patients at villages on the other side of the river. I felt fine the first day of his absence, but the next day, I started missing him so much that I would go to the boat landing, where I would peer across the river at the gathering dusk and try to scan for a black dot. If it was moving, I would know it could be Father getting on the boat to come home. I was not always lucky. I could make out several black dots during the evening, but not one of the returning travelers was always Father. I would, though, keep on waiting for him until everything—the landscape and the river—was engulfed in total darkness. Only then would I turn around and walk back to our place, moaning softly like a character in a children's book I had read years earlier in Dalat, "Ba, please come home now." That night I would lie awake into past midnight, crying until I fell asleep. During my childhood and early adolescence, Father substituted for my mother, and he *was* a great mother figure to me.

When Father came home, he always brought with him a big tuna. Wearing a black tunic and white pants, with a black umbrella and a bundle of clothes, rice, and foodstuff in one hand and the fish dangling the length of a string in the other, he walked all the way from neighboring villages back to Trung Quán, trying to make it home to be with us. How could I describe my joy and thrill when seeing him come back! It meant my brother and I would be safe with his protection, and it also meant we would have a delicious meal, a rarity to us in these tough times. I do not recall since our early teens Father ever hugged us, but during our meal just seeing his gentle look or hearing his gentle voice telling us stories of his venture far and wide for our sake was more than what I could ask for. He was always a father, a mother, and later a teacher to me after I was sent back to school the next year.

No sooner had we been on our feet than Father decided to send us to school. He did not want us to do housekeeping because he said that was intended for girls and because our schooling had been interrupted for almost two years now since our last evacuation from Văn La. By now the French had successfully installed a Vietnamese administrative system in major provinces and cities across the country. However, because small localities like Trung Quán were subject to Việt Minh guerrillas' control after dark, we could only attend school during the day. The school system at the primary level was based on the French one, its curriculum consisting of the three R's, civics, and French.

Father enrolled us in a local primary school. Because we had received homeschooling from him, we were allowed to skip two grades. My first day at a small village school in a northern province was very embarrassing. Because the class was full, I was put on the bench reserved for the girls. I heard some kids giggle in the back and a flush of shame rose to my face. Compared to my school in Dalat, this one was so boring. There was only one teacher, Mr. Phán, who taught all the subjects and often dozed off. His best subject was French which our class did not like because the students had no previous knowledge of the language. His worst subject was math, especially arithmetic. Not only did he confuse us, but he could not solve a simple math problem. My father was very worried because I was weak in math and my graduation exam was getting close. So, one day without giving prior notice, he came to Mr. Phán's class and made his request that math be given priority. During his encounter with Mr. Phán, my father spoke French. Mr. Phán, after his initial shock, also responded in the same language. My father, who had struck Mr. Phán as an illiterate countryman, later became his good friend. But I suddenly found myself a victim of my father's new friendship. Mr. Phán and Kim, his oldest daughter, seemed to take a special interest in me. He even moved me to the front row to sit next to her. She was a nice girl, a couple of years older than me, but I did not like her paying too much attention to me. The rascals in the class saw it as a pretext to make fun of me. Seeing no good in pressing Mr. Phán to become a good math teacher, my father took the trouble of coaching me in this subject. This was an extremely challenging task for my father because he was never strong in math. But he tried his luck anyway on his thickheaded son. He used a French textbook he borrowed from Mr. Phán and slowly walked me through the fundamentals of arithmetic. Despite my father's patience, I did not pass the primary school graduation exam held in Đồng Hới that year. Several students in my class who took the exam had no luck either. We repeated that same class for another year.

Midway into my second semester, Mr. Phán found a young man with a high school diploma who agreed to give us special math lessons during his vacation at home in Trung Quán. The man was knowledgeable but tough. His tantrum over my inability to quickly understand his teaching was frightening. One day, as I stood silent rather than trying to answer his question, he flew into a rage and cussed me out loudly: "You idiot, you know what you'll be doing when you grow up? *Begging for food in the street!*" Burning with anger and shame, I was telling myself I would prove him wrong, but did not know how then. One thing I did afterward to prove he was wrong about me was I got my father's approval to quit his class. Again, father and son resumed their toil of wallowing through the muddle of arithmetic for several more months. A couple of days before the exam, my father took me to see Mr. Trung, a proctor at the upcoming exam, and hired him to help me on the math test. As it turned out, Mr. Trung was more an impediment than an asset to me. At the close of the test, he showed up from nowhere and, standing in front of me, started making hand and head gestures which confused and scared me. Luckily, when he came in with such body hint language I was about to finish. (I later found out that Mr. Trung, himself not good in math, had memorized the test answers from other students and tried to make me understand with his strange gesticulations!) Fortunately, I passed the exam this time to my father's great satisfaction.

(I could not figure out why I passed that exam, for I must have flunked the math test again. My father attributed my success to his changing my name to a new name, which means good fortune. But I discovered later that that exam was canceled the following year. All students in Mr. Phán's class passed that exam that year.)

Our life took a new turn after my passing the primary school exam. My father had wanted to move the family to Đồng Hới for a long time. Trung Quán and the neighboring villages where my father practiced medicine were not safe anymore. Việt Minh guerrillas now came out even in the daytime to recruit soldiers and to punish *Việt gian*. One evening, I saw an old drunkard wobbling in the street and cussed the Việt Minh out for killing his son, an employee in the Vietnamese local government. We feared for the old man's life but thought he would be okay on account of his drunkenness. But the next morning, someone found the old man's head outside his home. Meanwhile, the French frequently executed Vietnamese suspected of collaborating with the Việt Minh. This was what I witnessed when they hanged a Việt Minh suspect in Trung Quán before we escaped to Đồng Hới. They rounded up the villagers at the market square where there was a big banyan tree. Next, they brought out from a GMC, a French army truck, a young man in his bloody white clothes and with his face bleeding profusely, made him stand on a highchair, and placed a nook of rope around his neck. At the commanding officer's signal, a soldier pushed the chair off. The man's feet wiggled for a few minutes then his body went still. Immediately after the executing squad left, an old woman, the victim's mother, emerged from the crowd, jumped on his body, beating her chest, shrieking, and wailing. Even after everybody had gone home, she was still there with her son, and we continued to hear her squealing, weeping, and laughing throughout the night. The old woman was by her son's body for two consecutive days. On the third day, we no longer heard her keening. She was found dead beneath the tree where her son had been hanged. The villagers were allowed to bury both mother and son. They began to burn incense at the site where the victims had died to comfort their spirit. Before we left Trung Quán five months later, hardly had a day gone by without witnessing or learning of a tragedy or a wrongful death here or from neighboring villages. Nobody left home after sunset. The guerrillas were the most active at night, and the French from their watchtower might want to try their shooting skills at any moving object. There was no guarantee that we would be safe even in the daytime, and we feared very much the Việt Minh and the French *Légionnaires*. Their presence would often mean imminent danger to us.

As time wore on, Trung Quán became the battleground between the Việt Minh and French troops. Việt Minh guerrillas now grew bolder as they came out even in broad daylight to attack French troops who were out on patrol. When chased by the enemy, they blended in with the peasants and stayed safe. But if they fired back at the French from their hideouts, the latter would retaliate by mopping out the suspects including civilians. French soldiers consisted of Moroccan recruits, who were very cowardly, and the Légionnaires, who were best known for their brutality. Woe to any woman they happened to find in their raid. In my neighborhood, a young man and his wife could not be evacuated because of her childbirth. When the man begged the Légionnaires to spare his wife's life, they killed him and raped the woman. The villagers later found their bodies near a dump site. They could not shut their eyes when they buried them. Their baby was alive.

Another victim of the Legionnaires that I knew of in Trung Quán was our landlord's aunt called Cô Ba (literally, Miss Three, so called because she was the second daughter of her parents. From Bình Định all the way to the Mekong Delta, family members are commonly called by the order of their birth, although in official documents they usually go by their given name. For many peasants it is easier to remember "common" names than given names). Cô Ba was an extremely attractive woman in her early forties. Her right leg was deformed, and she had great difficulty moving around in the house. At first, I had thought Cô Ba suffered poliomyelitis, but her nephew said that she and other women had been rounded up by the Legionnaires and put on a train to be taken to their barracks. Because of Cô Ba's fierce resistance, she was brutally beaten and thrown off the speeding train. She did not get killed but could not walk again. When her nephew told her story, she did not say a word, but I saw a glow of rage and determination in her bright beautiful eyes. It had been a long time since the assault, and yet Cô Ba did not seem to get over it. I could see that she was reliving the most horrible but heroic moment of her life during which she had acted alone to protect herself and her dignity. My landlord's narration had taken Cô Ba out of obscurity for a moment. During the remainder of my stay there, she resumed her life as an obscure, nondescript spinster whose infirmity would be attributed to illness rather than the result of her heroic resistance to the Legionnaires. But for her nephew's indiscreetness, I would not have known her extraordinary story. In the war there were many victims like Cô Ba, but who would care to listen to their stories or protect them when everybody's life was in danger? It was also because in their culture, the female body, like a temple, should be sanctified, and if for any reason it is sullied, then they would rather die than live and bear the humiliation or talk about it in public.

As the war was raging, the people of Trung Quán and neighboring villages witnessed tragedy happen to their neighbors or their family as a routine. Men who worked for the French or the government were assassinated by the Việt Minh, Việt Minh suspects were executed by the French, women were raped by the Legionnaires or Moroccan soldiers, and children were killed by stray bullets while tending their cattle in the rice fields. The dead were buried on a stretch of land which used to be a paddy field. In summer nights solitary dots of light would come out from the cemetery, fly around a little while as if they were looking for something, then disappear. Our landlord said these were the apparitions of war victims searching for food and their former home. A chill ran down my spine, and I stopped watching the scene and shut the window tightly before going to bed.

One night in winter 1950 (I do not remember the exact date, but it could be in late winter because it was wet and cold), Father woke my brother and me and told us to get ready to leave Trung Quán as quickly as possible. I did not realize that he had planned this secret escape to the city several months before I passed my primary school graduation exam and my brother finished grade school. He decided that living in the country not only was not safe but would deprive us of good educational opportunities. Never had I seen my father so determined to give us a better future until the moment I woke up on that night. As soon as we were fully awake, we got out of our house and silently filed out into darkness. Led by our guide who knew the shortest and safest way to the city, we were embarking on the riskiest journey ever. We were supposed to keep away from Việt Minh-controlled areas and French troops' barracks. But to get to the city, sometimes we had to pass those dangerous locations on our way. When emerging from hidden lanes, we ran as fast as we could but lay down in the cold muddy rice field every time a flare fired from a nearby French military post lit our passage.

We arrived at Aunt Em's home in Lương Yến, a small village on the outskirts of Đồng Hới, in the wee hours of the next morning. After my father paid our guide, he dismissed him. Today I still wonder how Father, a timid and withdrawn man, could plan and carry out our escape so well. First, how could we avoid running into the Việt Minh, who now became strong enough to attack French posts almost every night? Could our guide have been a Việt Minh insider? But one thing Father had done several days before we made the trip confirmed my faith in his ingenuity. One morning as we were on our way to a neighboring village, we saw a unit of French troops move in our opposite direction. Father stopped a young man who looked like the commanding officer and explained to him our situation in French. The soldiers were friendly to us probably because their leader was very polite to Father. One man stroked my brother's head, speaking to him in a gentle voice. The soldiers looked on while Father talked to their commander. They seemed very much impressed when seeing him engage in a conversation with their commander in their native tongue, which must be an extraordinary thing in this rural place. For the first time, I did not fear French soldiers. It was safe to be near them. My brother and I, from now on, would be protected by Father!

A few days later, Father went to see the French officer and was warmly greeted by him. He got what he wanted: a laissez-passer that would allow him to travel safely in French-controlled areas to practice medicine. Father showed me the precious document. "That young gentleman was very polite to me, always addressing me as *'docteur'*," he said proudly. The document was written in beautiful longhand and signed "Lt. Bernard De Lattre."

(In June 1951 after we had resettled in Đồng Hới, I read in the *Paris Match* about the death of Lt. Bernard De Lattre, the only son of General De Lattre De Tassigny, the commander of French troops in Vietnam. He was killed in Ninh Bình Province in a battle at River Đáy at the age of twenty-three. I mentioned the news to my father, and he was positive that it was the kind-hearted officer who had issued a laissez-passer to him on the eve of our move to Đồng Hới. Apparently, Lt. De Lattre had been transferred to Ninh Bình province in the north after his assignment in Quảng Bình. His death shocked my father tremendously.)

ESCAPE TO ĐỒNG HỚI

We stayed at Lương Yến for a while waiting for my father to work out his plans to settle eventually in Đồng Hới. Using his laissez-passer, my father traveled freely to the city to see his new patients and to rent a house close to school. (Even after he had retired to live with my family in Huế, he still insisted that we find a site near school to build our home so his grandchildren could safely walk to school.) But Lương Yến was not a safe place either. Though it was only three kilometers from Đồng Hới, Việt Minh guerrillas would come out in the daytime and pop into our residence for a random check. By now we had grown wary of the Việt Minh because of our recent departure from Trung Quán without their approval. I was smart enough to fool these hardened adults. As soon as I saw them, I would pretend that I was drawing the scene of a battle in which the French were wiped out by the Việt Minh. When seeing my work, those Việt Minh soldiers praised my patriotism and one of them by the name of Tiến sat down to teach me how to sketch common things such as trees, birds, clouds, houses, mountains, rivers, etc. This strategy not only allowed us to avoid their suspicion of our origin but helped me acquire the habit—and imperfect skill—of doodling to entertain myself. As our friendship grew, Tiến taught me to sing patriotic songs. It was a waste of time for him, for no matter how hard he tried and how much I liked music, he could not make me open my mouth. I would rather learn drawing than singing. To me, drawing was a pastime that I could do in my privacy and at my own pace. I could also be free from public pressure when doing the work. I was too timid, too self-conscious to try singing in front of a stranger!

The song I liked best was "Du kích sông Thao" ["River Thao Militiamen"] by the famed composer Đỗ Nhuận. I was mesmerized to hear Tiến sing that patriotic song. It made me love Vietnam better and feel more grateful to the men like my friend Tiến who were fighting the enemy. It made me change my mind about the Việt Minh, who not long ago filled me with terror and were the reason for our fleeing Trung Quán. When I was alone, I would hum the tune to myself and feel a wave of patriotic feelings well up in me. After that day, I began to miss Tiến when he did not come to see me. He was not only a close friend and a brother figure, but he became associated with the land I loved so early in life. Tiến did not come to see me for several days, then he disappeared for good. He might have been killed somewhere. There was a lot of fighting at that time around Lương Yến and in the suburbs of Đồng Hới and both sides suffered heavy casualties.

***

We managed to leave my aunt's village and settled in Đồng Hới after our daring escape in late August 1950 shortly before the new school year began. My brother and I enrolled in Chơn Phước, a private junior high school run by the brothers of the Sacred Heart. The principal, a sickly-looking, soft-spoken man in his forties, taught French and Catechism. Other brothers taught various subjects ranging from catechism to Vietnamese literature. The school also employed non-Catholics to teach math and history. Students from the city were wealthy as they wore shirts, trousers, and sandals. But those from the neighboring villages and refugee families like us were poor. We walked to school barefoot, in shorts, and often with no breakfast. The road from our home to the school was long, windswept, wet, and cold in winter. We had fun playing "car race" by pursuit, but our feet got badly frozen after the run because we had no shoes on during the race.

I had no happy memories of my educational experience at Chơn Phước. Perhaps because it was an all-boys school run by male priests with an all-male faculty and staff, the atmosphere was oppressive. Except for Mr. Phạm Kiêm Âu, our math teacher, a political exile from Saigon, who treated us like his own kids and teased us when we gave dumb responses to his questions, the rest maintained an absolutely forbidding appearance. I was most afraid of math and Mr. Lương, the man who taught this subject. He was a terror to us because of his use of corporal punishment to enforce discipline and to bring weak students in line with strong ones.

Since the medicine shop where my father saw his patients was across from the local *deuxième bureau* (French military secret police) building whence at night came piercing screams of Việt Minh suspects being tortured, I could not help peering in that direction when I was not in the shop with my father. One day, I happened to see Vietnamese *deuxième bureau* agents apparently preparing for an interrogation and torture session. Instead of quickly coming inside, I stayed in the middle of the street, riveting my eyes on the scene. A young man, apparently a Việt Minh suspect, was dragged out of a military truck. No sooner was he on his feet than another Vietnamese man, a security official working for French security forces, came over and started beating the prisoner on the face with a big stick. Frightened, I turned to walk away, but it was too late: that man had seen me. He ordered me to stop and, crossing the street to get closer to me, he grasped my shoulders and "whack! whack!"

slapped me in the face several times, cussing me out in his foul language. Luckily, nobody was around when that happened.

I had seen and experienced nothing but violence and terror since our moving to Đồng Hới. Having lived long enough in the city under government control and having seen so much terrorism committed by the Việt Minh, I lost my naive belief in them. Our small town was gripped with fear because of frequent assassinations of government officials by Việt Minh commandos. After performing the act, they would escape through the town's main gate to the suburbs. As soon as they reached the city limits, they were safe because in the 1950s, the countryside was under Việt Minh control. The townspeople buzzed about each assassination after its occurrence, their gossip ranging from the assassin's "exploit" in killing a major government official and his successful escape to the suffering caused to the victim's family. They seemed to enjoy doing it, not knowing that next time it could be their turn to mourn one of their relatives. (Most people living in Đồng Hới were government employees and were a target of Việt Minh terrorism.)

Because Đồng Hới was a small town, when an assassination took place, I knew immediately who the victim was and could hear the loud keening of his family and see his funeral afterward. I lost my faith in the Việt Minh, who in my young mind became associated with terror rather than liberation. At the same time, I hated French soldiers who killed our men they suspected of being Việt Minh collaborators and raped our women. I frequently heard of or witnessed acts of terror committed by both sides. The Việt Minh assassinated innocent people in broad daylight while the government and the French displayed the enemy's corpses for public view instead of burying them. On my way to school now and then I saw piles of blood-caked bodies in drab pajamas in an abandoned school on the roadside. Their eyes were open. There was still shock and horror on their faces. Because their eyes did not close all the way, I often heard old people say, it meant that they died of a wrongful death and many of them could be innocent civilians, not just Việt Minh soldiers. When we children first found out about the display, we would linger on to take a peep at the corpses out of curiosity. Later, as the war was raging and this occurred frequently and somebody suggested that the ghosts of these dead men might be lurking around to find a replacement, we grew stiff-scared and no longer wanted to see them.

My adolescence was the most critical period of my life. It is therefore easier to remember my four turbulent years in Đồng Hới before going south under the Geneva Peace Accords than any other moment of my young adulthood. My people's suffering affected me tremendously. The cry of the families whose relatives were frequently assassinated by the Việt Minh broke my heart. The blood-caked bodies of peasants and guerrillas with eyes open exposed in that abandoned school kept haunting me even in my sleep. The all-boys school where I could hardly see a smile was really depressing. My family's situation, furthermore, was no better. Because of lack of parental supervision (my father was at work all day), when not in school I would roam the streets with kids in the neighborhood or sneak into the city theater to see movies. When we were found by the usher and kicked out, we would puncture holes in the back wall through which we could still enjoy the show from the wrong side of the screen. During noontime when everybody was taking a nap, I was wandering in the marketplace barefoot, bare-chested, my shirt draped over my head to keep off the summer heat. It was during these outings that I accidentally came close to a brothel where I could not help peeking through the window at prostitutes with French soldiers. Seeing our women with these hateful Legionnaires and mean-looking Moroccans haunted and nauseated me.

As early as 1953, three years after we left Trung Quán, we began to see light at the end of the tunnel. My father's medical practice was prosperous. We bought a new home with land large enough for us to build an extra brick house which we later rented out to a family just repatriating from Laos. I still cooked for the family when returning from school because we could not afford to keep a maid. But occasionally we were able to supplement our ordinary staple with some luxury foods. We also dressed better when going to school. To top it off, I stopped hanging around with kids of dubious repute in the neighborhood to concentrate on my studies. Knowing that math was still my worst subject, my father bought me a subscription to the *Hiếu Học* [*Crave Knowledge*], a study guide magazine published in Hanoi, so that I could start preparing for my 9th-grade graduation exam the following year. I had little success with my math but derived immense pleasure from devouring sample essays on Vietnamese literature written by Mr. Nguyễn Đình Tế, a teacher at Nguyễn Trãi High School in Hanoi. For the first time I was exposed to a new world of knowledge and learning. Through this fabulous teacher's guide explained in the magazine, I learned to develop my own style of writing and oral presentation. I impressed Brother Thomas, my Vietnamese teacher, when I gave a speech on folk poetry using literary expression I had learned from Mr. Tế's sample essays. By the time I entered eighth grade, I had acquired the skills and habits of learning with an eagerness to follow my father in his footsteps—becoming an educated person.

The year 1953 would have been perfect but for a last mishap befalling my family. My brother and I took turns to fall seriously ill. First, I contracted typhoid fever when Quảng Bình had a big flood. When water began to flap against my bedside, Father evacuated us to our new brick house. Seating me on his back, he waded through the knee-deep muddy water on his shaky legs all the way to the safe location and came back to make another trip for my brother. After Father had cured me, a few months later my brother contracted the same disease. His condition was so grave that his skin and teeth grew black, his eyes yellow, his bowel movements dysfunctional. Father burned incense on our ancestors' altar and prayed for my brother's recovery in addition to ransacking all his medical books to search for a possible cure. It broke my heart to see how he cared for my brother. At night, every time he administered medication to my brother, Father would stay up to watch him. He also extracted meat broth to feed him. One day, I saw him blow pellets made of papaya seed powder into my brother's rectum to ease his bowel movements. This sort of treatment worked very well, but my brother's stool popped out and landed on Father's face!

My last year at Chơn Phước was the best I could ask for in my entire adolescence. Being graduating candidates, we became the apple of our school's eye. To make sure that we passed the upcoming exam that would qualify us for admission to covetous secondary schools in Huế, the brothers enlisted Mr. Nguyễn Hữu Thứ, a judge originally from Huế, to teach history. Perhaps because of his legal training, Judge Thứ was very strict, but his knowledge was awesome. We still had Mr. Lương for math, but he became humbler. He must have learned a hard lesson from Võ Khắc Mai, a math whiz in our class. This boy seldom paid attention to Mr. Lương's teaching, but instead his eyes were glued to a martial arts novel he was hiding under his desk. One morning, Mr. Lương made him solve a difficult problem on the spot, intending to set a trap for Mai to fall in so he could justify his premeditated punishment. The rascal did get away with it by presenting on the blackboard a step-by-step approach to the problem that we found so clear, so easy to understand! Mr. Lương left him alone ever since then.

I had fun in the two remaining classes: English and Vietnamese. Our English teacher, Brother Antoine, had a dignified look but he was too young and too handsome to be a priest. He drilled us in English pronunciation using the *Anglais Sans Peine* [*English Without Toil*] texts and voice recordings. My experience in the Vietnamese class was more educational. Brother Thomas had a vast knowledge of Vietnamese literature, except, as a priest, he had some difficulty dealing with texts that were romantic or slightly on the erotic side such as *The Tale of Kiều*. (Implicitly erotic texts by the 19th-century poetess Hồ Xuân Hương, which were widely studied at the secondary level in public schools in the rest of the country, did not exist in our school's curriculum). Later in his life, Brother Thomas left the Order, got married, and made a family of his own. I never had a chance to see him ever since we left Đồng Hới in 1954. As I am writing these lines, I regret that I did not try to visit Brother

Thomas and other brothers who, I was told, after Chơn Phước high school had been closed, moved to Huế and lived in the same seminary where I had stayed while taking the oral part of my junior secondary exam.

In April 1954, I took and passed the written test of the junior school certificate exam. Because at that time most rural areas from the north of Quảng Trị to Quảng Bình were under Việt Minh control, the only safe way to travel to Huế for the oral test was by airplane. We were all proud of our achievement, which won us a free trip on Air Vietnam to Huế, a dream city for country boys like us. It took our plane only an hour to arrive at Phú Bài Airport where we were put in an Air Vietnam van and whisked to the city. Though I came from Dalat and had traveled by car with my family before, this was the first time since my return to my father's country that I was driven in a luxury automobile and saw such a big city. There were so many houses, buildings, cars, tricycles, bicycles, and pedestrians. Everybody there went about their business in a carefree, happy manner. Boys and girls my age rode their bicycles in rows of three or four, with smiles on their radiant faces. War did not seem to affect Huế. A few days earlier, while in Đồng Hới, I had heard our teachers say that the conflict might end soon with the partition of Vietnam at the 17th parallel. For sure, Quảng Bình would go communist, they added. I suddenly felt envious of the safety and peace that Huế people were enjoying. Huế was not part of the Vietnam I was familiar with since the outbreak of war in 1946.

I continued marveling at the wonders of Huế, especially Đồng Khánh High School, an all-girls school, where our oral exams were being held. Never had I seen such a vast, gorgeous campus with huge buildings. It was so cool and green there that I could not help comparing it with my small school in Đồng Hới which was hot, windswept, and dry at this time. But it was the people I saw that greatly impressed me. Teachers here looked younger, but they carried themselves with more dignity than the brothers at my school. Students who were sitting their exams also looked wealthy, smart, and sophisticated. I felt ashamed of my origin.

After I returned to Đồng Hới, developments at the Geneva Conference confirmed the division of Vietnam at the 17th parallel. My father began whispering to us the possibility of fleeing the Việt Minh again, but he did not tell us how. Now that I finished school and had a lot of free time, I went to the city's public library to keep myself abreast of the news. Because of censorship, Vietnamese newspapers did not reveal much about the possible outcome of the Geneva Conference, but they could not hide the serious reality of war: General De Lattre was appointed as Commander-in-Chief of French troops in Vietnam, there were several major military movements ordered by De Lattre, and the battle of Điện Biên Phủ just began. To have a better grasp of the political and military situation, I consulted the *Paris Match* in the public library. The picture drawn by the French weekly was very gloomy: the French were losing the war and the evacuation of the Vietnamese government from Hanoi to Saigon was most likely.

But except for concerned citizens in Đồng Hới, most people went about their business as usual. I kept my father posted of the developments at the Paris Conference as reported in the *Paris Match* whenever I could, but I also wanted to enjoy life, not caring much about what was happening.

PANGS OF FIRST LOVE

Earning a junior high school diploma was an important purpose for boys who lived in Đồng Hới in the 1950s. First, we could not afford to go to Huế to complete our Baccalauréat (high school) education because it was too far and too expensive. Besides, in a small town like Đồng Hới, where junior high school graduates were rare and highly esteemed, we could easily get a teaching job in an elementary school, live a comfortable life, and start a family, a thing that most middle-class families like ours aspired for. Such a life could not be more ideal for me. Not only was my family not well off, but I also preferred to stay put because I was not smart enough for an advanced education.

It was by accident and perhaps through predestination that I fell in love with Trang whose house was in my neighborhood. At eighteen while my peers were preparing to enter a new phase of life, I was still living under my Confucianist father's strict supervision and did not have a girlfriend. One day in early summer 1954, I saw from across the street where I lived a girl and her mother getting on a pedicab. They seemed to be going to the temple as they wore a light blue dress and carried bouquets of flowers and bundles of joss sticks and candles. I knew Mrs. Giám, the girl's mother, whose husband owned an Oriental medicine shop and employed my father as an attending physician. But I did not know the girl. My cousin Tân told me I did not know Trang (the girl) because she had been sent to Hanoi for school before we moved to Đồng Hới. She was home for summer just recently.

I was struck by Trang's beauty and fell in love with her immediately. It was, as I often heard the adults say in French, a *coup de foudre* (love at first sign). I felt an instant, irresistible attraction for her though I did not know her. The French word *foudre*, meaning lightning strike, very aptly depicts my condition. An electrifying sensation shot through my body, one that gave me excitement, pleasure, and happiness that I had not experienced before. Suddenly, I realized that this was not a real joy, as it was followed by a painful presentiment that this would end up with nothing. She did not see me, nor did she know who I was. She appeared just like an image to me. And yet the image was so sharp, so lively in my mind. It haunted me, giving me more pain than pleasure.

I had trouble falling asleep that night. As her image sank deeply in my mind, it became alive. I did not see her face and hear her voice clearly, but her image now became sharp, lively, and real. I could not help thinking about her as if I had known her for a long time, as if she was my actual girlfriend.

Mr. Giám's house, which was usually quiet, became noisy when Trang was home. I saw girls her age come to her place apparently to visit her or get together with her. At such moments I heard animated talking and crystal-clear laughter inside her home. The girls' crystal-clear voice reverberated in the transparent air of the early summer evening.

I also saw Trang go out with her group a few times especially in late summer afternoons, which were hot and sunny. From the balcony of my home, I saw Trang and her band take their afternoon walk. I knew the time when they would go and waited with trepidation for that moment. I could hear their giggle and animated conversation and see their white *ao dai* (long dress) and pants fluttering in the wind when they passed by my house. Their crystal-clear laughter and twittering struck me like a musical scale that found an echo in my heart. They had been long gone, but I stood motionless at my balcony and cast my glance at their disappearing images and could hear their diminishing voices and see their vanishing images. They had been long gone, but their images stayed on in my mind, sharp and clear and poignant in the hot late summer afternoon. They had been long gone, but my mind was still abuzz with their giggling and crystal-clear laughter. I stood still for a while and did not get in my house until their images and their voices subsided, vanished completely. Just then a wave of sound melodious, mellow but sad rose from the flamboyant trees in full bloom along our street. The sound grew to a crescendo, was sustained, fell quiet (was it a *tacet* or just the notes were still being played but I could not hear them because of my obsession with Trang and her band?), then started over again. It was those cicadas that routinely came out at this time in late summer to sing until nightfall. As I turned to go into the house, everything fell into darkness. An immense sadness arose in me.

Things developed incredibly fast in my favor. One evening when returning from the medicine shop where he worked for Mr. Giám, Father told me to get ready to go with him to see Mr. and Mrs. Giám. I knew what was happening and was thrilled but afraid. I guessed Father might have talked to Mr. and Mrs. Giám about me, about my graduation from high school, and so on. It was obvious that Father had picked Trang for me, and her parents wanted to see me. I could not believe it. I was going to see the girl with whom I was secretly in love!

My father chose an auspicious day in early July to take me to see, as he said, "your future parents-in-law." (He did not say "your future wife" because, in our culture, seeing her parents would be enough). My heart pounded hard, my legs wobbled when we reached their home. Mr. and Mrs. Giám greeted us very warmly, so I felt much better. After we sat down and my father and Trang's parents exchanged their greetings, Mrs. Giám called out to Trang to bring tea to us, whereupon I saw her appear from the bamboo blinds connecting perhaps to the living room with a tray of tea and refreshments. She made a deep bow to my father and cast me a quick quizzical glance with a twinkle in her eyes as if she was teasing me, knowing why I came today. I was so embarrassed but extremely happy. This was the first time I saw her closely. Just a week ago, I contemplated her at a distance from the balcony of my house when she and her band marched in my street. She was very pretty, much prettier than when I saw her from my house when she was preparing to go to the temple with her mother. There emanated from her poise, intelligence, and confidence that characterized her as a modern Hanoi girl. This made a country boy like me feel ashamed.

Trang's parents permitted me to come to see her at their home. Still afraid and timid, I was tongue-tied so Trang did most of the talking. She had a beautiful Hanoi accent, which made her voice sound very sophisticated to me. She told me she was training to become an elementary teacher and wanted after graduation to teach at a private school at home. In our later meetings when we became closer to each other, Trang asked me a lot of questions about my school experience and about my plans. When I told her that my father wanted me to continue my education in Huế, she looked so sad. I also felt sad because there lurked in the back of my mind something ominous that told me that I would have to leave Đồng Hới and our union would not materialize. There were tears in her eyes. I awkwardly held out my hand to her, intending to wipe her tears but afraid to do so. She took my hand and briefly held it in hers. I felt like there was an electric current flowing through my body. How happy I was! I wanted her to hold my hand like that forever. But we could not go further than that. We were just kids growing up in a Confucianist-oriented society. We met under her mother's watchful eyes. My desire could be satisfied only in my imagination or in my sleep.

Since my visit to her house, I did not see Trang and her band come to my street. She told me she was not in the mood for enjoying herself anymore. Like me, she might have known something grave was going to happen to our future union. For me, the ominous sensation I had felt in our first date was clear now: it was the recent developments at the Geneva Conference. The breaking news was that world powers had agreed upon a cease-fire in Indochina and rumor had it that Vietnam would be partitioned at the 17th parallel.

People were talking about leaving Đồng Hới as the city would belong to the Việt Minh.

Trang came to fetch me at my house and asked me if my family would leave should the country's partition become a reality. She revealed that her oldest brother, who was a high-ranking officer in the Việt Minh army, was returning home and demanded that her family not go anywhere. I was stunned, shocked, and sad. I could not answer Trang's question because I knew that our relationship would end soon. My father had yet to make his decision, but I knew that leaving would be best for us in this situation. Father was afraid that the Việt Minh would punish him for fleeing Lương Yến, a village under their control, to arrive in Đồng Hới. He also wanted to take us to the South to have a better future for us. Poor old man. After so many years of moving around from place to place without a home of our own, he finally succeeded in building a house for us to settle in and for him to have a place to worship his ancestors. Now he was about to give up everything because of us!

The *Paris Match*, the only French weekly magazine that the public library subscribed to, revealed bad news about the outcome of the Conference. It confirmed the rumor that Vietnam would be partitioned at the 17 parallel. The Geneva Peace Agreements were officially signed on July 20th, 1954, dividing Vietnam at a small river called Bến Hải as a demarcation line and providing a timeframe for people to choose their preferred regime. People living in the North were beginning to leave.

The morning after the cease-fire we witnessed a shocking scene: emerging out of nowhere, Việt Minh cadres were roaming the streets of Đồng Hới. They also showed up at civilians' homes, demanding that they be taken in as guests. (They did not bother the Catholics who they knew did not accept communism.) Doing so allowed them to keep an eye on the people in Đồng Hới (and maybe in other small towns where the International Armistice Control Commission established by the Geneva Accords was not represented) and prevent them from fleeing. One of our distant relatives, who had lived with us as a house guest for some time and who had mysteriously disappeared for a few days, suddenly showed up with two guests. My father ordered us to stay at home when they were around, but we secretly packed our belongings in a small wooden suitcase and waited for the right moment. Occasionally, I stealthily sneaked out of the house and ran to the quay where a French military ship (people called it *"tàu há miệng"* because its side was gaping wide like a big animal's maw) was docking and waiting to pick up evacuees to find out what was happening. I saw lots of hilarious scenes here. Young men who succeeded in getting to the pier were often stopped by women and young kids who loudly besought them "not to abandon your loved ones." Apparently, it was the Việt Minh who organized events like these to foil our male citizens' attempts to leave. The French sailors had to disperse the crowd so the men could board the ship. One day, a man made it to the dock but missed the boarding, whereupon all the waiting women and urchins jumped on him, all claiming him as their man and daddy and dragging the struggling person off the port. If their victim was lucky enough to be rescued and escorted to the waiting ship, they would beat their chest and clamp their feet, crying bitterly as if they had just lost someone who was dearest to them!

As the deadline for evacuation out of Đồng Hới was drawing nearer, more and more people left home and camped out at the dock. Most evacuees were Catholics, but there were also folks who wanted to go south to seek a better future.

We were in a big dilemma during the two last weeks before the last ship left the port of Đồng Hới. My father could not make his decision right away though we had packed and hidden our luggage from our relative and his two Việt Minh friends. As familiar faces I had often seen on the streets of Đồng Hới gradually disappeared (I could not tell whether they had left or kept themselves indoors because they could not make their decision or were just waiting for the right moment), my father resorted to his favorite method: tossing ancient coins to consult our ancestors. He had used this method at least on two previous important occasions—before his return to his native Quảng Bình and before our fleeing Trung Quán. Though my father was extremely resourceful, he would turn to our ancestors for advice at his wits' end. In a short but very solemn ceremony conducted before our ancestors' altar with his *I-ching* book open, my father threw the coins three times. The arrangement of the coins after the throwing suggested that we would encounter a lot of difficulties, but it was important that we leave.

My father was thus determined to leave as soon as the next—and last—round of evacuation was announced and when our house guests were not around. Father was in great distress and pain since he had made that decision. He did not seem to get any sleep because I saw dark circles under his eyes. He was worried because at sixty it was too late for him to start over with two young children with no money and no relatives in a strange land. It was his fear of the Việt Minh and his vague dream about his children's future that made him make that decision to give up our comfortable life in Đồng Hới. Father said it was important that our schooling be continued and therefore we must leave Đồng Hới. *You would disgrace your ancestors and your father if you didn't care for your education,* Father said. *Be willing to accept challenges and even risks if they are worth it. Don't you remember,* he added, *four years ago had I not braved the Việt Minh and taken the family here, you wouldn't be a high school graduate today? Be brave, son, leave this place to seek freedom and educational opportunities. I want you and your brother to become doctors. Heaven, Buddhas, and our ancestors will protect good-willed people like us.* I was stunned and afraid. Father had never given me such a powerful lecture like this before. Convinced that the Việt Minh would deny schooling to children from families not loyal to them and that jobs involving manual labor would not suit us, Father believed that only through education could he secure a good life for us. *Besides, you know that it isn't safe to live with the Việt Minh. They will punish me for two reasons: they will find out through our former tenants and servants that I was trained as a mandarin at the Imperial Academy and that, I'm sure you still remember, on that dark cold night in November we fled Lương Yến village which was under their control and arrived in Đồng Hới, the only place under the government's control. Perhaps,* Father emphasized, *you're too young to know about their so-called denunciation campaign against landlords and French-educated intellectuals.* Father stopped. His voice quivered. I never saw him so agitated, but so passionately articulate when talking to me. I understood what Father said and agreed with him, but in the back of my mind, I felt that the adventure we were about to take would not end well, and I had a premonition that I would have a very tough time after our arrival in the South. But at eighteen I was too young to be consulted by Father about this important thing. Father was a very genteel man, but he was resolute in matters of raising his children.

I understood what Father said, but I did not want to leave Đồng Hới. Education was something too vague, too abstract, too risky. Suddenly, I thought of Trang. So much had been on my mind I had not thought about her since the breaking news about the partition of the country and my father's determination to leave Đồng Hới. I had not gone to see her these last two weeks. I did not know what to say to her nor did I have the courage to tell her the bad news. I missed her and everything related to her since I first saw her and later on when my father took me to see her and her parents—the band of girls under her direction marching past my house in the late sunny summer afternoon talking and giggling all the way, their white *ao dai* and pants flickering like butterflies, her deep bow to my father, and the teasing twinkle at me on her beautiful radiant face. I missed so much the moment she took my hand and held it in hers with tears in her eyes. Did my cousin Tân tell her all about me and she wanted to reciprocate my love for her? I did not know that when I thought I had found happiness it slipped out of my hand. Thinking, *So, I am going to lose Trang, am I not? If I was destined to lose her, why was I arranged to see her and become her would-be intended?* I do not understand, nor do I want to understand this terrible truth. I invoke Father's teaching about how to withstand the force of circumstances, which he calls fate: *"Don't resist fate.*

Bear it until it wears out and it will leave you alone." But what is fate? Isn't it the will imposed by the strong on the weak? Who caused the war, who decided the partition of our country that caused me to leave home and lose my sweetheart? Had the war not been waged and had the world powers in Geneva left Vietnam alone I would be united with Trang. I would be the happiest person in the world. In the end, I ought to agree with my father's plaint about his misfortune in life *"Con Tạo trớ trêu!"* (How malicious fate is). It arranged for me to see Trang and fall in love with her, for her family to accept me as her future intended. But it cuts short in the middle of our planned union. It kills my first love. How ridiculous, absurd, unjust, and cruel.

Đường Nhà Tằm street, where I live, is deserted now that people are preparing to vacate the city. I no longer see Trang. She and the girls no longer come in the sultry summer afternoon with their giggle and crystal-clear laughter. But the usual regular schedule of the invisible cicadas is the same in the late summer afternoon. They come out invisibly from the flamboyant trees in full bloom along our street and start singing. When their music reaches a crescendo, it is sustained for a moment and then continues until dusk. They stop singing as dusk falls, but I still hear its sad echo in the gloom of the twilight. In the gloom of the twilight, the echo grows thin but pervasive and poignant.

Lying in my bed, I think about many things. I think about leaving the comforts of home and plunging in an interminable journey full of uncertainty and risks. How can I support myself and go to school at the same time? What kind of thing can I do to live? Will I be able to put up with the derision of classmates in the new school when they find out about my family situation? Father said hardship is the gateway to success in life. But can I endure hardship by myself in the strange land with no resources, no relatives? Most importantly, can I endure the sorrow of losing Trang whom I have not seen since we heard news about the division of the country and my father's decision to leave home? My mind drifts to the remaining days of July, only ten days left before we will be going on that risky, unpredictable journey into the unknown. Never have I thought that much about home, paid that much attention to things around me.

At night things are livelier than during the day. Lying in bed at night, I feel that everything at home now becomes dearer, more important to me than ever. In the completely still, quiet, dark night, I can hear the feeble monotonous, melancholy cry of crickets around my house. I can hear the dogs far in the quiet dark night in the neighborhood and even long away from my home. *OuOuOu. OuOuOu. OuOuuuuuuuuuuu.* At night their high-pitched uninterrupted sound is sharp, piercing, and forlorn. It sounds like *Ôi,* which in Vietnamese means *alas*. In the night the dogs' howling drags out eternally, tearing your heart out. Then it dies away, but its clear sad reverberation continues in the air and in my mind for another while until I fall asleep. Is it because dogs carry a soul, a living force inside of them that machines do not? Father said that dogs' voice heard at night is doleful because they can see, understand, and sympathize with hungry ghosts searching for food at night. Not only do they feel sorry for the ghosts, they can also communicate with me and feel sorry for me tonight as I will be gone and my home will be permanently lost. The soul of your native land will follow you, will not let go of you wherever you go, Father said, when I asked him why his poems are about home and why they are so sad. He said that his poems are sad because they are about his native Quảng Bình he had left so early in his life in response to the call of adventure when he was about my age. I do not want to follow my father in his footsteps. I do not want to leave home and write poetry about it because I am not a poet like my father. I want to stay here with Trang. Just the two of us in this place. But it looks like I am destined to inherit that karmic debt from Father. It is an inherited debt imposed on me, mysterious and implacable.

A light rain starts outside tapping on the roof and on the windowpanes, waking up the lethargic and dozy crickets in this unusually sultry summer night. The steady taps of the rain on the roof on the windowpanes and the feeble doleful shrilling of the crickets get increasingly loud in my mind, inhibiting my thinking. Then it wears off, I hear Trang and her band sauntering past my house, laughing and giggling along the way. Then I hear Trang's voice with a delightful Hanoi accent because of her long stay in the North. When she talks about her dreams and hopes, especially our future union, her voice sounds like a singsong. I do not remember much of the contents of her talk, but I vividly remember her voice.

A series of thundering mournful whistles from the French military ship being anchored at the port wakes me from my reverie. Loud and threatening and melancholy, the blasts are the last call for people who plan to leave in a few days. They remind people of the last round of evacuation which will take place in no time. A train's whistles also remind one of separation, but they are not as menacing and painful as a ship's horn blasts. Loud, threatening, and gloomy, they signify I am going down the road from which I will never return, that I will have a tough life ahead of me, and that I will never ever see Trang again in this lifetime. The powerful horn blasts shut up all the sounds of nature, the howling of the dogs, the crying of the crickets which were vibrant in my mind a short while ago. A short while ago, I could picture in my mind Trang and her band passing by my house, their white *ao dai* and pants fluttering in the wind like butterflies, laughing, chattering, giggling garrulously along the way, in the late hot, sultry summer afternoon. A short while ago. I could still hear Trang sharing with me her dreams and hopes in her fascinating Hanoi voice.

Suddenly, all the sounds related to home and my sweetheart vanish after the emission of the horn blasts of the ship. The ship's brutal sound destroys my last daydream about home and my lover before the fateful journey. The crickets stop crying. I am clinging to the sounds of home and my memory of Trang's voice to alleviate somewhat my sorrow and depression when the ship's horn blasts bring me back to reality. The crying of crickets has died out. My room gets stuffy. Everything goes silent save the relentless ticking of the clock on my table. What is the use of trying to escape from reality when the dice is cast? Finished. All finished. What remains are tons of heavy memories I will be carrying in my journey to the unknown land.

During the last week of July, I undergo a strange phenomenon of memory. Present events stop existing, replaced by memories of the past. I have not left home, and yet feel I have lost home and am living with its memories. It has been a while since I left Trang and Đồng Hới. I feel remorse for leaving her and not trying to see her. I saw tears in her eyes. We both knew our union had ended. But suddenly, I seem to be opening a Pandora's box from which my happy past springs. Trang is my girlfriend. More than that, she is my intended. Images of Trang and her group are pouring out in my mind. She and her band march hand in hand in the direction of my street. They walk and laugh and giggle along their way, their white dress and pants fluttering in the summer breeze like white butterflies flickering in the hot afternoon sun. They flicker for a brief while in my mind like the images on a magic lantern. They move with the lantern but are not progressing and go out of my mind as fast as they came.

***

July 30th, 1954. Around 5:00 p.m. I ran home as fast as I could to tell my father the breaking news: the huge ship was being docked at the port with a big crowd waiting to be evacuated. I just learned from an old woman that this would be the last evacuation out of Đồng Hới by the French Navy. As our guests were out (probably because we might have gained their trust for making no attempt to leave thus far, our Việt Minh guests had relaxed their supervision of us), my father made the most important decision in his entire life: he gave us five minutes to leave. We had enough time to pack in a heavy wooden trunk a pair of clothes for each of us, a couple of medical materials and poetry books that my father authored (he was a physician and a poet), our academic diplomas to be used for application to secondary school in Huế, a copy of our genealogy records in Chinese, and a stack of dried cuttlefish to give our family's acquaintances in Huế as a gift from Quảng Bình. We carried some cash for food and lodging during the journey to what my father called *"xứ lạ quê người"* (the strange land). As the three of us got in a waiting pedicab in front of our house and it began to move in the direction of the river, we all looked down, just like ostriches, so that nobody could see us. But before we did so, I could see two tears rolling down Father's face. That was the second time in his life I saw him cry, the previous time in Bình Định when he learned about my mother not returning with us to Quảng Bình. My brother also looked shocked and was unusually still. I felt a pang in my heart, trying to control my sobs as images of our beloved home were surging in my mind. We were leaving behind a home my father had just built and his country that I had just come to love perhaps more dearly than Dalat, my birthplace. I closed my eyes in order not to see and not to be seen, but it only made the images of our home, our city, places I had frequently been to more vivid and poignant in my mind. Like an avalanche, those images burst out all at the same moment, swarming in my head, rather than gently working their way into my consciousness and allowing me to relish tender memories of living in Đồng Hới and seeing Trang. Tears began to well in my eyes. I missed my home and my sweetheart. Trying hard to control my emotions, I trembled feebly. There was a firm touch on my shoulder. Father drew a heavy sigh. He seemed to understand now my sorrow of losing Trang, his favorite would-be daughter-in-law. But his greatest suffering, I think, was that we were giving up our *"khúc ruột"* (entrails), our dearest, safest niche, as he would say. We were going to a strange land and did not know what would be in store for us. Had we known this, we would not have left Dalat. He seemed to realize the mistake he had made when relinquishing Dalat where he had enjoyed a very thriving business and a happy family. But it was too late to go back and start over again.

Immediately upon arriving at the wharf, we ran into the noisiest, most unruly crowd I had ever seen. People did not form lines for boarding, but they jostled one another into a narrow bridge connecting to the waiting ship. The throng consisted mainly of the elderly from Đồng Hới and wealthy country folks who perhaps might not want to leave at first due to their strong attachment to their native place but changed their mind at the last minute perhaps because they feared possible large-scale punishments by the new regime. The crowd fought their way to the ship with their bulky luggage, creating a deafening fracas with their crying, screaming, and cussing. With my father and my brother holding fast to one side and me to the other side of our heavy trunk, we tried to push it through the crowd with little success. Some women swore at us when we got in their way. Along with the rest, we finally made it, but only in tatters. Thanks to the French sailors' gracious efficient assistance, the refugees of this last evacuation finally got settled in on the deck. Soon a siren was heard a couple of times and suddenly the quay and Đồng Hới started receding slowly. Unlike a train which makes a lot of noise after it starts, this ship was gliding so quietly, smoothly, and imperceptibly that people hardly noticed it was moving. Because people did not get distracted, they could acutely feel the pain of permanent severance from home. All the ruckus and fracas suddenly died out, and the entire population on the deck sank into an eerie quiet. There was a frightened, shocked look on their haggard faces. I also heard suppressed sobs from somewhere. My father looked away, mumbling something, perhaps a prayer. Because I had been much preoccupied with my emotional life these months, only now could I observe Father closely. He aged so fast, looking so thin and fragile.

The ship ran a few more hours before everything was engulfed in darkness. A cool, gentle breeze was blowing, wafting to us the salty smell of the ocean. It was the same salty smell of Đồng Hới, the city by the saltwater Nhật Lệ river. The sky was clear and beautiful with myriad glittering stars. It was so peaceful that I found it hard to believe that we had just lost our home and our country and were on a long journey into the unknown, *thinking* how could that happen, how could that happen? *Thinking again* if we could just have a voyage like this at a better time—that is, at the end of it we could return to our home in Đồng Hới, my father could go back to work at Mr. Giám's medicine shop, and I could go and see Trang on my own after she became my intended....

HUẾ

At around 7:00 pm, we arrived in Đà Nẵng, about 300 kilometers from Đồng Hới. After going through a quick registration procedure at the harbor, we were taken to our shelter downtown. To avoid the inconvenience of staying at a Catholic church, Buddhist refugees were sheltered at a Buddhist temple. We were also provided free meals while staying in Đà Nẵng and a sum of money for traveling to Huế for our final resettlement if we wanted to.

Contrary to my first visit to Huế a few months earlier, my coming to the South now made me feel really depressed. Back then life could not have been better for me. I had just earned a junior high school diploma and had got ready to go to Huế for further education. Now I was a tattered refugee after the traumatic journey. I was burning with shame when seeing the way in which the boys and girls my age, members of the local Buddhist church, assisted us. I knew they meant well, but I felt they were taking pity on us. There were in this group some pretty girls who reminded me of Trang, and I wondered how they felt about me. These kids and I were from the same country, but I felt I was no more than a mountaineer who happened to be in their city for the first time. I felt bad and regretted that I had left Đồng Hới to come here.

We refugees owed Mr. Ngô Đình Diệm a great deal for our successful resettlement in the South. Soon after the Geneva Accords, he was appointed Prime Minister of South Vietnam by Ex-Emperor Bảo Đại, who had lived in exile in France since the start of the first Indochina war. Upon his return to Vietnam from a Catholic convent in the United States, with the support of the U.S. and the Free World, Mr. Diệm immediately set about bringing more than a million refugees to the South.

Because we had no relatives in Đà Nẵng and ran out of money, my father decided to leave. Refugees could get free transportation by train. But the map of Central Vietnam in 1954 resembled a leopard's skin with several provinces along the coast under Việt Minh control; therefore, we could not go further to Dalat by train to find our old home and had to return to our original plan of moving to Huế.

On the morning of July 31st. we boarded the northbound train going to Huế. It was the most crowded train I had ever seen. Our wooden trunk continued to be our curse. It was too heavy and too big for me and my father to heave onto the train. We finally made it, but it broke my heart to see Father's pajamas almost in tatters as a mark of success! At fifty-six, he was already very frail and pale, like a seventy-year-old man, even by Vietnamese standards. I was angry with these young folks who jostled their way to get onto the train ahead of us. What had just happened and many other occurrences I was to encounter later in Huế taught me much about the human race and soon made me lose hope in the new land.

We arrived in Huế very late that night. A kind pedicab driver agreed to take the three of us along with our heavy trunk into the city. We got off at Đông Ba Market to buy something to eat. As it was very late at night, all food stands were closed. We could not afford to eat in a restaurant across the street; nor did we have money for another trip to find the house of my father's friend at this time. As we were all tired, Father made a bed for us by juxtaposing two rows of stools we found at a food stand for each of us. We went to sleep hungry that night. I was woken many times during the night by the bad smells of the market and the mosquitoes. Father did not seem to get any sleep because I saw him flap his paper fan all the time to keep the mosquitoes off me and my brother. Tears gushed from my eyes. Father had made a similar sacrifice when, during our first evacuation from Văn La to a mountainous region, he had us eat his meal because our ration was too small. Far into the night, I thought about the tough times ahead of us and how we were going to cope with them. We had no relatives in Huế. My father had some patients here, but I doubted they would offer any help. Our savings and the money we received from the government were insufficient. Father brought us here because he cared for our future. But now he had second thoughts about it.

Next morning, my father told me his decision to send my brother to Nha Trang and we would return to Đồng Hới. Since there was no need now to give our cuttlefish to anyone, he told me to sell them. We needed extra cash to buy our way back home. The money we had then was only enough to purchase a plane ticket for my brother.

I was both scared and ashamed to be a hawker in this strange market full of mean-spirited, cruel women. At first, they seemed surprised to see a boy sell goods in the market, the job being restricted in their country to girls and women. When I explained to them our situation—that we were refugees who wanted to go home but had no money to pay for our fare and needed their compassion, et cetera, et cetera, they nodded sympathy for me in such terms as "Bless your heart, poor child," but would not budge on the cheapest price they could haggle over. Hawking around with no success, I was hungry, exhausted, and very angry. I did not need their sympathy. I sold our fortune to an old woman who was mumbling a prayer at a dirt-cheap price she could get from me and came back to where my family was waiting. Never had I wanted to return to our country so much. I had enough here. Had we still been at home in Quảng Bình, my father would not have let me do such a thing!

After seeing my brother off at the airplane booking office in the afternoon, we went to visit Mr. Nguyễn Văn Đẳng, the son of my father's late friend. (This old mandarin in the former imperial court, like my father, had been forced by the local Việt Minh authorities to practice for a parade in celebration of the August 1945 Revolution; even before his death, he could not bring himself to forgive his offenders.) My father also knew Mr. Đẳng, who became the mayor of Đà Nẵng a few years later, very well. He had come to Quảng Bình a few times to inspect the local government there and to visit my father. I did not know why, though my father had already set his mind on leaving Huế, he still wanted to see his young friend. Perhaps my father was still undecided and wanted to seek Mr. Đẳng's advice. Because my father deeply cared for my future, he probably thought that Huế would be the best place for my schooling.

Mr. Đẳng greeted my father very respectfully. During the entire conversation he never failed to say "No, Sir" and "Yes, Sir" when addressing his late father's friend. I was so proud of my father. He was not a simple refugee but an excellent doctor, a fine scholar who spoke French fluently, and I was his son. I felt better and forgot already my shameful experience at the market that morning. Mr. Đẳng strongly opposed my father's decision to return to Quảng Bình. "Don't you remember, sir," he said, "that you're a scholar and were a property owner in Dalat, a thing that those revolutionaries always dream about but can't achieve? Your status and achievement would be sufficient evidence for them to build a strong case against you. If, Heaven forbid, something happens to you, who would take care of this young man?" he said, pointing to me cringing in a big armchair. Knowing that to be able to stay in Huế we had to work, he offered to find me free room and board in exchange for tutoring grade-school kids. Thus, I could attend high school and my father would not worry about me so he could go to Đà Nẵng to find a job in a medicine shop.

Thus, our repatriation plan did not materialize because of my father's fear of the Việt Minh. I did not know if this was good or bad for me. Only I felt that things would be tough now that I was going to be alone making a living by myself. Our small family was already torn apart with my brother gone that morning to an unknown place and the two of us soon to go our separate ways.

We stayed at Mr. Đẳng's home that night. The following day in the afternoon, he took us to an acquaintance of his in Gia Hội, the city's second most prosperous area. We stopped in front of a big old residence in an attractive street lined with shady flamboyant trees at the peak of their bloom. Suddenly, there came a chorus of cicadas from the trees. It started with two or three disparate, equally spaced-out notes, soft and distinct like an overture to a crescendo of myriad cries, which then gradually faded out into total silence and emptiness. I felt a pang of sadness mixed with a feeling of anxiety. I thought about home and Trang and wondered how she was doing now. I had seen the same flamboyant trees and had heard the same cries of cicadas at home at this time. Back then, I was happy because our family was intact. I also experienced love for the first time. Things were so pleasant, so safe at home in our country.

That reverie came and went in a flash. We were greeted by a skinny sickly-looking man in his forties in his black tunic. It was hard to understand him because he was so soft-spoken and had a high-pitched accent. I learned from Mr. Đẳng that he was a government employee in Đồng Hới and a good friend of Mr. Đẳng. During their conversation, I heard Mr. Đẳng address him as *Mệ*, which means "Madam." My father later explained to me that *Mệ* Huy, the man's name, was so-called because of his royal origin. According to a tradition invented and faithfully observed by the Nguyễn, the last dynasty of imperial Vietnam, a male descendent from the royal family was to have this female appellation precede his name to signify his aristocratic status and what was related to it: disdainful and overbearing like a Nguyễn prince and snobbish like a Nguyễn princess. With the passage of time these people came to be known as belonging to a privileged caste made up of good-for-nothings who lived on public support but never admitted it. To be sure, they did not necessarily represent the royal family, many members of which carried themselves with dignity and high integrity. Mr. Huy, for instance, received numerous awards including the Outstanding Employee of the Year Award at Huế National Bank.

Moved by our sad story told by Mr. Đẳng, Mr. Huy agreed to let me stay in his home to tutor his two boys, ages nine and ten, and babysit his five-year-old girl. Our condition was so desperate that my father just thanked him profusely rather than asking him important questions, such as my tutoring schedule and monthly allowance to support my schooling. My situation now was like that of my family's servants before the war. My parents used to take them in an analogous manner. The peasants were so poor that they could not afford to raise their children, so they literally *sold* them to us for a minimal sum of money with no conditions whatsoever. Some of our servants stayed with us until my parents married them off. They managed, if they were still alive after the war, to come and see us in Dalat or Quảng Bình. In a reunion like that, they would tearfully embrace me and ask, "Do you remember me, *Cậu* (young Master)?"

My premonition turned out to be true. On the second day of my stay at his house, *Mệ* Huy in his unusually stern manner called me to his living room and handed me the following daily assignments: (1) tutoring Tuấn and Đoàn, 2 hours; (2) cleaning the living room, in the afternoon or when needed; and (3) playing with Cẩm Vân, his five-year-old daughter, 1 hour. It was hard to deal with the boys' serious learning problems. Tuấn worked hard and was polite, but he was such a slow learner. Đoàn was smart but lazy and impolite. Both were in danger of failing, according to their report cards. Mr. Huy wanted me to make every effort to turn things around for the kids. I took time painstakingly going over every subject they were taught at school, starting from the basics. They were improving a little, but I felt hurt because Đoàn often talked back to me, perhaps because he was aware of my status. Besides, working hard for them left me little time for school.

The hardest part of my daily assignments had to do with cleaning the living room. Except when Mr. Huy had a guest that he wanted to entertain here, this room was closely shut and kept dark all the time. The place with many antiques lying around, particularly its owner with his grim, sallow face and his habit of donning a black tunic all the time, vaguely called to my mind the ghosts of a glorious past era belonging to the Nguyễn dynasty of which Mr. Huy was a dark living symbol. I was scared when dusting the huge earthen vases. Because the room was pitch-dark, they could break if I wasn't careful. When Mr. Huy was home, he would inspect my work and offer suggestions, even criticisms.

A generous loving father to his own children, Mr. Huy was nevertheless very cruel to me. I remember one night, after tutoring the boys, I began doing my own study. We had been using an incandescent mantle that was bright enough for us, but as soon as the boys had gone to bed, Mr. Huy would replace it with a small one, still trying to dim the light as much as he could and hissing in his shrill, ear-piercing Huế accent with clenched teeth, *"Vặn nhỏ chút nữa nì"* (Turn it down a bit more, will you?). He did so every night. At the end of that year, I got near-sighted and could not make out what was on the blackboard at school. On another occasion, he interrupted my study, handed me a damp cloth, and told me to scrape off some ink stains left on the wall by his kids. I shook with anger and shame. After I finished the clean-up, I went outside and cried bitterly when nobody was around. Unofficially, I had become a servant at Mr. Huy's house! My status was worse than that of my family's former servants. Whereas we loved them, nobody here was kind to me.

I should say a few words about Mr. Huy's wife, whom I also addressed as Mệ, the female Mệ, as contrasted with the male one. She was an obscure, demure woman around her husband's age, with beautiful even dyed-black teeth and extremely gentle manners. She ran a grocery shop somewhere in downtown Huế, often leaving home early in the morning and coming back late in the evening. Before going to work, she would fix a quick breakfast for me by frying some rice leftover with old lard. I got food poisoning as a result sometimes, so I lied to Mrs. Huy that I was not used to eating breakfast. But every morning, I would stop by Đông Ba Market, where we had slept before, to buy some boiled sweet potatoes or corn and eat them on my way to school. I saved some for lunch because classes resumed early in the afternoon. During our midday break, those who lived too far from school ate their lunch on campus. I saw them take out their food wrapped in cellophane and eat together in small groups. I never joined them, nor did they ever invite me to join them. They were rich kids, always well-dressed and wearing nice leather shoes. For dressing, I only had an old white shirt and drab slacks. Rather than shoes, I wore wooden clogs, which made a funny noise when I walked up to the teacher's desk to recite my lesson. While they enjoyed their meal and friendship, I walked down the river across from Quốc Học High School to my private spot and hurriedly swallowed my potatoes.

Mrs. Huy treated me like her own nephew and with time I came to see her as my aunt. Seeing that I was so thin, she told me to take care of myself and even offered to cook medicinal herbs for me if I could get them from my physician father. Though I liked her very much, I was embarrassed by her obsequiousness. She always addressed me as *"anh,"* meaning "older brother," and even went as far as using the respectful expression *"dạ thưa anh"* ("respected older brother"), which is equivalent to "Sir." At first, I found her manners annoying, but I got used to them afterward, knowing that she must have come from a family with an excessively genteel tradition and was married to a member of the royal clan like *Mệ* Huy.

I do not know how Mrs. Huy would behave when she was alone with her husband, but in front of strangers or visitors she appeared very meek, even subservient, toward him. He seldom spoke but would gesture his order with a cold look that Mrs. Huy was quick to understand and execute in no time. Men of Mr. Huy's temperament were not rare in the imperial clan. Stories of their eccentric behavior and temerity often amused us. Viên, a new friend I met in the neighborhood, also a member of the royal family who, I am sure, must be privy to the secret life of his elders, told us that his great uncle did not pee the way we do, but he would go about it as if he was performing a ritual: first, he would pull down his pants, then with a pair of chopsticks he gripped his penis, raising it high enough so that he would not get wet, and began to release himself. Throughout the entire process, it was obvious that he tried not to touch his penis with his hand! Meanwhile, as Viên disclosed, his uncle had a wife and a couple of concubines who gave him a dozen offspring.

Because Viên was a notorious braggart and his tale was too weird to be true, I did not believe it a bit. But this extraordinary exploit by *Mệ* Sanh, another notorious prince, was on everyone's lips in Huế in the 1950s. A commoner heard his dog bark fiercely in the backyard. He rushed over to find *Mệ* Sanh clinging to a star apple tree, his body shaking and his face pale like a leaf. On seeing the house's owner, *Mệ* Sanh said to him peremptorily: "Clear out so *Mệ* can come down safely, or I will lock you up," using his honorific title to refer to himself. After getting down, he hobbled away, cursing the day he was born and the people who had caught him. Obviously, the prince-turned-pauper had resorted to stealing fruit for food, but this did not prevent him from acting like one who was in his heyday. I know now why Mr. Huy treated me like a servant. He, like *Mệ* Sanh, came from a lengthy line of powerful princes and dukes who had enjoyed a lot of special privileges and had kept a lot of servants. What I do not understand was why Mr. Huy was rich but so stingy, so unkind although he claimed he was a devout Buddhist. I guess I was unfortunate when landing in the house of a man who happened to carry in him the traces of a glorious past and the baseness of a normal human being.

Shortly after I became a tutor of Mr. Huy's children, he welcomed his brother and his family to his home. A sickly-looking man in his early forties, Mr. Tùng (he would not permit me to call him *Mệ* although he was Mr. Huy's brother and had every right to earn the title), who had joined the Việt Minh to fight the French in 1945, decided to come home instead of joining his comrades in Hanoi. Mr. Tùng escaped from a Việt Minh-controlled area in Bình Định with his wife, a young woman of Hanoi origin and their two children, Chính and Mỹ Lộc, ages ten and four, thanks to a kind-hearted Việt Minh agent's help. When I met Mr. Tùng, he was suffering from severe malaria. At Mr. Huy's discretion, I was to give Chính special attention because he had not been to school for a long time. But Chính was a good kid. He was smart, hard-working, and respectful toward me. He must have owed it to his parents who had shed their inherited aristocratic morass while living with the Việt Minh. I liked very much Mr. and Mrs. Tùng with whom I maintained a close relationship for many years until they moved to Saigon to live with Chính. The last thing I heard from Mr. Tùng was that Chính had graduated from the University of Saigon with an engineering degree, had a good job with the government, and had just gotten married. Mỹ Lộc was a sophomore at Saigon University.

My life in Huế had light moments, though. I made friends with Thịnh, Mr. Huy's nephew, who then introduced me to his buddies in the neighborhood who were members of a fitness club. A couple of years older than me, Thịnh worked at a bike repair shop. When he did not go to the shop, he worked around the house like a servant. He told me he had never been to school because he lost both his parents when he was five. He asked me to teach him how to read which I did in secret without Mr. Huy's knowledge. Seeing me so skinny, he introduced me to his buddies in the neighborhood and we would meet around 5:00 o'clock in the morning to run or to practice gymnastics together.

Knowing Thịnh and exercising with his friends, I felt less lonesome and my health improved. I began to develop a new hobby: keeping a diary and trying my hand at creative writing. Using my recollections of Quảng Bình, especially its lore, I wrote a story about Bàu Tró, a lake where supernatural beings were said to have been seen, and submitted to the *Đời Mới* [*New Life*], a Saigon-based literary magazine, under the penname Nhã Trang, which was my sweetheart's name. After I had sent it off, I went to a local bookstore regularly to check the result. A couple of weeks later, my heart started beating wildly and I almost fainted when I saw my story in the magazine with my penname appearing below its title, "Nét Đẹp Quảng Bình: Bàu Tró" ["Beauty of Quảng Bình: Lake Tró"]. A few days later, I received a cash of 10 *đồng* (piasters) in the mail and a note of encouragement and praise from the editor. Until now I still wonder how my story got accepted and published in a national literary magazine! I think I inherited my love of writing and literature from my father though I chose teaching English as my profession.

Around November 1954 my father moved back to Huế. Although he had some former patients in Đà Nẵng who continued to see him for medical care and brought him new patients, he wanted to live near me. Huế was not a good place for him to practice his art because people hardly knew him, so he went to the country to meet patients and I could see him only when he came to town to get a new supply of herbs. Our meeting place was a small restaurant in the Outer Citadel area near the Đông Ba Gate. When we met, I would eat with my father. He ordered only the delicacies and made me eat as much as I could. Though after this brief reunion, I was not supposed to see my father again for another month, I came back after two weeks to peek at that restaurant to find my father. Unconsciously, the pattern I had followed back then in Trung Quán—going to the river bank every evening to wait for my father's return though he had not been gone long—emerged again. Seven years had passed, and I was now a high school student, yet I still needed Father, an old man in his sixties, to protect me. It was hard to live in a strange, inhuman world without him.

Things took a bad turn for me at the start of winter. The wintry weather in Huế did not suit me. Months of living in deprivation, grief, anxiety, and humiliation were also taking a toll on my health. I got sick and missed school a few times. My vision was also deteriorating because I did not get proper lighting to study at Mr. Huy's house. Thịnh was very worried about me. He begged me to let him go and find my father for me. Since my coming to Huế, no one here was kind to me but him.

After getting Thịnh's message, my father came to see Mr. Huy and expressed his concern about me. Mr. Huy apologized to my father for his neglect of me but blamed me for not telling him I was not well. He swore he loved me like his own nephew and assured my father he would personally take better care of me from now on. But Father had already made up his mind. He thanked Mr. Huy and took me out of his house immediately. He whispered to me that he had saved enough money and could now move back to Huế to live with me permanently.

I said goodbye to everybody. Mr. Huy did not say a word to me, perhaps because he was upset that he could not keep me to tutor his children. Mr. Tùng said some very kind words to me and his voice was trailing. I also saw a tear in Mrs. Tùng's eyes. But it was the kids who broke my heart. Chính and Tuấn began to cry, followed by Little Cẩm Vân. Mỹ Lộc, Chính's little sister, who did not know what was happening, also blubbered. Chính made me feel bad because I had discriminated against him, knowing that I was not supposed to tutor him.

My father and I moved in to live with a young couple and their ten-year-old son near Nguyễn Hoàng Bus Terminal. The woman was my father's new patient. Her husband was also from Quảng Bình. They were glad we could live with them because my father could teach the boy Vietnamese and French, and I could tutor him in math and science. We paid a minimum rent for the room. We ate our meals at various food stands in the bus terminal.

As our landlady spread the word about my father's skills, he did not have to make trips to the country or Đà Nẵng to find patients anymore. In his free time, he would coach me in French. By drilling me in analyzing logic and grammatical errors, he helped me master the fundamentals of the French sentence, and by the end of the second semester, I became more competitive in Mr. Khánh's class than at the start of the school year.

The rest of 1954—the most traumatic year in my adolescence—would have gone by uneventfully had we not received news from my half-brother Sang. On his northbound repatriation, Sang, a high-ranking Việt Minh cadre, sent word through a female liaison that he would like to see us at an undisclosed location in Huế. He also asked my father to buy him a fountain pen. At first, my father wanted to go, but later he changed his mind. He was afraid that it could be trickery used by the government to check if we refugees had any connections with the Việt Minh. My father's sixth sense also influenced his decision not to meet Sang. Even if the person turned out to be Sang, who knows if somebody would not listen in to my father's conversation with him and report to the police? In Quảng Bình, I had heard and witnessed a lot of arrests and executions of innocent people by French and Vietnamese police by heartless, irresponsible informants. "A timid bird has a better chance to escape its hunter than a reckless one," Father would say, citing the motto as a golden rule of living. I could not agree with him more. At nineteen, I had lived long enough to realize that in life, a minor act of neglect, a lapse of mind, could cause a disaster. My father might not have been aware that our family became asunder because of his return to Quảng Bình to worship our ancestors instead of staying with my mother in Dalat. I was struck in the face by my math teacher because of my attempt to read his letter to my father out of curiosity. Even now, how can I forget that security agent at the *Deuxième bureau* office in Đồng Hới who beat me mercilessly because I was stupid enough to peep at his torture of a Việt Minh suspect? And there was no guarantee that good deeds would be appreciated and that well-thought-out decisions would bring success. Having experienced these traumatic months in Huế as a refugee, I wondered if our leaving Đồng Hới was worth it.

It was six months now since July 1954 when we left home to arrive in Huế. It was the last month of Year of the Snake, so Huế residents were excitedly preparing their welcome of the New Year, Year of the Horse, which people hoped for a prosperous year on account of the lively nature of the animal. The city was in a great festive mood with flags flown and banners hung across the streets or displayed on government buildings and at public places. A Tết fair was held at Thương Bạc, a major park in Huế, starting on the 23rd day of the month—the day the Kitchen God is believed to leave for Heaven to present to Heaven his annual report on the state of the earth—and ending a few hours before New Year's Eve. My school also took part in the festivities, with students putting on a show for the public on New Year's Day.

It was six months now since we had arrived there. Too long to endure hardship but too soon to feel at home in the new land. It was particularly difficult for my father because this was the time when preparations for welcoming our ancestors to our home would have been under way. Educated in the Confucian tradition with its emphasis on filial piety as a cardinal moral virtue, Father took upon himself ancestor worship as his most important commandment. Our shrine in Quảng Bình had an altar on which he placed our ancestors' *bài vị* (gold-painted tablets), with their names and titles crafted in scarlet Old

Chinese characters. Every night my father would light incense and pray for our happiness and safety. Tết is an important opportunity for us and all Vietnamese to officially show our indebtedness to our deceased parents and ancestors. According to a traditional popular belief, because during the Tết holidays the dead return for a brief reunion with the living, it is our duty and honor to show them our gratitude and love by making our food offerings to them as if they were still living with us. Failing to come home during Tết to visit one's living parents and to show one's respects to one's ancestors is considered a grave breach of the country's moral code and a disgrace for every Vietnamese. As our host family was decking their home and dusting their ancestors' altar to get ready for Tết, Father grew quiet and pensive, and at night, I could hear him sigh deeply. As his eldest son who was expected to step into his place after his passing, I knew how he felt at this time of the year when everyone was celebrating Tết at their home and we had no home of our own. According to him, not having a home to welcome and worship our ancestors on this important occasion was a grave violation of the principle of filial piety, as our ancestors could not enter a stranger's dwelling and would be condemned to being solitary wandering ghosts.

It was a year since I had left Đồng Hới. I began getting used to my new life. The praise I continued to receive from Mr. Khánh and later from Mr. Văn Đình Hy, my favorite Vietnamese teacher, for my essays made me immeasurably happy. The girls who sat in the front rows must have known who I was now because when Mr. Hy mentioned my name, some of them would slightly turn around and cast at me their sidelong look. The boys were even kinder to me: they started talking to me and inviting me to join them in their visits to our teachers during the Tết holidays. Since I wanted to become their peer as quickly as possible, I made a point to imitate their language. Occasionally, I unconsciously lapsed into the Huế dialect and accent when I talked to my father, and he must have noticed this as he raised his eyebrows sometimes. Slowly but surely, I succeeded in becoming a full-fledged Huế boy. I no longer felt attached to the land and the people that I had thought I would never forget as long as I lived.

On the second day of the New Year, I try to enjoy the flavor of Tết by going to a movie without telling my father. As it is still too early for the movie, I take a leisurely walk on Trần Hưng Đạo Street to watch Tết in its full swing. Because on New Year's Day, all shops, including movie houses, are closed with residents refraining from leaving home, all public celebrations officially start today. Streams of people, young and old, all wearing their best clothing, pour out into this main street and adjacent ones to participate in the festivities here and at the on-going Tết fair on the grounds of the Thương Bạc Park.

I admire the city in its pomp and beauty when I see marching in my direction a band of girls, hand in hand, jollying and bantering, giggling and laughing. Suddenly my head swirls, my eyes are dazzled: *Trang is one of those girls!* She is at her merriest, smiling, nodding, and shaking her head all the time as if tickled by her friends. I can hear the girls' crystal-clear voices as they get closer. Suddenly, they stop, turn around to cross the street, and disappear into the crowd pouring into the fair's direction. Trang and her friends disappear as suddenly and as fast as they appeared.

I cannot believe my eyes. It is just Trang and her band that I customarily saw in Đồng Hới in the past summer, except that their parade today is so short. Like a flash of lightning. My mind buzzes with questions. Is it really Trang? Did she leave Đồng Hới with her family before our evacuation? That was a possibility. My father had stopped going to Mr. Giám's medicine shop for at least two weeks before we left, so we might not be aware of her family's possible departure. Besides, Trang's parents were wealthy enough to start their new life here with ease, and that is why she looked so happy. But, if Trang is that girl, why doesn't she recognize me? My head swarms with questions and answers. Maybe Trang does not see me because she has such a good time with her company and does not bother to look around for anything. Or maybe—and this line of reasoning makes me feel terrible—she cannot recognize me or, even worse, does not care to recognize me because I have changed so much for the worse in such a short time.

But it cannot be Trang. I know that she is not that kind of person who can adjust so easily to a new life in a matter of months. Though she went to school in Hanoi, she is every inch a Đồng Hới girl—timid, demure, quiet, and thoughtful. It is hard to imagine her in company with those boisterous Huế girls that she might hardly know not long before, let alone her apparent familiarity with the Huế ways. It would be a great shock if that girl was Trang! It cannot be her and must *not* be her. Had it been Trang, she would have taken this stroll with her band on Đường Nhà Tắm street in a hot, sunny summer afternoon, not in such a strange place at such a wrong time. To convince me that it was Trang, she must be seen in the framework of a city by the sea in a late afternoon, hot and sunny and bright. No, Trang *is* still in Đồng Hới and right now must be having a rough time. According to the government's propaganda, kids of wealthy families who did not leave are sent to the country to perform forced labor. The girl I see must be someone who looks like her. I saw on more than one occasion people who looked like their twins, but they were not related in the least.

I am stunned by the incident and by what it all means. By the time I get to the movie, it is too late for the show. I walk back to our host family's house, feeling heavier in my heart than ever. I thought I had forgotten Trang with my discovery of the wonders of Huế, but suddenly this morning.... What happens this morning on Trần Hưng Đạo Street is like a dream, but it is more vivid and poignant than real life. It is like a dream one has about a loved one who is long lost. Our lost loved ones live in a different world. They become alive but act as though they do not belong to us anymore, they ignore our joy when we see them, they do not notice our grief when they depart, they even torment us if we are lucky to be briefly recognized by them. We are overjoyed to see them again, but they pay no attention to us. The instant they vanish, we are awake and overcome by inconsolable sorrow. Our eyes are full of tears.

Trang is my unconscious, long repressed, now coming back alive. She is even dead but is resurrected to me in my sleep. Due to my struggle for survival, I have not thought of her for a long time. I even forget her when my life gets better in Huế, when people begin to recognize me, when the girls here in my unconscious are more charming and elegant than a small-town girl like Trang. What happens today destroys the dream I just began to build in the new land. The incident brings back to me my past and what is related to it—my first love, my happy boyhood, my beautiful home, and my united family. I regret leaving Đồng Hới without trying to see Trang. Had I tried to overcome my fear, I could have gone to see her, could have been brave enough to tell her I cared for her, loved her, and missed her so much these days. The more I indulge in these thoughts of regret, the more I feel guilty. Who knows, when discovering I had been gone, Trang would not have grieved? Ours is not a kind of separation that promises eventual reunion, but a permanent, possibly eternal, severance. In a country torn apart by war and sharply divided along ideological lines like Vietnam, separation is synonymous with death. As long as the country remains partitioned, to think of a temporary reunion of loved ones living in the North and the South is merely wishful thinking. The trauma of separation due to never-ending ideological conflicts over the centuries is a common reference in the Vietnamese language and literature, hence the expression *"tử biệt sinh ly"* (death and permanent separation are the two greatest sorrows in life). Never will we see each other again in both cases.

The surging of Trang's images in my memory plunges me back into my former loneliness. That was a year and a half ago when I left home and Trang, a year and a half behind me when I left home and the girl I still miss and love. Returning to my loneliness and exile complex, I grow quiet and withdrawn again. During my lighter moments, I listen to music by refugee composers who write about memory and home. One of my favorite songs is Phạm Duy's "Tình hoài hương" ["Nostalgia"]. A year earlier, I went to see *Chúng tôi muốn sống* [*We Want to Live*], a film by Vĩnh Noãn that tells North Vietnamese refugees' heartbreaking stories of escape to freedom after the communist takeover of Hanoi. I was mesmerized by the song in the movie. Exquisitely executed by the famous vocalist Thái Thanh, herself a refugee, the piece moved me to tears. It evokes the countryside of North Vietnam in peacetime(both the artist and the composer were from Hanoi)—and Quảng Bình—as well as images of gentle, hard-working peasants who would never leave their home for any reason. The lyrical andante that depicts the ethereal beauty of the refugee's homeland breaks down into a repressed sob as the vocalist renders its fading into an unrecoverable past on board the ship that takes her and her fellow people into the unknown. The vocalist ceased, silence fell completely, but the music returned, its evocative power at its greatest. During Thái Thanh's performance, I only heard the song, but now I see a wave of beloved images so soothing and vivid rising in me. Suddenly, Quảng Bình, my home in Đồng Hới, my happy adolescence, and Trang all come to life inside of me, so real, so close, and so visceral as though they were always my identity, were inseparable from me, and I never left home. For the first time, I am astounded by the power of music. It emancipates me from the biographical and chronological time, the cause of my sorrow and suffering. The past I am reliving now is short but it is so dense, so vast, and so delightful that it makes me feel breathless. Forgetting my status as a refugee, I hum a favorite tune as if I was still living in Đồng Hới.

***

Beginning my junior year at Quốc Học High School, I grew more emotionally and politically mature than my classmates. As it might be the last year in school for some boys who might get drafted for the army (Mr. Diệm was serious about building a republic in the South militarily strong enough to resist anticipated North Vietnam's invasion) and also for some girls who might consider leaving school to find a job or to start a family (in the 1950s, it was not uncommon for girls in their late teens with a high school diploma to secure themselves a job and a family of their own), everybody began to pay attention to one another. They exchanged keepsake notebooks in which they were to express their thoughts and feelings about each other. It was a very nice custom that would allow graduating students to remember their class in their future journey of life. I was asked by a female classmate to write a few lines in her notebook and could not turn her down. But when glancing at lengthy sentimental thoughts crafted in their finest penmanship by her friends, I decided I could not compete with them. In many ways I was worse off than they were: my family was broken, I was a refugee, and we barely made ends meet. It was hard to sentimentalize friendship with people with whom I had nothing in common and to whom I could not relate. So, I just wrote a line or so, appreciating her interest in me and wishing her well. No other classmate bothered me with this thing.

Huế at the first anniversary of Mr. Diệm's coming to power was rife with political activities. Numerous huge rallies were organized by an emerging major political party called *Phong trào cách mạng quốc gia* (Movement for National Revolution) at Phú Văn Lâu Square (where Nguyễn emperors in the past would meet with his people's representatives to hear their petitions) to show support for *"Chí sĩ"* (revered patriot) Ngô Đình Diệm. This title, which had occasionally been used to refer to Mr. Diệm when he was in exile, unofficially replaced the title Prime Minister conferred upon him by Ex-Emperor Bảo Đại, then Chief of the State of Vietnam. Concurrently, another endearing appellation, *"Cụ Ngô,"* was in circulation among Mr. Diệm's loyal subjects. Like *"Cụ Hồ,"* the term *"Cụ Ngô"* is untranslatable on account of its emotional and linguistic complexity. We are trapped in a pitfall here: Mr. Diệm was in his mid-fifties, not old enough to be referred to as *Cụ*, a form of address used only for the elderly on account of their respectability and wisdom. In my opinion, Mr. Diệm's people used his surname rather than his given name to address him or refer to him because they wanted to elevate him to a national hero's status. A word should be said about some men and women who went by their surname in the country's history. They were first-rate national heroes who were deified by the people because of their successful leadership of the country against foreign invasions. In Vietnam's history, there were only a couple of names that were accorded divine status, viz., *Hai Bà Trưng* (The Trưng Sisters) and *Đức Thánh Trần* (Saint Trần), whose birth name was Trần Quốc Tuấn, the legendary general of the Trần dynasty who twice defeated the Mongol Yuan invasion in 1285 and 1288.

Politics also found its way into school life. By order of Mr. Lê Văn Hay, Director of Central Vietnam Education Agency, himself a member of Mr. Diệm's state party, all elementary and high school students, faculty, and staff were to participate in pro-government rallies and meetings. It was easy to mobilize us for those public events because we were in great numbers and always available. I recall those days when a rally was announced we would be dismissed from class at short notice to join the girls at Đồng Khánh High School for our march to Phú Văn Lâu Square. As a rule, we were more excited about class being dismissed and about seeing the girls than about showing support for the government. Our frequent loss of time for political events eventually took a toll on my studies, which worried my father very much.

I do not know who in the student body, the administration, or the faculty had suggested the idea of changing our school's name from *Quốc Học* (National School) to *Quốc Học Ngô Đình Diệm* (Ngô Đình Diệm National School). Since my enrollment less than a year earlier, the school had undergone a name change twice—from *Khải Định*, named after Bảo Đại's father, whom Huế people did not like because of his submission to the French rule, back to its original name *Quốc Học* after Mr. Diệm's coming to power. As early as the spring of 1956, Huế youths were caught up in the so-called *Ngô Đình Diệm* movement. A student came to every class exhorting us to sign a petition to change the school's name to *Quốc Học Ngô Đình Diệm*. I do not know if the petition had ever been submitted or what had happened to it, but I am certain that in traditional Asia dedication of a public monument to a celebrity is a posthumous honor and should not take place when he is still living. In ancient Asia, names with exalted meanings were not given to emperors, whether they were still living or not, but only to famous monuments, such as *Tienmen* (Gate of Heavenly Peace), *Điện Thái Hòa* (Palace of Heaven-and-Earth Harmony), etc.

After Mr. Diệm had consolidated his power, rallies in support of him tapered off. Still, we students were mobilized to greet the prime minister whenever he came to Huế for the anniversary of his father's death or just to see his mother who lived with his bachelor brother, Mr. Ngô Đình Cẩn. As usual, we lined up along Lê Lợi Street, where his motorcade would pass by. I was thrilled about the opportunity of catching a glimpse of the prime minister who made me proud because we were from the same country—Quảng Bình—and my father had always sung his praises as a great patriot and a mandarin of highest moral caliber in imperial Vietnam. But as time went by, my excitement gave way to frustration and disappointment. There were times when we had lined up from early morning till late evening to welcome the prime minister when we were told that his motorcade had changed its route. "If they just could keep the kids in school instead of wasting their time like this," my father would complain, looking around to make sure nobody heard him. My landlord, a soldier, reported that once his platoon had been lying for three days on the outskirts of the city in the freezing rain to protect Mr. Diệm when he was home for Tết. People began to whisper about Mr. Diệm's favoritism extended to his loyal subordinates and particularly to his family. His brother Cẩn, an unknown man, suddenly emerged as a sort of viceroy. I heard that his residence in Phú Cam was like a court where generals and major government officials who arrived from Saigon were expected to show up and kowtow to him. Rumor, confirmed by Vũ Văn Mẫu, Mr. Diệm's Foreign Affairs Minister, in his memoir *Sáu tháng Pháp nạn 1963* [*Year 1963: Six Months of Dharma Calamity*], had it that these dignitaries were so obsequious to Mr. Cẩn that at the end of their audience they would back up all the way to the entrance before they could turn around to depart. Huế residents had fun telling a story about a general who inadvertently hit and broke one of Mr. Cẩn's precious vases during his single-minded concentration on those rites. The general did get a stern scolding from the president's brother.

Stories like those made us feel disappointed about the image of the legendary Ngô Đình Diệm my father had instilled in my mind as I grew up in Quảng Bình. It is hard to imagine why my father gave up the land he deeply loved without realizing that he cared both for our education and his political freedom, and the only man who could offer such an opportunity was, in his words, *"Cụ Ngô."* "Without Cụ Ngô," my father said, "we wouldn't have arrived here safely." Immediately after the Geneva Accords, we read in the paper that Prime Minister Diệm had made several trips to Hanoi to direct the local government to mobilize all available resources to provide for the refugees a safe and smooth resettlement in the South. We felt confident we would have a better future in the new land now that we had a leader we could trust. And not only did we trust the man, but we admired two important precepts he exemplified as a statesman in the Confucian tradition: (1) loyalty to Ex-Emperor Bảo Đại (in all official documents he put this phrase before affixing his signature: *"Thừa ủy-nhiệm Đức Quốc-Trưởng"* ("For and on behalf of His Excellency the Chief of State," implying that he was still serving as a humble subject in the erstwhile imperial court in Huế) and (2) patriotism (no sooner was his government established than he officially asked France to withdraw its troops from the country). Unfortunately, this political system akin to Japan's that Mr. Diệm was trying to build never materialized. Less than a year after he had become the country's prime minister, a campaign to impeach Bảo Đại was launched in major cities. In rallies and demonstrations we heard speeches denouncing Bảo Đại as "a notorious, irresponsible bon vivant man unfit to lead the country" who should be replaced by the "revered patriot" Ngô Đình Diệm. We also saw posters and leaflets exhorting Huế citizens to participate in the referendum scheduled for October 26th, 1955. On posters and leaflets, there was also a photo of two men, Mr. Diệm and his ex-emperor, with a big cross on the latter's face! Bảo Đại's face was also smeared with black paint on the surface of major streets on the eve of the referendum.

Mr. Diệm proclaimed himself President of the Republic of Vietnam (RVN) on October 29th, 1955. The RVN Constitution was promulgated by him on October 26th, 1956. The president seemed determined not to honor the Geneva Accords, which would require the two regions of Vietnam to hold general elections in 1956, by setting out to build an independent South with its own army and political system. For Ngô Đình Diệm, a staunch anti-communist Catholic, reconciliation with Hồ Chí Minh was unthinkable, let alone placing his South Vietnam under the communist rule. But that was the last time I was concerned with politics. From 1956 to November 1960 when the first coup d'état against Mr. Diệm led by Col. Nguyễn Chánh Thi took place, South Vietnam enjoyed the most peaceful time I had ever known since I grew up. My family's condition also got better, with my brother reunited with us, my father having more patients, and myself finally garnering a high school diploma and becoming a full-fledged Huế student save my outlandish Dalat accent. I made friends, gained confidence, felt secure about the future, and seemed to totally forget my past and my former sweetheart Trang. No place could offer me a better chance for my future than Huế!

The year 1956 was pretty "eventful" before I came of age. My brother successfully challenged his junior high school exam and we both became seniors at Quốc Học High School. In Huế in the late 1950s, students with a high school diploma were considered the apple of their parents' eye, and we were no exception. I often heard my father brag about our accomplishments when he had visitors and patients at our house. There was a glint of pride and happiness in his eyes: our departure from Quảng Bình and the sacrifices he had made for our sake was paying off. Just as most parents took pride in their children whose success was the fruit of their labor, we boys were flushed with excitement because people were paying attention to us. Up to the middle of 1957, Quốc Học High School was still the highest educational institution in Central Vietnam. There were not many taking the high school exam, so people would know whether we had passed or failed the competition by just watching our demeanor as we were heading home on our bikes from the other direction on Trường Tiền Bridge! For example, if we were all smiles, looked poised and confident, and rode our bike fast (a sign that we were anxious to share the great news with our family), then everybody knew we were sure to have made it. Many years later, in his spare time surrounded by his children and grandchildren, my brother would tell them how he was allowed to see a beautiful girl in our neighborhood by telling her mother, a widow, that he was a senior at Quốc Học. To be sure, this time around next year, with the opening of the University of Huế, a college certificate would be a minimum requirement for any suitor of her daughter. For their part Huế girls, believe it or not—would raise their expectations even higher: *"Phi cao đẳng bất thành phu phụ!"* (No marriage is acceptable unless my man is a college graduate). An academic degree would bring him prestige and a comfortable living, which was every girl's aspiration. Unlike my brother, I was very shy of girls and gatherings, preferring to stay at home to read or wander alone where I could not be seen. I squirmed when told by my teachers to rise and express my opinion in class about an issue, especially in front of the girls. Although I had some close male friends, I would visit with them separately to better exchange mutual confidences.

During my three years of attending Quốc Học, there was a unique time when I successfully overcame that handicap. In the spring of 1956, an official from the Department of Education in Saigon arrived in Huế to inspect Quốc Học and Đồng Khánh secondary schools. One morning, Mr. Kiết, the inspector general, visited our Vietnamese class. I remember our teacher, Mr. Lê Hữu Mục, was lecturing on *The Tale of Kiều* by the famous 19th-century poet Nguyễn Du. Mr. Mục's topic was Kiều's reflections on Kim Trọng, her first love. When Mr. Mục referred to these two lines:

> "And who is he? Why did we chance to meet?
> Does fate intend some tie between us two?"

Mr. Kiết interrupted him and turned to our class, asking: "How does Nguyễn Du resolve the tension between free will and fate in *The Tale of Kiều*?" Feeling an uncontrollable urge to respond to Mr. Kiết's question, I raised my hand, looking at him, my heart pounding. The inspector saw my hand and pointed to me, saying: "Boy in the second row, you may speak." I decided I had made a big mistake, but it was too late. The shyest student in my class, I suddenly became the center of everyone's attention. My face must have turned scarlet as it was burning with shame. Everyone—Mr. Mục, the boys, the girls—was gazing at me, the only boy sitting in the girls' row. On the first day of class, our English teacher, for convenience's sake, moved me up there because all rows reserved for male students were full, and maybe he did not want to put a burly one on the girls' bench for fear that he might bother them.

This is the gist of my speech: "In accordance with strait-jacket Confucianism, young men and women in 19th century Vietnam weren't free to choose their partner. Kiều, a talented beauty in Nguyễn Du's *The Tale of Kiều*, is no exception. When introduced to Kim Trọng, a young scholar, by her brother Vương Quan, Kiều decides that Kim is her right man. At the same time, she feels that even if their chance meeting materializes into a relationship, this will lead nowhere. In marriage it is her parents, not the young woman, who have their say. So, when Kiều repeatedly asks herself what will come out of this, whether 'fate intend[s] the tie between us two,' she knows the answer is in the negative and it's a trick played upon her by fate, the formidable power of Confucianist culture. In matters of love, if free will exists, it is moral fortitude, the ability to endure adversity that would allow young people to prevail in the end, not their determination to fight for their inalienable right to achieve their matrimonial happiness." I spoke in a breath, feeling I was at my most eloquent when expressing these impromptu ideas. Impromptu ideas? No, I had pondered those thoughts before. Lying in my father's lap when I was a child, I had heard him recite line after line of *The Tale of Kiều* in our ancestors' shrine. These lines I knew by heart and curiously since my meeting Trang, I had subconsciously likened our condition, that is, our ill-fated love, to that of Kim and Kiều. Might the urge I felt to blurt out my remarks on the meaning of these two lines despite my terrible timidity have something to do with my unconscious desire to redeem our lot? Did it mean that, despite my excellent adjustment to my new life, deep down my past and my first love were still important to me and I still wished I had not left Quảng Bình? I do not know. All I know is these two lines from Nguyễn Du's poem, while they were casually read by my Vietnamese teacher, produced on that day the same evocative power as Phạm Duy's song I had heard in the movie *Chúng tôi muốn sống*. Not only did they bring back memories of my first love, but they allowed me to verbalize my subconscious thoughts, even articulate them.

In the summer of 1956, I suffered a bout of illness. What I had been through at Mr. Huy's house, my hard work at school, and perhaps my oversensitive nature took an enormous toll on my physical and mental health. Immediately after I took the high school graduation exam, I experienced symptoms of severe depression. For several weeks I did not get a wink at night. If I fell asleep out of exhaustion, even a very small noise would wake me up. I could not concentrate on my studies and was always in a state of despondency. This happened when my father was away in Đà Nẵng and I lived with my brother in Huế. Tuy, a childhood friend from Đồng Hới, took me to his home to stay with him and his family for a while. It was good to have a friend to talk to and a quiet place to spend the night. I felt better and could sleep a few hours at night after a few days. When my father returned, he put me on a course of herbal treatment, and I was back on my feet a month later. Thus, I was well equipped physically and mentally to endure the last year of my high school education and be ready to get a start on my college career.

I could not appreciate Tuy enough for listening to my love story which I told him in fragments. Embarrassment kept me from making a clean breast of it, but I knew he was aware of what had happened between me and Trang because he was her childhood friend and neighbor. I could realize how much Tuy sympathized with me when he seemed to be gazing into a distant past, mumbling: "I miss Trang, too. She's such a nice girl." Tuy and I continued visiting each other regularly for several years until the Tết offensive when I lost contact with him. He was a true friend who knew my story and who deeply cared for me.

Tôn Thất Điềm, another friend who helped me get through this post-depression trauma, was a member of the royal family. In 1956, we still lived in the Inner Citadel and, to commute to school, I boarded a rickety sampan used to carry students to the *Hữu Ngạn* (right bank) of the Perfume River where Quốc Học and Đồng Khánh high schools are located. It was Điềm who broke the ice when he saw me hold fast to the boat's side by assuring me that it was safe enough. We soon became close friends and I discovered that we had lots of things in common. We both were timid, poor, and did not have a mother. Like me, Điềm was contemptuous of the wealthy and the privileged. I liked

Điềm best for this most important reason: he was a good swimmer, and he swore if the boat sank, he would rescue me first before he would consider the pretty girls. He seemed to know all the girls on the sampan, whispering to me their names, their family backgrounds, where they sat in the boat, and so on. I believed Điềm because I knew he was very honest and sincere. He did not seem to hold anything from me, even the history of a small scar on his left cheek. He said it used to be a mole, but he had it removed because a necromancer had told him that it signified misfortune. When discovering that Mr. Diệm had a similar cyst on his cheek and he was still President of the Republic of Vietnam, Điềm wished that he had not done it. "Hadn't I had my mole removed, someday I could become President like Mr. Diệm," he guffawed. Before we were dismissed for the Tết holidays, Điềm came to see me and showed his draft summons. I did not see him off the day he left and have not heard from him since. I worried about Điềm but was comforted by the thought that he should be all right because his name is pronounced like the president's.

The 1956-1957 school year started with a bang. We were told that a ceremony to commemorate the 60th anniversary of the founding of Quốc Học would take place by year's end and students would be in charge. The selection of December 26th, 1956 for the event was important because it coincided with the date on which the late Mr. Ngô Đình Khả, President Diệm's father, had assumed his position as the school's first principal. The ceremony, therefore, would be an appropriate way to honor the elder Ngô. More important, it was a politically correct course of action since Mr. Khả's son was the current powerful President of the Republic.

I did not know much about what was being planned for the big event, but the hustle and bustle of it could be seen everywhere. What kept the entire school on edge was the news that the ceremony would be presided over by President Diệm.

On the morning of December 26th, we were dismissed early to assemble on both sides of the campus entrance. The girls in white *ao dai* were in the front rows. We stood behind them in white shirts and blue trousers. The president's motorcade arrived in late morning. Upon getting out of his limousine, Mr. Diệm ambled toward the podium, followed by his big entourage. I was able to catch a glimpse of the man my father admired. He was bigger and shorter than the average Vietnamese man but looked extremely dignified in his white suit. His gait was fast and nimble despite his stature. Overall, he struck me as a very imposing political leader. Because he looked young and full of energy, I was a little surprised that people referred to him as *Cụ*, an honorific title used to address an elderly person. As everybody's attention was riveted on the president, someone shouted "Long live President Ngô!"

Instantly, we roared back the slogan, excitedly waving our flags. We repeated our response at that person's cue, and this went on for a while until Mr. Diệm arrived at the podium. The so-called stimulus-response sequence reminded me of rallies I had witnessed in Dalat in 1945 and afterward. It was an effective technique used by the Việt Minh to get public support for a plan or agenda of which the crowd did not have a slightest inkling. The denunciation campaign against the so-called landlords launched by the Việt Minh in the North in 1955, so graphically depicted in *Chúng tôi muốn sống*, employed the same strategy.

Something unusual happened that morning, and today it still stays vivid in my mind. In the president's long cortege, I observed a man in his traditional uniform—green tunic and white pants—with a black turban on his head. He looked embarrassed and lost probably because he donned this traditional costume while the president and his party wore suits. A student behind me whispered to his neighbor, "Look, it's Mr. Hay." Mr. Hay was the head of the Central Vietnam Education Office. Rumor had it that he was the mastermind of that day's organized events. A brilliant but ruthless man, he was feared by everybody in his jurisdiction at that time. Because Mr. Diệm had served in the former imperial court as prime minister, he adopted, when he became president, a traditionally mandarin dress style in his appearance at national commemorative events. Mr. Hay's dress code was very appropriate; unfortunately, it was out of sync. The president and his entourage wore suits for the ceremony on that day.

Because December 26th was an all-day celebration, classes were not held. Except for the morning activities we were required to attend, we were free the rest of the day. I went home after the morning ceremony, not interested in things that had little to do with my personal life. Having resettled in Huế for over a year now, I still did not feel at home, still seeing Huế as *their* city, Quốc Học as *their* school, and activities like these as *their* business. Though we were better off now, materially we were not much different from a poor family in Huế, whereas most of my classmates, according to my observation, belonged to the middle and upper class. I was embarrassed when my classmates came to find me at our small flat in a low-income neighborhood. In those days, it was not uncommon to have an unexpected visitor when you were in the middle of something. I had nothing against the custom but did not want my classmates to know about our poverty and share what they saw with everybody. I shrank from appearing in public, worrying that I might be seen by people who might have known our condition because they had been to our place. Being present with everybody at an all-school gathering where they were all excited and happy was not much to my liking.

Late in the evening, Điềm came over to fetch me. We both got bored and decided to stop by the school to see what was happening. As we arrived, we were kept out of the auditorium because it was packed, and the president and the VIPs were inside. Listening to the live broadcast from loudspeakers, we gathered that the play *Giảng sách dưới trăng* [*Interpreting Literature in the Moonlight*] was being performed. Written by Vũ Hân, a high school teacher from Đà Nẵng, the play is about Qin Shihuang's brutality against Chinese scholars under his reign, but clearly it was meant to warn Mr. Diệm not to step into the ancient Chinese emperor's shoes. Except for the student playing the scholar, the cast was predominantly North Vietnamese refugees. I could not help wondering why those folks were adjusting so well to their new life in the South and why they were so happy, so gregarious as if they had never left their native land.

It was frustrating to hear the sound bites of the show because we could not get in the auditorium. Occasionally, there were jarring noises that interfered with our enjoyment of the program. Luckily, when the last item of the show came up, the sound system had been fixed. Điềm showed me the program: it was "Tình ca" ["Love Song"] by Phạm Duy, and the vocalist was Nguyễn Thị Minh Cầm, the daughter of Mr. Nguyễn Đình Hàm, Quốc Học High School's principal and our math teacher. Despite its title, the song is not about lovers' affection and tenderness but about love of one's country and people. There strikes a feeling of nostalgia in the song as if Phạm Duy, who composed the piece in 1953, a year before the Geneva Accords, had a presentiment of his people's emigration to the South a year after. Whereas "Tình hoài hương" and "Tình ca" deal with a similar theme, they are structured differently and did not evoke the same emotions in me. The slow, regular beats distinctly spaced in "Tình hoài hương" are the refugee's recital of her remembrance of a paradisiacal past that is no more. The music is soothing, like a lullaby, but heartbreaking, with each note striking to the marrow of the refugee's anguished soul. I do not know the lyrics, but I can hum the tune along with the artist spontaneously, as though the song was unlocking in me echoes of what it tries to convey—love of our lost native land, and the feeling of uncertainty about our journey to an unknown region. The song's power is derived as well from Thái Thanh's virtuoso execution and the unique setting in which it is performed: on board a ship of refugees uprooted from their native land. "Tình ca," by contrast, as I listened to it tonight, while evoking my pleasant memories of the Quảng Bình countryside and Đồng Hới, also triggered a plethora of elevated sentiments toward Vietnam, including Huế, as my country in general. The relatively fast-paced movement of "Tình ca" took the audience, as its lyrics state, on a journey through the country's turbulent but heroic history condensed into a five-minute presentation. The singer's last chord ended in its highest pitch and the orchestra fell into complete silence, but the tide of its vibrations could still be felt outside where I was standing.

That was the second love song I heard in the same year. But it was the first time since I left Đồng Hới that I was carried away by a medley of positive emotions. In lieu of the nagging feeling of alienation I had felt until recently, I was overwhelmed now with a sense of *belonging*. Didn't my classmates, male and female, get out of their way to make friends with me and call me by my first name? Didn't some of my teachers mention me by name and sometimes praise my work in class? I owed these people a lot for accepting me, and I too wanted to reply in kind. Suddenly, an immense gratefulness and elation started up in me. Here in this safe and peaceful part of Vietnam I could plan my future in my fashion, or I could just dream high. Now that I was in my final year of high school, next year I would be in Saigon, probably to attend medical school or study to become a career diplomat. Both options fascinated me. I wanted to follow in my father's footsteps but with a difference: I could boast of my excellent skills in Western medicine and my knowledge of valuable traditional medicine I would inherit from my father. I also wished to get into the Foreign Service because I wanted to have an opportunity to get to know the world. But to do so, first, I would have to earn a *Cử nhân Anh văn* (Baccalaureate degree in English). I was studying both French and English but wanted to specialize in English for an important reason: now that the French were gone, there were fewer opportunities for French graduates except for teaching high school, which I hated. With an English degree upon graduation from the Foreign Service School in Saigon, I could be assigned to a Vietnamese consulate in an English-speaking country and practice English, my favorite foreign language. I became so infatuated with this degree that I would often type its name under my name on an improvised business card. Though I had not been there yet, just seeing the printed lines would puff me up!

It was so wonderful to live in a country and at a time when I could dream as high as I wished. I did not have to worry about tomorrow. Like everybody, I realized the importance of working hard for my future, but occasionally I could make room for a little imagination and daydreaming, which had markedly shaped my character since I was a child.

***

Fall 1956 was a turning point in the life of the Class of 1957 at Quốc Học. As early as August, Father Cao Văn Luận, our philosophy teacher, had told us about his intent to establish a higher education institution in Huế to meet the demands of students from Huế and other provinces in Central Vietnam who, for various reasons, were unable to attend college in Saigon. Our reactions to Father Luận's idea were mixed. We desired to pursue our higher education in Huế but would feel uncomfortable about graduating from an institution not as prestigious as the University of Saigon. Since Father Luận wanted an overwhelmingly favorable response from us and we were too shy to make known our pleasure, we made him upset sometimes. Some of our classmates who were close to him reported that he was furious when they, tongue in cheek, told him they planned to go to Saigon after graduation. But Father Luận worried too much about his future university. President Diệm's coming to Huế to preside over a commemorative ceremony at a high school like Quốc Học, while motivated by his filial piety, should also be seen as his government's commitment to a distinctive higher education system, the first of its kind in South Vietnam since the departure of the French. (Founded during colonial rule and until 1954, the University of Saigon was still modeled after the French higher education system.) Shortly after Mr. Diệm's return to Saigon, Father Luận was notified that the University of Huế was officially established by a presidential decree.

I do not recall if we were ever excited about the breaking news. We were still too young to understand the implications of Father Luận's project as well as the government's propaganda about a so-called humanist, liberal education system upheld by President Diệm and pioneered by the University of Huế, the first higher education institution next door to the communist North. After all the excitement about the commemoration had passed, we fixed on our study for our high school graduation exam. For male youths like us, it was extremely important that we pass this hurdle, otherwise we would be drafted for military service. As late as 1956, after Mr. Diệm's refusal to hold general elections, the North started its sporadic attacks on remote areas in the South, which made it necessary for him to declare an emergency state in the country. The war between the North and the South had begun. We were afraid of getting drafted and killed when we were so young.

What I had worried about turned out to be true. Two months away from the high school graduation exam, I received a summons for military service at Mang Cá Fort in two weeks. The sky seemed to come down on my head. It meant that my education was finished, my coming to Huế for a better future became useless, and all my dreams cherished thus far were merely fanciful things. Some of my school friends also received similar summons and for several reasons felt the same way about their bleak future. We would get together to comfort one another and discuss the rumor that Father Luận would intervene with the government for those who were willing to stay in Huế and enroll at his university.

Close to the date we were to report for the physical exam, we got word that our conscription had been called off. We did not know if Father Luận had intervened on our behalf or if the notice had been sent to us too early when our graduation exam was still two months away. On hearing the news my father felt relieved and immediately lit candles and incense on the family altar to thank our ancestors for answering his prayer. The nightmare was over, and I could go back to my studies, but gone also was my dream of becoming a doctor or a diplomat. My family could not afford to send me to Saigon and, given what had just happened, it was too risky to live so far away. By May 1957, I had been pretty sure about my staying put in Huế but did not know what I would do next. While I was certain that I would pass the exam and my military service would continue to be waived, my father might want me to find a job to help him support my two brothers who were still in school. The prospect of becoming a teacher—the only option for any high school graduate who wished to work then—frightened me. Being called out by the teacher in class would make me squirm, let alone teaching a mixed class of boys and girls who were by and large not much younger than I was!

I swallowed my tears the day I graduated from high school. It broke my heart to see my father at the end of his tether. Despite his advanced age, he still toiled away to keep us in school. Being the eldest son in the family and the only one qualified to work because I had a high school diploma, I could not let my father down by doing nothing. But I was in an impasse. I did not want to be a teacher because teaching did not suit me. But enlisting in the army was the riskiest thing to do at that time because it was wartime. Unfortunately, this seemed to be on my father's mind now. He was swayed by his acquaintances' advice that I replace him in providing for the family and that enlisting was the best choice. I had no qualms about my father who wanted me to help him raise my brothers, but thought it was cruel of his advisors to recommend enlisting as the best thing for me. Would they do that to their children? Didn't they try to get their kids exempted from military service by bribing government officials? But while I was angry with these people and even with my father for being misled by them, I was reminded of my role as his eldest son. In the Confucian culture, one of the most desirable qualities the eldest son or daughter is expected to exemplify is his or her unconditional devotion to younger siblings. In the past many young men and women had passed up their marriageable age for taking so long to fulfill this parental role after the death of their parents. It was a formidable task for me because my father insisted that I make sacrifices for my brothers' sake, that is, to make sure their education was not interrupted. "As you're my eldest child, you should be as exemplary as you can be," he would quote his favorite dictum.

While I was being torn apart by the conflict between Confucian straitjacket morality—seeking a full-time job to support my family—and going to college, something happened and turned around the course of my destiny. I was admitted to the university's high school teacher training program with a three-year scholarship. Since I was not required to live in the dorm, the stipend was sufficient to cover basic expenses for a family that was used to living within its means like ours. I saw the event as an important turning point as I came of age. Now that I had given up my fantastic dream about medical school and the Foreign Service, I was safe to reorganize my life and rethink my career goals. I was still scared about teaching high school students. I was told they were rude, rowdy, and undisciplined compared with us at my Chơn Phước school in Đồng Hới back then. But what about doing research and teaching at the college level? What about finding a scholarship to study English overseas since I loved the language and wanted to master its essentials? But to get these done, I would have to earn a Baccalaureate degree in English besides my teaching diploma.

I enrolled at the University of Huế in August 1957 and graduated in May 1960. These three years were my most pleasant time since I came of age. Politically, South Vietnam under President Diệm was very stable. Most communist attacks were sporadic and took place in remote areas. There were rumors about Mr. Ngô Đình Cẩn's ruthless behavior or his condoning his subjects' atrocities, such as torturing to death a wealthy local contractor after extorting his money and then staging a suicide scene by throwing him off a high-building balcony. Stories like this and the emergence of the arrogant, spiteful first lady, Madame Nhu, President Diệm's sister-in-law, gradually changed my mind about Mr. Diệm as our ideal leader, but it never occurred to me that his regime would fall and the South would be lost to the communist North someday. Like everybody, I concentrated on my studies and looked forward to my future with hope and confidence.

English was a new but important subject in our university's curriculum. Now that the French had left, there was a great demand for learning the language of Vietnam's new ally, the United States. A believer in the domino theory, U.S. President Dwight Eisenhower was convinced that should South Vietnam fall to the communists, the rest of Southeast Asia would gradually go under in its wake. North Korea's China-led invasion of South Korea in 1950 and, most recently, the French defeat at Điện Biên Phủ in 1954 were still fresh in the minds of U.S. policymakers. Under Eisenhower's pressure and in the face of the communist threat, Mr. Diệm had to accept the presence of a limited number of U.S. military advisors in Vietnam. Vietnam's economy was booming thanks to U.S. aid. Through the United States Agency for International Development (USAID) and other U.S. government-sponsored agencies,

Vietnamese students received scholarships to study in America. Americans under the International Voluntary Service (IVS) Program were sent to Vietnam to teach English. There was in every major Vietnamese city a United States Information Agency (USIA) office with adequate library facilities to serve the Vietnamese reading public eager to learn about America. In just three years after the French departed, an American presence was already visible in Vietnam's most conservative city.

Despite Father Luận's ties with the Americans, resistance to U.S. interference in the academe was strong. Most of our faculty were Father Luận's former students who were educated in France. Our academic system, including the curriculum, was a clone of the French one. Our degree coursework lasted three to four years but was condensed into four to five *certificats* instead of splitting into numerous short-term courses. Chances were if you got sick halfway through the year or took the *certificat* exam but failed it, then you would have to wait another year to start over again. The strict application of the French grading system—for example, assigning a superlative work a grade no higher than a B equivalent in the American system—would hurt those who wished to pursue their graduate study in the U.S. Furthermore, unreasoning rote learning, repeating lecture notes word for word, a sure way to get high marks, was widely practiced in Vietnamese secondary and higher education institutions.

Though we were dying to practice speaking English with Americans, we preferred to do so with Britons. Having been accustomed to British English as taught by French authors in textbooks like *L'Anglais vivant* [*Living English*], we found it hard to understand American English pronunciation. Never could I regret enough the harm we inadvertently did to an American couple who had volunteered to come to Huế to teach us conversational English at Father Luận's invitation. Due to cultural differences on their part and miscommunication on ours (we understood little of their Massachusetts accent!), we made them angry. Instead of apologizing to them, we boycotted their class. We learned later that they submitted their resignation to Father Luận and tearfully left Huế. Personally, I was more biased against things American than my classmates. Misinformed about America and "brainwashed" by French textbooks, I formed grave stereotyped views of Americans. The two captioned cartoons in *La Vie en Amérique* [*Life in America*], my favorite high school textbook, "He stands for Parliament" and "He runs for Congress," reinforced my naïve perception of two markedly opposite cultures—British and American—one characterized by leisure and laid-backness and the other by a gung-ho and get-up-and-go attitude. But my most serious *misperception* of America had to do with American authors. I thought it was easy to get published in America because most textbooks (they were used ones and donated by the

Asia Foundation) I saw at the university library were nothing but a compilation of various texts with a brief introduction by the editor. This led me to naively believe that it was easy to become an author in America!

Shortly after our graduation something happened that still stays vivid in my memory today: our audience with Mr. Ngô Đình Cẩn. I do not remember specifically what occasioned this extraordinary event, but some time before our final exams it was rumored that Father Luận would present his university's first batch of graduates to President Diệm's brother and powerful advisor. If that were true, then it could be Father Luận's pleasure, or it could be initiated by our dean out of his belief that being granted an audience with the viceroy would best protect us in our new job.

On the appointed day, accompanied by our dean, we were taken in a van to see Mr. Cẩn at his summer residence on Thuận An Beach, about thirty kilometers east of Huế. Father Luận had arrived there ahead of us. Upon our arrival we were brought in to see Mr. Cẩn. In his early fifties and dressed in a black tunic and cotton white pants, Mr. Cẩn greeted us with a gentle smile. Contrary to rumors, Mr. Cẩn did not strike me as a ruthless man. Overall, he resembled Mr. Diệm but was taller and did not look as dignified and "intellectual" as the president. (Contrary to rumors, I did not see him chew piper betel in our audience either.) At first, he seemed timid in our presence, but after Father Luận had introduced us to him he went out of his way to ask Father Luận about us and the university. As Mr. Cẩn was lovingly, respectfully, or fearfully known to his subordinates as *"Ông Cậu,"* literally meaning "Mr. Uncle." (Out of respect for Mr. Cẩn one did not use his given name to address him or refer to him.) Father Luận, at the start of his speech, greeted him as "Respected *Cậu.*" When addressing us, Mr. Cẩn also used the same appellation to refer to himself. English has only the term "uncle" for the loving Vietnamese *cậu* and *bác,* the former denoting one's mother's older or younger brother and the latter one's father's older brother. It was Hồ Chí Minh who initiated this affectionate kinship identification by calling himself *Bác* as though we were all his own younger brothers' children. Mr. Cẩn also referred to himself as *Cậu* as if we were all his sisters' children. To win our hearts and minds, politicians like Hồ and Ngô Đình Cẩn treated us like children of their brothers and sisters. But what particularly struck me was before the end of the audience he said: "Good luck in your career, brothers and sisters. *Be sure to write Cậu if you encounter discrimination at work.*" He had little formal education, we were told, but the thought he expressed then seemed to come from the bottom of his heart. It was a rare opportunity for us, a bunch of greenhorns, to be seen by the president's brother, the most powerful political figure in Central Vietnam.

DALAT

Home Sweet Home

As part of the university's summer activities, graduates were provided a free trip to Dalat to participate in Dalat University's summer workshop. I was very excited about the opportunity to visit my birthplace that I had not seen since my return to Quảng Bình in 1947. My father also wanted me to see Aunt Hoa, his adopted sister. I had seen her only once when I was seven or eight. She had come to our home in Dalat to visit my father when he was gravely ill and disappeared for good afterward. My father never told me about the nature of his relationship with Aunt Hoa but occasionally he mentioned her name very affectionately, so I guess he must have known her before marrying my mother. It appeared that after his marriage and eventual return to Quảng Bình, my father no longer communicated with Aunt Hoa. Luckily, I had the address of Uncle Gia, my father's friend, who also lived in Dalat and knew Aunt Hoa's home. Being curious about what had happened between Father and Aunt Hoa, I was determined to find out from Uncle Gia who I thought could provide a clue to their relationship. Feeling like a prodigal son returning home after a long absence, I burned to explore as much as I could my father's "past," vaguely knowing, despite my young age, that it was inextricably intertwined with my past.

My ten-day long trip to Dalat was one of the most memorable times in my entire life. I skipped most of the scheduled activities to revisit my birthplace and previous hometown before the first Indochina War. Uncle and Aunt Gia gave me such a warm welcome. Their children, including their five-year-old daughter who was born after I had left Dalat, not only knew me very well but also treated me as if I were closer to them than anyone in the family. Hiếu, the little girl, was especially attached to me. She would not let me hug her at first, but after a day or two, she would not let go of me. Aunt Gia prepared her best dishes for me, Uncle Gia would not let me alone with his repeated questions about my father and my brothers in Huế and about my new name. "There, there," he teased me. "That's *not* your name. Your name *was* Ty Anh. You were just a little kid when we came to see your parents at your home here." He was very proud of me, congratulating me all the time on becoming a high school teacher at twenty-three! His sons took turns to show me around their neighborhood, which also used to be mine. We talked ceaselessly, and I was shocked to discover that my pure Dalat accent finally came back so fast. A tremor of joy like that of homecoming swept through me though I no longer had a home here. Only children of broken families can appreciate that kind of bliss. Living in a perfect family condition, the children of Uncle and Aunt Gia, I am sure, could not understand my tears when I entered their home.

***

My first night at Uncle Gia's home is so pleasant. I curl up in my blanket, relish the lingering delightful moments in the afternoon, and fall asleep only past midnight. Lying in my warm bed in the absolute stillness of the room, I come upon my childhood experience right here in this city. As sleep is approaching and consciousness is suspended, the light taps of the rain on the roof and the windowpanes and the soft cry of crickets outside are shockingly familiar to me. I heard them during the night shortly before we left Đồng Hới. Lying in bed and unable to fall asleep, I heard the crickets outside my old home. I had not left home yet, but the mournful cry of the crickets aroused in me such a profound nostalgia as if I was already living far away from home. I am thinking about home and about Trang and can not fall asleep.

Tonight, at Bác Gia's home as I lie in bed, I hear the chirrups of the crickets and other insects outside differently. It is an uninterrupted chorus, soft but clear, ethereal, and harmonious. Unlike the cry of the cicadas, it does not gradually grow to a rousing crescendo but is consistently soft, light, intermittent but sustained throughout. It sounds like a warm welcome extended to a prodigal son, a celebration of the revival of my idyllic childhood. I seem to have heard this music before here in my former Dalat home a long time ago before my family was broken but I was too foolish to not appreciate it. Hearing these insects again tonight arouses in me an uplifting boundless joy which was not lost but stored away somewhere and is now being released for me to enjoy and appreciate better the importance of the past. I fall asleep like the child I was fifteen years ago.

I wake in the shining glow of a sunny morning. Outside the window is a range of distant hills shrouded in gray mist. Far below is Uncle Gia's plantation with stretches of lush vegetation. I open the window to get a "feel" of my childhood hometown after so many years of absence. The rain has stopped but it is still wet and chilly. The ecstasy of homecoming, of returning to childhood, is still strong. I feel a tug at my heart. I saw these things before. We used to own a two-storied home and stretches of land like these. Every morning upon wakening, I would see the same hilltops hidden in the same gray mist. Ngành would come by and we would walk to school together. My recollection of school in my first grade is very vague: probably my mother would walk me to school. But, starting with my second grade in 1945 because of frequent air raids, Ngành would take care of me at school at my mother's request. When not in school, I would spend the day reading and dreaming with my characters or roaming the woods nearby. It was the sleepy, mystical Langbiang mountains I saw every day that made me pensive and romantic at such a tender age.

As I watch out the window the landscape rolling in front of me, I'm overcome by a surge of sadness. My past becomes alive with its ghosts reincarnated: *chị* Ngành, my little sister Như Cẩm, the tortoise at Linh Sơn Temple, the old monk, my participation in the chase of the French kids at an elementary school, my half-brother in his *Vệ Quốc Quân* (Protecting the Fatherland) uniform, my parents before their separation, and myriad other beings and events, all competing to surge back into life from every nook and cranny of my memory. Because their resurrection is short (my whole past in Dalat is condensed into a span of five minutes) and my memory is flimsy, these recreated past events, things, and people rapidly disappear into emptiness afterward. Because they are no longer in the flesh, permanently severed from me, and not within my reach as they were in my childhood, it is hard to completely recreate and keep them long in my mind. I cannot relive my past just as I had lived it when I was a child. Finished. Finished is my dream, my wishful thinking, my paradise. The soul of Dalat and my happy childhood through my involuntary memory became alive only for a short interval. They will not come back again. From now on I can only remember my former hometown piecemeal, in fragments. My childhood is recalled as separate events subject to the whim of my voluntary memory, not as a whole with its sounds, scents, and images.

I visit two more places of my childhood before saying goodbye to Uncle and Aunt Gia and their children. Aunt Gia takes me to see our former property first and, knowing that I need to be left alone to relive my old memories, she goes back to her home. I cannot believe that I spent my early childhood here. Our big two-storied house is gone and in its place is a rundown shack. Weeds grow in abundance where stretches of lush vegetation used to be. Aunt Gia says that my mother sold our place to a wealthy woman who lives in Saigon and rarely comes here to visit her property. After a moment of shock, I can recognize the panorama of my birthplace. Next to the shack is a row of tall pine trees which used to be in front of my childhood home. Farther to the left where I am standing now is the same tortuous brook where my brother and I would play floating paper boats. Beyond the fence and uphill is a deserted winding road where, every now and then, a small group of hill tribe people with bamboo knapsacks on their backs would trudge in silence to Dalat Central Market to barter with city dwellers. Across the second hill in front of me is the city's cemetery, its marble tombstones gleaming under the afternoon sun. My baby sister was buried there. Twenty years have passed and yet I still love and miss her so. For the first time in my life, I witnessed the death of a loved one in my family and knew what suffering was like. It seemed like something on my body was missing (my father would liken a person's siblings to his or her limbs) and, since then, I have always felt the need for a sister-figure in me. This probably explains my continued attachment to Trang whom I still see as my sweetheart, childhood friend, and sister.

Contrary to the brief but delightful moments I experienced the night before, images of the past I try to evoke now are painful. Things do not change much, but the people who were inextricably associated with me and who lived with me are gone, and I feel lonelier than ever. In the past, I never had to invoke memory because *these people were my identity,* and I felt no need to remember them. I was surrounded with love, joy, and happiness without knowing it, let alone appreciating it. Now it is my loss of innocence that makes me aware of the importance of my loved ones. Phantoms as they are now, I still feel the necessity of turning to them for continued sustenance. They do not have to be my family. The *montagnards* (highlanders) on their way to the central market were not my people, and yet they participated in my process of growing up happy and carefree. They formed an integral part of a time whose significance I understand only after I was uprooted from my birthplace by the war and disruption in my family. I miss them as much as I miss my own people.

Being back in my birthplace allows me to conjure up briefly my idyllic past. My body is like a wind chime that vibrates at the slightest stir of a gust of wind. These privileged moments, I am sad to discover, not only are short but far from purely pleasurable. No sooner am I thrilled to recognize my lost paradise than I am overcome by vague feelings of melancholy and uncertainty. Will I be able to recapture my past when I return here next time? Does this precious moment occur only once in my lifetime? Would I have another chance to come back to recover my paradise when my life takes root somewhere after this trip, will I forget Dalat, and will my search for the past not be needed?

The last thing on my schedule is visiting Aunt Hoa. Thạnh, Uncle Gia's son, takes me on his Honda and lets me off at a little cottage on a pine hill drive off my parents' former plantation. A lady a little older than my mother, looking very dignified and attractive despite her age, answers the door. Instinctively, I know that she must be Aunt Hoa.

I am a little nervous about meeting Aunt Hoa face-to-face for the first time. She strikes me as aloof, timid, sort of forbidding as if she was not used to seeing strangers. Uncle Gia tells me that since her husband's death, she has lived with her daughter, a student at the Couvent des Oiseaux, a French Catholic high school for girls. When I introduce myself and tell her my father's name, a gleam of joy sparkles in her eyes. Immediately she gives me a very warm welcome. "You take after your mother," she says. "I saw you once at your home when you were around eight. I went to see your father when he was very ill. After he had been sent home by the hospital, he prescribed himself his own medication. Thank Heaven, he recovered quickly afterward. The last thing I learned was your father had taken you and your brother to Quảng Bình in 1941 and I haven't heard from him since." Aunt Hoa speaks almost in one breath, as if she was rehashing what she might have repeated to herself several times, obviously to avoid telling me (her friend's son) what happened to my family that she, I am sure, knows too well. My father's serious illness she witnessed in her visit some thirteen years ago and his departure from Dalat must still have an impact on her mind. I can easily see her concern about my father's well-being as she bombards me with more questions about him. "How's your father's health now? What's he doing? Is he still practicing medicine? Who is he living with? With you, am I right?" Then switching her attention to me, she asks repeatedly, "I suppose your father is living with you. But are you married, *son*? How old are you? What's your name? We used to call you Ty Anh, but that was when you were a small boy. Uncle Gia told me you've been appointed a high school teacher in Nha Trang, and I'm happy for your father." Throughout her "solo speech," Aunt Hoa talks incessantly about my father, briefly addressing me, and hardly mentioning my mother. What touches my heart is that she keeps calling me *son*. Since I've grown up, I have not heard anyone, except my father, address me that dearly. I am dying to hear with my own ears that heavenly sound from Aunt Hoa's lips. She has a Quảng Bình accent but it is lighter than my father's because of her long stay in Dalat. I enjoy the flavor of both my ancestral land and my birthplace in her speech. Suddenly, I wish that Aunt Hoa had been my mother! She would not have left us, our family would not have fallen apart, and I would not have had such an unhappy childhood.

As I am about to say goodbye to Aunt Hoa to return to Uncle Gia's home, a very pretty girl emerges from an adjacent room. Dressed French style, she seems to be going on a date or something. Aunt Hoa tells her daughter I *am* her cousin. There is a surprised look on her beautiful face, and quickly she flashes a friendly smile at me. I am too embarrassed to respond. Compared to

Trang, Elizabeth strikes me as too bold and brash, and I wonder why in the world my father wanted to pick her for me. A short moment later, the bell rings. To my surprise, her date is Quang, the boy who played the scholar in the play *Giảng sách dưới trăng* four years ago at Quốc Học in an opening ceremony presided over by President Diệm! I saw him a few times at my former school. He was glib, loquacious, and extremely popular with girls. What makes him travel 830 kilometers from Huế just to date Elizabeth? Did she know him before? Why is Aunt Hoa so permissive? There is a touch of sadness on Aunt Hoa's face. Does it mean it is too late to revive her relationship with her old friend through a union of her daughter and his son? I do not know. But even if Elizabeth did not have a boyfriend, I would not consent to Aunt Hoa's plan. Elizabeth is not my type. Attending the Couvent des Oiseaux Lycée, she is too "French" for a country youth like me. My father would agree with me. He would not want to have this "fast" girl for a daughter-in-law. Suddenly, I feel so sad. I have found Aunt Hoa for my father; I have briefly experienced a taste of paradise when visiting Uncle and Aunt Gia and my former birthplace. *But that's about it.* I cannot help feeling sorry for my father who could not renew his friendship with Aunt Hoa through me and her daughter. When I returned to Dalat forty years later, it was all too late. All the witnesses of the past—my father, Aunt Hoa, Uncle and Aunt Gia—were dead. Elizabeth was also gone. The only place which I was familiar with and which still exists is Dalat's cemetery where my sister was buried but there were no landmarks to help me locate her grave. Every living thing is gone. What exists is perhaps the soul of the dead.

THE ROAD OF LIFE

One week before the start of the 1959-1960 school year, I left Huế to take a teaching position at Võ Tánh High School in Nha Trang. It was the first time I had come to a strange place since I came of age, so I was very worried. According to my appointment letter, I was to teach upper-level classes with students as old as or even older than I was. What happened was Võ Tánh High School was the only high school for students from Nha Trang and southern provinces of Central Vietnam who had lived under the Việt Minh regime and had little schooling or started school very late. By the time the government took over those provinces vacated by the Việt Minh, they had barely begun middle school.

With a letter of introduction from an old acquaintance of my father in Huế, I knocked at the door of a beautiful villa on Biệt Thự Avenue in Nha Trang. My new host family gave me a very warm welcome. At twenty-three, I was already on my own, working to support myself and my family. That night, I could not sleep a wink. I thought about my father. Late into the night, I seemed to be thinking a lot about Trang for the first time in a few years. It was strange that I thought about her whenever I had a rough time. Maybe she was still important to me though I had permanently lost her. I thought about her at this time because the difficulties of life were in store for me in the days ahead and I did not feel I was ready for this threatening real world.

My first day of work was very stressful. As I said earlier, teaching was the wrong career for me. Being terribly timid and self-conscious, I was never comfortable in front of a crowd. I remember when attending Chơn Phước school in Đồng Hới, to combat my shyness, I volunteered for the role of a young beggar in a play. I had been expected to walk across the stage and recite the line, "Please take pity on this poor child. He's cold and hungry." When it was my turn to show up, I was so frightened I forgot the line and wobbled all the way instead. There was a roar of laughter, and I could hardly finish the trip. Just a year earlier in my first teaching practice at Đồng Khánh (an all-girls school before 1975) in Huế when I first stepped onto the platform and started taking the roll, I heard some giggle followed by a comment: "Look! That teacher is no older than my kid brother!" I wished I had vanished off the face of the earth at that moment!

That morning at my new school in Nha Trang, as I entered a packed class with many eyes fixed on me, my heart started racing, my knees were shaking, and my face was burning. Taking a quick glance at the threatening crowd, I sized up the situation to determine a pertinent course of action. It was a huge class with the first two rows cram-full of girls and the rest bulking with husky boys whose demeanor struck me as though they had been more interested in getting even with me than in welcoming their new teacher. Suddenly, a roar came out from the end of the classroom. "Hey, guys. He's fresh out of the oven!" followed by a peal of laughter. I was so shocked to see the girls join this game with their unabashed giggles. At this most critical moment, my survival instinct came alive. I blurted out, *"And therefore beware of his heat!"* not knowing how on earth I could make such a rapid-fire retort. Suddenly, the class grew silent. Some bowed their heads who a short while ago might have created the hullabaloo.

I quickly took advantage of the momentum to influence the class by showing off my English skills, having been convinced that English was the most popular foreign language in Vietnam at that time. Using the British accent I picked up from the BBC, I said a few sentences in English for the sheer purpose of impressing the class, knowing well that they did not understand what I was saying. But my strategy was working. Not only did the students grow quiet but they were listening. Trying to perform my overkill, I occasionally paused to write out on the board some English expressions alluding to the students' rude behavior and explained in the student's native language what those expressions meant. While the class attentively copied down the new vocabulary, there was a touch of remorse on some students' faces.

Things got into their usual rut after my first encounter with students on that day. Though with time I gained confidence as a teacher and gradually won my students' respect, I was not satisfied with my performance. I decided that I was not adequately prepared for my teaching career. Like them, I predominantly used the translation-grammar method, which made me a lazy teacher by not requiring myself to prepare carefully for class. All I did was have student after student read aloud a few sentences and translate them into our native language or lengthily explain an abstract grammatical point, almost never touching on the language as it was spoken. Oral English skills had been neglected while we were in college, which was why now we often found ourselves tongue-tied in a live speaking situation. The University of Huế had used some American GI's from Phú Bài Base as part-time instructors of English conversation, who had no success because our classes were too big. We came to class, therefore, to hear the instructor speak English rather than to practice speaking English with him. Thus, we were left to solve our problem on our own by either listening to the BBC World Service or forming various

English-speaking clubs, which, for lack of native speakers' participation, did not produce much benefit.

Despite the increasing presence of Americans in the country, the university's foreign language curriculum was heavily French-oriented with its concentration on writing rather than on oral skills. Ironically, after three years of intensive training in the School of Education, I was employing similar teaching techniques my teachers had used in secondary school. Instead of having my students engage in live conversations and debates, I had them translate passage after passage from textbooks. They were also crammed with grammar and vocabulary, which enabled them to write some correct English sentences, but which proved useless as far as speaking the language was concerned.

Once I underwent a humiliating experience due to my limited oral skills. One day, I visited the British Council in Saigon to inquire about a scholarship opportunity. A Vietnamese woman at the information desk asked a few questions in English. Knowing that I was struggling with oral English, she switched to Vietnamese and dealt me such a blow: *"Tiếng Anh yếu như thế làm sao đi du học Anh được?"* (How can you go to study in England when your English is so poor?) I was so ashamed that instead of waiting for an interview, I stealthily walked out and never passed by the street where the British Council was located ever since. I was angry with myself, with my English teachers in high school and later in college who had taught us how to use synonyms, when to use *commence* and when to use *begin*, etc. rather than teaching us conversational skills. How useless, impractical stuff like that was to me! It was the cause of my humiliating experience at the British Council.

Things began to fall into place after a while. I grew accustomed to the routine of teaching five classes a week, being one of the school's homeroom teachers, and participating as required in a weekly meeting to study Mr. Diệm's political thought which always started with the faculty's chanting "Suy tôn Ngô Tổng Thống" [Hail to President Ngô]. At twenty-three, I already became a full-fledged government employee and felt very old! Worse, by sending home two thirds of my monthly salary to support my family, I no longer missed my father. I was also amazed that Quảng Bình, Đồng Hới, and even Trang had ceased to haunt my memory.

***

Life got better for me in this small town. I moved into a luxury villa with some colleagues originally from Huế. I came to know the world of male singles who called themselves "Huế expatriates" and who acted like "Old Mr. Confucius," a euphemism for educators, so called on account of society's expectation of teachers to observe the highest moral principles prescribed for those who are ranked second only to the king in Confucian culture. To this end, a teacher, no matter how young he is, must behave like a parent to his students. It is not uncommon for a student to refer to himself or herself as *con* (your child), when addressing a teacher who is his or her older brother's age! Because it was imperative that young male teachers like us watch our conduct, trying to keep a solemn demeanor would be the best policy especially in the presence of female students. My housemates released their repression at the dinner table by criticizing the codes of conduct for teachers or cracking jokes about women and sex, which made it hard for me to imagine how they could perform their dual role so well. Luckily as time went by, Confucian morality lost its battle. Shortly after I left Nha Trang, I received an invitation to attend the wedding of my former roommate whose bride, to my amazement, was the student he had secretly fallen in love with. Since then, I also heard that some other colleagues married their former students, who, I am sure, must be their secret sweethearts.

Because I did not plan to live in Nha Trang permanently, it never occurred to me that I would follow my colleagues in their footsteps. Nevertheless, I was drawn against my will into the battle with Confucianism for a while. One day, in one of my classes I discovered that the girl on the right end of the first row was gazing at me. At first, I thought she was just paying attention to my lecture. But my intuition told me that I was wrong because it happened frequently throughout the class and lasted several seconds before she cast her final glance at me and resumed her notetaking or pretended to do so. She looked so sad. There was a flash of reproach in her sidelong glance. This went on for a good while until she stopped showing up in class. I thought about asking her sister, who was a student in my other class, about her sudden absence but was too timid to do so. One day in March 1961, I received a letter postmarked in Saigon. It announced her marriage along with a short note in her own graceful handwriting inviting me to her wedding. I understood the reason for her leaving school but could not figure out the meaning of her sad, reproaching look she had been casting on me those months. Maybe I had misinterpreted her demeanor, or maybe she had done it but in a thoughtless, unintentional manner, or maybe she might have wanted to tell me she would miss me and my class. Suddenly, I discovered that I missed her beautiful gray eyes and sad look.

As time went by, I became fully adjusted to my new life in Nha Trang. Its people were genuinely warm and friendly. My students were very affectionate and loyal to me. As I lived by myself, students often came to see me. In January 1961, I fell ill and was bedridden for several days in my boarding house. One day, I ran a high fever and slept several hours. Someone poked me in the toes. When I opened my eyes, I saw my students gathered around me, all looking worried and some with tears in their eyes. A boy brought me a dozen chicken eggs that I knew was a fortune to his family. Most kids in my classes were from the country and were very poor. I owed my recovery to their kindness and dedication to Vietnamese culture that taught them to treat their teachers like their own parents. Although they referred to themselves as *your children* when addressing me and I could not correct them, deep down I saw them as my own brothers and sisters by virtue of my age. Until May 1964 when I was transferred to Pétrus Ký High School in Saigon, we had spent time together in various extracurricular activities, especially outings and picnics.

Though North Vietnam had started its invasion of South Vietnam as early as the late 1950s, its attacks were sporadic and on a very small scale. We could travel safely by car or by train on Route 1 and almost everywhere in the Mekong Delta without worrying about getting blown up by Vietcong mines. The first three years of the 1960s was the most pleasant period of my young adulthood. For the first time since my emigration to the South, I could enjoy the fruits of my father's sacrifice and my own efforts—a well-paid job, a respectable social status, and a potentially bright future—things unthinkable to my family when we first came to Huế. Still seeing myself as a refugee, I appreciated the opportunity of living in a free and peaceful country. On Saturday evenings right after I got out of my last class, I got on an express train that ran through the night and arrived in Saigon when I was barely awake. How delightful to nestle myself in my snug berth and look out the train window at the slow-moving silhouettes of thatched-roof houses and palm trees until my eyelids grew heavy and closed at the onset of sleep. Sleep was not an accurate term to call my state of being. Though my visual perception was shut down completely, I could hear the steady chug of the train regularly and rhythmically pouring into my ears, and felt a delicious sensation, the same one I would feel when traveling by train at night with my father and falling asleep in his lap. In my slumber, I could also tell where I was. If I felt a cool wind streaming in from the window, inundating my entire berth and the rattle growing louder and sharper because of the impact of air currents on the fast-speeding train, then I knew it was crossing a river. When I heard the drawn whistle accompanied by heavy, short puffs, then I knew we were climbing the steep Langbiang Pass and would be home shortly. The train then would ease itself into a slow ride, and I could see dark shapes of tall telephone poles coming into view then passing, passing. Shortly, the brakes would hiss and screech, sending the carriage jerking forward, and I would be fully awake, feeling a knot in my stomach. A few minutes later the train would come to a standstill. "Wake up, Ty Anh dear," Father would cuddle me. "We're home."

It was a heavenly bliss to be on a train and comfortably restive in my dreams while the world outside was awake and restless at work. I was able to relive and relish what was endearing to me. The train, because of its long connection with my dear father, my happy past, and because of our frequent use of it, became my identity. To see it again meant to rediscover my lost self because everything associated with it I could easily recognize on the train. The magic lay in the train. Somewhere in the middle of my night ride when my consciousness was suspended, its acoustic quality and hypnotic motion wakened the dormant world in me. Like a harp or a chime, my mind vibrated with every stir of wind. The train drifted me back effortlessly into a recognizable faraway time and place before the war in my travel with my father to Quảng Bình. I had not dreamed of him in years since he took me out of Mr. Huy's house, but that night in my dream, I saw him ride the train with me. At one point I snuggled in his lap. As the passenger carriage was so warm, he always fluttered a paper fan to keep me cool. He did not seem to have a wink throughout the night.

As soon as I got off the train and left the station, I was swept off by a powerful swirl of life coming from all directions. Throngs of people huddled along or crossed the streets at express speed, hawkers cried their ware, taxis and motor tricycles scurried around honking noisily. Saigon, the capital of South Vietnam, as I first knew it, was bursting with a raw energy, a mighty life force that could not escape the attention of a small-town citizen who saw it for the first time. Overlooking momentarily the glaring flaws of the Diệm regime, I suddenly grew sentimental, feeling grateful to it for bringing order, security, and prosperity to my adopted land. Had I chosen to stay in Đồng Hới, I would have lived only a drab life and would not have witnessed right in this city what was associated with youth. It was no wonder then that all the former refugees from the North not only had integrated themselves so well to the South, but also here in Saigon many of them were proud owners of the prosperous commercial hub on Lê Thánh Tôn Street. Given such promising prospects for the South, it was difficult to imagine that some disaster would ever happen to me, my family, and my people.

The South was also a haven for artists, writers, and intellectuals from Hanoi who did not accept communism. Shortly after their arrival, they set out to resume their interrupted activities in great earnest. Since 1954 we had witnessed a boom in the publishing industry hitherto unknown in the South. Literary magazines, journals, and newspapers with significant titles such as *Sáng Tạo* [*Creative Arts*], *Văn* [*Literature*], *Văn Học* [*Literary Studies*], *Tự Do* [*Freedom*] all founded by intellectuals originally from Hanoi quickly became forums for all South Vietnamese artists and writers who not only cared for their freedom of expression but wished to experiment with new stylistic and thematic innovations. There was also a flourishing of women's literature, and some writers went so far as to fight rigid ethical and social restraints placed on their sex by traditional culture. Two writers who caused a stir in the literary scene were Nguyễn Thị Hoàng and Túy Hồng. Whereas in *Vòng tay học trò* [*In the Student's Embrace*]), for example, Nguyễn Thị Hoàng celebrates sexual freedom by unabashedly exploring the intimate relations between a female teacher and her teenage high school student, Túy Hồng accuses Confucianism of turning all young women into saints before marriage. Born and raised in Huế before she moved Saigon and became a writer, Túy Hồng was privy to the lives of ex-princesses, courtesans, maids of chamber, and their female offspring who had been taught to put a highest premium on their pre-nuptial virginity. Those women in Túy Hồng's well-known novels *Vết thương dậy thì* [*The Wound of Puberty*] and *Tôi nhìn tôi trên vách* [*I Am Looking at Myself on the Wall*], end up being neurotics as a price they've to pay for their compliance with social and cultural requirements.

This bold treatment of female condition and sexuality by female authors is a far cry from Nguyễn Du's *The Tale of Kiều* which dramatizes the brutal victimization of a woman in Vietnam's feudal society but falls short of dealing with her most intimate needs. These women writers' concern with female sexual freedom was inspired by Françoise Sagan's *Bonjour tristesse* [*Good Morning, Sadness*] which expounded hedonism and amorality rather than by Madame Nhu's *Phong trào phụ nữ liên đới* (Women Solidarity Movement). According to critics, the "emancipated" woman the movement claimed to have promulgated kept her from performing domestic duties by enlisting her in uncalled-for paramilitary activities. Rumors flew around that Madame Nhu was the author of the Family Law that prohibited divorce, which made her original intent to free women a paradox. Clearly, Madame Nhu's so-called "liberated" woman does not fit Nguyễn Thị Hoàng's and Túy Hồng's portrayal of their female characters.

So many random thoughts on women's literature in the early 1960s. Its importance stems from the fact that, for the first time, women writers, when exploring the complex realities of women's lives, asserted their need to develop an independent sense of identity and their freedom to work out their own destiny. Though censured by society because they candidly portrayed—rarely in Vietnamese literature—women's sexual feelings, Nguyễn Thị Hoàng's and Túy Hồng's fiction was widely read by young men and women of my generation. If we are to define artistic freedom as the artist's right to talk about issues that he or she deems important to himself or herself, then only in the South could it be found. And, as noted earlier, most refugee writers from Hanoi joined their fellow refugees in their journey to the South and their new southern colleagues for the same cause. Though it turned out to their great disappointment that the Diệm regime was politically repressive, writers in general could at least freely practice their art in their new land.

It was this congenial atmosphere that promoted and fostered a healthy development of art and literature in the South after the partition of the country in 1954. But the chief factor that contributed to the literary flowering, as mentioned earlier, was these writers' desire to create a distinctly South Vietnamese literature of its own, one that they could be proud of in their non-communist South. Anxious to make their movement a success, these men and women exhausted their creative talents on the one hand and explored various European schools for their literary experiment on the other.

To understand better the reason of Vietnamese writers' turning to the West, particularly France, for inspiration in literary innovations, it is important to provide a brief rundown of the French occupation of South Vietnam beginning in the late 19th century. *Nam Việt* (literally, the South of Vietnam), a name used to call the southern part of the unified Vietnam from the time it was conquered from Cambodia by the Nguyễn lords in the early 17th century down to the partition of the country in 1954, consisted of Saigon and the Mekong Delta. When the French came to Indochina in 1858, they quickly took over Nam Việt and turned it into a French colony in 1862 with a new French name *Cochinchine.* Immediately the French set up an administrative system in Cochinchine, including training selected Vietnamese to assist them in ruling the new colony, replacing the imperial court's mandarins with French-speaking high-level *fonctionnaires* (civil servants), awarding privileges including French citizenship to loyal locals, etc. In an obvious attempt to emulate imperial China's policy toward its Vietnamese colony in the past, the French francized educated South Vietnamese adults and school children. I remember at our primary school in Dalat we were required to salute the French flag and chant the *Marseillaise* every morning. In class we were also taught to say *"Nos ancêtres les Gaulois"* (Our ancestors the Gauls). This practice also applied in Vietnamese-run schools, where *Annamite* [sic] kids dressed in white pants and black tunics were required to rehash the same rituals.

Although at Mr. Diệm's request, French troops had withdrawn from the South by the end of 1954, French schools were still allowed to operate. Shops selling French merchandise and run by French-speaking Vietnamese owners continued to abound in Saigon and major cities. The best restaurants in the capital of South Vietnam showcased chefs who had cooked for their former French masters. Even hawkers, in most cases, used French and body language when haggling with American GIs on the streets of Saigon. Although the South had become independent, French was still the medium of instruction in law, medical, and technical schools, as well as the official language used by the government in its correspondence with foreign countries. Most educated Vietnamese were fluent in French. The French had left, but their culture and lifestyles stayed almost intact.

Using their knowledge of French, Vietnamese writers in the 1960s absorbed and applied European modernist innovations that best suited their literary interests and vocation. Against the backdrop of a civil war that already showed signs of unprecedented brutality in the country's history, they explored themes echoing Kafka, Sartre, and Camus, like the absurdity of the human condition, the ironies of moral commitment and life realities, and man's futile quest for meaning in an ice-cold universe. A quick glimpse at the work of representative authors of the Sáng Tạo group, in particular Thanh Tâm Tuyền and Dương Nghiễm Mậu, reveals modern man's condition at its worst: desperate, lost, lonely to the point of insanity. To dramatize all this, these authors borrowed the techniques of *avant garde* schools such as the *Nouveau Roman* (New Novel) and Surrealism. In his story "Dọc Đường" ["On the Road"], for example, Thanh Tâm Tuyền writes about a character who arrives at a rubber plantation to visit his brother. It turns out that because his brother is not there, or he may have taken the wrong bus, or something is wrong with his memory (which is reminiscent of Kafka and Camus), he ends up in a war zone and cannot find transportation to get home in time before the curfew. At the story's end, as everybody in the small town has turned down his request for shelter, he can be seen clinging to a barrel of water by the light of flares amid loud explosions. Throughout the story, the war, the ice-cold world, and the character's condition are rendered through a completely detached camera-like representation of reality. And yet Thanh Tâm Tuyền's use of Alain Robbe-Grillet's favorite technique produces an entirely different effect: against the background of a war-torn world the seemingly cold optical description of things only makes the sense of loss, bewilderment, and helplessness experienced by the character—and shared by the reader—viscerally acute. Though society enjoyed relative political stability, its moral values were threatened with an imminent collapse due to the escalation of the war and massive U.S. military intervention. The Kafkaesque seeker of an ideal in the previous decade gave way to a delusional escapist living in a nightmarish world. Most characters in Dương Nghiễm Mậu's *Kinh cầu nguyện* [*Prayer Sutra*], for example, because they are unable to reconcile their professed moral values and the exigencies of the practical world, flee into their dream world only to discover that it is nothing else but their horrible unconscious. In Thanh Tâm Tuyền's poetry, reality is a series of nightmares where nature is evil and man is desperate and horrified to the point of insanity: "When pouring out misty rains / the wind, the howling wind / across disappearing green regions / You are back, you must be back. How distraught you are / just like tattered reeds / paths are labyrinthine puzzling / deserted like a cemetery completely deserted / graves' weeping stops short somewhere" ("Mais désespérément"). Given the prophetic nature of their writing, can we say that these two writers, as early as the early 1960s, had predicted the condition of their people during and after the war?

It is important to add to my preliminary remarks on South Vietnamese literature from the 1960s to the fall of South Vietnam in April 1975 a large group of young writers, most of them poets, who directly participated in the war and wrote chiefly about the war. Poetry was their choice because they had little free time and it suited their sensitive mind. Young, educated, full of idealism, and free of political ideology, they demonstrate in their writing a stark representation of the terror of war, as well as a touching sensibility about the country's tragic condition. The destruction caused by war is beyond words: "The country is blown up by bombs and rockets / Wilderness inundates the soul / Does this mean flares will forever light the way like torches?" (Chu Tân). It means loss of opportunities, loss of paradise for young people: "All childhood dreams destroyed / like a balloon breaking loose, soaring up, disappearing into the high sky / Dreamy eyes fixed on old school memories / The summer bird stopped singing" (Vĩnh Lộc); "Gone forever is my tender age" (Thụy Văn). While condemning the war, they commiserate with their enemy whom they see as "companions in sorrow" (Ý Yên). The soldier poet expresses his anti-war sentiments in a very humane manner when he addresses his enemy thus: "Oh, how can we hate each other / when you call your country Vietnam / and I also call mine Vietnam?" (Đỗ Ngọc). Cao Tiêu has a better reason to commiserate with the enemy. "The prisoners are a string of teenagers / Born in the North and expected to die in the South / They call me "Grandpa" / I didn't know I have grandkids / Here's your food, dears / My heart is lacerated and bleeds." Trang Châu, a military doctor, has an important message for warmongers: "In the present-day war / please allow me to fight without hatred." He writes these extreme moving lines when caring for a wounded VC and seeing him shed a tear of gratefulness. It's the same VC who gave him a glare of anger when he was first captured: "allow me to trade one hundred victories / for a tear from the enemy." The soldier poet dreams of peace while fighting the war: "Whether peace is at hand or remote / please, darling, do not give up hope" (Phạm Cao Hoàng). What touches my heart is the combat soldier often reveals his romantic mind when he has a chance. In the 1968 Tết offensive when there is a lull in fighting, Phan Bá Thụy Dương writes home to ask his lover "if our place is still there / so I can wrap it with my loving heart." Trần Hoài Thư, who represents the romantic trend at its greatest in South Vietnamese combat soldiers' poetry, uses writing to protest the terror of war. In "Thank You, War" he romanticizes life on the battlefield: "Thank you, war, for giving me a mansion / Its roof is the sky laden with stars / Its walls are grandiose heaps of bricks / The starlit night sky helps me become poet / Graves around me allow me to befriend ghosts." Like his romantic peers, Trần Hoài Thư celebrates memories of pre-war peacetime and happy childhood: "I can see clouds in your eyes / young children in white shirts and blue trousers awaiting / dismissal from school pouring out like a kaleidoscope of small butterflies." Similarly, Vương Tân encourages his sweetheart at home "to dream more / to forget about nights of flares and bullets / to appreciate the joy of life." Despite the country's desperate situation, dreaming about the return of peace and keeping hope alive characterize the poetry of most South Vietnamese combat soldiers.

While there was no clear evidence of the influence of French existentialism on combat soldiers, the philosophy of this school was in vogue in South Vietnam in the 1960s. Interestingly, the poetry of those who directly participated in the war is reminiscent of the mood of French intellectuals in the 1940s, particularly Albert Camus and Jean-Paul Sartre, save that existentialist mood in Vietnam war literature is very intense because it is derived from young Vietnamese soldier poets' raw experience. Thus, the absurd is not an abstract philosophical concept of life but a concrete representation of the most irrational and unfortunate thing that has ever happened to a peace-loving people. Thus, Thi Vũ Hà Như writes: "[Y]ou dig deep the earth / which buries unlucky men / in a fratricidal protracted war / that is *sickly, senseless, dirty, shameless*" (emphasis added). For Hoài Lữ, who had a book of poems published when he was only nineteen and who was killed in a battle two years later, the war is absurd, inhuman, and tragic for a soldier because "it has destroyed his youth." For Hoàng Hà, the Vietnamese youth have no future, only "an emptiness before them, one with claws as sharp as a knife blade." This is how Đỗ Ngọc explains "existence precedes essence": "It must take twenty years to make a man / it takes only a very small bullet to pierce through his heart." Things in war-torn South Vietnam become absurd, irrational, meaningless since the coming of the war. Not only does it happen on the battlefield where senseless killing is a survival mode; it turns an entire society upside down, makes things unpredictable, and destroys time-honored social and moral values. For example, the massive presence of U.S troops in Vietnam provided generous employment opportunities for married women, but it was the cause of many disastrous consequences to the Vietnamese family.

The war in Vietnam grew more complicated every day because of the massive U.S military intervention. In his poem entitled "To My U.S Allied Soldier" Hoài Ziang Duy explains to his American colleague what Americans do not know about Vietnam. It is the apex of suffering: "First, you must know the name of my country / Because it is here / That misery, misfortune, poverty

/ And overflowing tears exist." It's death: "sad death, tragic death / Mines blowing up buildings, crowded streets / Any time, morning, evening, night / Every one of us is expected to have a similar fate." The poet's country is deeply divided; language is used not to promote understanding but to cause feuding and disunity: "There is that river that divides the country / There is that small dreary canal / Such a country, such a language / the extended hand will never be held." These are the basic things about Vietnam that American soldiers can never understand. Nor can they comprehend, as Hoài Ziang Duy observes, why the Vietnamese maintain an amiable demeanor and cheerfully accept their condition in the face of war: "When you stop by / A certain place / You will see / On a barge that transport people and goods across a river / A child who greets you in a friendly manner / A blind beggar / Who calmly tells his story / And a disabled man on crutches / Who very indifferently watches the water flowing." It's beyond the American soldier that, while the so-called "Vietnam War syndrome" is a nightmare to him and his buddies after their return, his former Vietnamese comrade in arms seems immune to it and lives like a philosopher.

Americans were sent to serve in a country that was literally unknown to them. They were also confused about what they were fighting for. As mentioned earlier, the war was also fuzzy to young Vietnamese men who participated in it. By a twist of fate, young Americans and Vietnamese were brought here to face death, a truth that was clear, certain, friendly, equal, and liberating: "It's like once a day / The water flows on the canal now shallow now deep / It's like we hear gunfire every night / It's like we thought we weren't ourselves / Because it's so dark we couldn't recognize each other / The accidental bullet greets us cheerily / Each of us has our way of life / To die is to laugh awhile / Peace." This eloquent "existential" view—life is absurd, and death is a fun game—explains the Vietnamese people's survival after such a long and devastating war.

Combat soldiers' literary contribution to the brief flowering of South Vietnamese literature was important not only because of the magnitude of its production (thousands of poems by more than four hundred poets in less than a decade), but also because their work exhibits great humanistic themes. Due to the scope of this memoir, it is hoped that future researchers and scholars will study this brief but important literary phenomenon.

***

It is important to offer some brief observations of those who were directly involved in what Americans called the Vietnam War, as well as their impact on Vietnamese society. A frequent visitor to Saigon, I was struck by looking-alike crop-haired foreigners on Saigon streets. Taller and bigger than French men I had seen in the old days, these Americans looked rugged and awkward in comparison with French colonists. They also appeared naïve as they were easily fooled by Vietnamese urchins who stopped them to ask for cigarettes with their unchanged litany: *"Ô Kê, Sa-lem?"*("Give us Salem cigarettes, okay?"). They would either pause to give some, or walk on unruffled, followed by the kids who shouted obscenities at them.

In the early 1960s, Saigon was safe one hundred percent while the war was raging at remote outposts. Americans could go virtually anywhere, but their favorite spots were the bars on Tự Do Street, formerly *Rue Catinat* (the meeting point of the characters of Graham Greene's novel *The Quiet American*) which served *Saigon tea,* a euphemism for alcoholic beverages. It was at these places that they met local women who worked as servers and whose lives were affected by these foreigners' presence in their country. The well-known female novelist Nguyễn Thị Thụy Vũ has skillfully depicted these young women's adverse condition in her heart-wrenching book, *Mèo đêm* [*Night Cats*]. Thụy Vũ's characters sell their body to make a living in these tough times. And yet they also sacrifice for a worthy cause: supporting their family and sending their younger siblings to school so they can get a better future than theirs. In many ways they resemble their soul sister Kiều that Nguyễn Du has immortalized in *The Tale of Kiều.*

Coerced into an unwanted intimate relationship with the GI's when working in barrooms or at U.S. military bases, many women got pregnant. Unwed and with a child fathered but abandoned by a foreigner, these women were subject to public scorn and humiliation and had no chance to find a husband in their country. But her situation was far much better than that of my relative who worked as a house cleaner at Phú Bài Base to support her family and was raped by a black GI. When found pregnant, she was beaten by her husband and scorned by her own children and relatives. When my relative's half-breed child grew up, she suffered an even worse fate than her mother because of her skin color. Contrary to official reports, during the war the number of Amerasian kids who were accepted by their American fathers for resettling with their Vietnamese mothers in America was insignificant compared with those who were left to scrape for a living at such an early age. Barely in their early teens by the 1968 Tết offensive, they already joined the army of Vietnamese orphans who made their living by rummaging through U.S. military dump sites for leftovers or by selling candies or lottery tickets at bus stations. Oftentimes, they were often greeted with racial slurs by some adults.

No place was more biased against the marriage of Vietnamese women with American men than Huế. Viewed as vulgar, uncivil, and foreign, they were in the eyes of Huế people incompatible with their beauties raised in the former imperial city's aristocratic tradition. An American soldier from Phú Bài Base who taught conversational English at the University of Huế fell in love with one of his students. While the girl and her modern-minded parents accepted him, her relatives strongly criticized his marriage proposal. Whereas Huế culture did not favor the marriage of its women to American men, it would sing the praises of a Vietnamese man who happened to have an American wife or European wife. In traditional Huế culture, a woman, regardless of her national origin, was supposed to subjugate herself to her husband's will. Due to the massive resettlement of Vietnamese people in the West in recent decades, traditional culture has become lax. Intermarriage is no longer a taboo for young women of Huế origin.

In February 1963, I received a cable from home that read: *"Papa gravement malade. Retourne immédiatement"* ("Father gravely ill. Return home immediately"). I had a previous appointment with an American couple, who were missionaries living in Nha Trang, with whom I regularly practiced speaking English at their home. Because I had no access to the telephone, I went to see them to share the news and cancel the meeting. The missionaries immediately asked me to rise with them and, holding hands with me, they prayed for my father's recovery. With eyes closed and in an extremely devout manner, the missionaries recited their memorized prayer with such articulateness, vivacity, and earnestness as if they were delivering a sermon. They addressed God as if He was a *real* Being, was in the room with them, and was listening to their prayer. I had seen my father pray many times, but the way he did it was quite different. Except for the extremely sincere and respectful look on his face, I could hardly hear what my father was saying to *Trời Phật Ông Bà* (Heaven, Buddha, our ancestors). "To pray effectively," Father said, "you must keep calm. Noises, whatever their source, are an impediment to successful communication with the supernatural world." There was a fervent look on my father's face when he was praying, but unlike the missionaries, he did not strike me as though he was communicating with Heaven and the latter was promising to him that his request would be granted.

The missionaries went on praying steadily and zealously. I did not understand everything they said because they spoke so fast. But I could catch the flavor of their prayer. It was vehement and eloquent, just like a sermon. When they finished, the missionaries opened their eyes and turning to me, the husband asked, "Would you like to accept Jesus as your Savior?" Caught off guard by what transpired, I was frightened and tongue-tied. The missionaries saw my panic but could not read my mind, so they comforted me, telling me they would pray harder, and my father would be okay. I stopped visiting the missionaries to practice my English after that incident.

On the train home, I had plenty of time to reflect on my father's cable and its mystery and felt pretty sure that he was fine. If my father was sick, why hadn't someone in my family signed the cable instead of him? Also, why did I feel calm despite all this? If something had happened to my father, I would have felt it because I loved him so much and felt inseparable from him. A thought flashed across my mind: the old man must have gone to the post office to send his cable and he should be all right now. I could not figure out the purpose of the *télégramme* but vaguely realized that it must be something very important, otherwise the old man would not have done it.

In the early 1960s, it was relatively safe to travel by train. It was not rare, therefore, to see foreign and American tourists explore the country by train. I happened to see a young American looking out the train window as if to enjoy the Vietnamese landscape. Wanting very much to practice my English, I struck up a conversation with him. We talked about various things and, knowing that he was a medical doctor, I mentioned my brother, a medical student at the University of Huế, and my father, a physician in the Sino-Vietnamese medical tradition. Though my father's practice was limited to herbal medicine, I bragged about his knowledge of acupuncture. Unfortunately, my interlocutor, a hardcore believer in Western medicine, was not impressed at all. He said he sympathized with my father's practice because herbal medicine was allowed in America but abhorred the idea of inserting needles into your body. To him, this sort of treatment was senseless, unhygienic, and dangerous. He might not know that ten years later, in the wake of Nixon's China visit, acupuncture, Chinese herbs, and *Chi-k'ung*, i.e., methods for developing vital energy, made an uproar in America.

As soon as I got off the train, I rushed home to see my father. As expected, nothing had happened to him. He was entertaining his favorite guest, a famous astrologer from his hometown in Quảng Bình, and looked healthier and more cheerful than ever. When seeing me, my father mumbled something apologetically, which was very unusual of him: "Home that soon? Thought it would have been another while before you could get back."

Then turning to his friend, he explained the purpose of his cable: "I just wanted him to have a little more time with the family this Tết." Good heavens! Just to have me home early for the holiday he had given me such a scare! But seeing his astrologer friend with him today, especially his nod to my father's utterance along with his quick glance at me, I knew with certainty why he had sent me the cable.

My father's criteria for selecting his most senior daughter-in-law (so called because of my status as his eldest son) were very strict. She must be raised in a Confucian family. Whereas he would consider the girl's grace, her beauty was out of the question to him. I could understand why he set his mind to it that way. Being the only surviving heir in the Trần clan and extremely devoted to the wordship of our ancestors, he wanted me to continue that tradition. In his judgment, I could not do it without a woman raised in the same faith, nurtured by the same roots, and more importantly, willing to serve my father as faithfully as she had served her parents. Though an ideal bride, in my father's opinion, should demonstrate other qualities, such as an exceptional knowledge of the rules of propriety and household governance and an unconditional loyalty to her husband, what he emphasized was her willingness and ability to assist me in caring for him in his old age. What was more, if my father outlived me, this most important task would fall on this most senior daughter-in-law.

I went to see my future bride with my father purely out of obedience. I wanted to please my father, to make him feel happy as much as I could when he was living. But deep down I did not take the visit seriously. I wished that this would fall through as it had a few times in the past so that I could return to school as soon as I could. Another reason for my apathy to this sort of thing was I was still struggling to get over the shock after my breakup with Liên, a girl I had met and briefly dated while serving on a high school graduation exam committee in Huế.

As anticipated, while my father seemed to know that family well, I was a total stranger subjected to everybody's scrutiny. My prospective parents-in-law were talking with my father, but I noticed they looked squarely at me from time to time. It seemed the girl that we were to see might not be home. "It couldn't be better," I told myself, feeling relieved about the possibility of getting away with my father's plan with my departure tomorrow. At the same time, however, I felt hurt at the thought of being taken so lightly by this girl who, I suspected, might not be interested in me. We had been waiting to see her for half an hour; still, she did not show up. I began to feel fidgety and embarrassed and wished we had not come. This had never happened to me before. I had had no trouble with Lan, the daughter of my father's old friend at the former Imperial Academy, because she showed up shortly after our arrival at her home. As for Liên, she seemed to have been waiting for me to give her my first English lesson.

As I was drifting off in thought into the pleasant past, my future bride suddenly emerged in a great hurry from the door connecting the lounge where we were sitting to the family room. I was shocked to find her so familiar. Hadn't I seen her hand in hand with some other girls on New Year's Day just a few months after our arrival in Huế and foolishly taken her for Trang? As I was too embarrassed to fix my eyes on her, I looked away, but maybe because of that, I could recall this girl—the girl I had mistaken for Trang on that New Year's Day—more vividly than ever before. Blushing terribly, the girl greeted me with a nod and quickly made her way to her motorcycle in a corner of the lounge. Now I could watch her closely. She must be the girl I had seen with her company on that New Year's Day in 1954 on Trần Hưng Đạo Street after my arrival from Quảng Bình! But how could she resemble Trang that much, that is, pretty and graceful, except that she struck me as more sophisticated than my sweetheart! She was wearing a white silk *ao dai*, white pants, and white gloves. She was also holding in her hand a blue wide-brimmed cloth hat that I found out later she would be wearing for paramilitary exercises which were required for young women who participated in Madame Nhu's Women Solidarity Movement. In this formerly imperial city, which still emphasized female decorum and propriety, it was not suitable for women to be seen in public in their military uniform because this outfit would make them look too masculine. Like her colleagues, my future bride carried in her motorcycle her uniform which she would change to only when she arrived at the city stadium for paramilitary training. As a rule, Huế women always went out in their fluttering *ao dai* and white conical hats that would serve to heighten their grace, beauty, and femininity.

On August 30th, 1963, Nga and I were married while a curfew was enforced in the entire city following demonstrations by Buddhists and students against the government. There was a good drizzle when we went outside with my father-in-law to light candles and incense on the altar of the earth god to ask for his blessing. It lightly rained during our wedding, a rare thing in this driest, hottest month of the year in Huế. My father-in-law said it was a good luck sign for our eventual union. I did not understand the meaning of his cryptic pronouncement until 1975 when my plan to return home from a study in the U.S. failed due to the fall of South Vietnam. My eight-year long separation from my family ended in September 1980 when the new communist regime finally allowed my loved ones to leave Vietnam to reunify with me in the U.S.

SAIGON

Upon returning to Nha Trang from my Tết holiday in Huế, I received a letter from the Ministry of Education notifying me of my new post at Pétrus Ký High School in Saigon. I was thrilled and afraid at the same time. I had applied to transfer to Saigon to complete my bachelor's degree in English at the University of Saigon. With a second English degree in hand, I would have a better chance to get a scholarship to study in America or England. But the appointment also put me in a Catch-22 situation: Nga was pregnant. I wanted to return to Huế to be with her and to care for my old father, but at the same time, I wanted to relocate to Saigon to have a better future.

I wrote home to tell my family the news. A week later, I received a cable from Nga encouraging me to accept the appointment because it was the family's wish. She assured me she would be fine as her family would take safe care of her. I knew very well how my father felt in this situation. Education and better career opportunities for us were his most important concern in his whole life. Unlike my father, my wife was not so education-oriented. Besides, because I had a good chance to transfer to Huế for family reasons, accepting the appointment in Saigon would forfeit the opportunity. But being the daughter-in-law to a scholar who would trade everything for his son's education, Nga learned not to contradict her father-in-law.

I left Nha Trang after four pleasant years of teaching just because of my hankering for a second degree in English literature! And this was the price I had to pay for transferring to Saigon. The city was too big, noisy, and unsafe. It was a place to visit, not to live. Nga's sister lived here, but her home was too small to accommodate me. Besides, it was too far from my new school. With her help I found a small room near school, but the rent was twice as expensive as my luxury room in Nha Trang. The evening before moving in, I ate a cheap meal in a shabby restaurant. Suddenly, I missed my good old days in Nha Trang as a teacher at the most prestigious high school in the city. I had lived with my colleagues in a mansion-like boarding house. For the first time, I had to live within my means to save money to support my family. Pétrus Ký High School, named after Pétrus Trương Vĩnh Ký, a 19th-century Vietnamese scholar who converted to Christianity after the South had become a French colony, was an all-boys public school. Compared with my students in Nha Trang, they were by and large unruly, rarely sitting still and often exchanging notes rather than paying attention to me. They also seemed to get a kick out of my relapse into the Huế dialect now and then when I lost my temper and talked fast although I could manage to speak with a southern accent. Today, I still do not understand why, in a linguistically homogeneous country such as Vietnam, vocabulary usage in some cases can be so different that a term considered refined in Huế may have a vulgar meaning in Saigon. One day, I was shocked to notice that a student did not orally repeat my correction of his mistranslation of an English phrase but instead stood still, his face turning red. I heard some muffled giggling from the back rows when I shouted the corrected phrase, thinking he did not hear me. At that point, I discovered something wrong was happening, so I told the student to sit down and switched to something else, feeling my face burning with shame the rest of the class period. A few weeks later, out of curiosity, I asked a student in private the cause of that incident on that day, but he, too, looked embarrassed and would not answer my question. So, I guessed I must have used an expression that Southerners would use as a slang word to refer to something improper or vulgar. I learned my lesson, and from then until I left Pétrus Ký, never used the translation method again in class.

My living and financial conditions got worse every day. I had to split my salary for multiple expenses: supporting myself and my brother who was attending college in Saigon, paying back a loan for our new home in Huế, etc. Having given up his dream to return to Quảng Bình, my father now had a fervent wish: to die in our own home. Since our coming to Huế we had moved around so many times that my father, who was in his early seventies now, started worrying about not being able, as he said, "to close my eyes" before we could settle down in a home. In his opinion, when dying in somebody's house, one risks becoming a homeless ghost condemned to roam about for eternity and, therefore, incapable of being redeemed by the Buddha. In traditional culture this is a disgrace for the family, and if the deceased person happens to be a parent, his or her children will be regarded as having committed a grave crime. As young kids, we had been taught to love and honor our ancestors and parents—even after they die—as if they were still living at home with us. For this reason, an altar, on which our ancestors' names are inscribed, is placed in the center of our house where we would regularly offer incense, tea, and food to their spirits. Another reason for our belief in our ancestors' continued presence and concern about our family was that when something of utmost importance arose and my father was unable to make an immediate decision about it, he would seek our ancestors' advice by lighting incense on their altar, softly stating the query, tossing the coins, and consulting the *I-ching* for the ultimate answer. Now that I had a job and got married and my father was over seventy, the need to have a home where he could worship our ancestors and teach us to fulfill our filial duty toward them and him became more urgent than ever.

With part of Nga's dowry, all my savings, and a high-interest loan from one of his friends, my father bought a piece of land and started to build a small house. Already with a mind on his grandchildren's education, he had selected a site close to school for our future home. It used to be a swamp and therefore was expensive to level with dirt. It cost us a fortune and so much pain to complete the construction of our residence in accordance with my father's criteria.

I had to tighten my belt by reducing my personal expenses to a minimum. I had my meals at a temple that were so cheap they were considered free of charge. Most guests were low-income taxi and pedicab drivers and students. To save on the rent, I moved out of my apartment and took a small room with much less physical comfort. Four years of living in relative luxury in Nha Trang as a wealthy high school teacher had made me forget those tough times of my refugee life until now. Relocating to a city big but short of space, I came to realize how important space was to me. Being born and growing up in the vast hill country of Dalat and the countryside of Quảng Bình, I had taken for granted the great privilege my parents, especially my father, had worked hard to provide for me. Living now in a small sultry room where I could hardly breathe, I hated wealthy folks who owned so much space, who had too much room to move around at will, too much air to breathe while many people were suffocating in their slums, swallowing their mortification and anger. Men like Lenin, Mao, and Hồ had no difficulty winning the peasants' hearts by promising them an opportunity to own their own land, to breathe more freely. It was the same desire to provide us with adequate space to live and to grow that had prompted my father to take us to the South in 1954 as Việt Minh troops were entering our city.

Despite her late pregnancy, her teaching at a local secondary school, and her taking care of my father, Nga wrote me regularly. I worried very much about her, but she always said she was fine and told me instead to take care of myself. I wanted very much to go home to see her, but traveling by train was too dangerous because of Vietcong attacks and I could not afford an air ticket to fly home.

On July 12th, while visiting Nga's sister in Chợ Lớn, a postman came to deliver a cable to my name. My heart was beating wildly and I knew the cable must be about Nga at home. I shakily ripped open the green sealed slip and quickly glanced at the Morse transcribed French message all in caps, signed by my father's name: "*Bébé garçon mère fils bonne santé*" ("Baby boy mother okay good health"). Though knowing what the cable was about, chị Thúy asked me about it. I handed her the cable, saying, choked with emotion: "It's a boy."

How did I feel about being a father for the first time in my life? It seemed I was suddenly taken out of the fantasy world I had been living in since my early boyhood and was plunged into a real one with its unexpected exigencies. While I was thrilled about the new arrival that I saw as an important achievement of my own and my family (because of the dearth of male heirs in the Trần's clan, the birth of a male baby was everybody's great joy and pride), I felt that I was not free anymore to explore the fantastic world that had captivated my imagination since the early years of my life. Yes, that romantic dream, if you wish, was replaced by worry, anxiety, and fear about huge responsibilities that I was afraid I might not be able to fulfill due to my immaturity, inexperience, and financial difficulties. On the contrary, Nga was well-equipped to assume motherhood despite her age. To me, the word "fatherhood" still sounded unfamiliar and funny, let alone my unreadiness to meet its terrible requirements.

On my way back to my boarding house, I was solely preoccupied with my new baby and my role as a new father. Because my father's cable was so short, I wondered whom the baby took after, how he was doing, how much he weighed at birth. That was basically how I felt about my firstborn; other matters related to fatherhood—love, responsibility, devotion— were vague. Suddenly, my heart grew heavy with anxiety and guilt when I thought about Nga. Because the baby's arrival had preoccupied my mind all afternoon, I had almost forgotten his mother! Besides, as I was too young (was it a good excuse?) to be a devoted husband and depended too much on her family for caring for her, I had not thought much about her until now. I felt guilty about not being with her during the most critical moments of her life. What if something wrong had happened to her? The cable was too sketchy (to save money, when sending a cable my father would keep it brief by using French) to tell me clearly how she was doing. Because we had no access to the telephone, our only communication was by mail which would take several days to reach us. "For sure, she's all right and I'll hear from her soon," I kept telling myself. This did not help me much. I kept feeling terrible for several days.

Though we were more fortunate than many people, we lived in the worst of times. Nga's condition was not better than many other women whose husbands were stationed at a remote base and could not get a leave to come home when they were in a critical condition such as childbirth. And this seems to have been the Vietnamese woman's fate to brave this danger by herself and in silence since time immemorial. An unknown author laments her tragic condition and celebrates her heroism in these words:

> *Đàn ông đi biển có đôi,*
> *Đàn bà đi biển mồ côi một mình!*
>
> (Men go to sea together.
> Women go to sea alone, like orphans!)

In Vietnamese literature a woman in labor and delivery is compared to a fisherman braving the sea to eke out a living for his family. But whereas he has several other men for his company, his wife braves all the risks alone. Because healthcare was non-existent or very primitive in the old days, she gave herself and her baby totally to fate. Tears rolled down my face. It was only now that I was able to think of Nga. Final exams, work, politics, and—just the day before—news of our baby's arrival had left me no time to think of her.

It was a great relief and blessing to receive Nga's first letter since her "going solo to sea." I could now see for myself her peculiar way of addressing me. "*Mình ơi!*" (the phrase can be roughly translated as "darling," but literally it means "my darling self" as if I was her own life) and the graceful feminine slender curves of her letters that I had missed for several weeks. She told me it had been quite a big scare for her. "*Mình ơi!*" she wrote, "I went into labor on Sunday when most doctors were off, A young nurse was assigned to me. She had done a good job until a male voice called at the door and guess what? It was her boyfriend who came to pick her up. At that moment, I heard the baby's cry, but suddenly it went silent. The nurse pushed the baby back in and rushed to the door to answer her boyfriend. It was like a flash of lightning. She went back to work instantly, and this time I heard the baby's strong continuous cry. Thank Heaven and Quan-yin, our son was born safe. What a scare! I sweated profusely."

Though knowing that both Nga and the baby were safe, I was out of breath by the end of her letter. I felt awful though I heard from Nga regularly and learned that she and the baby were well. My wife and my son almost lost their life, and yet I was roaming the streets of Saigon and hanging around bookstores, not knowing what was happening at home! My stomach was in knots. Overcome with shame and remorse, I wanted to cry but my eyes were dry.

Things improved after my first semester at Pétrus Ký. Students behaved better, some even going out of their way to assist me in maintaining class discipline. Having mastered the Saigon dialect, I was able to go back to my translation method. Weekend outings with my classes to the Botanical Garden as assigned by the school also helped us get along better. Once in an informal get-together, a student remarked that he had seen me eat at that temple canteen a few times. I blushed, but quickly recovered myself by telling him that I was a vegetarian. I was trying to get out of the dilemma when Toàn, a former colleague from Nha Trang, who had transferred to Saigon before me, and who lived within walking distance to school, invited me to stay at his house for free. I jumped at the offer. By staying with Toàn, I could save my money to eat at a regular restaurant without being seen by anybody.

Toàn introduced me to his wife Huyền, an attractive woman in her early thirties, who was a nurse at Hôpital Grall. The couple told me they had no children and were going to adopt a baby girl from an orphanage. If I still wanted to move in, they said, I would be expected to stay in a room on the first floor where the baby's crib would be placed. I accepted their terms immediately, even knowing that the baby's cry would disturb my sleep at night. A week after I had moved in, Toàn and Huyền brought home a cute small baby, who whimpered intermittently like a kitten just removed from its litter. Just as I had anticipated, the baby woke me several times during the night. Toàn and Huyền did not let her sleep in their room, but they came down to care for her at night. I was impressed with Huyền's nursing skills and great affection for the baby. She sang her nursery rhymes to lull her back to sleep in a very tender and sweet voice. It was so moving to see a childless young woman, who just the day before had known nothing about motherhood, become a mother in her own right that night. Her husband had gone back to bed, but Huyền was still holding little Tee Tee in her lap, humming her nursery tune until the baby fell asleep, then left the room on tiptoe. Suddenly, I thought of Nga and missed her tremendously. During her pregnancy, she shared with me in her letters her excitement about becoming a mother for the first time. She also told me that all preparations were made for the baby's arrival and, knowing that I would not be able to return on time, assured me that she could take care of herself, the baby, and everything. I loved Nga very much, but I knew there were lots of things beyond my power. I could not return home to see her because it was not safe to travel by train and I could not afford to fly. There were so many things on my mind then—teaching at school, taking classes at Saigon University, worrying about the home loan—that I almost forgot what Nga was going through as an expectant mother until I saw motherhood in action that night.

A tragedy prevented Huyền from fulfilling her role as an ideal mother. One month after her adoption, Tee Tee was taken to the hospital because her health deteriorated. I could see the enormous toll Tee Tee's grave illness exacted on Toàn and Huyền when I visited them at the hospital. They looked haggard, completely exhausted. Tee Tee was soundly asleep, her face rosy and beautiful because of her high fever. She reminded me of my sister Như Cẩm in her death throes twenty-two years earlier in Dalat. She looked so beautiful when she drew her last breath in my mother's lap. When I came in, I saw Toàn comforting Huyền who was crying softly. They had done the best they could for their baby, but it seemed hopeless now.

Tee Tee died shortly after my visit. I stayed with Toàn and Huyền a few more days to comfort them, then decided that it would be best for me to move out and leave them alone. I witnessed something that made my brief stay at their home one of the most memorable experiences in my life. One morning, I left school early after giving the semester exam. When I was about to get in my room, I saw Huyền drooping on Tee Tee's empty crib, her face buried in her outstretched arms, her shoulders shaking. In her white uniform and with a cross on her chest, she was truly an Oriental version of *The Pietà*. Stunned by what I saw, I quietly turned around and walked back to school.

I moved out of Toàn's and Huyền's house a few days later. Before I left Saigon, I went to see them to say goodbye. Never had I seen them so happy. Huyền's face was radiant with joy and pride. She told me at her request she had been transferred to the hospital's pediatric section. I understood why Huyền had chosen her new job and was happy for her. Not having the opportunity to be Tee Tee's mother, Huyền now devoted all her time and efforts to many babies Tee Tee's age.

***

In January 1965, the principal of Pétrus Ký High School saw me privately in his office and told me that my application for transfer to Huế had been approved by the Ministry of Education, pending the availability of a teaching opportunity in Huế, which would take several months. Rather than congratulating me on the news, he asked me to reconsider the move, telling me that Saigon was the safest haven in the country, that everyone at the school liked me and wanted me to stay, and that, if I so wished, he could ask the Ministry to cancel the transfer. I thanked him for his concern and kind offer and told him I had no other option. However, since the new school year would not start until next semester, I assured him that I would change my mind if I could bring my family here.

I went back to the Faculty of Letters and attended a few class lectures to better prepare for the oral exam if I was lucky to pass the written one. Trying to complete the semester at the university and teaching four classes a week at Pétrus Ký left me literally exhausted.

I had mixed feelings about my possible return to Huế. I missed my family and wanted to reunite with them as soon as possible, but at the same time, I did not want to spend the rest of my life there. Huế was peaceful but too conservative. That was why many young people my age and older had left their native Huế to seek freedom and better opportunities in Saigon. Ironically, after they had settled down in Saigon, they started getting homesick. At Pétrus Ký, several of my new friends originally from Huế shared with me their fond memories of the former imperial city. However, they all tried to persuade me to change my mind, citing many reasons, one of which had to do with safety and better opportunities in Saigon. Suddenly, I found myself caught in a Catch-22 dilemma: reuniting with the family or giving up what was important to me: job security, potential career advancement, personal freedom, students' respect, and more.

Because Nga and the baby were well taken care of by her family, I took advantage of my remaining time to explore Saigon more. In the past, my visits to the city had always been full of fun. When I first came there to teach, I found it very threatening. Now Saigon suddenly fascinated me more than ever. I began to miss the city's vigorous life, its cultural richness, its invigorating noises. Because time was running out and yet there were lots of things I did not know about Saigon, I grew lax in teaching. I spent time exploring the city. I visited bookstores, mostly used ones, to buy books whenever I could afford, or just to browse them. Chợ Lớn, Vietnam's famous and largest Chinatown, continued to attract me with its exoticism. Again, I was never tired of hunting for curiosities illegally smuggled from mainland China via Cambodia. I particularly liked fountain pens, watches, perfume soap bars, life energy cultivation books, and herbal tonics. I was greatly taken with medicinal herbs because my father was practicing traditional medicine. Even today, the fragrance of sandalwood soap still puts me under its spell. Every time I happen to smell it, images of my favorite places I was roaming in search of curios become alive in me. The resurrection of that period of the past, however, fills me with an unassuageable melancholy amounting to enduring sorrow. With time the sandalwood fragrance comes to permanently stand for something very precious that is lost but paradoxically continues to exist in me and is always available whenever I happen to smell its scent. Nevertheless, its evocation brings me anguish rather than pleasure. I feel I cannot live without that pervasive sense of anguish and sorrow that has pursued me since my childhood.

My free time in Saigon also allowed me to enjoy one of the three things a famous proverb encourages every Vietnamese man to try—dining in a Chinese restaurant (the other two wishes being residing in a French villa and marrying a Japanese girl). I could not afford to eat in an expensive restaurant, but I was able to visit cheap food stands in remote alleys in Chợ Lớn that served the best delicacies in the world at a price I could afford. Tips were not required because you were not waited upon and the food stand owner, who was also the cook, did not seem interested in such stuff. No other people could beat the Chinese in the art of pleasing customers. Places where I ate posted menus with fancy titillating names like *Cơm chiên bát bửu* (Eight Treasures Fried Rice), *Cháo long nhãn* (Dragon Eye Congee) which made an ordinary diner like me feel extremely special.

I also dropped in various classes and hung around on the Faculty of Letters campus to get a feel of what college life in Saigon was like. After the assassination of President Diệm, the U.S. succeeded in influencing South Vietnam's politics but was kept at bay in the country's educational system, which was a French replica. Classes, regardless of size, were confined to lectures. There was no communication between the instructor and the students. Attendance was not mandatory because roll taking did not exist, but rote learning was essential for passing final exams, both written and oral, the latter being a real killer for those who, like me, seldom showed up in class and did not know what the instructor wanted. The most humiliating, devastating part of the ordeal was the moment the results were posted. You could see all the personal information about you displayed in public: date of birth, passing or failing grade, whether you would be eligible to sit for next year's exams. God forbid, if you did not pass it or, worse, if you were not permitted to retake the test because your grade was too low, you might want to kill yourself or disappear for good because of humiliation. The Americans had little success in influencing the system run by die-hard French-trained leaders although the French had been gone for a decade already. Dr. Trần Anh, my anthropology professor, and a French-educated physician, was shot in broad daylight when he was on his way to work. His strong advocacy for replacing the obsolete French curriculum with the more practical American one in the School of Medicine was the reason for his murder. Dr. Anh's message went unheard, and until the collapse of South Vietnam in 1975, along with its French-oriented higher education system, nobody had come forward to defend or advance his worthy cause.

But formal French lifestyle still had a strong influence on the Vietnamese academic community in the 1960s. Everyone was dressed in an old-fashioned manner—women in flowing *ao dai*, men in long-sleeved white shirts and slacks but no jeans, professors in black or gray suits despite Saigon's sizzling and sultry weather. There was no running, no bumping into one another, just leisurely strolling. But for fierce fighting in the neighboring provinces, one would have thought the country was at peacetime.

On some nights, the campus had a different scene. The escalation of the war due to the U.S. military intervention stirred an anti-war movement involving many students in Saigon and Huế. The Faculty of Letters campus was a magnet for young people who were electrified by the legendary Trịnh Công Sơn accompanied by vocalist Khánh Ly who performed his famous anti-war songs. By the time I prepared to leave in December 1965, the movement had spread to most university and high school campuses in Saigon. Regardless of our stance on who was responsible for this absurd war, we were aghast at its destruction of our people and could not but agree with Trịnh Công Sơn's outcry when he sang one of his top hit songs, "Hát trên những xác người" ["Sing on Human Corpses"], which depicts what the speaker sees after a raid—corpses of civilians strewn over a rice field and afloat a river. The song struck a chord with Trịnh's young fans who hated the war and the presence of foreign troops in their country. When executed by the talented Khánh Ly, the best artist to render Trịnh Công Sơn's musical genius, these little phrases from the song would move even the coldest person to tears.

Because he was against the war, Trịnh was accused of being pro-communist. In my opinion, an extremely sensitive artist as he was, it was natural that he was outraged by the presence of foreign troops in his country that he thought was the cause of his people's suffering. Artists live by the dictates of their conscience and passionately defend what they believe, paying no attention to possible political implications or consequences of what they did. I had sat through a couple of gatherings on the Faculty of Letters campus and must confess Trịnh's music strikes at the core of our heart, bringing out our most primeval emotions connected with what nurtures us, with what is vague but so dear and important to us that we do not want to lose. As we grow older, these instincts evolve into lofty feelings of emotive and moral order known as patriotism, i.e., love for and loyalty to our land and our people. Because Trịnh and his audiences were young and idealistic, they were unafraid to display their patriotism, to make the voice of their conscience heard.

Shortly after Diệm's assassination, the country gradually slid into instability. By mid-1965, it plunged into real chaos after a series of coups and so-called *chinh lý* (political readjustments). There was no capable leader to head the junta, so the young generals that the U.S. press called "the Turks" put one in the top position only to take him down a few months later. A member of the ruling junta, Gen. Nguyễn Khánh, appointed himself head of state and wrote up a new constitution for the country himself only to be forced into exile by student protests shortly afterward. But what scared me was the show of force by a Catholic militant group in the streets of Saigon. Just as the Unified Buddhist Church under monk Thích Trí Quang's leadership had played a key role in overthrowing the Diệm regime, it was now rumored to be involved in appointing government officials. This angered a Catholic community originally from the North which had resettled in the suburbs of Saigon since 1954 after Diệm's coming to power. Armed with sharp weapons such as knives and spears, they poured into Saigon in a potentially violent show of force, fiercely shouting anti-government slogans and denouncing what they called political favoritism. Fortunately, it was only a brief show of force and there was no reported clash with the Buddhists.

Saigon was literally anarchy in 1965. Anti-government demonstrations provided enticing opportunities for high school students to break school rules. This was a common occurrence at Pétrus Ký High School. Though students did show up for class probably because of their parents' influence, they wanted to get out to join an ongoing demonstration or just to have fun. We teachers found ourselves in a dilemma. We were instructed by the administration to keep our students in class, but often we failed to maintain class discipline. Their protest ranged from silent boycotting to all-out disruption. For example, they would refuse to rise and respond to your questions and the whole class would keep a complicit silence, making you feel very humiliated. Or they would violently disrupt your class. One day, no sooner had I finished taking the roll and turned around to write an assignment on the board than a firecracker exploded behind me. Its loud explosion made me cringe with fright while the class roared with laughter. I felt terrible because the incident occurred in my favorite class! Wanting so much to get out to demonstrate or to have fun, they treated me so cruelly.

Saigon did not appeal to me anymore. I wanted to leave any minute had I had the opportunity. I liked my students very much, but they betrayed me shamefully. I loved to continue seeing the city more but had no mind to do such a thing. Curfews began too early at night, several streets were blockaded, and clashes between police and students occurred daily. Every day we teachers reported for duty at school, but we all had great difficulty maintaining class discipline. To cope with the situation, when things were out of control, the administration closed the school and dumped the kids on their parents. Meanwhile, I received shocking news from the Ministry of Education: due to the critical situation, all personnel transfers were canceled. That meant my chance of reuniting with my family was very slim for now.

By late January 1965, things had returned to normal a little. My classes resumed with no trouble, and I was also able to come to class occasionally at the Faculty of Letters to attend lectures and buy lecture notes to study for my final exam in Vietnamese Civilization, a required course for my *License d'Enseignment d'Anglais*. There were students like me who could not find time to attend class and had to buy study materials at the student union. The notes helped me a great deal because they were close to the professor's lectures (apparently the note taker obtained them from the instructor). I studied for my final by trying to memorize as much as I could the class notes. Based on my experience at the University of Huế, I knew that our professors here also enjoyed hearing us rehash their lectures word for word.

As anticipated, I easily passed the written part of the course exam. In my orals the professor, a friendly-looking old man, asked me if I had attended his class regularly because I did not understand his question well. When I explained my situation, he allowed me to select another one. He seemed content and amused, then visibly touched by my parrot-like rehearsal of his lectures. I passed both parts of the exam and was very happy. Finally, I earned an English degree from a prestigious institution—the University of Saigon!

With a dual English degree in hand, my dream of garnering a scholarship to study in the United States or England could be a reality in the near future. Filled with optimism, I sought an audience with Dr. Nguyễn Khắc Hoạch, Dean of the Faculty, to explain my request that I be issued the degree. Unfortunately, he gave me the cold shoulder and accused me of taking advantage of the system's leeway by transferring all my course work from the small, little known college of liberal arts in Huế to his prestigious *Faculté des Lettres*. I understood his feelings but asked him to consider my inability to fulfill my degree requirements at my university because of my living and working in Saigon. However, when he began to belittle my former school, I decided I had enough of it. He had no right to belittle my university where I learned he was a visiting professor. So, I thanked him for the appointment and left, my face burning with shame and anger. Two years later, after I had returned to Huế to teach at the College of Education, one day I received a registered letter from Saigon Faculty of Letters. To my great surprise, it was a diploma conferred on me and signed by Dr. Hoạch. This occurrence touched me tremendously. When he came to the United States in 1975 as a refugee, I did not have a chance to thank him for his kindness and find out about the mystery of his change of heart and mind. In 1998, on a trip to California to attend a conference, I saw him stand in front of a Vietnamese supermarket, seemingly lost in thought. Perhaps he was thinking about his glorious past as Dean of the famed Faculty of Letters or perhaps he was dreaming of his beloved Vietnam that was far gone (he had published a collection of beautiful poems entitled *Thành phố trong hồi tưởng* [*The City in Memory*]. I wanted to get close to him and introduce myself then thank him for the favor, but I didn't make the move probably because I was timid or was dissuaded by a friend who apparently had an unfavorable opinion of him. After I left the café and went outside to find him, he was gone. Last year, I happened to see Dr. Hoạch's obituary in a paper and felt a pang in my heart for passing up my only opportunity to express my heartfelt appreciation to him. Had I not let my friend interfere with my decision, Dr. Hoạch would have been pleased to know that there was a former student at his school who still remembered him. Despite his tough stance at that meeting, I feel that, as a poet, he must have had a tender heart. Otherwise, he would not have granted me that degree and would not have written so many touching poems about home. His death still touches me today.

It was the worsening of the political situation that caused my delay in returning home. Buddhist-led demonstrations in protest of the ousting of the newly appointed civilian government and the re-establishment of the junta led by Lt. Gen. Nguyễn Văn Thiệu and Air Marshal Nguyễn Cao Kỳ and the show of force by Catholics and Buddhists were a common scene in Saigon. Buddhist youths organized themselves into security guards to watch their temples day and night. Luckily, the tension tapered off after a short while. Sporadic demonstrations continued, but people bothered little about it. There was a lull in Vietcong attacks probably because the communists were wary of the mass landing of U.S. troops in Đà Nẵng early in 1965. In May, the ban on government personnel transfers was lifted and I was ready to go home.

OF HEARTH AND HOME

My first impulse when getting home was rush in to see my ten-month-old son. I must have unconsciously grown attached to him though lately I had thought more often about the adults—my father and Nga—than about him. Did I do so out of curiosity to see a brand-new little being we had just brought into the world or by a fatherly instinct that just shot up from the innermost recesses of my soul? I did not know then, nor do I know now. I greeted my father, who responded in his usually casual manner, "You're home, aren't you?" and called out to Nga, who must be with the baby somewhere in the house, "Nga, *thằng Cu*'s daddy is home." I heard Nga's voice coming from our bedroom, "Yes, Sir. I'll be right over." It did not take her long to emerge from the bedroom with *thằng Cu* (meaning "little penis," a common nickname for male infants, believed to scare evil spirits away because of its vulgar connotation) snugly cuddled on her shoulder, smiling broadly. On seeing me, the smile on his chubby face turned into a scowl. He shrank back and started whimpering when Nga tried to hand him to me, cooing all the time, "Pa is home now. Don't you like Pa to hold you?" Her encouragement worked after her second try. Still softly whimpering, he suddenly leaned forward in my direction and this time let me hold him. It did not take him long to recognize the inseparable relationship between him and me. "You *are* lucky, son," my father told me. "He won't let anybody touch him but his mother."

The following day, I reported to Trường Kiểu Mẫu (Pilot School), which was affiliated with the College of Education, for duty. Unfortunately, because my transfer occurred in the middle of the academic year, no position was available. It was too late to return to Pétrus Ký. Luckily, when I was in danger of being sent to a school in a remote area, a former professor at the University of Huế, now an academic dean at the College of Education, my alma mater, offered to keep me to work at his school's library. I jumped at the opportunity.

It was a customary practice in South Vietnam then that government and government-related agencies were overstaffed. The College of Education was no exception. Its small library held no more than 500 titles but employed three workers—a secretary, an office boy, and me—all with no previous library experience. The secretary, who oversaw the library, a pale-looking but attractive woman in her mid-twenties, was knitting something when I arrived. The clerk, a skinny man in his early forties, dozed off at his desk too early in the morning. The woman greeted me warmly and then hollered at the sleepy man about my arrival. Probably because they had been told that I would be their supervisor, they knew my name and treated me with some respect. I happened to discover later that she was the singer Kim Lan whom I used to hear over Radio Huế before moving to Nha Trang. Lôi, my other associate, also knew my wife's family as they were from the same hometown.

No sooner had I arrived than I set out to get the library out of its primitive stage. My two associates were cooperative but had a long way to go before they could get in gear. Kim Lan would still spend more time knitting her sweater and reading popular magazines than helping me catalog the books. Lôi was hard at work for only an hour then ran out of gas and fell asleep again. I excused him so he could go out to recharge himself with some caffeine, but he would not come back until after lunch.

The three of us got along well, and I would have happily accepted my new lot had I not been harassed by Mr. Hành, the College's Associate Dean, a science man who did not like English people and who disapproved of the Dean's showing favoritism toward me. He often came unexpectedly, apparently to check if I was in the office, and rushed me to open the library for students' use as quickly as possible. A short, stocky slant-eyed man, cold and mean-spirited, he spoke with a high-pitched voice that reminded me of Mr. Huy, who had given me hell during my stay at his home after my arrival in Huế. Kim Lan told me that though she had been with the college for a year now, she had never seen Mr. Hành set foot in the place. She agreed with me that his frequent visits were because of me. But he was not the only source of my stress. To Kim Lan's surprise and my frustration, several students walked into our library unceremoniously, though we had put the sign "Closed for Inventory" on the door. One day, because Kim Lan and Lôi were not around when they came, I had to handle their inquiry. Perhaps not knowing who I was, they addressed me as *anh*, an ambiguous term used to address a male slightly older than you but whose identity as well as social status is unknown to you or is not quite respectable. Should your interlocutor be younger than you are, his or her use of this second personal pronoun *anh* can be interpreted as a lack of deference. Embedded in a culture that overemphasizes the importance of age and social distinction, I found these young people's demeanor unacceptable and silently reacted with anger. Suddenly, I was angry with myself for leaving Saigon where I had enjoyed popularity and high esteem from students, with Nga for bringing me back to this hellhole, and with my father for his idea of building this house here, which put us deeply in debt and mortification. I hated that associate dean, who must have sent the students over to punish me for being there without clearing with him. He treated me like a low-class employee and yet addressed me as "respected brother" though, in fact, he did not respect me in the least.

Perhaps out of pity for me doing a hackneyed job or because the college needed someone to teach introductory English to non-English majors, my dean made me a new member of the teaching staff six months after I had successfully cataloged all the books and trained Kim Lan and Lôi to run the library themselves. My family rejoiced over the good news. But my misfortune was not over yet. Because I got the appointment through the dean's favor, some colleagues, while accepting the latter's decision, in my presence alluded to my odd situation. One even attempted to harm me by telling students that I voted down a proposal to increase the number of candidates for graduation. I was sure he did that not because of his envy (there was nothing in me that could make him jealous because my appointment was temporary) but because he resented my fortune. Vietnamese society in the 1960s still functioned like a feudal system in which subordinates cried craven to their superiors but intimidated those who were inferior to them for no good reason. As a rule, being successful by good fortune or through your own effort without securing a powerful person's sponsorship invites only trouble and even danger. But to have this powerful person's protection, you must belong to his inner circle and faithfully serve his interests. I was too timid to seek favor from the powerful and too mediocre to be considered by them. Luckily, after Mr. Hành left our college, his people stopped harassing me.

Incidents like these after my return to Huế rekindled my erstwhile longing to get a scholarship to study overseas. A husband just reunited with his wife after one year of separation and a new parent barely acquainting himself with his baby, I nevertheless felt that a successful career would be more important to me than my family, ignoring the fact that the situation was growing from bad to worse due to renewed Vietcong fierce attacks and continued political instability in Saigon and other major cities in the country. In all fairness, most colleagues at the University of Huế, especially those who were singles and who felt discriminated against on account of their "second-class" status, believed that going overseas to study and returning a few years later with an advanced degree would be the only way to save us from our present impasse. We forgot or ignored the fact that our city, which was only one hundred kilometers from the DMZ, could be attacked or invaded by the enemy at any time. Amazingly, that kind of insouciance was a general trend in Huế. People went about their business as usual. There was even a boom in the city's economy due to the smuggling of goods from the American PX in nearby Phú Bài base. The university was expanding with its implementation of important programs, including sending its faculty to the U.S. and Europe for advanced training. All these signs plus the common daily scene of unending U.S. military convoys loading at Thuận An Beach and rumbling all the way to Phú Bài with happy-go-lucky GI's naked to the waist waving to kids and young women dissipated a rumor of the partition of the country—this time at the 13th parallel. We nourished that naïve belief owing to the South Korean precedent in which the North Korean invasion had been driven back by the U.S. and South Korean forces. Seoul, South Korea's capital, just fifty-three kilometers from Panmunjom, had stood ever since as a symbol of the Free World's determination to defend South Korea's freedom. But since we had been through so much adversity and had no choice but to stay put in this most dangerous place, we were either burying our heads in the sand to avoid facing reality or just trying to let go and leave it to fate.

In March 1966, Huế was embroiled again in political chaos like the aftermath of the Diệm coup but on a much larger scale. The so-called *Biến động Miền Trung* (Central Region's unrest), which was the continuation of the Buddhist protest against the military regime of Nguyễn Văn Thiệu and Nguyễn Cao Kỳ in Đà Nẵng, was shifted to Huế, the cradle of Buddhism. Under the leadership of monk Thích Trí Quang, the renowned orator and skilled leader of the successful movement against the Diệm regime, the protest this time involved large numbers of Buddhists from different walks of life—lay people, students, teachers, government officials—in Huế and Đà Nẵng. Huge demonstrations, silent processions, and prayer sessions happened almost daily, demanding the resignation of Thiệu and Kỳ, the establishment of a civilian government, and the election of a democratic congress. The movement also published a political magazine called *Tuần báo Lập trường* [*Our Political Stand Weekly*], perhaps the best of its kind in the country with a group of prominent Huế University faculty on its editorial staff. With the participation of the military and the local government whose members mostly practiced the Buddhist faith, Huế, Đà Nẵng, and most provinces in the Central Region were facing the possibility of total isolation from the central government. Thiệu and Kỳ took strong measures by replacing the defecting commanders with their own generals from Saigon, but as soon as they arrived, they sought asylum at the U.S. Marines Base in Đà Nẵng.

Developments like these threw central provinces into a state of semi-anarchy, causing Kỳ to take stronger measures. U.S. cargo planes transported government troops to Đà Nẵng to retake the city from the dissidents. Threatened by an all-out offensive including air strikes, Buddhist leaders called off armed resistance to avoid bloodshed and ordered instead the moving of domestic altars out to the street, hoping that this would deter the advance of government troops. Meanwhile, in Huế, in a separate show of force, students burned the U.S. Consulate and demanded that President Lyndon Johnson intervene for a cease-fire and the withdrawal of troops back to Saigon. The government said that there were Vietcong infiltrators in the student protest. (In fact, after the student movement was defeated, some leaders fled to the Vietcong and later returned to the city in the Tết offensive. Most recently, Nguyễn Đắc Xuân, a former prominent Huế Buddhist student leader has signed a joint petition asking the communist government to release jailed dissidents. What shocks me is that he had joined the Communist Party before the fall of South Vietnam.) On Radio Huế we heard Ven. Thích Trí Quang's urgent appeal to students to exercise self-restraint, but he did not fail to accuse Johnson of "breaking the promise he made a few hours ago that Thiệu Kỳ would launch no attack against us."

Buddhists in Huế employed similar tactics to resist government troops' advance from Đà Nẵng. They blocked up streets with their ancestral altars, even burning incense and keeping their vigil all night. Press conferences were held for foreign reporters, and some of my former classmates had the opportunity to show off their English skills by translating for Buddhist leaders. For their part, students were more committed to their cause than ever with sit-ins, vigils, and hunger strikes in front of the Faculté des Lettres building where foreign journalists could easily see them.

Huế returned to normal for a short while after the unrest. At the start of the new school year 1967-1968, I officially became an instructor of English. I was fortunate to have the confidence of the new dean, Dr. Lê Trọng Vinh, a French-trained scholar, who often turned to me for help in preparing correspondence with British and U.S. cultural agencies in Saigon. (Dr. Vinh, his wife, and his children later perished at sea in their unsuccessful escape from Vietnam after the fall of South Vietnam in 1975.) My mania for academic degrees, which I had thought long dead because of the high price I had paid for them and the ordeal I had gone through since my arrival in Saigon, now began to raise its ugly head. Though it was a natural trait of my personality, it stemmed from my desire to keep my current job, improve my future, and advance my professional career. Though deep down I—and my colleagues at the university—were concerned about a communist attack, we brushed it off. Maybe, during the war, we had seen so many deaths and survived so many Vietcong mortar attacks that we became immune to fear, or maybe we put too much trust in the Americans who were only a few miles away, not suspecting in the least that just a few months later in January 1968, most of the city would fall to the communists and we would finally come to know what terror meant!

After things had returned to normal, Huế students' resistance was challenged by Nguyễn Cao Kỳ's surprise visit. We teachers were ordered to accompany our students to Đồng Khánh High School campus to greet him. A commotion began as soon as Kỳ and his cortege arrived, and I could hear a muffled shout of *"Đả đảo Thiệu Kỳ"* ("Down with Thiệu Kỳ clique!") coming from somewhere in the front rows of students at the campus entrance. I do not know if Kỳ or anyone in his group heard it, but perhaps because he knew that Huế people did not like him due to his recent crackdown on the Buddhists, his face wore a very stern, unpleasant look. General Nguyễn Ngọc Loan, Kỳ's national police chief, one step behind his boss and with two pistols strung across his shoulders, looked more confrontational than ever. (Loan later gained worldwide attention for footage shot by AP cameraman Eddie Adams showing his summary execution of a captured Vietcong in Saigon during the Tết offensive). The students stood silent, refusing to wave flags to cheer Kỳ. Having heard about the man who had defeated Thích Trí Quang, who had threatened to cross the 17th parallel in a warplane to bomb North Vietnam, who had scared the Taiwanese government in his state visit by climbing into the cockpit of a Taiwan Air Force plane and flying off, I was curious to take a good look at him. He wore a very chic suit, carefully tailored to fit his size, his thick black mustache making his face look dignified, full of confidence, but cold. He struck me as a character in a John Wayne movie because of his bravado and his admiration for the American film actor.

I came home with a heavy heart, my mind buzzing with miscellaneous thinking and memories. Since my first arrival in Huế from Đồng Hới for my high school exam, I had seen so many things take place on the campus of this school and its neighbor, Khải Định Secondary School, an all-boys school. I remember vividly my being there as an eighteen-year-old country boy awestruck by this campus in its summer splendors that became livelier than usual because of the gathering here of so many students for their oral exams. I had felt insignificant, small, but thrilled about the wonders I had seen for the first time in my life. It was the same campus I had gone to during part of my freshman year (our school then had shared with this girls' school the same campus but was located at its opposite side). Fresh from a small country, I felt timid and embarrassed to be placed in the same class with rich, sophisticated boys and girls for the first time. Then my mind leaped to a cold, overcast afternoon in November 1954 when we were ordered by Mr. Nguyễn Văn Hai, the school's principal, to carry posthaste benches and desks to our new campus, which was a short block away just vacated by French troops. The campus bustled for a short while with youngsters eager to reclaim what had belonged to them before it returned to its quiet after we had completed our move. One year later, alumni from all over the country and current students celebrated the fiftieth anniversary of the opening of this so-called National School, the name suggesting the fame the institution had claimed, with President Ngô Đình Diệm presiding. He and many, many of his contemporaries and predecessors including Hồ Chí Minh and Võ Nguyên Giáp had left their footsteps here, our fathers and older brothers had left their footsteps here, and now the controversial Nguyễn Cao Kỳ who had vanquished the redoubtable Thích Trí Quang and whom Huế Buddhists hated so much also left his footsteps here (though in a different capacity). Not long ago, I also spent my high school years here. I could have evoked other incidents had my train of thought not been interrupted by another round of protest and derisive applause as Kỳ and his cortege were leaving Đồng Khánh High School campus. So many things had happened, so many people had come and gone in such a brief period, leaving no trace after their departure except in my flimsy memory. History is a representation of the law of mutability and impermanence.

November 1967 brought my family some wonderful news: the arrival of our second baby, another boy! As Nga had had a miscarriage the year before and her third pregnancy this year had been rough on her due to her occasional bleeding, the baby's safe delivery and the mother's wellness made the entire family happier than ever. My father had every reason to thank Heaven, Quan-yin, and our ancestors for bestowing on him another grandson, thus making his dream of seeing the clan expand a reality.

Because this baby was born when I was home, my father told me after he had calculated the boy's horoscope: "Son, it's your fortune that the boy was born to you and your wife. He's bound to be by your side because he was related to both of you in some previous life. You weren't around when *thằng cu* (our first-born son) was born. You won't be away from home again when your next child is born to you." Thus said, he gave his new grandson the name Gia Thụy, which means family's glad tidings. Part of what my father was saying came true. Except for his *khóc dạ đề* (all-night crying) during his entire first month, which was miraculously cured by Nga's geomancer cousin (whose precise prediction of our marriage Nga always admired) by hanging a talisman over our infant's crib, he was *dễ nuôi* (easy to raise), as shown by the massive birthmarks on his buttocks which had given his mother a big scare (being half asleep and half-awake after giving birth to the baby, Nga thought she had seen the birthmarks on his face). He has grown from a healthy baby into a handsome young man, and his grandfather was right; he has been available to us at the most critical moments in our lives.

THE TẾT OFFENSIVE

The remaining months of 1967 were quiet except for sporadic night mortar attacks, which did not concern us much because we had within our reach a covered shelter right in the house. We decided to make big preparations for the approaching lunar New Year (January 31st, 1968) to mark my reunion with the family and the arrival of our second child. Huế during the last few days before New Year's Eve always bustled with vendors and buyers who wanted to make the most of the occasion, the former trying to make a bid of their leftovers so they could get home on time for last-minute preparations for Tết, the latter—people like us—attempting to strike a bargain for stuff we could not afford under normal circumstances. But this year we noticed that Đông Ba Market on Trần Hưng Đạo Street and adjacent areas were more crowded than usual. I felt something eerie in the air, but very quickly the inkling evaporated when I got home and went about my business. Later, when I mentioned this to Nga, she said that she saw the same thing but thought that this year people were making unusually big preparations for Tết because both sides had agreed to a three-day ceasefire for everyone to enjoy the traditional holiday.

The following day on New Year's Eve, it was almost nightfall when we came home from our final shopping trip. The odd feeling the day before came back when we saw at twilight men and women in black pajamas (the uniform of South Vietnam's rural reconstruction cadres) huddling along or leaning over the ramps of Trường Tiền Bridge as if they were enjoying Huế's night scene on the Perfume River. I pointed out these people to Nga. "Maybe they're Rural Reconstruction guards," she responded with confidence. "Don't you remember that Vietcong have declared a three-day ceasefire in celebration of Tết this year?" I accepted Nga's theory, but on our way home still felt ill at ease about what we saw tonight.

Nga prepared a tray of food and fruits on time for my father's midnight offering to our ancestors. It was still early for the ceremony, so I went outside and secretly tuned in to Radio Hanoi for Hồ Chí Minh's New Year message. It was a plain poem in which Hồ stated that this year would be much different from the last year, urging the Vietnamese people to march on as "total victory will be ours." I did not pay attention to the meaning of Hồ's message as he had said the same thing over the years. I turned off my transistor radio when

Nga signaled that my father was getting upset because I was late for the ceremony.

After the ceremony, Nga woke up our four-year-old son and we began to express our New Year's greetings to my father. Suddenly, there was a loud explosion somewhere in our backyard and a lot of gunfire coming from the direction of the Police Station. As soon as we got in the shelter, there was another explosion in the outer house where fortunately our maid Hạnh was not sleeping because she had been up in the house all evening helping Nga prepare for the ceremony. All the lights in the house and in the street went out, the pitch-dark night and continuous gunfire close to us increasing even more the terror of an all-out war. Because our shelter was built for temporary use only, it was too small for our family. The baby woke up and cried, so my father and I rushed out of the house and squeezed inside the vault of our temporary kitchen shack. It was wet and very cold here, and though I was trying to cover my father with the heat of my body, he still shivered. I had to take him back inside and this time we took shelter under Quan-yin's altar. Meanwhile, we continued to hear loud explosions across the river, in the *Thành Nội* (Inner Citadel). There seemed to be some more in our backyard.

There was some letup at dawn. I turned on my transistor radio and tuned in to the BBC to learn that the Vietcong, supported by the North Vietnamese, had launched a big offensive all over the South since midnight. Without letting my father and Nga know, I stepped out of the house to inspect its premises. To my terror, the kitchen shack where we had taken shelter the night before was gone, with splinters of bricks, tiles, and mortar lying around everywhere. What if my father had not had a chill that had forced me to take him back into the house? I told him what I had seen, and he looked up at the altar, mumbling his thanks to Quan-yin.

The serene, cool atmosphere of springtime lured me to the front gate of our house despite Nga's warning. The street was empty. Had there been no Vietcong attack last night, people dressed in their best would have poured into the street on this New Year's Day. But since it was so quiet, could the enemy have already been driven out of the city? When I was about to venture further toward the street to take a good look at it and the neighborhood, I could make out a small group of people in black pajamas at an intersection of about two short blocks from our house not too far from the Police Station. Judging from their uniform, I thought they were militiamen assigned to protect our area. Because of the short distance between us, they seemed to see me. Suddenly, a shot rang out. By instinct, I dived down and crawled all the way back to the house. Nga opened the door to let me in, and my heart almost leaped out of my chest out of fright. It was now clear to me that these people were the

Vietcong that we might have seen on Trường Tiền Bridge the night before. I was so lucky because only one shot was fired in my direction. I could have gotten hit had they emptied at me a string of bullets from their machine gun.

We had little time to calm down after the incident when there came from a plane flying above our area with a broadcast ordering all residents living on the *Hữu Ngạn* (Right Bank) where we lived (it did not mention the Citadel and its adjacent areas, so I guessed they might have been taken by the enemy) to evacuate to the campus of the College of Education as the city would be bombed in an hour. Now it was all panic. We interpreted the lull in fighting as a possible complete occupation of the city by the Vietcong. The concentration of half of the city's population on the premises of a small campus would be an easy target for the enemy's shelling or final assault. But there was no time for us to think. In half an hour, we packed as much as we could. The broadcast did not tell how long we should be staying at the shelter, but we gathered that if Huế had been completely occupied, the liberation of it would be hard and long. Because Nga had thought this Tết would be peaceful, she bought just enough food for a few days. Our biggest problem was we were short of cash. We had deposited all our salary in our bank account and kept only a small amount of cash for the holiday expenses.

My family was among the first to leave. As we were getting out of the house, we saw a woman whom Nga recognized as our neighbor who lived across our street staggering in our opposite direction, her hands holding fast her bloody belly, wailing intermittently. "O Heaven! What have I done to be punished like this?" I saw to my horror that her bowels were out, and she was trying to push them back in. She was a plump woman with light skin who was wearing her best clothes for New Year's Day. Blood soaked through her expensive white *ao dai*. We cast a quick glance at her and hurried on to our safety, not bothering about what would happen to her. My father kept reciting the Quan-yin's name to pray for her safety and for ours. That was the best we could do for our neighbor under these circumstances. I wondered if she could make it home on her own to die. Later, when Huế was liberated and things returned to normal, Nga revealed to me that there was a new grave in the backyard of our neighbor's home.

About two hundred meters from our home, we bumped into the corpse of a Vietcong. He was bigger than an average Vietnamese male. He wore a gray uniform made of light cotton that fitted his body tightly, and his legs were bound with strings obviously to help him move with ease. There was on his right arm a red-and-green ribbon perhaps to help him and his group recognize one another. Unlike South Vietnamese soldiers who wore heavy boots, he just wore a pair of sandals made from tires. He must have run all the way from the

Police Station, where the attack had taken place, to our area and fell dead at the gate of a neighbor's home. His eyes were still open. There was a look of shock on his lifeless face.

As we passed the Police Station on our way to the shelter, we saw more bodies all clad in gray uniforms with colored ribbons on the arm. They were tall, big, bareheaded, and armed to the teeth, so I guessed they could belong to a commando squad. Some of them died in a standing or leaning position in the vacant police sentinel booths. They must have been fatally hit while taking cover there before attempting to launch their attack. The scene struck me like a dumb show with dead men still trying to dodge invisible bullets fired from the now entirely quiet police station, with a faint grin on their contorted faces. I was frightened but mesmerized by what I was seeing. The Vietcong, whom I saw for the first time, did *not* belong to our world because they were very much different from us in their dress, physical appearance, and dazzling stunts.

Evacuees quickly packed the university campus. Shortly afterward, all classrooms were taken, each family assigned a space the size of a small mattress. As we were moving in, I looked at the other side of the river before us. An immobile NLF flag could be seen on top of the Citadel Tower against the dreary overcast sky. It meant the entire Inner Citadel and the Left Bank were now under Vietcong control. The Vietcong had also blown up Trường Tiền Bridge to prevent the Americans and government troops from advancing to retake the city. While people from the Right Bank, where the enemy had stayed after a short occupation, were streaming to the shelter, no one from the Left Bank could reach here. Because of the sporadic exchange of firepower between the Vietcong and the Americans, one could tell how dangerous it would be even for the best swimmer to cross the river safely. In fact, this would never happen under these circumstances. Because the NLF flag was flying on the Tower, it meant that the enemy was still there, and they were not allowing residents in the Inner Citadel to flee.

Our first day at the shelter was full of tragedy. No sooner had we settled in than I heard some folks weeping in a corner of our room. It was a family who had just arrived with an old man who was gravely sick and was now in his last moments. He died shortly afterward. Because the family could not take his body home, they buried him in the nursery lot in the back of the college building. His family mourned him by wearing on their head a band of white cloth torn out from a white dress. Probably because they did not want to disturb us, they stopped crying, but I could hear their muffled sobs far into the night.

There was another tragedy on the same evening. Just before sundown, we heard a gunshot in the back of the building where the refugees were cooking their first meal. Our maid told us that a young girl had been hit in the head and died instantly. She said that he heard people say that the shot had come from the watchtower behind the campus. The girl was immediately buried, there was no investigation, and nobody bothered to find out who she was. Accidental deaths like these for which no one was responsible were common in wartime. Nobody would know the university campus had become a temporary cemetery with two fresh graves within one evening. I was thankful that this did not happen to our maid, a cute fifteen-year-old girl whose mother had begged us to adopt her because her family was too poor to keep her. I felt both guilty and ashamed for staying inside all the way instead of going out there to do the cooking myself. What if the girl who was killed were our maid? How could we answer her mother should she come to inquire about her daughter? In a culture that puts such high premium on noblesse oblige, we men often act cowardly, selfishly, and irresponsibly with impunity.

The warning about bombing the entire city did not go into effect. U.S. Marines from their base in Phú Bài and government troops from Đà Nẵng began to retake the Right Bank and met only sporadic resistance from the Vietcong. Refugees were pouring into the shelter from liberated areas, in tatters and with horror still written on their faces. A small first-aid station was set up in a room that used to be my office. On the evening of our second day at the shelter, a woman came with her baby who was bleeding badly. Despite her injury, there was a smile on her angelic, serene face. I heard the doctor tell the woman there was no medical equipment available he could use to save her baby's life. Minutes later, the beautiful smile on the little child's face was gone, her eyes closed for an eternal sleep as her blood, the source of her life, had run dry. On seeing the doctor shake his head, the woman jumped upon her child, let out a piercing scream, then fainted. I immediately left the scene, afraid to pass by my office again. As the number of fresh graves continued to grow on the campus nursery plot, there must have been more wounded victims, children included, who did not survive after arriving at the shelter.

We ran out of food after the first day. Our in-laws offered a slice of rice cake for my father, but he told us to give it to our little boy. It broke our heart to see him devour the piece of cake which, under normal circumstances, he would not touch. Earlier, he had caught his mother off guard by yanking the bottle of milk from his baby brother's mouth and taking a long gulp before giving it up. He was smart enough to realize that it was not right for him to consume entirely the food reserved for his brother. It was funny to see mother and son fight over the bottle of milk. But it was so sad to watch him devour the little piece of cake as though it was the best food he had ever eaten.

With some neighbors, Nga and Hạnh made a quick trip home to get food. The Americans, who stood guard at the intersection, pointed their guns at them. They were checking the refugees' *căn cước* (ID cards), and it was easy to know what they wanted because they held up a sign with the Vietnamese words with no diacritic markings apparently copied from an English-Vietnamese dictionary. In her memoir, Nhã Ca tells a hilarious story about an old woman's success in rescuing her group from a big dilemma. They were stopped by the Americans and one of them shouted something that sounded like *"ken kuck!"* Not knowing what he wanted, the group thought he was using a Vietnamese cuss word and cringed out of fear. As the group stood silent, the American soldier went on shouting angrily. Suddenly, an old woman in the group excitedly exclaimed, "I know what *Ông Mỹ* (Mr. American) wants. He wants to see our *căn cước*!" It turned out that the group had mistaken the American soldier's pronunciation of *ken kuck* for the Vietnamese expression *con cặc*, which means "penis," a common swear cuss word used when one gets very angry. The puzzle having been solved and the GI's desire satisfied, everybody was relieved thanks to the old lady's great ingenuity!

The following day, Nga and I returned to check the condition of our house and to secure what we thought valuable but could not take with us in our previous evacuation. The Americans had been gone, probably because our area had been cleared of the Vietcong. But the road was empty and so quiet that I got goosebumps all the way home. A strong unpleasant odor came from the corpses that were beginning to decompose. The body of the big Vietcong who passed out in front of our neighbor's house was still there, with swarms of flies. When we reached home, I found that the gate was open, and though Nga insisted that when leaving she had forgotten to close the gate, I still hesitated a moment before going in. A thief, a stray animal, or even a wounded Vietcong might be lurking somewhere in the house.

It was shocking to see our own home in such bad shape. There were big holes in the roof and broken tile pieces were everywhere on the floor. The glassware on our altar was all broken except the Kwan-yin statue. Our house looked like what remained after a battle. There might be fighting in our neighborhood after our evacuation. Days later after our return, the man who lived behind our house told me he saw the body of another Vietcong in his backyard and that some people working for the government had been taken away by the enemy. "You must be very lucky," he added. "They wanted a person like you to translate for American prisoners. There are spies in our neighborhood, and I wonder why they didn't tell on you." Yes, I was very lucky. They could have found me had they just lifted the latch on our gate and broken into our house. Nga attributed my fortune to her father's installing a new gate for us just before Tết. She did not realize that the gate was a makeshift used only to discourage a petty thief, not to prevent a break-in.

Contrary to the devastation in our home and our area, spring had come to Huế early. It was now only the third day of the New Year, and yet the trees and the grass looked so green, so full of vigor. I shuddered a little when thinking of decomposed corpses lying around. Nature owed the dead its unusual burst of vitality this year. Suddenly, I felt that our home belonged to the other world.

We hurriedly packed all the essentials and were about to leave when there was a muffled sound coming from the shelter. Nga jumped into me, screaming her head off, her face pale with fright. I was also numb with fear, believing that an injured Vietcong was hiding in our house. When we turned around to look, it was our dog Rê. He could not get his muzzle out of the jar of candies that the other day Nga had forgotten to take to the shelter for our older son. Poor Rê, he must have hunted for food and accidentally pushed his muzzle in the jar and could not get it out. Our being home awakened him and the sound we heard was his muffled bark when he recognized us. We could not help laughing when seeing him in this condition. After getting his muzzle out of the jar, we fed him some candies. Before we left, we patted Rê on the head, trying to comfort him. He responded by lying down, wagging his tail, and making a long soft wail.

We stayed at the shelter for another two weeks. During that time, a trickle of residents arrived with harrowing stories about their experience with the occupiers. Except for some areas on the Left Bank and 1st Army Division Headquarters, Huế was literally taken over by the Vietcong. People were rounded up to hear their propaganda and even to watch shows by the Cultural Performance Troupe from Hanoi. Meanwhile, with the assistance of informers, numerous military people and government workers were identified, arrested, and taken away. Public executions of so-called "criminals who owed the people blood debts" were also conducted in some areas. Vietcong sympathizers and infiltrators began to show up, telling on "reactionary elements" or revenging themselves on their enemy. Stories flew around about a former teacher at a Buddhist school in the Citadel whose brother, a well-known scholar and anti-war activist, had been previously dumped in the DMZ by the Diệm regime in 1956. After expelling the scholar, Diệm's police arrested and tortured his brother. After his release, he took to the *Bưng*, a euphemism for VC headquarters. Now back in town with two pistols buckled at his waist, he was hunting for his former offenders. I met him in 1960 when we both taught at a school in Huế. He was a very gentle person. But I understood why he acted that way. It was wrong to punish him simply because he was the brother of the man you had severely punished for advocating a political position that you did not like. He defected to the Vietcong because he was cornered. When he had the opportunity, he turned his repressed outrage into a burning desire to avenge the wrong that the government had inflicted on him. Brutal revenge, a common practice in feudal Asian society, continued down to modern times during the war or after a change of regime in Vietnam. Considering himself above the law, the victor could mete out with impunity the kind of punishment he saw fit for his vanquished enemy.

I heard very sad news after the liberation of the city—the death of Nga's cousin astrologer. The Vietcong arrested him while he was sleeping at his home in his village and his body was found in another mass grave. His death was a great shock to us. He had never worked for the government. But as an astrologer, he had enjoyed discussing politics with customers and might have said something unfavorable about the NLF. His death was a blow to Nga. After his forecast of her meeting me and our subsequent marriage had turned out absolutely accurate, she made him her special spiritual advisor.

With the support of the U.S. Marines, government troops recaptured most parts of the Citadel and the Left Bank, but Vietcong snipers were still digging in to houses and buildings, slowing the city's total liberation and posing grave threats to civilians who were trying to escape. But what I could not understand was fighting had gone into the fourth week and yet the NLF flag was still flying over the Citadel Tower. U.S. warplanes had heavily bombed the Tower and yet assault after assault from the RVN Marines was driven back by Vietcong firepower. It took several more days to completely silence their last pocket of resistance. When the first government troops moved in, they found bodies of NLF soldiers chained at their ankles to their machine guns with artillery pieces lying around. They were the commandos who stayed and fought to the end while all the regular forces had long withdrawn from the city.

We returned home after spending four weeks at the shelter. A monk at our local temple started doing the cleanup on the street. Since nobody volunteered to help him with the corpses, he burned them with gasoline. A true Buddhist practitioner, he did all the work alone out of compassion for the dead, regardless of their origin and political adherence, unafraid of possible grave consequences that he could face due to his tending to the enemy's souls.

Now that the long nightmare was over, we were back to work and tried to repair our lives. There were quite a few people—faculty, staff, and students—who did not return. Very shortly we learned what had happened to them. First, Dr. Lê Văn Hảo, Director of the University Library, had defected to the NFL.

During the offensive, he called for Huế's people to uprise against the Americans and their "Thiệu-Kỳ regime" on Radio Hanoi and Radio NLF. In the end-of-the-year talent show, I saw Dr. Hảo cry when the students performed a piece dramatizing the Vietnamese people's resistance against the French oppressive rule. After that night, he disappeared with some of my students who were in the cast of the play. During the offensive, other anti-war leaders who had not been seen in a long time suddenly emerged armed to the teeth and started to hunt for their former enemy. They all disappeared again after the Vietcong and the North Vietnamese had withdrawn from the city.

Those who had been taken away by the Vietcong during their retreat did not return. A couple of months later, a mass grave was found in a remote area in the country and many victims were identified by their relatives. Thanks to the information provided by villagers. many victims' remains were found, and in the end, hundreds of missing people were accounted for. Most victims had cracked skulls, which suggested that their heads might have been struck by hammers or hoes rather than by bullets. It was believed that NLF and North Vietnamese forces in their hurried retreat had disposed of their prisoners as quickly as possible.

After the Vietcong had withdrawn, the same tragic human drama continued in the freshly liberated city. Redbaiting that had discontinued after the toppling of the Diệm regime now began to raise its ugly head. As the police began to hunt for Vietcong suspects and sympathizers, it was time for some folks to settle accounts with their foes. The police arrested my university's business manager on an unfounded accusation by one of his employees. The man was jailed and tortured. A colleague of mine who taught history did not show up for his class one day. When we learned that he had gone through the police's harrowing interrogation, we all understood that it was his indiscretion that got him in trouble. When he came back to work a few months later, he was a completely changed man. He shunned all social gatherings and grew quieter than ever.

It had been a while since the school reopened, but still we had not recovered from the great calamity. There was horror, shock, and fear on the face of everyone, especially those from the Citadel and areas that had been under Vietcong control. Almost every home had a loss, and often the dead were buried in the backyard. My classes met in a room with windows facing the soccer field with fresh graves that served as a daily painful reminder of the recent tragedy. Some students were missing. Perhaps they were dead now, or perhaps they had fled with the Vietcong. Some others wore a small black ribbon on their shirt, a mark of mourning for their loved ones, but I was afraid to ask.

Classes were tedious and dismal. My lectures fell flat. We had no heart for doing anything.

The city, once so beautiful, was now in ruin. The main bridge was cut in half by a Vietcong mine explosion and submerged in the middle. Even during daylight, Huế struck us as a ghost city. Trần Hưng Đạo Street, the busiest and liveliest place just a month earlier, was deserted with charred roofless buildings. Some people claimed they found a tunnel inside their houses that zigzagged through the main street all the way to the suburbs, and this was why the Vietcong could hang on so long and no casualties were found after their retreat from this area. Because the offensive came suddenly and took everybody by surprise, some incredulous folks elevated the Vietcong to an almost legendary level, claiming that they could build a tunnel noiselessly within hours with their portable Soviet-made machines!

The Citadel Tower was the hardest, bloodiest spot for the U.S. Marines and government troops to conquer. It miraculously remained almost intact despite heavy U.S. artillery and air strikes. Nevertheless, the Forbidden City where the Nguyễn emperors had lived and held their court and where the Vietcong had dug in was in ruin. The gates of the Citadel, the target of intensive American air power, also collapsed. Because the enemy held out in these places only, most private residences could avoid U.S. bombing. But because the Citadel, like the suburbs, was the Vietcong commandos' last stronghold, its residents had experienced their longest nightmare ever. Added to the hell of living through a month of ceaseless American bombing was the survivors' grief and agony of seeing their relatives, who were local government employees or military personnel on leave for Tết, being taken away by the Vietcong in their retreat.

It was unusually cold that year. The sky was always overcast, bleak, and dreary but there was no rain. The clouds were so low they submerged the Tower, which was still breathing smoke after RVN Marines' bloodiest battles with Vietcong commandos. With a 24-hour curfew strictly enforced, Huế was a ghost city. At night, it was in total darkness.

Huế people call the 1968 Tết offensive the *Tết Mậu Thân*. The event took place when the Vietnamese celebrated New Year's Day of the year of the Monkey. Vietnamese, in general, is less precise than English and other Western languages when naming major historical events. But the event, which had no parallel in Vietnam's history and to which a short reference would suffice, will not fade in the survivors' memory as long as they live. The city had fallen to the French once in 1885. But the war then was nothing compared with the *Tết Mậu Thân*. At that time, the French used only rifles in their attacks. The

Vietnamese army, armed with bows and arrows and spears, littered the streets of their city with bananas, hoping that French soldiers who wore boots would slip and fall and thus their advance would be hindered. We can guess that sort of warfare did not cause as many casualties as it does today. The destruction wrought upon Huế by the communist offensive and the retaking of the city by the U.S. and government forces and their consequences were more than its people, well known for their gentility and devotion to a quiet, peaceful life because of their royal origin, could bear or imagine.

The offensive had a lasting, more disastrous impact on many individuals and families than on the city. While there was a general revival—shopping and business transactions resumed right on the grounds of the destroyed market—innumerable heartrending stories of isolated tragic cases came out. The killing of a teacher that Nhã Ca mentions in her memoir *Giãi khăn sô cho Huế* [*Mourning Headband for Huế*] turned out to be Tú Y, one of my high school friends and a math teacher at Quốc Học High School. The night of the offensive, the Vietcong came and arrested him at his house in the suburbs of Huế. His remains were found months later in one of the mass graves after the city was liberated. His death broke his family apart. Because his wife was sick and unable to provide for her children, they quit school and worked to make a living at such an early age. One of the most shocking and tragic things about the Tết offensive concerned the murder of four foreigners: Father Urbain and three Germans on the teaching staff of Huế Medical School. A Franciscan priest and scholar in French literature, Father Urbain left Thiên An Monastery to join the French department at the university's request to help out with its faculty shortage. His body was found in a shallow grave a month after the offensive. According to a witness, Father Urbain was taken away from their monastery with some other priests. Along the way, he tried to come back to get a coat for a sick colleague without telling his guard. He was suspected of leaving secret signs to reveal the prisoners' whereabouts and was killed instantly. At the same time, the remains of Prof. and Mrs. Rainik, Prof. Discher, and Dr. Alterkoster, a young handsome assistant to Drs. Rainik and Discher, all affiliated with the University of Freiburg, were discovered near a temple on the outskirts of the city, their arms tied in the back and their jaws severely broken. Rumor had it that the NLF soldiers had mistaken them for Americans. The university declared a week-long mourning for its benefactors. As the memorial service was about to begin, a tearful young Vietnamese woman wearing black appeared with a wreath carrying this message: "To my dear Dr. Alterkoster with my sacred and humble love." She wrapped Dr. Alterkoster's coffin with her outstretched arms, breaking down in sobs. She was one of his close associates.

Not all stories were sad. My student told me that his American instructor was arrested by the NLF soldiers but miraculously escaped death. When he was brought before the local commander, the latter recognized him and secretly set him free. It turned out that the Vietcong officer was one of his former English students at the University of Huế. Another moving story concerns *Bác Siêu* (Uncle Siêu), so-called on account of his seniority and prestige in the local Buddhist community, who risked his life by bringing rice to people trapped in areas that came under heavy fighting. Today we still wonder how he managed to stay safe and get his work done in such dangerous situations. He continued his charity work for several more years until his passing in 1975.

The destruction of lives in the offensive was so enormous that years later the freshness of its horrors is intact in the fiction of some writers. Michael Herr's depiction of his narrator's gut reaction in *Dispatches* when he sees dead civilians on a street near his Marine base at Phú Bài on the outskirts of Huế would be viscerally real to any Huế resident who lived through those hellish times; it surpasses the stark realism of Stephen Crane's *The Red Badge of Courage*: "[A]n old man arched over his straw hat and a little girl riding her bicycle, lying there with her arm up *like a reproach*. They'd been lying out like that for a week, for the first time we were grateful for the cold" (emphasis added). I did not see as many civilian dead as Herr might have, but I recall it was unusually cold during the one-month-old offensive. Perhaps because of the chilly weather, corpses did not decompose quickly. But having been there, I can add to what Herr could have said more about what he really saw. *We in Huế, you know, see the exposure and decomposition of the remains of our people, especially those of women and the elderly, in public as our greatest humiliation, a most heinous crime against both the dead and their living relatives.* Herr partly senses this truth when observing that the little girl is lying out "with her arm up *like a reproach*." We see it more than a reproach. It *is* an accusation and a demand or plea (depending how you interpret her gesture) that *she be buried immediately, or her spirit will not rest*. This explains why, in his novel, days later, though fighting is still raging, when Herr's narrator returns to the scene, the old man and the little girl have disappeared. This is also why the backyard of many houses in Huế was a temporary graveyard for many survivors' loved ones killed in the offensive. The dead must be buried as promptly as possible, must be kept out of public view as much as possible.

The horrors of the *Tết Mậu Thân* defy human comprehension and imagination. The happenings were real, but they strike us as *unreal* or *surreal*. I had lived through the siege of the city but could not imagine such horrible things until I heard stories that came out after the offensive.

The will to live—no matter what form it takes—always remained strong in the survivors. We set out to rebuild our lives in earnest immediately after the liberation of the city. Due to the destruction of Đông Ba Market, small markets emerged everywhere, even in alleys. Private homes destroyed during the offensive were rebuilt thanks to the government's support. An American colleague told me when his plane was preparing to land at Phú Bài Airport, he looked out the window and was struck by a spectacular scene: covered with metal shingles donated by the United States, houses and buildings below glittered like myriad points of light in the bright afternoon sun. Huế's economy suddenly experienced a boom with transactions of goods smuggled from the Phú Bài PX. Our favorite place was *Chợ Trời*, a popular open marketplace that emerged after the Tết offensive and was held every day from 5:00 pm until dark, where things stolen from the PX that we saw only in Sears's catalogs or magazines were sold at cheap prices. We bought what we could afford but particularly liked canned food and butter because they were cheap, delicious, and *American*! *Chợ Trời* always attracted a huge crowd, contributed to the growth of Huế's economy, and provided a temporary respite from our grief over the recent tragedy and worry about insecurity in our city. Life went on. But we seemed to cheat ourselves out of the hard reality we were facing by indulging ourselves in as much distraction as we could and by redoubling our efforts to repair our broken lives and broken city. It was touching, for example, to see the University of Huế try to recover from its near-total destruction. We worked under primitive conditions with an almost empty library and laboratories, in classrooms with leaked roofs and no furniture. Some students were missing, and those who did return, especially those who lived in the country and had relatives killed in the offensive, looked sad and grim, but all were determined to salvage their life and their university's future from ruins. When classes did not meet, they took part in cleaning up the wreckage caused by bombs and mortars or helping with providing relief for war victims. Under the remarkable leadership of Professor Lê Thanh Minh Châu, a Cambridge graduate and a Ph.D. from the University of Chicago, the University of Huế quickly became a first-rate higher education institution in South Vietnam. Moved by the great tragedy that had befallen the Huế people and impressed with their extraordinary courage, the Free World poured its aid to the city and our university. Professor Châu and his staff set out to implement important long-term plans for their institution. Grants were awarded to selected faculty for advanced training in the U.S. and European countries as part of the university's faculty development program. New academic programs that met the country's educational needs were also introduced into its curriculum. There was a remarkable increase in student enrollment. The campus became livelier than before the Tết offensive.

Huế, which had been thought unable to recover from the catastrophe, underwent a remarkable revival after just one year. The two major streets that had suffered the greatest damage during the offensive now wore a new face with beautiful shops and buildings. The destruction gave Huế people an opportunity to build or remodel their dwellings and business facilities. Having lived through all the hellish times, I was shocked to see my people's apparent quick oblivion of the horrific tragedy. But I was wrong about it. They did not forget the tragedy nor their loved ones who were dead or still missing. As it turned out, the Tết of the following year, Year of the Rooster, which fell on February 16th, 1969, was more lugubrious than ever. As soon as the New Year holiday ended, every family began a month-long commemoration of their loved ones killed in last year's offensive. Because people knew only when their loved ones were taken away and never returned (generally the offensive claimed at least a victim in every household), not when they were killed, they just commemorated their deaths every day. During the entire first month of the Year of the Rooster, incense was burned and candles were lit every night in every house's shrine to mark the survivors' remembrance of their dead relatives. Memorial services were also held at Buddhist temples and Catholic churches for the victims. The Vietnamese, especially the Buddhists, believe that if their dead are not remembered, their souls will not be saved, and they will be condemned to wandering endlessly in this world full of sorrow and suffering.

One month after our return home, my father fell ill. He suffered from a stomach ulcer with occasional bleeding. We could not take him to the hospital because it was closed. Fortunately, his mind was still sound enough for him to self-treat his condition with herbs. I had seen many dead people before, but this was the first time I feared death because I worried it might happen to my father. Every night after he fell asleep, in the dark I groped toward him, held my breath, listened for any vital sign in him such as stirring or breathing, and only went back to sleep after making sure he was all right. With a time-consuming teaching job and a family with a wife and two young children to care for, I found little time to be with Father except when the family ate meals together at noon and in the evening. The thought of not seeing him anymore scared me and made me feel guilty. Many times, I wanted to show him how much I loved him but did not know how. An extremely doting father who was unfortunately toughened by his situation as a single parent and inhibited by a stoic strait-laced Confucian culture that views the display of emotions as unsuitable for men, Father had never taught us to show our affection to him. I had thought I would never be able to express my love to him until one day when I came home from school, I saw him staggering into the bathroom and caught him on time before he fell. As I was rushing to hold him up in my arms, I let out a moan, "*O Ba!*" and tears gushed out of my eyes. That was the only time I embraced my father. I saw disbelief and shock in his eyes. He did not seem to realize how much I loved him, nor did he understand why I could express my love to him in such an unbecoming way. When he died sixteen years later, I was stuck in the United States with a visa problem and could not return to see him in his last moments to embrace him again, to tell him that I loved him more than anyone in my entire life and that I would become the most unfortunate orphan in the world after his death.

Except for the horrific offensive, which was over now, the last month of the year 1968 brought us some great joy: the birth of our third son on December 22nd. His arrival made my father the happiest person in the family: he became the patriarch of three grandsons. But I owed Nga my third child's life and my father's happiness. Her pregnancy occurred when our family fortune was at its lowest because of the war. But while, like many Huế women, Nga provided the best for us, she denied herself any well-being she could afford. She was so devoted to her children that she insisted that she, not me, care for them alone. Arguing that she was fine, she refused to follow a regimen recommended by the doctor because she thought it was too expensive. She would spend her money on food and other basic needs for the family. This and many other sacrifices she has made in her life are motivated by her boundless love for us, one that is absolutely unselfish and unconditional. To her, I and the children are more important than her own life.

To this day, I am still amazed by the act of love Nga performed on the evening of December 22nd, 1968. Shortly after returning home from work, she complained of pain in the belly. Suspecting that she was going into labor, I got ready to take her to a clinic, but she insisted that she was all right and went back to caring for the children. Only when she could not endure the pain anymore did she let me take her to a local maternity clinic. When we arrived, there was not much time left before the curfew went into effect. Instead of letting me stay with her, she begged me to leave, insisting that there was no adult at home to watch my ailing father and the children. I had to leave her at the clinic with the midwife. I could have stayed with her, but the curfew, the creepy silence of the night suddenly raised in my mind the specter of another offensive, urging me to come home for my father and the children and let Nga embark by herself on her extremely dangerous adventure. It was a long night with a lot of nightmares. I could not sleep a wink. There was no way to find out if Nga would be all right that night, and the only thing I could do for me, for her, and for our children, was pray for her safety. At thirty-one, I was already the head of a family with an ailing father, a wife in danger, and two young children. The burden was too heavy for a young man like me to bear.

If something happened to Nga, how could I cope with it? How could I care for my family without her?

As soon as the curfew ended, I hurriedly rode my bike to the clinic to see Nga. Along the way, I prayed continuously as though I was now taking Nga to the clinic and praying could turn things around when the worst might have already happened. As soon as I arrived, I dashed into the clinic office, my heart jumping out of my chest. To my greatest joy, the midwife greeted me with a smile. She took me to Nga's room. She was awake, looking pale but obviously extremely happy. The first thing she asked me was how my father and the children were doing and whether they had been up. Then smiling, she pointed to the crib by her bed where the baby was sleeping. Born prematurely, he was as tiny as a kitten!

During our eight years of marriage, Nga "crossed the ocean" by herself two times, to use an old saying, this time and in 1964 when she gave birth to our firstborn. At both times I was not around to face the danger with her. We almost lost our firstborn because of the nurse's mindless irresponsibility. Had things not gone smoothly this time, I could have lost Nga and our baby. One year after the Tết offensive, healthcare facilities except for the Central Hospital, which was too far away for me to take Nga to, were not adequate to manage complicated cases that might require blood transfusions or surgery.

Since the birth of our third son, things started getting better for us. Nga got a permanent job at a local high school, I taught private English classes at home, our oldest boy started kindergarten, and my father's health improved significantly. Finally, I was promoted to senior instructor with some increase in salary and academic prestige. All my relatives were safe. The horrors of the 1968 offensive gradually grew distant in my memory. Though news flew around about the strong pressure of the North Vietnamese forces on the city, like most people, I deliberately put my fear aside, partly because there was nothing we could do about it, but mostly because we had a lot of trust in the Americans. We had no doubt about their intention to stick with us to the end when they had half a million combat troops in Vietnam. Fighting communism in our country, we would argue, must be related to American interests. Though at that time we knew little about the domino theory, we knew that the United States wanted to contain the spread of communism from the Soviet Union and China. To help the South resist the North's invasion meant to prevent a country in the Free World from falling to the communist bloc. Inspired by the successful intervention by the United States in the Korean War and witnessing the amazing revival of our city after the offensive, we brushed off the thought of a possible communist takeover of the South.

The period between 1969 and the spring of 1972 was my happiest time as the head of the family. I enjoyed many moments of small but real happiness. Every day on my way home, I stopped by a small grocery store to get a C-ration for my children. When spotting me from a distance, they would stop playing and rush out to the gate to greet me excitedly, "Pa is home! Pa is home!" knowing that I would have candies or cakes for them. My small but *real* happiness also came from helping Nga take care of our three little ones. Catering to my father's needs, such as occasionally taking him to a temple or typing his translation of Chinese poetry into Vietnamese, was one of the most memorable moments I had ever had before I left my family and began my fateful life-long exile in America.

The heart is such a strange thing. It controls our intellect and emotions, arbitrarily imposing on us various modes of conceptualizing and feeling at various stages of our lives. Because our life does not stay the same, our perception of it changes with time. After my graduation from college, happiness for me was reliving my privileged but ephemeral moments of the past in Dalat and Quảng Bình. Now my happiness consisted in living these *simple*, *real* present moments of my life—loving my loved ones and being loved by them. There was no need for me to evoke these precious moments because they existed right now and right here.

While I enjoyed the greatest bliss I had ever had in my life, I occasionally felt a pang of sorrow in my heart, a foreboding that misfortune would happen. Though Huế seemed safe, it was in time of war with a curfew strictly enforced and troops armed to the teeth guarding major points and military convoys rumbling on Highway 1 on the outskirts of the city. There were rumors that another communist attack was imminent, that the Americans were negotiating with the North Vietnamese for a pullout at the Paris Conference in exchange for peace, and that the current demarcation line would be shifted down to the 15th or 14th parallel, well beyond the Hải Vân Pass on the outskirts of Đà Nẵng. Most affluent people were leaving Huế. We were on edge, afraid to hear of a possible division of Vietnam with Huế belonging to the North.

VIA DOLOROSA

May 1972. The dice was cast for me and my family. For the first time, the U.S. Fulbright Program offered scholarships to study in the U.S. to the University of Huế faculty. Because there was no interest from the senior faculty in my department, I was encouraged to apply. In truth, while apprehensive of the significant risk, I was thrilled about the opportunity. Pursuing an advanced degree in the U.S. in my field had always been my dream before I graduated from college. As I said earlier, I got the job thanks to a former professor who kept me when I was about to be sent to a remote area, and since then I became a target of some fellow faculty's backbiting. I do not know if these people had reported anything about me to the new provost of the university, but his secretary, who was a friend of mine, told me that the provost was aware of my "improper" appointment. Because he was a petty and malicious man, my friend's warning scared me. She advised that I should not pass up this opportunity. "When you return with a Ph.D. from an American university," she said, "not only you could help yourself and your family, but you could also protect your other junior colleagues, people like yourself today."

I sought the advice of my father and my father-in-law who both urged me to accept the opportunity, if offered. Nga, who knew best the dilemma I was facing, also encouraged me to leave the country, though I saw tears in her eyes. Our union was indeed a strange one. We had undergone a long separation after our marriage. Now it looked like I would leave home again, for my sake and my family's. With an advanced academic degree in hand, I would be able to help my loved ones better. Though a possible communist takeover occasionally loomed in my mind, I often shrugged it off. Many people I talked to assured me that there would never be another communist offensive because Huế was now well-protected by the Americans and the elite 1st Army Division consisting of soldiers from Huế who were committed to defending their families and their native land at all costs. The NVA (North Vietnamese Army) and Vietcong had gained no new ground in the Huế vicinity since the Tết offensive. If, God forbid, Huế was to come under another assault, which would take years for the communists to prepare, by then I would have completed my study and returned home. But this was only a worst-case scenario. Because the last offensive was still fresh in our memory, it was natural that we were prone to that unfounded fear. Given the amazing revival Huế was experiencing and the pouring of the Free World's aid to the city's reconstruction program, only skeptics could imagine the occurrence of another communist offensive.

That was the state of mind of those who were desperate, who could not go anywhere or do anything but stay put. To survive, we employed many strategies including maintaining a strong faith and often immersing ourselves in make-believe, wishful thinking, and even delusions. In a country torn by constant war and political violence where the worst was expected any time and we were helpless, it was better to adopt this strategy of living than give in to despair and forgo our responsibility toward our family.

In April 1972, one month after I had submitted my application and gone through the selection process, the U.S. Fulbright Program offered me the scholarship and gave me one month to decide. No sooner had I chosen the school to study in America than the so-called *Mùa hè đỏ lửa* (Assault of Summer 1972) began. After their withdrawal from Khe Sanh, now vacated by the U.S. Marines, the NVA concentrated their assault on Quảng Trị and easily took over the city's old citadel. Again, chaos and panic broke out with thousands of refugees fleeing from Quảng Trị to Huế on Highway 1. Though short, the retreat was very tragic. Weeks later, I happened to see an issue of *Time* magazine in an American colleague's apartment that covered the military debacle. There was a photo of a small child standing by the bodies of civilians strewn on the roadsides. He looks stunned, astonished, or frightened when seeing the people fleeing past him. Maybe he cannot find his parents, maybe they are among the dead, or maybe he is too young to know what is happening. Because of news censorship, we were kept in the dark about the fall of Quảng Trị until Đông Ba Market was burned and looted by thugs. Thinking that the Vietcong had come, Huế people fled the city in panic. After putting all my family on a packed bus, I got on my Honda C-50 and, for the first time in my life, went to Đà Nẵng by motorcycle. Luckily, it was only a false alarm and we returned home shortly afterward.

The panic of the *Mùa hè đỏ lửa* dampened my excitement about the Fulbright scholarship. How could Nga, now pregnant with our youngest child, handle by herself a family with three young kids and an ailing old man in an emergency like this most recent exodus in my absence? Which was worth my attention? My career or my family's safety? Naturally, my family's safety came first. But at the same time a thought occurred to me that the recent panic was only a false alarm triggered by our fear of another communist offensive. The local government never issued an evacuation order and all government employees reported to work the day we civilians fled the city. Besides, the old citadel of Quảng Trị was retaken only a few days after the enemy's occupation. At Nga's suggestion and in my naïve belief that Americans knew best what was going to happen, I asked an American colleague if it would be all right for me to leave the country at this time. While he encouraged me to accept the scholarship, he was evasive (I do not know whether he did not have the answer, or he did not want to disclose a top secret to which only Americans had access) about the U.S. intention in South Vietnam. Mellowed by my disappointment, he later told me that he saw no threat of a communist invasion of Huế soon. Desperate as I was, I clutched at his response as a saving grace, something that I used to justify the course of action I was going to take. After several sleepless nights, I came to make the hardest decision in my entire life: accepting the scholarship. *I will not pass up this excellent opportunity to improve my future. I will work hard to finish my studies and return home as soon as possible.*

August 20th, 1972. This was the saddest day in my life. Before we went together to the airport in the afternoon, we had a picture taken together. My children were excited whenever I took pictures of them, but now they all looked sad. Even our four-year-old son, who smiled all the time, when woken from his nap today to go to the airport with us, started crying when I held him up. I succeeded in having a picture taken with my family, but everybody just stared at the camera. There was shock, fear, and sadness in everybody's eyes. It was Nga and my father who had encouraged me to apply for the scholarship, but I knew deep down they did not want me to go. They could not hide their feelings upon my departure. I felt the same way about leaving them. Things developed so fast (it took me only two months to get accepted for the scholarship) that I felt unprepared for our separation.

I wanted to take another picture of my family at the airport before boarding the plane, but Nga's eyes were already wet with tears. That was the only photo of all my loved ones present on that day that I still have today. This picture of my family and the folk music I later bought in Saigon before I left Vietnam were the saddest memorabilia I was to take with me in my longest journey to exile.

It took me two weeks in Saigon to get through the visa application hassle. The long, idle waiting period without my loved ones by my side plunged me into a deep depression. I missed my father, my wife, and my children so much. My stomach was in knots every time I thought of them. I wanted to go to the post office to make a call to Nga but changed my mind. She would have to get to the post office to get my call, which was impossible because working and taking care of my father and the children took up all her time. Writing was my only way to communicate with my family, but because mail was so slow, they would not hear from me until I had left. Sorrow, loneliness, and particularly fear of a possible communist assault that might happen while I was away with no relatives around to help my family disheartened me and dampened my enthusiasm about going to America. To make myself feel better, I visited downtown Saigon—my favorite place in the past—but it only made me feel worse. My eyes brimmed with tears when I saw young parents leisurely leading their kids by the hand, their faces glowing with pride and happiness. I could have been one of such happy parents had I not abandoned my loved ones and brought myself into this impasse.

Three days before my departure, Khoách, a colleague from my university who had virtually moved to Saigon with his family after the Tết offensive, invited me to his home for dinner. Because I wanted to ask him and his wife to help Nga in my absence when they returned to Huế, I accepted his invitation. At some point during our conversation, Khoách and Tâm expressed their concern about my leaving the country at this dangerous time. Khoách's wisdom, courage, and care for his own family as shown in his getting them to safety in Saigon made me realize now how reckless, foolish, selfish, and uncaring I must be to leave my loved ones in Huế in harm's way. Just like a levee that could not contain an all-too-powerful tide, I broke down into sobs when Tâm, a very compassionate woman who knew my father well, asked me bluntly, "Should something happen to your father, do you think Nga could handle it all by herself without you?" Yes, I had thought a lot about it and almost turned down the scholarship, but my father had told me because he was a physician, he knew his health was fairly good and that he could live many more years, I felt emboldened by his words. My father-in-law, a well-known astrologer, also had given me a green light after consulting my horoscope about my chance for an eventual reunion with the family. But that night, this couple's remarks caught me off-guard and dashed all my hope. Suddenly, I was forced to face the reality I was running away from or trying to ignore. My friends were right. I should not have taken the scholarship. Now that my father was past eighty, could he live until I returned? How could Nga, who was pregnant, care for the family without me? Though the NVA was kept at bay, it was still posing a threat to Huế and its vicinity. It was dangerous then to leave my loved ones in harm's way at this time. How foolish, how cruel of me to trade my family's safety for a little fame and reputation. It was not worth it!

But it was too late. There was nothing I could do to reverse the situation. I started blaming fate for my dilemma. But should I blame fate for the opportunity I had sought and prayed for so passionately? Wasn't it fair to say it was because of my inability to put up with the so-called injustice in the workplace, my desire for career security or, more accurately, for a name for myself? My shameful experience with Mr. Hành, my fear of being kicked out of the university by the new provost because of my improper appointment, etc. were still painfully fresh in my mind. I had to move forward, or my future would be in danger. I, for one, knew better than anyone at the University of Huế that a Ph.D. from an American university was a weapon to fight injustice and advance myself. The fear of losing face was another reason for my rushing into the decision. It would be a great disgrace to give up the scholarship, cancel the flight to come home and face scorn from friends, colleagues, and students. I shuddered to think of the ordeal recently experienced by a young colleague at my university. He got a scholarship to study in France, but not long after his arrival, he quit and came home. Backbiters claimed that he abandoned the opportunity because of his language problem. I could understand why these people did that to their colleague. They got bored and needed to work up something for fun, or they could be jealous of him, an intelligent man, and making him painfully aware of his weakness would give them pleasure.

Nowhere do people care more about saving face than in Huế, the former capital of imperial Vietnam. Emulating the ideal of noblesse oblige practiced by the descendants of princes and princesses, they would rather die than go begging. My father, my father-in-law, and Nga also adhered to this tradition; they loved me and yet desired to see me succeed in life. With this hope and courage rekindled, the next morning I went out to buy a few souvenirs to take with me to America. I bought some music albums and was eerily drawn to one with a curious title: *Quê hương và kỷ niệm* [*Home and Memories*]. I felt like something bad was going to happen but did not know how soon. A creepy feeling traversed the length of my spine. Why memories of home when I was expected to complete my study in two years and would return home immediately after that? As you can see, the day of my departure from Huế was a fateful day. It turned out that I was not to see my wife and my children in eight years, could not go home to see my father at his deathbed, was not able to see his grave until the normalization of diplomatic relationships between the Socialist Republic of Vietnam and the United States, until all my dreams and hopes I had set out to build before my leaving home went for nothing. In fact, home and memories, or rather memories of home, was an anguished question on my mind since the fall of Huế on March 26th, 1975 and upon my realization that I could not go home again.

The evening before my departure, the president of my university invited me to have dinner with him. He put me much at ease by assuring me that the university would provide Nga as much assistance as it could in my absence. I refrained from telling him what I was most concerned about—my family's safety—because I felt that the university was already too kind to us. In addition to my Fulbright scholarship, I was granted a paid leave of absence.

Overwhelmed by gratitude and thrilled about the good future in store for me upon completing my studies and returning to Vietnam, I put aside all the worries that had beset me to concentrate on practical matters ahead. I found myself completely ready for the adventure.

Chị Thúy, who supported my decision in this matter, saw me off at Tân Sơn Nhất Airport. Looking around and seeing most departing passengers surrounded by their relatives, I felt depressed, lonely, and terribly homesick. The same apprehension, anxiety, and worry about my family's safety came back. I was gripped with a vague fear that something wrong would eventually happen and that this trip would be my permanent departure from home. *Chị* Thúy must have seen me shaking. She wiped a tear when I made for the departure gate to board the plane.

As the plane took off and flew higher, I peered out at Saigon below, trying to take in the familiar images of a city—and a country—that were getting dimmer and dimmer. When everything had gone dark and I could not make out anything below anymore, I pulled down the window shade and stared at the dark void in front of me, the dark void of a future I already perceived too soon. Out of the dark void came images of my children, my wife, my father, and my home in Huế. They were sharper, more vivid than they had appeared before I boarded the plane. Suddenly, the wonderful world I had lived in with my family that I had thought would last as long as I lived ended abruptly. Too soon it became a past full of sorrow that was beginning to haunt me. Would this past accompany me to America in my academic pursuits? Would it prevent me from realizing my cherished dream of becoming a literary scholar and returning home to reunite with my family as scheduled? Would I be able to realize the same dream my father had successfully realized when he took me and my brother to the South to seek better educational opportunities? Or would I end up seeing all my dreams thwarted, everything that was dear to me—family, home, Vietnam—becoming memories, as the title of the music album I purchased on the eve of my boarding this plane might forebode?

VIA DOLOROSA (continued)

America

Honolulu was my first stop to change planes en route to Austin, Texas where I would be attending the University of Texas. A representative from the International Institute of Education (IIE) met me at the airport. This was the first time I was on the American soil, saw such a huge American airport and American passengers, and encountered an American official. America was an extraordinary country in size, orderliness, and efficiency. Americans looked rich, poised, and imposing. I was being exposed to a country and a people that I only caught a glimpse of in movies and textbooks.

My second stop was San Francisco. Another IIE official met me at the airport and took me to a Hyatt hotel where I was to stay overnight before catching a domestic flight to Austin the following day. Being a fresh arrival in America, I had trouble telling the two IIE officials apart. They were big, fair-skinned, and full of energy; they were also nice, friendly, and professional. They gave me handouts with oral instructions on how to get around at the airport and the hotel. I was a little upset when they asked, "Do you like it here?" I mumbled "Yes, madam," wondering if this query was in their agency's manual because the two IIE ladies asked me the same question. (I discovered later that in nine cases out of ten officials representing U.S. government agencies overseas speak out of their prepared manual.) I thought the question they asked was unfortunate for a Vietnamese national like me. I came here to study, not to have a fun time. I left home most unwillingly, and though this was a great and fascinating country, I did not have the heart to enjoy it now.

The IIE lady helped me check in at the Hyatt San Francisco. Before she left, she handed me $50 for food and miscellaneous expenses. She also gave me instructions on how to get to the airport to catch a flight to Austin in the morning, then quickly left. *My being in America is real. This is the beginning of my permanent exile. I cannot go home again.* Tomorrow, I would be on my way to Texas, half a globe away from Vietnam. The feeling of loneliness and sadness I felt on the plane was intensified by an overpowering sense of shock and anxiety. In the days, weeks, and months ahead (I was afraid to mention "years" because I could not endure our separation that long), I would be facing myriad problems. Overwhelmed by my being in America for the first time, I forgot to ask the IIE representative if she had arranged for somebody to pick me up at the airport and if she had found a place in Austin for me to stay. I was also extremely worried about arriving one week late for school. Being a foreign student minimally prepared for study in an English-speaking country, I did not know if I could meet the challenges of graduate work or would end up returning home and suffering humiliation. But my greatest concern was my family's safety. I had left them in harm's way to come here. Should another assault like the 1968 offensive occur, how could I get home to be with my family? How could I live without them?

I closed my eyes, trying to drive away the dark thoughts.

It was still early in the afternoon, so I went to the hotel office to buy some postcards and stamps to write home. Though my heart was heavy with sorrow, I could not help admiring San Francisco—and America—that I had heard much about, had wished to see, and was now seeing with my own eyes. The "mythical" city was unrolling before my eyes with its breathtaking green foothills stretching until they blended into the waving skyline dotted with skyscrapers glittering in the afternoon sun. The sky was a limpid blue, without a cloud, without an aircraft. It was so cool, pleasant, and tranquil. On the hotel's walkway, I saw people, some with children my little ones' age, taking their afternoon walk in a leisurely manner. They looked confident, content, and happy. What a blessing to be citizens of such a beautiful, peaceful, and safe country! How envious I was of these Americans! Poor Nga, since we got married and before I left Vietnam, I had never seen Nga take one day off to rest. Nor had we had a chance to go on a pleasure trip together. As for our children, I could not recall how many times they had been roused from sleep at night by mortar explosions since they were born. How I wished my children to grow up normal, full of self-confidence, free from fear and threat like those American kids I saw today!

I wrote three postcards each addressing my father, Nga, and our oldest son Hùng, who was in second grade and could write. I told my father that I was well and safe and asked him not to worry about me, ending with the salutation expected of every child raised in the Confucian tradition: "Your undutiful son." In observance of Confucian propriety, I did not say I missed and loved him. It was unbecoming for children to verbally express their affection to their parents because Confucian culture viewed parental sacrifice as too great to be described in words. The rule, however, did not apply to Nga and Hùng whom

I could address in affectionate terms. Though I had not started school yet, I tried to comfort them by giving them a specific date for my return. I told Hùng to help his mother take care of his grandpa and his younger siblings and promised to send them toys and clothes as soon as I got to Austin. As it was late afternoon in San Francisco and it would be a little after nightfall in Vietnam, my children would not be asleep yet, I guessed they would ask Nga about me, and she would assure them that I was all right and would come home soon. Everybody at home surely must have missed me. Suddenly, I felt terrible. All the arguments I had used to justify my leaving home could not keep me from blaming myself for coming here. I slumped onto my bed and cried like a child.

I took the postcards to the front desk. An attendant told me to drop them in the mailbox in front of the hotel. There was a big blue box with a bald eagle icon on a sidewalk, not a small box with the French word *Lettres* and a slot to slide in the mail that I used to see on the front wall of a post office at home. Seeing that no one was around, I mustered the courage to lift the handle. Trying as hard as I could, it would not move. How embarrassing! After the second try, I gave up, deciding to mail the postcards later when getting to Texas.

When it rains, it pours. And it was because of my lack of resolve and inability to adjust to the new culture. I had eaten lunch on the plane, but that same evening, because of my excessive self-consciousness, I went to sleep fasting instead of eating at the hotel restaurant. I spent my first night in America in a luxury hotel tossing around in bed and having lots of nightmares.

UNIVERSITY OF TEXAS AT AUSTIN

I arrived in Austin on the afternoon of September 6th and experienced another grave shock of recognition. Before leaving Vietnam, I had thought that all places in America would be on the cold side, just like San Francisco, not realizing that Texas would be so hot. As soon as I walked out of the airport building, I was greeted by a massive heat wave that came upon me from all directions, engulfing me, dazzling my vision. My body evaporated. Streets were empty. American space—cars, homes, office buildings—was entirely insulated, whereas at home, we were exposed to the inclemency of nature, bareheaded and barefooted. Another shocking instance was, contrary to my expectations, nobody met me at the airport. At first, I thought the IIE representative was late, so I just kept waiting for him or her. Still, there was no sign that anybody in Austin knew of my arrival. Fortunately, a young Asian man who was on the plane with me and who knew I was under duress offered to take me to the International Student Office to get help. Mrs. Elizabeth Keed, the Assistant Director, told me she was notified of my being accepted as a graduate student in the American Studies Department but was not asked to provide any assistance upon my arrival. I felt shocked and hurt, not knowing which caused my plight—the IIE that failed to contact the International Office for assistance on my behalf or the International Office that did not heed the IIE request. I felt better when she thumbed the pages of a UT student directory and found the number of a Vietnamese student for me to call. Minutes later, a young man showed up and took me to his apartment. Ziệp and his wife Yến, an attractive, soft-spoken young woman from Huế, invited me to stay overnight at their apartment. In the morning, Ziệp took me to see a group of young Vietnamese students who were kind enough to invite me to stay with them until I found a place to live.

There were about thirty Vietnamese students at UT at the time of my arrival. About half a dozen were officers from the Dalat Military Academy. They were graduate students on USAID scholarships. The group I was staying with were engineering and business majors and were on student visas. Though I was much older than they were, they quickly took me into their circle, treating me like their big brother.

Due to my late arrival, I was one week behind schedule. Something hilarious happened before I went to see my academic advisor. Because I left my luggage at Ziệp and Yến's apartment and the people I was staying with slept late, I had to borrow a shirt from someone whose owner happened to be big and short in stature. Because I was small but taller than that person, his shirt was too large and too short for me! Yet, I still went to see my academic advisor in that funny-looking shirt, wondering if he noticed it.

Dr. Robert Crunden saw me in his spacious office which looked like the library of my English department at home. He was a well-known scholar with numerous publications in the field of U.S. intellectual history. I later discovered that all my professors here were of Dr. Crunden's caliber and that they all cared for professionalism and scholarship. My first encounter with Dr. Crunden made me worry about my inadequate preparation for graduate study, but it planted a seed of scholarly curiosity which was to shape my future academic career in America.

Compassionate but blunt, Dr. Crunden asked me some very candid questions about my academic background and interests. When I told him Jack London was my favorite author, he wittily remarked: "But only high school kids read him today!" I did not know if it was because of my dumb response or because of the Fulbright Program's request that I would be allowed to take only general courses in American culture (might the U.S. government have brought me here for "indoctrination," as one of my classmates later suggested?) Dr. Crunden recommended only courses in American culture and U.S. diplomatic history, not even one in American literature, which was my favorite subject. I made a deal with Crunden, successfully persuading him to let me have half of the course load in literature and half in history, telling him that if I had trouble with literature, I would be happy to concentrate on history during the rest of my study program.

It was the roughest time I had ever had in my college life. Arriving one week late because of a visa problem, I was lost in classes that had already covered so much material in a language I did not feel comfortable with. I sat tongue-tied and ashamed through discussion sessions that spiritedly engaged everybody. In the undergraduate course "Main Currents in American Culture" that Crunden had me take as a refresher, I could hide myself in the back because it was a big class and participation was not required. Graduate courses, however, were my worst nightmare because students, not the professor, conducted the class. I cringed when it was my turn to do a presentation and afterward answer questions from class members. They must have seen me in pain, because occasionally they—especially the women—cast a sympathetic and tender glance at me. Deborah, who later became a good friend, during a break invited me for a cup of coffee, obviously out of compassion for my plight. She had to repeat her invitation because I did not understand her at first. Naturally, I should not blame her Texas twang for my problem!

During the first few weeks, continued stress over school coupled with homesickness left me demoralized. A few times, I thought about quitting and returning to Vietnam. When I was in such low spirits, Nga's first letter arrived and turned things around for me. She shared with me lots of good news: everyone at home was well, our eight-year-old Hùng was now a Boy Scout, and most importantly, Nga's health was good and her pregnancy normal. Though she said she was lonesome and missed me very much, she encouraged me to stay on to complete my study program. Uplifted by great news from home, I went back to work with great resolve and exhilaration. I did not want to let my family down, nor did I want to disgrace myself by giving up. I wanted to swim, *not* to sink.

By borrowing lecture notes from my classmates and meeting with my professors during their office hours, a thing that did not exist in the Vietnamese system, I began to understand their lectures. My solid knowledge of English grammar and style was also a big help. But what made me successful in writing essays was my reasoning ability—the *esprit cartésien*—which I owed a great deal to my father's tutoring me in French.

I survived my first semester, doing better in literature—the subject I planned to teach when returning to Vietnam—than in history in which I had little interest. Dr. Crunden now permitted me to concentrate on U.S. literature as my major field of study.

I adjusted better to American campus life, getting used to American food and starting to make friends with American students. I tried as much as I could to get to know America by keeping a journal in which I recorded my observations and impressions of its culture and people and planned to use them for my teaching when I return to Vietnam. America was not only important to us because, tragically, it was involved in our destiny, but it fascinated me just as it had fascinated famous French authors who had written about it like Alexis de Tocqueville, Jean-Paul Sartre, and Simone de Beauvoir. Like these writers, I wanted to write a book about it. My book should be very interesting from a Vietnamese perspective because of my unique experience of living and studying in America.

AMERICA DAY BY DAY

October 15th, 1972

I start my journal with some bad news from home. I already had an inkling of it shortly before I left Vietnam but didn't realize it would happen that soon. Today, I received a letter from Nga in which she tells me that my university at home has taken me off its payroll. I'm shocked, saddened, angry, and extremely disappointed. I was sent here with the understanding that my wife would be allowed to receive my salary on my behalf. If my family did not get my salary, how could I support them when I barely live with a monthly stipend of $300? I presume my university's new provost must have given that order, but have no idea why he did that. Perhaps, like some colleagues at my School of Education, he was jealous of what they called my "good fortune."

I immediately send Nga a telegram, telling her not to worry and everything will fall into place for us. I advise her to see President Châu and explain to him our situation. A week later, I have great news: my name is back on the payroll! Nga tells me that Dr. Châu is a kind man. He assures her that the university will do whatever it can to help my family so I can concentrate on my studies.

The recent incident teaches me a lesson. It makes me rethink what I had planned to do when I return with my doctoral degree: Never challenge people like the provost, but live in humility. If you still want to make any reform, work with those who have the power to protect you. Suddenly, my father's advice comes to mind: "A fearful bird has a better chance to evade its hunter than a bold one. Foolhardiness could cost you your job, your future, even your life!"

***

Thanksgiving 1972

Through the University of Texas International Office, the Clarks, a couple living in southwest Austin, expresses their wish to be my host family. Today, they take me to their home for Thanksgiving. Dick works for the city of Austin and his wife Shirley is a homemaker. This is the first time I have visited an American family. I am touched by their hospitality that I find not only generous but genuine. Though they are rich—most Americans are—they are very humble. They thank me for the privilege of being my host family. They also ask me to call them by their first name. Since Shirley isn't working and I don't have a car, she offers to drive me to the grocery store and wherever I want to go. She encourages me to call her any time if I need help. The kindness Dick and Shirley show me is natural with them, with Americans. Just a few weeks ago, Deborah in my U.S. Literature class invited me to her home for dinner. Both she and her husband comforted me when learning about my condition as an older married foreign student. Compassion and generosity are spontaneous and natural with Americans because it's rooted in Christian culture and stems from their desire to share part of their fortune that they see as divine favors—enduring peace, unrestricted personal freedom, the bounty of the land. I can't help thinking about my unfortunate family and people and our war-torn, poverty-stricken Vietnam when seeing my host family enjoy, as they say, "God's grace," reserved only for the American people. God's grace is reserved for me too, as I'm now in America, eating good food, not being roused at night from sleep by mortar attacks like my loved ones at home. Suddenly, I'm overcome by remorse and sorrow and want to go back to my room to cry a little.

***

November 28th

My first semester is over. As things have gradually calmed down, I begin to observe what goes on around me. In addition to those who occasionally cast on me their sympathetic look, there are some who seem amused, even contemptuous, to see an older than average student from Vietnam in an American Studies class. My being here from a country where the war has cost America some 56,000 lives must be the reason why they raise their eyebrows. There is a streak of amused disdain on the face of a colleague when I tell him my program sponsor wants me to study U.S. diplomatic history. Later, when he knows me better, he confesses he had thought I was here for "American indoctrination."

American government officials serving in Vietnam don't represent the American public here. Americans, especially intellectuals and students, see the U.S. military involvement in Vietnam as an act of aggression against the Vietnamese people. Somehow, the government of South Vietnam has failed to educate the American public about its country's need for American assistance in fighting communist aggression. The U.S. recklessly goes beyond its role as an ally by conducting the war as if it were the American war without taking into consideration its political consequences. The indiscriminate napalming of villages suspected to be VC hideouts and the terrifying B-52 bombing campaign expanded to North Vietnam, for example, shock the American people's and the world's conscience, providing legitimacy for Hồ's so-called resistance to the "U.S. aggression" and "liberation of the South." Furthermore, the American public has gotten tired of supporting a war too expensive in terms of human and physical resources.

I arrive in America at a time when the U.S. government has already heeded public opinion by disengaging itself from its previous commitment to its former ally. The U.S. has completely pulled out its troops. It also cuts back its military aid to South Vietnam. The Paris Conference, which is to decide South Vietnam's fate, is in the making. The dice is cast. Something—partition again or even the North's complete takeover—is going to happen because we have easy access to the latest news here, only I don't know when. Would I have enough time to complete my studies and go home before it happens? What would happen to me if I could not make it? Suddenly, I feel the futility and irony of coming here, to quote again a friend's amused observation, for "American indoctrination." Is it still important when the U.S. has bowed out of its commitment to helping South Vietnam defend itself against the communists? When we get to know each other better and become good friends, his criticism couldn't be more to the point: "Buddy, I think you must be insane to leave your family in harm's way to come here to study American studies—a subject that has no value at all for a foreigner in your condition!"

***

December 1st

My moody thinking of the worst thing that might happen arises when I watch the news about Vietnam. Because to most South Vietnamese, the fate of South Vietnam is in the hands of the United States, you can guess what is going to happen by just hearing what reporters and journalists are saying here. The Nixon administration has washed its hands of the Vietnam business with its Vietnamization policy and substantial reduction of military and economic aid to the Thiệu government. Something ominous is in the air that my fellow students in Austin and I can easily feel as we are deeply concerned about our family's safety at home. Could I return home before the worst happens or would I get stranded here and never see my family again? Is the worst thing I always feared when I was at home going to happen that soon, when I'm only three months into my study program?

***

December 5th

I'm overwhelmed today by what I get from home: a long letter from Nga, a short but carefully crafted note from my eight-year-old son, and a newsletter from my university. Nothing but good news! Nga writes me regularly despite her late pregnancy, her full-time teaching, and her taking care of the family, among other things. But this is the first time she writes me at length and so assuredly, as if she knew of the tough time I'm experiencing and wanted to lift my spirits. "*Mình ơi,*" she always begins her letter with this affectionate greeting every time she wrote me when I was in Saigon. "I'm taking advantage of my little free time after the children have been in bed to write you. Please don't worry about us, darling," she pleads. "Father and I are well. Our little ones *eat and play fine*" (Nga's special expression used to refer to the children's being in good health). Next, she gives me nothing but good news: everybody at her new school she was recently transferred to treats her very well, she can walk to work because the school is close to home, and, most important, the NVA pressure seems to be off as there are no more mortar attacks at night. Nga's chatty letter reminds me of the short but pleasant peacetime the South enjoyed after we got married and after the birth of our first child. Before I was transferred back to Huế from Saigon, she used to write me in this chatty voice to tell me how my father and our baby were doing at home. Though I know Huế's security as she reports is her wishful thinking, I cling to it to live. I know it makes little sense to hang on to a flimsy hope to live, but in a war-torn country where what we hold as valuable suddenly becomes valueless, where we are denied the right to organize our life the way we would wish, then we can say what Americans find unacceptable, such as wishful thinking, make-believe, and deception that we Vietnamese often see as positive assurance.

The good news in Nga's letter allows me to concentrate better on my study. It's little Hùng's message that drives away my despondency and revitalizes me. On a separate envelope he might have created from a notebook page and carefully sealed, Hùng puts in print "Top Secret: To be opened and read by Pa only." This is his "Top Secret": *"Please send me as soon as possible a new fountain pen. I've broken my old one. I also need crayons to draw with. Also, don't forget to send home toys for my brothers."* His request makes me cry. It justifies my coming here because of the simple things—a fountain pen, crayons, toys—that most children of middle-class families in our city take for granted but that obviously are not accessible to our little ones; it tells me how important it is, as my eight-year-old puts it, to *"finish your studies as quickly as possible and come home."* I feel particularly encouraged by the kid's "candid" description of the festive atmosphere that permeates the city before this year's Tết. *"Everywhere in Huế people are preparing for Tết, Pa,"* he writes.

"There are a lot of decorations at my school. There are also free movies. My brothers Mạnh and Long enjoy the movies very much. I help the school sell lottery tickets. The proceeds go to annual funds to support our soldiers in the front." It sounds like nothing grave is happening. Maybe American reporters and journalists are making up stories about communism winning. Regardless, I must grasp the flimsiest hope I derive from my son's candid but naïve report that everything will be all right until I finish my studies and go home. I must not let my family down.

To top it off, I received a newsletter from my university with a short article about my attending the "University of Texas in America" [sic] on a Fulbright scholarship, along with an extracted line from my private correspondence with the president: "I'm doing well in all my classes and expect to complete my degree program sooner than scheduled." The idea that everybody at home must have seen my story and that my family is proud of me puts me in a euphoric mood, dispels my anxiety, and revitalizes me.

I feel much better now. Further, I continue keeping my journal with entries on America as I see it every day, trying to emulate Simone de Beauvoir's technique in her *America Day by Day*. I still want to turn my diary into a book and publish it in English when I return to Vietnam.

***

December 10th-15th

I find a room for rent in an ad in the *Daily Texan* and go to see the landlady today. Located on 32nd Street, it's about a 15 minute walk to campus and on a UT bus line. Mrs. Onstot, the landlady, is a heavyset woman in her sixties. She makes me go through a list of questions about my age, marital status, national origin, and study major. Then she sets tenant rules for me, such as no consumption of food and beverage in the room, no visit from female friends. I accept all the requirements and move in the same day.

Mrs. Onstot acts like a mother figure to me. Seeing that I'm skinny, she urges me to eat more and even allows me to cook breakfast in her kitchen. She makes me keep her posted of my family news, reminding me to write home regularly. She's extremely strict, insisting that I address her as Mrs. Onstot, whereas her husband, a skinny, soft-spoken, friendly man in his seventies, wants me to call him by his first name, Howard. I get along with the Onstots well and like living here because the rent is reasonable, except that Mrs. Onstot enforces her rules very strictly, sometimes even interfering in my privacy. For example, every time I come home late at night, most often from the library, she asks where I was. I can't put up with her anymore and want to move out immediately when I have a chance. One day, on my return from school, she tells me I have a phone message from a girl. Despite my explaining to her that it is Yến, Ziệp's wife, who invited me to their apartment for dinner, Mrs. Onstot scolds me for not being a faithful husband by knowing another woman. I know Mrs. Onstot wants to protect my family but find her too intrusive and annoying. Enough is enough. I must get out of here as soon as I can.

***

December 16th

I'm lucky to find a room in a house on Jacinto Street. Two graduate students placed an ad at UT Student Union looking for someone to share the house. The rent is a bit higher than what Mrs. Onstot charged me, but it's only ten minutes from campus and there are no house rules to follow, so I move in immediately.

I begin to enjoy living and going to school in the States. It's fun to be a student again, though I'm older than most classmates. The liberal, relaxed atmosphere of the American campus rejuvenates me, making me feel younger, full of exuberance and energy. I still miss my family very much, but the thought of making them proud of me when I get my degree and go home convinces me that the sacrifice they are making will pay off. I have Mike, my housemate, a good photographer, take a picture of me on my way back from school with my backpack of books on my back and with an air of self-conceit on my face. I then write this line of dedication on the back of the photo before mailing it home: "*To Pa's little loved ones: This is Pa on his way back from the University of Texas at Austin! Pa misses and loves you all.*"

I concentrate better on my studies every day. When I have time, I also jot down my observations and thoughts about America. I treat my journal like a travelogue—the more I witness or experience, the better for my writing. For this reason, though Mike and Tom often entertain female visitors in the house, they don't bother me much. Here is my entry on Mike and Tom and my classmates:

***

December 17th

It seems to me that except Mrs. Onstot, a southern lady of the old generation, who's kind but strict, young Americans are very morally relaxed. Sex, for example, a taboo for Vietnamese young men and women before marriage, is a natural way of life I observe in my roommates and other students living in the Laos House on Jacinto Street. They live together like man and wife, but nobody bothers to know about them. They adopt a lifestyle marked by unaffected naturalness and simplicity. Free from the restraint of decorum and etiquette, they dress very informally—usually an old tee shirt, shorts, or a pair of blue jeans are what they need—when they go out. Even professors come to their classes in blue jeans! I can't help thinking of our dress code at home—a three-piece suit for professors, white shirt and gray slacks for male students (for teaching assistants like us, a dark or blue tie is an additional requirement) and a white *ao dai* and pants for co-eds. Living in a Confucian culture that stresses the importance of maintaining propriety in public, the Vietnamese always dress formally when going out on most occasions. They are also expected—though less often nowadays than in pre-industrial Vietnam—to adhere to a specific dress code as a mark of social distinction.

Here in America, as I observe in my classes, the Asian—and European—concept that familiarity breeds contempt doesn't exist. In one of my classes I hear a co-ed address Dr. Crunden by his first name, and yet she doesn't step out of her bounds as a student, nor does he appear to get offended by what in my culture would be tantamount to loss of face. (I was shocked when I first heard a classmate in a conversation mention a professor's name without his title. In my culture, even if we don't like a professor, we wouldn't refer to him or her improperly even in his or her absence, thus Mr. A. or Mrs. B rather than his or her bland name).

American democracy is characterized by the fact that everybody is entitled to power and what it entails, like wealth and prestige, if they have the ability and determination to attain it. U.S. history abounds in stories of heroes and self-made men who proceeded from rags to wealth like Franklin, Ford, and Rockefeller. Because in America, power is vested in the institution that Americans believe can protect their rights, not in the people who represent it, no one can use the power he or she is temporarily granted to oppress others. This perhaps explains why Americans show little respect for those holding power while zealously committing themselves to protecting their social, political, and religious system. I can't help thinking of Asian rulers who a century ago had their entire nation and people at their disposition. Just a decade ago, Ngô Đình Cẩn, Diệm's brother and the self-claimed lord of Vietnam's Central Region, exercised a similar feudal authority. It was rumored that members of Diệm's cabinet kowtowed to Cẩn when they were admitted for an audience with him, and that they stepped backward all the way to the door without turning around when they left. Such a display of obsequiousness is a course of action usually taken by cowards who wish to kiss the dust off their master's feet to court his favor, but who will soon betray him when they can. Diệm and Cẩn were killed by the people who had served under them.

***

December 20th

My grades for the first semester are posted today. I did well in literature and in American studies except in Professor Elspeth Rostow's class, "Heroes and Anti-Heroes in America." There is too much history stuff in this course, and history is not my strength. I need to ask Dr. Crunden to allow me to take more courses in American literature and culture which I plan to teach when I return home. There is not much time left before I complete my program. I hope Crunden will agree with me.

Now that things have settled down and I have become familiar with graduate study in America, I want to jot down some reflections on my educational experience, particularly graduate study, for my future memoir. I think it will benefit my students and colleagues in Vietnam, who might be sent to the U.S. for graduate study.

Most graduate classes are seminars. At the start of the semester, the professor hands out a syllabus with a detailed course description, required reading, and assignments. Students are required to read and do oral reports on several books on a topic listed in the syllabus. The professor doesn't lecture but acts only as a facilitator. The seminar format is designed to get all the class involved and to discourage dependence on the professor. Topics under study are covered thoroughly through presentations, discussions, questions, and comments. There's no exam, but we are expected to demonstrate our knowledge of the study materials in 3-4 papers and a research project. Independent study, which requires a lot of reading and research, is a must for students when writing a paper. In short, scholarship, a term unfamiliar to us at home, is what graduate students are expected to demonstrate before they're qualified to do doctoral work.

***

December 23rd

This year, Dick and Shirley go home in Massachusetts for Christmas. With students gone home for the holidays, the city looks almost deserted. Homesickness and loneliness return to me, now that young men and women full of energy and always on the go are gone. They are not my people, but I suddenly feel that they are important to me. They "keep" me busy, leaving me little time to think of my family.

I visit my Vietnamese friends and we spend time cooking and eating together. There are no more than twenty of us at UT, so we are very close to each other. Not having eaten Vietnamese food for quite a while, I enjoy very much the delicious meals prepared by the girls in our group. We have much in common—homesickness, concern about the worsening of the military situation at home, and the desire to finish our studies as quickly as possible to return home to our family.

Now that I know my fellow people better, I'm saddened to hear their stories. Loneliness and love bring some couples together and, like Americans, they end up living like man and wife. This is forbidden in Vietnamese culture which requires not only prior approval from parents on both sides but compatibility in the financial and social status of the couple's family. They're in a Catch-22 situation. Holding student visas, they can't stay permanently in the U.S. But would their parents accept their living partner when they return to Vietnam? Because in Vietnamese society, cohabitating before marriage is considered a disgrace, especially to the woman's family, chances are she will have difficulty getting her parents' approval.

Young women who have children born out of wedlock and who now want to leave their live-in partner have more serious problems. Mai, an undergraduate student at UT, tells me she wants to separate from Phát with whom she has a child. But in tears, she says that she didn't get her parents' consent. To them, living together out of wedlock is fine, but living as a single mother, that is, having children but no husband, is unacceptable in Vietnamese society.

Traditional culture has an important influence on Vietnamese at home and abroad alike. In the 1970s, there're still numerous moral tenets that they, especially women, are expected to comply with. An ideal woman must be a virgin before marriage, and after she becomes a wife, chastity is her new identity. Sexual freedom is taboo for "good" Vietnamese women.

Because of the presence of American GIs in Vietnamese society, purists at home, in their desperate attempt to protect their traditional culture, redefined sexual morality, making it stricter, by condemning—more so in private than in public—women who are married to Americans. Echoing the derogatory public view in the early 20th century of women married to French men as "*Me Tây*" (Frenchmen's wives), they call them "*Me Mỹ*" (American men's wives). A friend, a graduate student in Ohio, tells me that her parents are still objecting to her marrying her American lover, a medical doctor, whom she met in Vietnam. Though my friend's sweetheart has recently survived her parents' thorough investigation which shows that he never married before and that she would never be his "second wife," her hope for a union with him is still remote, she says.

I have mentioned Mai as a victim of traditional culture which sanctions sexual freedom for Vietnamese women. Because Mai is expected to uphold the Confucian concept of female chastity under any circumstances, she's barred from seeking a divorce from Phát. Phát, it seems to me, is a good husband who loves Mai and their child, and I suspect Mai wouldn't want to leave him except for causes of an extremely intimate nature that only my two young friends know. There's another couple whose marriage is considered over, but both the man and the woman cling to it. Hồng, an attractive young woman and a graduate student at UT Department of Education, met and married Fred, an American citizen, with their parents' consent. The young couple enjoyed their happy marriage for about a year. Suddenly, their union takes a bad turn. Fred comes home very late on weekends on the pretext that he works on a group project. This goes on for another while and finally, somebody tells Hồng that he has seen Fred visit a bar on Congress Avenue where gay men meet. When confronted by Hồng, Fred admits he's gay, but since he loves her, he can't leave her. Hồng also finds herself in a similar Catch-22 situation. Young, attractive, and being a U.S. citizen who isn't bound by Vietnamese law, she tells me she has thought about divorcing Fred. But because she's a Catholic and a Vietnamese woman, leaving her husband is out of the question, at least for now.

***

Christmas 1972

With everybody gone for the holiday, I'm the only one who stays in the house. Americans celebrate Christmas in their homes, whereas Noël is a public event in Vietnam. Austin is empty, while in Saigon on this day, all the streets must be thronged with people. Because Vietnamese Catholics are few and don't have their own church here, they attend Midnight Mass at a local Catholic church, which is held inside, not in the open as at home. Last night, I went to church at Hồng's invitation, and I really miss that ceremony at my Catholic school in Đồng Hới. I also miss my family. This year is my first Christmas away from home. Hồng also shares with me her homesickness which she says is greater than mine because she can't go home anymore. I feel sorry for her, but suddenly an eerie feeling of loss and sorrow and emptiness greater than homesickness rises in me. I don't know what it forebodes. I still have three more semesters to go before I finish my study. Time goes by so slowly. I've been here for only three months and yet it feels like ages!

***

January 6th

I stop by the American Studies Department today to check my mail. There's no news from home. But I find birthday cards from Professor Rostow, Deborah Mills (who invited me to a cup of coffee when seeing how distressed I looked on my first day of class), the American Studies Graduate Program, and Julie Hale, the department's graduate secretary. I'm shocked and then feel overwhelmed. I didn't know that today was my birthday. Before coming to America, I had never celebrated my birthday! I had been through so much since I was a child that I didn't remember my birthday, nor did I see it as an important date worth celebrating. The kindness and thoughtfulness extended to me by Mrs. Rostow and my new American friends touches my heart. It's a nice American custom that shows people who know you remember and respect you, and care about you. I'm grateful to these Americans who make me feel important. Except for my family, nobody in my country has made me feel special!

I'm going to a restaurant this evening to have a good dinner to celebrate my own birthday! I don't know if I will enjoy it or not when my loved ones are not here with me.

***

January 7th-8th, 1973

St. Jean de Crèvecœur observes that early American settlers were "ferocious, gloomy, and unsociable" because they lived on hunting and had to defend their property against wild animals and intruders. Part of their character was passed on to Americans today who place such a high premium on their privacy and personal freedom. In their early years, children already exercise their right to organize their life without parental interference. When visiting my friend Jeff at his home the other day, I was amazed to hear his six-year-old son Jason tell me his interests and career goals in such a serious and confident manner. He expressed himself assertively, using phrases like "I want" and "I don't want." I can't help thinking of Vietnamese children, my eight-year-old son included, who are closely watched for any deviance from proper rules of conduct, who are taught to take orders rather than to freely speak their minds. Granted, it's not wise for American parents to treat their kids like adults when they are not mature enough to exercise their freedom in a responsible way, but the other extreme approach to child rearing at home surely hampers the development of our children's personality and character.

American kids, as I observe in Jason, are brash and a little aggressive, probably because they are overconfident. But they are sincere, friendly, and sociable. It's easy to strike up a conversation and make friends with them. It's even easier to gain their confidence if they find you honest and trustworthy. American adults, by contrast, tend to be cautious, reserved, and withdrawn. An American home is an islet, its owner rarely seen outside except when mowing or watering the lawn. He's nice to his neighbor but minds his own business and loathes any attempt to interfere in his private life by strangers.

I don't mean that Americans resent social gatherings and public events. Throwing and attending parties is an American custom, but at the parties I attend here, there isn't the kind of enthusiasm and excitement you would find in Vietnamese social gatherings back home. Americans would break into small groups and talk only with those they know well or feel comfortable with. A Vietnamese "party" (I would call it a "gathering" because attendees know one another well and have similar interests), by contrast, is quite an event featuring all sorts of entertainment—music, poetry and prose reading, storytelling—that you can't help getting involved in one way or another. Here we have two cultures diametrically opposed—one asserting the individual's right to be apart from the public and the other stressing the submergence of self in society.

The pursuit of personal freedom and a distinctive identity has a significant impact on the American mind. It makes Americans noncommittal, afraid to involve themselves in others' business for fear of getting in trouble. Minding one's own business, a common way for Americans to enjoy their personal freedom and to protect themselves, makes them appear too "practical" to foreign visitors. They wouldn't hesitate to speak their mind straightforwardly and bluntly, or act in a like manner if their interests were at stake. Asians who first arrive in America are shocked by the paradox of the American character. Americans go out of their way to help stranded immigrants but shrink from getting emotionally entangled with the latter because they fear responsibility. Unlike Vietnamese and other Asians who are caught up in the maze of private and public relations that consumes all their resources and energy, Americans set a limit where the public cannot cross the private and see their obligation to society usually in contractual terms. This is a very practical approach to the problems of life. By keeping the wall that divides oneself and others, as Robert Frost advises in his poem "Mending Wall," one can protect his personal freedom and play it safe. This is American wisdom in action at its best.

***

January 16th-19th

For my course, "U.S. Modern Diplomatic History," taught by Dr. Divine, I do my research paper on Vietnam's relations with the U.S. since 1945.

Though history isn't my interest, this course is fascinating. First, it enlightens me on American scholarship on Vietnam's history. I don't know if Dr. Divine speaks Vietnamese, but his pronunciation of Vietnamese names and his knowledge of Vietnam's modern politics are impeccable. My classmates also demonstrate an excellent grasp of the history of United States-Vietnam relations. They know the subject much better than I do. I'm ashamed that I have underestimated them.

David Bloom, a friend and classmate, suggests that I consult *The Pentagon Papers* for my paper. It's quite a revelation to me. *The Papers* reveals a lot of things about Vietnam after it became independent, about Hồ Chí Minh's desperate attempts to get the U.S. intervention in the Franco-Vietnam conflict and recognition of his new government. From October, 1945 to February, 1946, through the Office of Strategic Services (OSS) channels, Hồ pleaded to Harold Truman to grant Vietnam "the same status as the Philippines." To show his sincerity and serious interest in becoming a U.S. ally, Hồ unconditionally proposed to send a first group of students to America for training. Unfortunately, Hồ's plea and goodwill gesture met with U.S. opposition or indifference because of Truman's suspicion of his communist background. To fight the French who were trying to restore their colonial rule in Vietnam, Hồ turned to the Soviets and the Chinese.

What would have happened had Truman accepted Hồ's request? Could the decade-long Franco-Vietnam war, the French debacle at Điện Biên Phủ, the partition of Vietnam, and the bloodiest Vietnam War leading to the U.S. military intervention have been avoided? Even now nobody can decipher Hồ's intention when he made that plea for help to Truman. The course of history can never be predicted. But some American scholars at the time, *The Papers* reports, criticized the U.S. for failing to recognize in Hồ "a potential Asian Tito." Hồ did say that he was a Marxist, not a communist. In March, 1946, he had accepted France's proposal to maintain a military presence in the Democratic Republic of Vietnam for five years in exchange for its vague promise of a status known as "a free state within the French Union." But instead of giving that status to Hồ, they granted it to Bảo Đại in 1949. The Franco-Việt Minh war broke out after Hồ's negotiations with the French and overtures to the U.S. failed. With American support, critics of American policy argued, "Hồ would have adopted some form of neutrality and maintained the DRV as a natural bulwark against Chinese expansion southward and would have served the larger purposes of American policy in Asia."

But there are numerous lessons about the history of Vietnam that Vietnamese politicians have failed to learn, and consequently they are leading their country to this impasse. Starting in the early 19th century before Western powers initiated their conquests in Asia, Vietnamese emperors had turned their deaf ears to some scholars' plea for modernizing the country, lulling themselves into the fantasy that Confucianism could defeat "White Devils." It turned out that just after a few engagements, Vietnam was quickly subdued by the French expeditionary army and became a French colony for nearly a century. Though the country was proclaimed independent by Hồ Chí Minh in 1945 after Japan's surrender to the Allies, his affiliation with the Soviets and persecution of Vietnamese nationalists who had fought the French alongside him alienated him and weakened the country. The partition of Vietnam in 1954 cast a shadow on the Việt Minh's Điện Biên Phủ victory because, soon afterward, the whole country was plunged into the longest, most brutal war in its history. With the North established as a communist state after 1954, the South became a symbol of hope for all Vietnamese who love freedom. Ngô Đình Diệm received the mandate to lead the South to that goal after his return from the U.S. in 1954. Unfortunately, he was overthrown and murdered in the 1963 military coup. Since then, the South has been going downhill and a possible communist takeover is looming.

The root cause of constant turmoil in the South is the lack of shrewd leadership. The Diệm regime collapsed because Diệm, who had accepted to play the democracy game, didn't stay the course. Though we can understand why he backed off in the middle—an application of unrestricted democracy, according to him, would foil the country's efforts to fight communism—his dropping out of this Western-style democracy game in favor of autocracy brought him to his tragic end. His successors have learned Diệm's lesson and stay safe, but because they are not leaders of his caliber, the war against communism is getting increasingly difficult. Unlike Diệm, who didn't want the U.S. to intervene in the war, South Vietnam after him depends too much on its ally which is seeking to bow out as has been seen here in the U.S. Congress and the ongoing Paris Conference.

***

February 27th-28th

In his famous memoir *Letters from an American Farmer,* written in 1769, St. Jean De Crèvecœur suggests that the first Americans' national identity consists of material welfare. *"Ubi panis ibi patria"* ("Where there is bread, there is one's fatherland)" is the motto of all emigrants, he explains. But to have bread, one has to work. Therefore, the only way to achieve the American dream of material success, as Benjamin Franklin declares in his *Autobiography,* is industry and determination.

No place is like America where labor is elevated to the level of ethics. Being employed is an honorable pursuit that every American strives for. Getting rich—the ideal worker's most desirable goal—earns him high social esteem, regardless of his origin and background. A CBS presentation of the Rockefellers I watched recently teaches me this truth about America—only the rich have the right to do what they please, and the method for gaining this right is hard work and, in the case of these New York titans, big ideas. In Vietnam, by contrast, anyone who proceeds from rags to riches, no matter how smart he is, is called "*trọc phú*," a term disparagingly used to refer to someone who is rich but considered disreputable because of his limited education. In Vietnam, Franklin wouldn't be as much esteemed as he is in America.

Probably because industry is a moral quality, one of Franklin's thirteen personal virtues, the application of it at the expense of one's mental and physical health is often praised. Americans speak of "workaholics" as though they were heroes! Because of my limited experience, I don't see these "heroes" at other places, but at the University of Texas often observe many "workaholics" in action at the Perry-Castaneda Library. They are pale-faced eggheads and graduate students deep in research or study all the time. Their intense devotion to knowledge amazes and intimidates me, a foreign student who is both physically and mentally unprepared for intensive graduate work in a language in which he is not totally at home. I feel sorry for my colleagues and my students at home who can't devote themselves to scholarship despite their great passion for it.

To write the preceding entry, I consult *Webster's Third New International Dictionary* for the term "work." I'm amazed at its numerous meanings depending on the context in which it's used. "Work" is a magic word because its newly formed expressions carry meanings that depart from its original meaning, "the labor, task, or duty that affords one his accustomed means of livelihood." The Vietnamese lexicon also has many terms equivalent to the American English "work," but its range of meanings is much limited. This means the Americans take Franklin's concept of industry seriously, whereas we Asians only look at its face value.

***

March 4th-6th

The idea of fate as something inevitably destined for a person or for a country is alien to Americans. Everything they do goes through a meticulous process and is followed through every step of the way. If it doesn't work, they blame it on human error rather than on the interference of a mysterious force.

The foiled project then is subject to a thorough investigation to determine the cause of its failure. Americans aren't bashful about making public their foibles if doing so keeps them from erring again.

This is my reaction to Professor Elspeth Rostow's lecture on U.S. foreign policy under John F. Kennedy and Lyndon B. Johnson. I'm amazed at the high degree of practicality with which U.S. policymakers develop and implement their plans. In South Vietnam, for example, originally U.S. policy had been designed to contain the influence of the Soviet Union and China, but when its military intervention became too costly, the U.S. reassessed its policy and disengaged itself from its previous commitment.

The Vietnamese mind vastly differs from the American mind. Coming from a culture based on intuition rather than on reasoning, on a strong belief in determinism (because we are defenseless in the face of so many deadly forces, we believe we could escape our fate only through mere luck) rather than in self-determination and careful planning, I'm amazed by the way Americans do their business. Their basic principle of living is based on pragmatism, the official philosophy of America. Founded by William James, pragmatism rejects unproven abstractions, fixed principles, and moral security in favor of the concrete, the factual, and the expedient. A practical mind, as shown in the United States' disengagement from its South Vietnamese ally, can easily solve problems that a befuddled mind bogged down in sentimentalism cannot.

Nevertheless, a culture that sanctions ruthless habits can provide plenty of leeway for people in the field of politics and business enterprise to deviate from James' teaching. Pragmatism as practiced by these Americans, as Henry Steele Commager has lamented, has "watered down to an acquiescence in cash values or a justification of business efficiency, associated with a series of shabby compromises and concessions, translated into a cunning technique for outwitting Providence." Nothing is more appropriate than Commager's accusation in an election year when strategists of both parties meticulously and aggressively develop plans to help their candidates win. By citing statistical evidence and facts (whether these are accurate or not, there is no way for voters to know) about people who run for public office, strategists make their candidates look great and their opponents look bad. For the sake of efficiency, politicians sacrifice the humane part of James' thought. But nowhere is James' philosophy more blatantly abused than in business. Big companies lay off or reduce their employees at the slightest sign of slow business. Hospitals and doctors refuse to treat patients with no health insurance. During the Depression, farmers killed their livestock to boost meat prices. They did it again a few days ago in Wisconsin by slaughtering their calves to raise both meat and milk prices! As pragmatism has lost its idealism, ruthless practicality takes over the American business enterprise.

It's unfortunate that the U.S. government, which is responsible for propagating the ideals professed by the founding fathers and eloquently articulated by John F. Kennedy in his famous 1960 inaugural speech, strictly adheres to the principle of "business efficiency" widely applied in the corporate world. U.S. foreign policy, therefore, boils down to this brutal notion: *whatever works is not necessarily moral*. South Vietnam is a case in point. At first, the U.S. was militarily involved because its interests were at stake in Southeast Asia. Should South Vietnam fall, the rest of the free world would follow suit. After Nixon's historic trip to China, which paves the way for Americans to do business with their former foes, the U.S. skillfully works up an exit policy through its so-called Vietnamization of the war with the total withdrawal of its troops and the substantial reduction of military aid to South Vietnam. Further, the U.S. forces Thiệu to sign the Paris Peace Agreements with many concessions to the communist North. The change of the Vietnam War into the *Vietnamese War*, which surely will lead to South Vietnam's ultimate defeat, would disengage America from its commitment to its former ally.

***

March 14th-24th

Religion in America

My host family invites me to go to church with them this Sunday. Shirley tells me her family wants me to participate in activities that are important to them, like going to church and celebrating Thanksgiving and Christmas. I accept their invitation. I want to make the most of my limited stay to get a firsthand experience with America, especially its culture, of which religion is an important part.

There are striking differences between the Catholic Church that I used to attend when I went to Chơn Phước middle school in Đồng Hới and my host family's church, which is Presbyterian. The first difference is the way the liturgy is conducted. Catholics, who are primarily taught that man is depraved and only through God's grace can he be saved, regard praying as the main thing not only at church but at home. At church, Catholic devotees intone word for word their priest's lament of man's sins and begging for God's pardon. The priest's sermon is also a sad litany of confession and supplication that amounts to making the congregation more acutely conscious of their innate depraved condition.

What I saw in a Catholic church's Sunday service back home I don't see in this Protestant church in Austin today. There is a lot of music and singing in praise of God and Christ. Though God's pardon is asked, man's frailty is slightly touched upon. The pastor, a ruddy smiling man with a robust voice in his late forties, delivers an eloquent sermon on man as God's choice to realize His will on earth. To signal that the service is ending, baskets are passed around for church members to contribute donations. The worship ends with a fanfare of trumpets as the congregation, with their faces glowing with joy and pride, gets up and files out of the building.

This may be due to, as suggested above, the character of the modern American mind. Whatever its denomination, the American church does away with the theology of Calvinism that controlled the Puritan mind three centuries ago to be in tune with the optimistic and pragmatic mood of modern America. American Christians now go to church not to hear preachers shout jeremiads about Doomsday or to beat their chests for unpardonable sins, but to celebrate their good life and to thank God for being Americans. In the 1970s, such a need is not merely addressed at a local church on Sunday or through personal and family visitation programs. One can tune in anytime to the radio for the teachings of Christ. Through the newly developed cable and satellite TV network, and particularly Billy Graham's "crusade for a wholly Christian empire," the Christian gospel is made accessible to all Americans and the world. The church also makes huge investments in educational and healthcare areas. Today, the names of such famous church-affiliated schools as Harvard and Princeton, and first-rate hospitals operating under the auspices of the Methodist, Presbyterian, and Lutheran churches, are all too familiar to every American. The services provided at these facilities are excellent but extremely expensive.

The distinction of church from state is the chief trait of the American democratic tradition. The Puritans who arrived in 1620 didn't want to establish in the new land the same autocratic system the Church of England had imposed on them. The founding fathers also saw to it that the church be vested with no political power in the U.S. Constitution. But in this century the church, which has become a major part of corporate America, is powerful enough to force the government to listen to its voice. Not only does the church have its authority on social and religious issues such as abortion, gay marriage, the Pledge of Allegiance, and school prayer, it can sway an important national election. Candidates for some public offices must have the endorsement of the church or church-related organizations whose interests they are expected to serve faithfully if they are to win.

While the church's departure from its purely religious goals is lamentable here, it helps to uphold the image of America abroad. For example, American missionaries who went to China before the communist takeover, besides teaching the gospel, operated dispensaries, taught school, did charity work, and even worked and lived with Chinese peasants. These men and women were living examples of Christian ideals in action—poverty, humility, compassion—which are hard to find in modern America. Pearl Buck's novel *The Good Earth*, for example, which describes the lives of these people, isn't entirely a work of fiction. It mostly deals with the writer's parents who were based in a rural area of Anhui where Buck herself grew up and attended school along with poor Chinese children. In Vietnam, Americans do their missionary work in the Highlands where the Vietcong often show up at night to collect food. My English tutors in Nha Trang are Presbyterian missionaries from Pennsylvania. Finally, the clinic that provides free service for the Vietnamese in Saigon and where I got my free physical exam to complete my application for study in the United States is run by a group of doctors and nurses belonging to the Baptist church. Unlike European missionaries who went to Asia early in the 19th century to prepare for the arrival of their conquering army, American missionaries in Vietnam work hard to win the hearts and minds of many Vietnamese, especially the poor, the underprivileged, and the less educated. To these Vietnamese, Christianity must be good simply because the people who practice it are so good to them.

I should add a few more words about "other" religions to my short presentation of religion in America. In the seventies, with the emergence of numerous ethnic communities, Christianity isn't the religion of every American anymore. The civil rights movement of the early 1960s didn't go away without leaving a deep impact on the way that Black people worship. Rejecting their American identity, many of them claim their African roots and practice Islam. A notable example is the legendary American boxing champion Cassius Marcellus Clay Jr. who changed his name to Mohammad Ali to indicate his adoption of Islam. In literature, LeRoi Jones became Amiri Baraka as a mark of his awareness of his African roots and a new frame of religious reference. As many Americans become alienated from their society, they find in Asian religions and philosophies a source of spiritual comfort. These alternatives to Christianity range from ancient traditions such as Zen Buddhism and Taoism to quasi-religious forms like the Hare Krishna and TM (Transcendental Meditation). They appeal particularly to young Americans who become increasingly dissatisfied with the uniformity and materialism of their culture.

***

My friend Mary Ann Pauken introduces me to Ted, a Vietnam vet, at a party at her house. Ted is jolly with his friends, but his face turns sour when Mary Ann tells him that I am a Fulbright student from South Vietnam. He doesn't bother to hold out his hand to shake mine, but mumbles something then continues chatting with Mary Ann's guests, seemingly trying to ignore me. It's obvious that he is disgusted with me. Embarrassed and hurt, I stay with Mary Ann's group for a few more minutes, then excuse myself.

I learn later about Ted from Mary Ann. He was stationed at Phú Bài around 1968 and lost one leg in one of the U.S. Marines' bloodiest battles to recapture Huế. He returned to the U.S. immediately afterward and changed from a happy-go-lucky youth to a sullen, morose, withdrawn man ever since. Mary Ann apologizes to me for his rude manners, saying that she thought Ted would be happy to meet someone from Huế, not realizing that my presence stirred up his memory of his old wound of war.

I begin to understand why some of my classmates seemed hostile to me when they first discovered that I came here on a Fulbright scholarship. It hurts them to see someone who reminds them of the loss of so many lives and resources for a foreign civil war that has nothing to do with their country. Luckily, I'm able to change their perception of me from someone who was sent here "for indoctrination" to a simple kind of student with an appetite for knowledge and scholarship like them!

The war is over for the U.S., but the scar it left on American society is still fresh. The news occasionally covers crippled GI's returning home and suffering what is called "the Vietnam syndrome." Flashbacks of their hellish experience, of their friends brutally and absurdly killed, of harmless peasants and their homes napalmed by U.S. warplanes, drive these vets insane. The war also makes many Americans misunderstand Vietnamese immigrants and students. My American friends' suspicion of me is a case in point. Hồng, who's still living with her gay husband, is also subject to the same sort of prejudice. She says she's very angry when her professor tells his class that Vietnam (he should have said "the Vietnam War," or "the U.S. involvement in Vietnam") is impoverishing America. "He made me mad and ashamed," Hồng cries. "Maybe he didn't know I am from Vietnam, but some people in the class might know who I am because I saw them cast their furtive look at me. I wanted to say something to protest the professor but couldn't open my mouth. How terrible! I wished I hadn't been in that class then."

I try to comfort Hồng by telling her that we're in the same boat, feeling, however, that I'm better off than she is, because I'm going home in December after graduation. As for Hồng, she must stay here to endure people's unjust perception of her native country. Poor Hồng, though she's a U.S. citizen because she's married to an American, she *is* too Vietnamese. She's still living with her gay husband, depressed and lonely, but not assertive enough to leave him.

***

My journal writing gets more irregular, sparse, sometimes interrupted for several days, probably because I need to focus on my study. But the main reason is that I'm losing interest in writing about America. It isn't worth doing something that you know would bear no fruit. Who at home would care to read your book when everybody is preparing for the worst, when they see no advantage in learning about America? De Tocqueville and Simone de Beauvoir were lucky enough to have an audience that shared with them the same culture and was their most trusted ally in the two world wars. I wouldn't have that sort of audience. Because of my American training, people at home will look at me with suspicion and contempt and will not bother to read my book. And, God forbid, should the North succeed in taking over the South, the book would be seen as added evidence of my collaboration with "the U.S. imperialists," let alone my American studies background, which the communist government would readily tie to part of CIA training.

I receive today, April 20th, Nga's letter, dated March 30th, which says our baby (it will be a boy, according to my father's traditional diagnosis) is due in a month. Because it usually takes two weeks for the mail to get here, his birth is expected any time and I'm waiting for a telegram from home to confirm it. For two months now, so much has preoccupied my mind—school, thesis research, worrying about my future when I return home—that I find no time to think of the family. There were moments when even the thought that Nga is expecting a baby didn't cross my mind.

I'm worried about Nga and the baby because there is no update on their condition since her most recent letter. This is the third time she "crosses the ocean" without me. What has driven me to this situation is because I wanted to come here to pursue my foolish dream of becoming a scholar. It frightens me to imagine what might happen to Nga when everybody knows that going into labor is a woman's riskiest thing, especially when no relatives are around. My guts feel like burning. I can't concentrate on my studies, anxious to receive the coming telegram and yet afraid to see it because you never know, it could bring bad news. Unable to wait any longer, today (May 2nd) I send a cable to Nga's sister in Saigon. Except for Nga, there is no dependable adult at home who can go to the post office in Huế to send me a reply. Besides, I fear that a cable from me would worry them, especially my father. I don't know if communicating with Nga's sister rather than directly with my family is wise, but the truth is I only want to hear the *good* news! Or, God forbid, if it is the bad news, then it should be delayed until I am ready for it—I know I will never be—or the news would be conveyed by a close relative who can comfort me. I imagine it's hard for Americans to understand this type of thinking, but people of my generation and older who have witnessed all the turbulence of our country's history and who have little or no control of their lives would act in a similar way. Because we're helpless, we rely heavily on chance or act recklessly as I did by abandoning my family at home to come here. There is no one to blame but myself for coming to this dreadful predicament.

On my way to the post office, I stop by the American Studies Department's office to pick up my assignments when Willa Beach, the Department's secretary, tells me she has a telegram for me. My heart beats wildly. I know immediately that it must be from home, but have no idea who sent it. It couldn't be Nga because she would have used my street address. When Willa hands the cable to me, she knows what it's about because I've told her all my story. She turns away when she sees me so shaken when I read the cable. She only turns back and asks, "How's home?" when I regain my composure. "My wife and the baby are okay," I beam. Instantly, Willa throws her arms around me and gives me a big hug. That's the best news I've ever received since my coming to the United States!

In her telegram, *chị* Thúy says that she was in Huế when the baby was born, which means Nga was taken care of very carefully because Nga's older sister is an RN. What a great relief! Now that all my worries are gone, I can concentrate on my study. With a thesis halfway finished and two more classes to take, I'm expected to get my MA this summer. Then I will be home with my family!

But my life's trajectory isn't always a smooth one. Its many twists and turns have become a familiar pattern since my coming of age. No matter how much I've tried to organize my future in my own way, a certain sort of chance always interferes with the course of my life and career, acting like fate by forcing me to face—but often accept—its ironic verdict. For example, I never wanted to be a teacher because speaking to a crowd scared me to death, but still I ended up teaching in high school and here I'm training again to become a college instructor. The Fulbright scholarship arrived at the wrong time (my family desperately needed me home), and yet I couldn't turn it down. Though in principle, I was free to weigh the pros and cons, my decision was hasty rather than through exhaustive reasoning. As a rule, I had no way to predict the outcome of the course of action I had chosen.

After the Paris Peace Conference in February 1973, there is a lull in fighting in the South that some people naively interpret as the weakening of the Vietcong and North Vietnamese forces. I accept this line of reasoning too, but more out of a desire to fool myself than out of conviction. Owing to their easy access to accurate information, most Vietnamese who live in America are convinced that the Paris Peace Accords gives the Vietcong an edge by allowing them to stay in the South so they can prepare for another major offensive in a near future. While we believe this will happen, we don't give much attention to it, or rather we act like ostriches which bury their heads in the sand, pretending everything is fine, because we don't want to face the ugly reality. We see peace, no matter how temporary or false it is, as a great relief from the misery that's past endurance. Many people at home celebrate the transient truce as permanent peace though they are aware of its illogic and irony. The war has been so long and costly that we accept peace at all costs. We even celebrate it. Trịnh Công Sơn, who enjoys great popularity among many young people and students in his recent songs, not only hails the end of war, but fantasizes a journey he's making through a newly reunified Vietnam, without being harassed by police. Victim of my own naiveté, I committed a grave blunder for which I'm not going to forgive myself as long as I live.

I go to see Dr. Crunden today (August 28th, 1973) to hand him my completed MA thesis and ask him to write for me a recommendation for a travel grant. I have three months before the scholarship expires, so I want to travel for a few weeks to see America as much as I can, then return to Austin to spend Thanksgiving with Mary Ann and her family before going home in December. Dr. Crunden praises my idea, saying that it's important for me to reinforce my knowledge of America through books with my first-hand observations of the country. Before I leave his office, he says something that's destined to change the course of my future: "I see that you've completed your study sooner than scheduled. Have you ever thought about requesting an extension of your stay for a Ph.D.?" Seeing that I'm caught off guard by what he says, my advisor puts me at ease. "You only need to stay for another year to complete the course work, and then you can go home to write your dissertation."

The idea of staying for further study never crossed my mind before. I only wanted to finish my master's degree as soon as possible and return home because I didn't want to leave my family in harm's way. I left Vietnam when the summer 1972 offensive was still raging with the fall of the old citadel of Quảng Trị and the Vietcong's ambush of fleeing civilians on Highway 1. Although Huế is now well protected by the elite RVN 1st Division, its people are still haunted by the specter of the Tết offensive. My two semesters and one summer here have been very pleasant but too long for me. I can't wait to get on the plane and go home after I officially receive my M.A.

Dr. Crunden's offer comes at a time when I'm preparing to return home, so it troubles me quite a bit. Suddenly, I find myself in a Catch-22: to stay or not to stay. To stay wouldn't be a big problem. Dr. Châu, my university's president, has always supported my academic endeavors, and I'm sure he wouldn't mind having another Ph.D. for his institution by granting me another year's sabbatical leave in the United States. The State Department, though maintaining its one-degree policy for all Vietnamese scholarship grantees, would consider my application for scholarship renewal favorably because I have Dr. Crunden's endorsement and because they have my family as "hostages" in Vietnam. The chief issue is my family. If I tell them of my intent this time, they will concur with me, but I don't want to fool them again. They have already suffered too much because of me, and I have no right to make them suffer anymore.

But the idea of staying one more year appeals to me as well. One more year won't be a long time; I will be halfway through my Ph.D. program, my career prospects will be brighter, my family will have a better future, etc. Also, as things stand now, the worst-case scenario would be a neutralization of the South, not an entire communist takeover. For fear of losing face, the Americans will *not* let this happen. My family will be safe, at least until I return.

Swept by a strong wave of euphoria, I find the idea of seeking an extended stay instead of going home immediately irresistible. I don't bother to consider possible adverse consequences should something happen to my family at home. I go to see Hồng to seek her advice. "You must not pass up this once-in-a-lifetime opportunity," she beams. "I'm sure your family will be able to bear another year." Then she says something that moves me to tears: "I have $3,000 in my savings. You can use it for your expenses now and pay it back to me later when you get your scholarship." What a friend! She must realize that it's very important for me to stay, so she offers to let me have all the fortune she has saved for my education.

I write home to tell my family of the possible opportunity, explaining its benefits and seeking their opinion. Since I have shortened my original study program to one year, I only need another year to complete my Ph.D. coursework before returning home to be with my family and work on my dissertation.

I also write Dr. Châu and solicit his endorsement. Two weeks later, I receive a reply from home. Everybody supports my new move. The application process starts in no time. Within a month, I get word from the IIE, the scholarship agency which represents the State Department, that I've been approved for doctoral study at the University of Texas. Things have things developed so rapidly, so aggressively, that I'm left with no choice but to follow their direction. Can it be an intervention of fate? It can't be, to be sure. Fate is usually blamed for a tragic, desperate situation one encounters in life. Here, I'm being presented with rosy prospects of a bright academic career when I return home as an ABD (All but Dissertation). People like Mr. Hành will not look down upon me, my colleagues and students will treat me better, my family will be proud of me. The swift turn of events leading me to this unbelievably fantastic situation, however, makes me feel uneasy. As happened to me before, an unnaturally auspicious thing was often followed by a series of misfortunes, so I wonder if this is good fortune or merely an ominous albatross.

I start my Ph.D. program with excitement and anxiety. I'm thrilled about the opportunity to make my big dream come true, but for the first time since this venture began, I'm given to doubt, worry, and remorse. When I applied to stay, I didn't consider much the question of security at home. Nor did I allow for my family's voice in the process, but rather I imposed my will on them. Nga will have to continue playing my role in addition to hers for another long year, and I'm not sure that she will be able to do the job alone. And who knows for sure nothing will happen to my eighty-year-old father, my wife, and my four little ones until I return? Is there any guarantee that Huế will be spared another disaster like the Tết offensive?

It's my family that lifts me out of the new bout of depression. Nga writes me often to motivate me to study. Her letters in which she tells me my father, our children, and herself are doing well are truly inspiring and comforting. Hùng, who is nine now and a third grader, also writes to tell me about school and activities as a Boy Scout. Mạnh and Long, ages six and five, through their brother, ask their daddy for "cowboy costumes with guns" (they ask for these things perhaps because in my previous letter I jokingly told them that I'm a Texas cowboy!) and "slow-moving movies" (this is our five-year-old son's request and I don't know why he wants these). Our five-month-old baby, Nga says, is growing fast. She reports that he says "Pa" when she shows him a photo of me. She also shares her good news about my father. He eats and sleeps well and enjoys writing poetry and translating medical texts into Vietnamese. How happy I am! How easy now to focus on my studies! You know how important the good news from home is. My success at school and my survival in America depend upon my family's safety, well-being, and happiness.

Things continue to go well for me at school. With Dr. Crunden's approval, my study program is geared to meeting my future teaching needs at the

University of Huế. To that end, my concentration on U.S. literature is reinforced by coursework in U.S. intellectual history. In addition, I'm allowed to do independent study in modern French literature to prepare for my dissertation, possibly in comparative studies of Franco-American literature. Demanding work leaves me little time to immerse myself in depression. I'm able to pull through after the two most trying semesters of my Ph.D. program. Short of a couple of courses to complete my required coursework in Fall 1974 (I'm one semester behind schedule due to the ambitious training program I choose), I will be well on my way to getting ready for my comprehensive exam in Spring 1975 and be home by next summer at the latest.

Fighting breaks out again in many places in South Vietnam less than a year after the signing of the Paris Peace Agreements. I worry when Đà Nẵng, where the U.S. Marines first landed in 1964, comes under attack for the first time. This causes alarm to everybody. Two years ago, Đà Nẵng was a haven for Huế refugees who fled here when Quảng Trị fell to the VC.

THE GREATEST CALAMITY

On March 10th, 1975, Vietnamese students in Austin are shaken to learn that Ban Mê Thuột, a major city in the Central Highlands, is captured by the North Vietnamese forces. The setback is followed by the mass pullout from this most important strategic point ordered by Thiệu. TV clips show the horrors of the most serious military debacle that South Vietnam has ever suffered. It is not a pullout; it is a tragic rout where thousands of soldiers and civilians on the retreating convoy are fired at by the VC from ambush. Route 7 looks like an immense junkyard strewn with military vehicles. Casualties must be extremely high as the convoy getting stuck is an easy target for VC firepower. The girls who watch the news with us cover their faces, shrieking and weeping.

While my Vietnamese friends from Saigon are clinging to a slight hope that there will be a reversal of the situation (they interpret Thiệu's pullout order as an attempt to pressure the U.S. into renewing its military aid, which was cut off after the signing of the Paris Peace Accords) and Saigon and the southern provinces will be safe, I am dealt another blow that leaves me completely devastated: two weeks after the loss of Ban Mê Thuột, NVA tanks roll into Huế which is totally deserted. Route 1 and Thuận An Beach are strewn with corpses, ammunition, and abandoned military vehicles. A friend tells me he gets a phone call from his mother in Saigon telling him his brother's family has arrived in Đà Nẵng from Huế, and I wonder if my family is among the lucky ones or among those who end up getting stranded on the China Beach. It must be very hard for Nga to handle all this alone with an ailing old man and five young children, the youngest only one-year-old (two months before the fall of Huế, at my father's counsel Nga adopted her from an orphanage, so now we have five kids). I pray that they make it to Đà Nẵng which would be safer because Thiệu swears to protect the city at all costs. I send a telegram to my brother and ask him, if he by any chance sees my wife, to tell her to stay in Đà Nẵng because it is very dangerous to flee to Saigon by car.

But Thiệu does not keep his promise. Đà Nẵng is abandoned only five days after the loss of Huế. On March 30th, North Vietnamese forces enter the former home of the U.S. Marines' largest base in Vietnam without firing a shot.

All communication with home is completely cut off, and I cannot do anything but watch the news to locate my family! TV clips show shiploads of refugees from Đà Nẵng with children dying of starvation and dehydration. And they die like flies. A close-up of the face of a dead boy instantly makes me think of little Hùng. The boy wears a blue felt hat, a white shirt, and gray shorts that my son also wears in his most recent picture. I peer into the clip. It lasts less than a second, but it stays vividly in my mind forever. Is little Hùng the boy in the clip? Could my family be onboard that ship which, according to the reporter, was docked at Nha Trang port? Was it possible that Nga might have put my family on that ship so that they could get to Nha Trang to stay with her other sister? It is safe to be here. If things get worse, this sister will take my family to Saigon. I do not know why I cling to the hope that my family has arrived in Nha Trang. Maybe I want them to be safe so that I can see them again. I close my eyes, trying to block from my mind the view of dead children when I picture my family onboard that ship. What if they are all safe except my little Hùng? How can I accept the news if it turns out to be true? Of Vietnamese students at the University of Texas, I am the only one who has little children at home and who has not heard from his family since March. My situation is worse than anyone else's here, and I am facing it alone. When a tragedy strikes, it is easier to cope with it collectively than by oneself. When we share our mutual sorrow as a family, we can derive comfort and strength from one another, and our misfortune is more bearable. I am not that lucky.

The scene of many refugees arriving in Nha Trang gives me a slight hope, but this hope quickly vanishes and gives way to fear, worry, and finally, total despair. The military situation deteriorates so fast that Nha Trang and all the remaining central provinces are abandoned a couple of days after the fall of Đà Nẵng. The familiar locations where I suspect my family might have been all sink into darkness, vanish, disappear. The all-out communist offensive this time resembles a tsunami. It comes from all directions, so suddenly, so fast it wipes out everything. Very few people escape. They are either wealthy, have connections with the United States, or are just lucky. My family, headed by a woman with six dependents—five young children and an ailing old man—does not fit any of these categories.

As early as April 1975, politicians and journalists here predicted that the Republic of Vietnam would collapse in a matter of days. Things are worsening on all fronts. Gerald Ford goes to Congress to ask for $300 million in military aid to the Thiệu administration, only to be confronted by a stony-faced assembly. Only Ted Kennedy speaks, but not in favor of Ford's request. "I won't give them a dime," he furiously lashes out at the idea of trying to save the country in which his brother, the president, got the U.S. involved militarily to contain China's expansionism. It is too late now, and there is nothing Ford can do except order a chaotic baby airlift out of Saigon, apparently to keep a fraction of the future Vietnamese generation from falling into the communists' hands. Ford's symbolic gesture of sympathy is a clear message to the South Vietnamese that the U.S. has washed its hands of the Vietnam business. In the wake of this evacuation and the pullout of the U.S. embassy, utmost chaos breaks loose in Saigon, hastening South Vietnam to its anticipated doom.

Two decades of American involvement have caused many Vietnamese to look upon the U.S. as a psychological crutch. While the Republic of Vietnam is in its death's throes, some friends and I still cling to the hope—which we know is no more than wishful thinking—that the U.S., which created all this mess, would somehow be able to prevent the communists' final assault on Saigon and negotiate for a political solution. We just want to have a chance to return home instead of pining here for the rest of our lives. After the end of the first Indochina war, there were many heartbreaking stories about Vietnamese expatriates reunited with their loved ones. A relative of mine had arrived in France in his early twenties, and by the time he secured a visa to return to North Vietnam to see his family, he had become a gray-haired man! Given the Vietnamese communists' animosity toward the U.S., if Saigon falls—and very likely it will—American-educated people like us will have no chance to see our family again.

In our utter despair, U.S. Senator Mike Mansfield's statement gives us a glimmer of hope. The prospect of a "bloodbath" in the wake of the fall of Saigon must be shaking the conscience of many Americans, including those who previously wanted to write off South Vietnam immediately. As North Vietnamese troops are preparing their final assault on Saigon, the Senate majority leader calls for an end to the hostilities in exchange for an offer of a multi-billion dollar aid package for North Vietnam's reconstruction. To put the North Vietnamese leadership at ease, Mansfield proposes that South Vietnam become a non-aligned state. Two years ago, Mansfield's plan would have been favorably considered by North Vietnamese negotiators, who persistently cited war reparations as their chief condition. Who knows, if granted a non-alignment status at the Paris bargaining table, South Vietnam's future would have taken a different course, the 1975 catastrophe could have been avoided, and I would not have lost my family! It is not difficult now to realize that South Vietnam was used as a testing ground for superpowers' contention that has caused our people in the North and the South untold suffering and devastation. The two Vietnams were pitted against each other because each was forced to follow a different ideology that was entirely foreign to our people. So, you know why we hold our breath for Mansfield's overtures of peace. We hope that at least the North will accept the war reparation proposal and temporarily refrain from imposing its rule on the South, and we can go home and find our family. Unfortunately, Mansfield's plea falls on the victorious communists' deaf ears. The Republic of Vietnam becomes history on April 30th, 1975.

I have not watched the news or read the newspaper ever since. What I have tried to build for the last twenty-one years from the moment I left Đồng Hới for Huế, then my new land of freedom, to my coming to America to prepare for a better future, ends up in smoke. It is all over. Nothing is left to repair, to begin again. To begin again, one must have something important worth living or suffering for, as in the case of my father, who took us to Huế for a better life. He was happy because we were never separated from him. After many years of working hard for us, he enjoyed watching us grow, mature, and start a family of our own. I followed in his footsteps but failed to understand the meaning of his sacrifice: *happiness does not mean abandoning your family in pursuit of a foolish dream but being with them, loving and protecting them, not letting them suffer because of you.* If my loved ones are alive, they must be suffering immensely now. How can they survive with no subsistence—the new regime must have cut off Nga's salary on which the whole family depended to live—but with so much sorrow, fear, and worry about me (they worry about me more than I worry about them even under normal circumstances). But seeing so many violent scenes on TV and being shaken by U.S. reporters' prediction of a possible bloodbath, I am not sure they are safe now or will be safe in the coming days.

What is happening confirms my suspicion of the intervention of a cruel fate in my life now. I remember three years ago in a letter Nga said that my astrologer father-in-law had told her I was not to return home after completion of my training program. I wrote back to her, dismissing his prediction as outright absurd though there lurked an eerie premonition of something wrong in the back of my mind. This nagging fear recalls another instance I mentioned earlier. Before leaving Vietnam, I stopped by a music store to buy some music albums. I was irresistibly drawn to one titled *Home and Memories.* When the visa hassle was over and I finally got onto the plane and started crying quietly, this album triggered my reflection on what had led me to this venture and what it would hold for my future. Why memories of home when I would return home in just two years as planned? Was the album's title an omen of misfortune like what had befallen us in 1954 that had sent us into exile? Not wanting to be distracted from the purpose of my leaving home, I brushed aside this idea, convincing myself that it was merely a coincidence. Later, after I had arrived in the States, I was too busy with school to think of the possibility that home and family might turn into mere memories. What is happening now confirms the appalling truth of what I thought was a superstition. I now come to believe that the course of my life—and by extension that of my loved ones' life—is under the control of a whimsical, inexorable force that steers us with its twists and turns to this tragic end. Why were we as a family brought together to share a mutual destiny only to be separated from one another in the middle? Why did I leave home when I knew that there was no guarantee of protection for my family? It is me who is to blame for the tragedy, but what was it that brought me that fateful opportunity to leave home when Huế was under siege? And why did I run headlong, impulsively, thoughtlessly to this place for a better future, only not to see my family again?

Since the fall of Huế in late March and the disappearance of my family, I have not missed a single class. There are a couple of reasons for my "acting normal" as if nothing is happening, which my American friends confuse for courage. First, I do not want to be "different." Timid and terribly self-conscious, I shrink when being talked to or being shown sympathy. This so-called fear of losing face I inherited from my father, the son of King Hiệp Hòa's teacher, who, despite heavy odds, had sent us to school rather than seeing us become hired men or servants. But the chief reason for my pretending to act normal is that I want to distract myself from my dark thoughts. Though I am trying to live for my family, the death drive becomes compulsive in me especially at night when I am alone. While I shrink from meeting people, seeing them and the live world keeps me from toying with dark thoughts. It makes me feel I *am* still alive.

Is it common in human beings that the death instinct is counteracted by the life instinct? I do not know. But when I feel I want to die to get rid of fatigue and depression, the will to live gets stronger than ever. I cannot help thinking of Quentin in Faulkner's *The Sound the Fury.* Moments before his suicide, he is very fascinated with life. Like him in the little Italian girl episode, I have a natural affinity with little children because they remind of my little ones at home and because they represent life.

Something extraordinary happens. As I cross Guadalupe Street on the drags to get to the Perry-Castaneda Library, I seem to hear car brakes screeching. I find myself in the middle of the street, the red light is on, and yelling and honking are directed at me. I come to consciousness and remember that I did clearly see the red light but felt an irresistible urge to plunge into the street, completely unaware of the meaning of the warning sign. It seemed like I was under the influence of a powerful tranquilizer because I felt so calm and relaxed.

If suicide is an act committed when one is most desperate, when one has nothing (in my case, no one) left to live for, when nothing matters, then my condition fits the definition except that the act is not carried out yet. Except for Nga's last letter postmarked in Đà Nẵng before the fall of the city in which she says that the family is fine and tells me not to worry, I get no more word from her since April, though most people here are beginning to hear from home directly or through relatives in France or countries that were not allied with the U.S. during the war. I live in worry and sorrow, neglect the necessities of life, and lose weight. I fear so much for my family's safety all the time that even in a short sleep, I see them dead or injured. Sometimes, it is my little Hùng who is among the dead children in the horrible TV clip, but he seems alive as I can hear his weak murmur *"Pa!"* I let out a piercing scream and wake up sweating profusely, my heart pounding. I am fully awake but so shaken that paradoxically, while I know it is a dream—the most frightening dream ever—I feel that it is *not* a dream, but a real thing. I continue to see my little boy in agony and hear his feeble voice as if the scene was unrolling before my eyes. Awake or asleep, I only have nightmares.

When checking my mail today (June 15th) at the UT Post Office, I find an envelope postmarked in Paris and addressed to me. I do not know the sender's name and wonder why he has my address. When I open the envelope, I am shocked to see a short message written on a small piece of old lined paper in a graceful style so familiar I can recognize it right away: it is Nga's message! It reads:

Darling,

We're home. Father is fine. The kids are well. I've returned to teaching. Please take care of yourself. Love and miss you.

It is the shortest letter Nga has ever written me. But it is the most wonderful, the most comforting one I have ever received from my wife because it tells me my family is safe! Tears are swelling in my eyes. Not wanting to be seen crying in public, I try to hold back my tears until I get to my cubicle in the graduate library. With my head down on the desk, I weep bitterly but noiselessly. My hands are wet with tears. These are the tears of joy you shed when you learn that your loved ones who were thought dead are found alive. These are also tears of remorse and sorrow. Never can I forgive myself for coming here for such a futility as education while knowing that this calamity would eventually happen. Though tremendously relieved to find my family, I cannot help worrying about their wellbeing in the months and years (not days) ahead of them. How are they going to survive with no regular income from my salary? (Before the change of regime Nga was still allowed to receive my salary.) If my father gets sick, how can Nga get medical care for him? Will she be able to manage the double task of raising five young kids and caring for an old man all by herself under such circumstances? These questions swirl in my head, extinguishing the joy just kindled in my heart.

While not promising any chance of a reunion with my family, the news from home saves my life. I now feel a powerful desire to live for them just as I feel they also live for me, and therefore I have no right to give up living. *"Please take care of yourself,"* Nga says in the short message. She cannot say much in the space provided (the person who currently lives in Paris and who forwarded Nga's message tells me his father in Huế had sent him several short messages for him to relay to their relatives in America, so I guess each writer was allowed a limited number of lines), but it is very clear that Nga knows I am badly hurt both physically and morally by the recent calamity and begs me to heed my health for our eventual reunion, however long it takes. Yes, I ought to take better care of myself because of my father, Nga, and my five young kids. I must have lost a lot of weight because of lack of sleep and not eating properly. Then, I must go back to preparing for my comprehensive exam. While knowing that everything has become meaningless, I must do it just as I must live because my father, Nga, and my children want me to. That is the only thing I can do right now to prove that I love them and deserve their love.

I telephone Mary Ann and we immediately set up a schedule for our study together. Early last spring semester, we had started doing some review for the exam when it was interrupted by the catastrophe. Mary Ann is particularly instrumental in keeping me alive these days. Not only does she not mind my interfering with her study schedule because of my sudden bowing out of it, she has given me her most careful attention since learning of my narrow escape from death on Guadalupe Street that she naively calls "a suicide attempt." She fetches me at my apartment and has her husband Phil take me to her house for dinner every week. Knowing that sheer expression of sympathy only makes me feel worse, she quietly and gently cares for me. She has a four-year-old son whom she teaches to call me Uncle. I quickly get back on my feet and can start preparing again for my qualifying exam.

I manage to cover mostly the assigned reading material, and, by the end of the summer, feel ready for my orals rescheduled for October. I prepare for the exam with no anxiety, and take and pass it with no excitement. Friends in the American Studies Department right after the exam whisk me to a party to celebrate my success, and they are happy that I seem to have a good time. But later that evening as soon as I get back to my apartment, I slump onto my bed, breaking down completely. This is too much for me to bear. What is all this endeavor and achievement for? What is going to happen next? My future looks gloomy as it is deprived of hope, and I am now relying entirely on illusions—a futile wistfulness for family reunion—for my emotional survival. But does it make sense to live only in illusions?

Nobody in America can live in illusions, and I am no exception. After the loss of South Vietnam, everything that happens points to many difficulties awaiting me. Early in June, the Fulbright Program cancelled my scholarship. Today (October 16th) I am dealt another blow by the Internal Naturalization Service (INS). Because of my failure to register for a refugee status required for all Vietnamese aliens who came to the U.S. before 1975, the INS says I am subject to deportation. I report to the INS Office in San Antonio and request, as suggested by a lawyer friend, a status called "docket control," one that would permit me a temporary stay in the U.S. renewable every six months. I do not want to become a refugee because it would jeopardize my chance of going home. Despite my explanation, the INS official who questions me does not relent. He threatens to take me into custody before sending me back to Vietnam. "I'm sorry, sir," I say to him politely but resolutely, "but I can't accept your offer to change my status. I'd rather be deported to be able to see my family than experience a slow death here." Seeing that his threat has no effect on me, he goes back to his office, apparently to consult with his supervisor. After a while, he comes back and gives me a form to fill out. It is obvious that they cannot deport me to a country that sees the U.S. as its enemy. This regime, which sees all American-educated Vietnamese as spies for the U.S. government, will *not* accept me. Nor will any other country accept me.

When I see Professor Rostow and tell her about my experience in San Antonio, she is very angry. "They have no right to treat you like that," she says. I am angry, too, for being treated like a criminal just because I want to go home to be with my family. Had I known this would happen to me, then I would not have come here. It is better to suffer with my loved ones than live by myself in remorse, sorrow, and humiliation. This is the price I am paying for training to promote mutual understanding between America and Vietnam!

***

A month after my orals, I appeared before my dissertation committee to present my thesis proposal. The topic of exile fascinates me probably because deep down, I feel that I have no chance to return home in this lifetime. For my thesis, I propose to examine a group of famous writers like Ernest Hemingway, Scott Fitzgerald, and Gertrude Stein, who left America in protest of the decadence of American civilization. The topic would require a lot of research, and I do not know if I have any more stamina to get it done. Lingering depression and the recent orals have drained me of all energy. My dissertation committee saves my life when it rejects my proposal, saying that much has been covered in the field.

I toy with the idea of quitting this intellectual business which has led me to this impasse but which I had held so important for many years. I need to rethink my career goals, if any, and adjust them to my new condition as a permanent exile. But I do not know what to do. I cannot switch to engineering or sciences because I have no background and previous training in these fields, nor can I change my career to selling homes or insurance policies because I am a very timid and self-conscious person. The only thing I can think of is completing my dissertation and finding a teaching job in Canada or somewhere in the world where communication with my family would be easier.

To do all this, I must find a topic for my dissertation. Drawing from my recent experience with my dissertation committee, I try a field less known in America. Using my background in French, I think about exploring a topic like Franco-American literary relationships. While researching the subject, I hit upon a review by Jean-Paul Sartre of William Faulkner's *The Sound and the Fury* in the *Nouvelle Revue Française*. Sartre likens time in Faulkner's novel to what we feel when traveling in an uncovered car and looking backward. Just as things on the sides of the road will not be perceived clearly until they have receded into a backdrop, the more distant a past grows, the sharper our remembrance of it becomes. According to Sartre, because in Faulkner's novel, time is shorn of the present and the future, it is represented only by the past. Deprived of hopes and dreams, the hallmark of the present and the future, Quentin Compson lives with haunting memories of sorrow, shame, guilt, and remorse. It is the past that kills him.

I can easily relate to Quentin. I do not have a future now. What I worked so hard for—completing my study and returning home as quickly as possible to be with my family and to serve the country—suddenly becomes useless and meaningless. I live in grief and guilt. Seven months ago in March, my folks at home were the most important motivation for my study because they were my joy, hope, and happiness. They are still my reason for living, but what is associated with them are only sad memories.

Another reason for my fascination with Faulkner is his dealing with the unconscious. Before March 1975, when I read *Absalom, Absalom!* I was particularly interested in the novel's exploration of the dark region of the human heart with its violent impulses that crop out and explode at the slightest sign of the collapse of consciousness. Most of Faulkner's dark characters, in their utmost desperation, tear off their masks and break down into insanity. I thought that my interest in Faulkner would be only a scholarly one, not realizing that since March 1975, I have suffered a quasi-breakdown of consciousness like what Faulkner describes in his fiction. Though I no longer sleep with a bright light, I still have nightmares now and then. The near-death incident on Guadeloupe Street happened only once, but occasionally I suffer a lapse of memory. When absorbed in study I am all right, but no sooner do I take a break from work than something happens. I would forget to return to work, my mind would drift home, and I would instinctively let out a muffled grievous moan. It is a release of pent-up sorrow when it is too much for me to bear. But the release does not help me much as my sorrow increases even more, is pent up and released again. What my friends might call my strength of will when seeing me work so hard is merely my attempt to forget my sorrow and suffering. When not doing anything, when walking a long way from the campus to my apartment alone, or when lying down in bed to rest for a few minutes, I let out a groan. The grief I have tried to repress bursts to the surface and torments me for hours.

Sartre's comment on Faulkner's use of the past fascinates me because it (the past) is linked to something I always long for but will never attain—*home*. Home is unattainable but its image gets sharper than ever because, as Sartre might say, I constantly look backward, because I constantly concentrate on what is no more, and because for me, time has been shorn of the future since that fateful day of March 26th, 1975. To study and write about the past, about home and memory, a subject in which I have a unique personal experience, seems easier than to delve into a totally unknown field. Besides, anything related to my present ordeal—pain, sorrow, guilt, and most importantly, the frequent unconscious wail that comes from the dark recesses of my soul—becomes my way of daily living. To talk or to write about this dark force, strangely enough, is a temporary release from its persecution.

Enough of my depending on Faulkner's fiction for my survival. When doing research, I happen to find the "French Faulkner," Claude Simon, whose work reverberates *Absalom, Absalom!* and *The Sound and the Fury*. Simon's acknowledged indebtedness to Faulkner allows me not only to define his American master's influence on him but to broaden my research into Faulkner's impact on the so-called school *Nouveau Roman* of which Simon is a prominent member. Just as I seek in Faulkner a sort of release therapy for my emotional trauma, so I find in Simon's fiction about France's military debacle in 1940 an echo of the South Vietnamese army's ultimate defeat in 1975. Just as the ghosts of the French troops still go on parading in the mind of Simon's narrator in *The Flanders Road*, twenty years later, the frantic, disorderly retreat of the Vietnamese army with their families trapped in a Vietcong ambush in the Central Highlands is still a fresh wound in my unconscious mind. Just as in Simon's fiction, the dead are always present and always demand they not be forgotten by future generations, so my home, my family, my South Vietnam, my happy past, as well as the horrors and brutality of war, will never fade in my memory.

I go back to my dissertation committee with the new thesis proposal about Faulkner's influence on modern French literature, particularly the *Nouveau Roman*. Because the University of Texas does not have adequate holdings on the subject, my department gives me a small stipend to travel to Harvard and Yale to conduct research for my dissertation. The opportunity to sit on a bus to see America that my academic advisor suggested after I got my MA finally materializes but at a wrong time and with such irony! Had the tragedy not occurred seven months ago, I would not have taken this bus trip and would have been home by now! But the ironic situation has its positive side. I need to get out of here for a while to alleviate my long depression which is taking quite a toll on my health.

AMERICAN TRAVELOGUE

October 25th, 1975

My friend Chip Dameron gives me a ride to the Greyhound on Congress Avenue. I buy a three-month round-trip ticket for $70. To see things better when the bus runs, I secure a seat near the window. Most passengers are elderly people who don't drive or don't want to drive. They all mind their business and don't seem curious about the "Asian boy." (Many Americans my age and older call me "young man" because, like many Asians, I don't look my age.)

As the bus rolls out to the suburbs, I peer at the city in its morning rush hour. Streams of vehicles flow on Highway 10 in both directions. On both sides of the freeway there are no pedestrians, only man-made things like buildings, shopping malls, and cars. America is a society that is safest, tidiest, but most isolated. Even on this bus, which is a small world, passengers keep to themselves except those traveling together, whose communication still sounds like a whisper. Human interaction in public is uncommon in America. Everyone is an island. It gets so still around me that I feel depressed and lonely. How much I miss a bus or train trip I took in the far past with my father from Dalat to our ancestral home in Quảng Bình! Public transportation at home offered no privacy and comfort, but the hubbub of noisy, animated passengers traveling with us was truly enlivening.

After three hours of running, the bus stops shortly in Waco, Texas. Some passengers, most of them elderly ladies, get off. They are met by their relatives who quietly hug and kiss them. Then they all get into their big waiting limousine and take off. Americans, as I observe, don't seem excited when seeing each other after a long time.

When the bus arrives in Dallas around noon, we have a one-hour break for lunch. To save money for my research expenses, I have a small hamburger for fifty cents and a glass of cold water for free. I'm very impressed with the way Americans conduct themselves in public. Though the bus terminal is at its peak hours, you're hardly disturbed by its activities. After eating my lunch, I sit down on a chair and almost doze off because things around me are so quiet. In Vietnam before the war, when my father and I boarded a bus or a train in our travel, we heard earsplitting fracas of different kinds.

The bus rolls again on Highway 35 en route to Oklahoma. My excitement about the first bus trip I've ever taken since I came to the U.S. cools off. I get bored of watching Texas' invariably flat landscape. Sitting next to me is a man in his early forties with long hair, a bushy beard, and a forlorn look. We boarded the same bus, and off and on, he dozed off since we left Austin. He glanced at me a couple of times as if he had seen me somewhere before, wanted to strike up a conversation with me, but then decided not to and went back to his meditation. After a long time, he opens his eyes, turns to me, and timidly ventures, "Speak English?" When I nod, he continues sounding me out, "You're from 'Nam,' aren't you?" No sooner do I say my nationality than he cusses out, "Damn it! Your country made my life a hell on earth!" He rolls up his sleeve, revealing his artificial arm. "I can't live a normal life anymore," he continues venting rage and grief. "My buddy Bill returned in a body bag, and I'm going to Oklahoma to see his mother." I try to comfort him, telling him my condition is worse. He has a family, relatives, and friends to turn to, but I have none and continue to live in nightmares. Brought up in a culture that teaches compassion as an appreciation of the Providence's special blessings for their country, Americans possess a natural sympathy for the less privileged ones. The Vietnam vet seems moved by my story as he now looks at me with his gentle eyes, telling me he's sorry about my condition. When I tell him the purpose of my trip to New England, he rolls his eyes in amazement, "What're you doing such a thing for?" I say I need to do something that keeps my mind preoccupied so I can live until I reunite with my family. He seems impressed with my way of coping with reality.

Before he gets off at Oklahoma City, we already become friends. He shakes hands with me and introduces himself as Gordon. He gives me his address in Austin and asks me to drop by to see him when I have time.

(When I returned to Austin after my trip, Gordon came to look for me. Despite my protest, he insisted that I accept his monthly contribution of $10 to help my children. He wrote me regularly to inquire about my loved ones' wellbeing. This lasted until my family came to reunite with me. I lost contact with him afterward. My mail sent to him was returned.)

***

October 27th, 2:00 a.m.

The wee hours at a small American bus station are very depressing. The brief commotion caused by the bus's arrival is over, and I fall back into my isolation. In the wan streetlight, the bus depot looks dreary and gloomy. People here go about their business in their American way—perfunctory, quiet, and perfectly accurate—making the need for human contact superfluous. As human communication isn't prioritized in American society, Americans fiercely protect their privacy, abstain from reaching out to strangers. Crèvecœur's remark that the early settlers were "ferocious, gloomy, and unsociable" can also apply to modern Americans. Not only is the frontier character alive and well in today's American society, but it's also fed by a culture that's getting more mechanical every day. The practice of isolationism, I think, makes Americans self-confident and self-reliant but lonely at heart. I can't help comparing them to the Vietnamese I came across in the trips my father and I took to Quảng Bình in the late 1940s before the Indochina war. The passengers were too friendly, always taking upon themselves the right to mind others' business as though it were their own. Given the extremely limited space Vietnamese are entitled to (it isn't uncommon for several members of a family to sleep in one bedroom), privacy to Vietnamese is an exotic notion. The crowded train where many passengers sit together on a long trip, therefore, is an ideal place for Vietnamese to confirm and exercise their cherished belief that "all men from the four oceans are brothers of the same family" (*Tứ hải giai huynh đệ*). Their way of addressing strangers using kinship terms is all too common to the Vietnamese people. By the end of his or her long trip, a Vietnamese passenger will have formed, it's safe to say, a pretty good knowledge of his or her fellow traveler's personal life, and vice versa. There is no guarantee that the acquaintance newly formed would develop into a lasting relationship, or if it would be simply added to the travelers' trove of tall stories.

***

October 28th, midnight

The bus rolls into Mississippi at midnight. In my half-awake, half-asleep status, I feel that I'm going through, not an actual southern state which was Faulkner's country, but the legendary Yoknapatawpha County, the Old South that Faulkner immortalizes in his fiction. Twenty years ago, when my father and I were traveling by train to his native Quảng Bình, once during the night I dreamed that I was traveling backward to my fantasy island of childhood. Likewise, tonight the Greyhound coach's steady, rhymical motion plunges me into this extraordinary region abuzz with the chorus of Faulkner's characters, the dead African slaves. Their voices sound now doleful and heart-breaking like a dirge, now joyful and uplifting like a hallelujah. In the still dark night, the chorale, now near now distant pours into my deep unconscious uninterruptedly and interminably, humming me to sleep and keeping me awake. I'm submerged in this sea of tunes. Though I'm a foreigner and can't participate in American history, I sympathize with this imagined invisible community of sorrow and suffering that goes out to sing tonight. Unlike the grievous ululations I heard at night in a dream after the holocaust of the Tết offensive, the song I hear tonight is sad but its tunes are rhythmical and melodious like the tunes of a requiem.

My reading of Faulkner's novels is the cause of my imaginary encounter with black slaves and their singing. Just as Marcel, Proust's narrator in *À La recherche du temps perdu* [*Remembrance of Things Past*], in his sleep falls out of chronological time and can "hear the echo of great spaces traversed," in my half-asleep, half-awake state, as I'm engaged in a visionary temporal quest for my own past, I happen to land in Faulkner's legendary land whose people share a history of sorrow and suffering with my people at home.

Music is also an important theme in women's African American literature. In Alice Walker's *The Color Purple,* the character Shrug Avery sings her blues songs for a living. Toni Morrison's *Song of Solomon* is about a young black man's odyssey into his ancestral past through music. His quest is inspired and guided by the children's songs he hears along the way and involves several female characters whose singing is a way of life. For Pilate Dead, the novel's central character, music is the apotheosis of the black soul. As she lies dying in Milkman's arms, being shot by her nephew's enemy, she asks him to "sing a little somethin for me." Like the female voices I hear tonight, Black characters use music to intone their sad fate and transcend their condition. Sadly, they can do so only on the outskirts of modern American history and in the reader's imagination.

The vision is a rare momentary respite from my long depression since the start of the trip. It's the result of my being exposed to the magic of Faulkner's writing and my deep sympathy for the victims of slavery described in his work. The vision also is the result of my long toying with escapism from the unbearable reality of a person who has lost everything and, to live, must cling to a world that is no more. He must nurture that world with his illusions and fantasies and pretend that it still exists so he can live. This is what happens in Claude Simon's *The Flanders Road* when the survivor/narrator imagines participating with his dead comrades-in-arms in telling their imagined exploits in a new light. Haunted by their memories of a defeat too shameful for them to accept, the narrator and the phantom cavalry soldiers are convinced that they *are* still fighting the war, that France doesn't accept its defeat, and that there is still hope for liberation from the Nazi occupation. Similarly, my brief vision of the dead in Faulkner is triggered by my asleep-awake state as my bus is rolling through Falkner's country, by my reading of Simon's novel, and by the haunting story of the most tragic, most humiliating debacle of the now defunct South Vietnamese army on Highway 7B in the Central Highlands in March 1975. Those who wrongly lost their lives aren't silent; they want us to hear their voices so we can understand them, know why they died, and whom and what they died for. Literature allows us to remember the dead, and America and France are fortunate to have great mediums like Faulkner and Simon. It's so sad that so many of my people at home have died heroically but futilely for their cause and for whom the bell never tolls.

***

October 30th

I arrive in Boston at 5:00 p.m. today and am met at the bus station by Jeff's parents. Mr. Jenkins, Jeff's father, who insists that I call him Mike, was an Air Force pilot stationed in Đà Nẵng before his discharge and return to the U.S. after the Tết offensive. Jane, Jeff's mother, is a retired English high school teacher. Because of the warm welcome and special treatment extended to me by the Jenkins, I gather Jeff must have told his parents about what I've been through these months.

Americans are very compassionate and kind to those who are less fortunate. They may be awkward when expressing their feelings, but clearly their feelings come from the bottom of their heart. Having lived in the States long enough to know this, I'm deeply moved by their hospitality and even go so far as to entertain a wish that I was a member of their family.

Jeff has a sister who is married and lives in Boston. Shortly after my arrival Frances comes to greet me. She's a part-time graduate student at Boston University. She hugs me warmly and kisses me on the forehead when we meet. There is a tear in her eye, and I guess Jeff or her parents must have told her about me.

The Jenkins take me to a Vietnamese restaurant for dinner. Jane says I must have missed food from home because I don't cook and have been on the bus quite a while. It feels like a family reunion dinner though this is the first time I've this family. During the meal, the Jenkins and Frances ask a lot about my trip and research project. They hardly ask me about my family. Their tactfulness and compassion touch my heart deeply.

It's the first time I stay overnight at the home of an American family. I keep tossing in bed, thinking about a lot of things. I envy the Jenkins and the Americans their fortune of living in a safe, peaceful world. Until my coming to the States, I had never spent a night without being woken up by bomb or mortar explosions that sent me and my family scurrying to a nearby shelter. The war is over, but the nightmare of its aftermath continues for me, my family, and many people in the South. The number of South Vietnamese fleeing their country, many of them perishing at sea, increases at an alarming rate. Why wasn't the Vietnamese conflict resolved the way the American Civil War had been resolved, that is, with less suffering, disunity, and animosity? Why aren't the Vietnamese communists using reconciliation to heal the wounds of their conflict like the Americans after the end of their civil war? Why aren't the people of the defeated South allowed to take part in rebuilding their war-torn country to the best of their ability but instead are sent to re-education camps and new economic zones to perish?

But it's silly of me to be envious of the Jenkins and other Americans. Blessed as they are to be living in a country that's the envy of the entire world, Americans are humble, compassionate, and generous. They always want to share what they have with people who are less fortunate. I'm so privileged to visit the Jenkins who are going out of their way to treat me like a member of their family. Deep down I even wish I was their adopted Vietnamese son and Frances' brother. More than ever, I want to have a family to turn to for comfort as a replacement of my absent one in Vietnam.

Cuddling myself in my warm bed as the snow falls outside, I fall fast sleep. For the first time in seven months, I sleep well that night.

***

November 2nd

I move to the International House today. It's hard to leave the Jenkins, but they understand why I make that decision. I need to stay on campus to do research at the library. Besides, I need some privacy which I don't have at the Jenkins'. When not at work, I want to have some free time to think of my own family, which has become my way of life since the fall of Huế in March.

Harvard University has excellent holdings in the field of Franco-American literary relations. But I find its environment not suitable for my research. For example, I'm not allowed to use the library stacks but can only get the material from a staff member at the reading room. It's very hard for me to get the work done in two weeks' time because I'm allowed to request only two items at one time, while I suspect I would have to browse tons of journal articles for information.

My difficulty in getting research material and the puffy manner displayed by some staff members here disappoint me. I cut short my stay in Boston, call the Jenkins to say goodbye, and leave for New Haven, Connecticut, the next morning.

***

November 4th

Yale University is an ideal place to do research for my dissertation. It has large holdings in French literary journals and newspapers published from the 1930s to 1950s, the period of my study. The library staff is helpful and friendly. After seeing my credentials, they immediately issue me a visiting scholar ID card that allows me to check out books for two weeks and to use the library stacks freely. Best of all, I'm assigned a carrel in the stacks where I can keep items reserved under my name.

The articles I'm reading might not have been touched since their purchase. As I thumb through the brittle yellow pages, an acrid smell wafts to my nostrils, making me sneeze repeatedly. I'm amazed by the great mass of holdings the library has on the French reception of American literature after the war. In the wake of the liberation was the French fascination with the *roman américain* whose robust flavor, candid expression, and bold techniques French writers wanted to imitate to better depict the violence and crude materiality of France's postwar society. Thus, by drawing inspiration from American literature, French authors hoped to revitalize their literature.

Faulkner was the French public's best-loved author. His fiction captured their contradictory postwar mood of despair and hope. French critic Jean Vagne noted in 1945 that what was important to France after the liberation was "not cigarettes nor candy bars, but Faulkner's books that we imagined lying in the trunks of American soldiers' Jeeps." Faulkner's world, like France under the Nazi occupation, is very tragic, but his characters calmly accept their lot, never losing hope that they will prevail eventually. The French people needed to apply this Faulknerian lesson to their life to pull through the long winter of spiritual depression after the liberation.

French critics and translators of Faulkner claimed they found the American writer just as their predecessors a century earlier had taken Edgar Allan Poe out of his obscurity in America by turning him into the founder of French symbolism. For this reason, when Faulkner won the Nobel Prize, they unabashedly applauded the event as a "French" writer's accomplishment. For example, to celebrate the "French" Faulkner's success, the *Figaro* carried the letter "F" on its front page with the headline: "F: Faulkner; F: France" as if the American Nobel Prize laureate *was* a French writer!

***

November 11th

My research trip pays off immensely. After one week of "digging in" at Yale University library, I've found enough to start on my dissertation as soon as I get back to Austin. With Faulkner as my focus and with a trove of French material on him, I know now what I'm going to do in my dissertation.

***

November 13th

I have $300 left and wish to use the remainder of the grant for more travel. My restless passion for adventure, interrupted by the trauma of separation from the family, becomes alive when I have the opportunity. I call Bryan, a former classmate who lives in Endicott, New York, and ask him to put me up for a couple of days. Bryan says he would be happy to welcome me at his home.

I'm met at the bus station by an elderly lady who tells me she's Bryan's mother and that her son is out of town. She's a quiet woman, on the unfriendly side. Throughout the drive, I try not to say anything untoward that could upset her. Suddenly, I remember Mrs. Onstot, my former landlady in Austin, a woman in the Old South tradition. She was strict and rigorous but treated me like her son. With Mrs. Steward, the last leg of my trip isn't going to be as pleasant as I anticipated.

When we get to her home, Mrs. Steward gives me her son's letter. Bryan writes that due to an unexpected business he's sorry that he can't entertain me at his home. Probably knowing his mother isn't a good host, Bryan suggests that I stay with his cousin, a Vietnam vet, who he says will come to get me when I call him. I have no choice but do as Bryan proposes.

David, Bryan's cousin, comes to pick me up right after I call him. He's in his early 40s, very pleasant and full of energy. I warm toward his friendliness, and we talk all the way to his home in Binghamton, which is a good thirty minutes' drive from Endicott. As we get off his truck, I notice David has an artificial leg as he limps when he helps me carry my suitcase into his home. "I almost got blown up by that damned mortar explosion during the Tết offensive," he guffaws when noticing my gaze at his leg.

David reveals to me that his aunt never forgives whoever was involved in the war that caused her nephew to lose part of his body. She blames the U.S. government for sending young Americans to die in an unknown region. Though she sympathizes with Vietnamese refugees who lost their land and came here, they painfully remind her of those who never returned or who did return but not in one piece like her nephew, and this makes her feel bitter about those who came from that country. I understand now why Mrs. Stewart held a grudge against me this afternoon, and wonder if Bryan, who was in my history class and knows all the mess, its causes and consequences, had told his mother about my condition here. But it might be difficult for her to understand all that because the war was such a complex, absurd, and tragic thing.

David asks me about what went on after the Tết offensive, but I hesitate to tell him. I'm afraid that might remind him of the cause of the pain I'm sure he still suffers now. But he doesn't seem to bother about it at all. He jokes about his narrow escape from death which costs him his leg as if it was just a fun life experience. He says since that accident, he has learned to use his remaining one dexterously. "What the heck," he gives a hearty laugh. "You lose some, but you win a lot." He knits his brow, and then suddenly a shadow of wistfulness flashes on his face. "I won't brag much about the knack I learned since I got this crafted onto my body," he points to his artificial leg, sighing. "I saw lots of folks in your country in much worse shape, and yet they never complained or blamed anybody for their lot. The fact that their limbs were missing didn't seem to interfere with their living. Those little folks really shame me and many Americans."

David's self-forgiveness, which I think is the cause of his natural joy and optimism, makes me rethink the way I'm living now. I've punished myself too much and am afraid that it could be detrimental to my health. Maybe I should try to enjoy myself a little. Besides, I ought to take better care of myself for the sake of my loved ones. It's difficult to do so, though. My condition is worse than David's. He lost one limb, but I lost everything—my country, my future, my home, and the opportunity of seeing my family again.

***

November 16th

I find David's warm and exuberant personality very congenial and feel tempted to leave Texas with its exorbitant heat and boring unvaried flat landscape to come here. I don't want to live in a place that reminds me of the period my family went missing after the fall of Huế. Besides, it's so depressing to see the same Vietnamese folks and hear their same litany of plaints about their family's condition in Vietnam and their uncertain future in America. I've enough of that stuff.

At David's suggestion, I go to see the head of the English Department at SUNY-Binghamton and ask him about the possibility of getting a teaching job here after I complete my dissertation. A very friendly and nice man who is a specialist in the comparative study of American and French literature, he's interested in my dissertation and says he'll support my application for a part-time position in his department while working on my thesis.

***

November 18th

Thanks to David's generosity, my money is almost intact, which allows me to make a trip to New York City. I would have done it last summer had the communist victory been delayed a few months. The would-be trip would have been important for a book on America I had planned to write before the fall of South Vietnam.

I check into a cheap hotel in Chinatown to see better the world's largest Chinese community. Chinatown has always been my favorite place since I grew up. While living in Saigon, I was never tired of exploring Chợ Lớn, Vietnam's most populous Chinatown, to buy prohibited Chinese curios secretly smuggled from Cambodia. When I was in Singapore on an ESL training program in 1971, I frequently went to a famous spot called the People's Park where people could gulp down bowl after bowl of greasy food without worrying about their arteries getting clogged because the chef served a special tea that would wash away the fat so they could eat to their heart's content!

Chinatown is the only place where I seem to have found my identity as an Asian since I lost my home. It's an Asian world with Asian faces, Asian mores, and Asian eccentricities, so you can't help feeling a sense of belonging here. In Austin and even in small towns, I always feel estranged and lost though I will soon become a full-fledged U.S. citizen. The loss or lack of identity is the most devastating problem every sentient has to face eventually. Even birds of the same flock fly together. Vietnamese refugees, who spread over America when they first arrived, now begin to migrate to states with large Asian communities like California and Texas.

New York's Chinatown, at first sight, resembles Saigon's Chinatown in many ways. Probably because of the town's limited space or because of the Chinese concept of efficiency, Chinatown's people shop at "mini" markets held mostly on street pavements. More notable are its restaurants that serve mouth-watering foods at prices low-income people can easily afford. Being the son of an herbalist in the Sino-Vietnamese tradition, I like the aroma wafting from ginseng herb shops on Canal Street. A Chinese ginseng herb store operates like a pharmacy and clinic combined. Behind the counter is a large cabinet with drawers, each with a label showing the name of a specific herb. The doctor, usually an aged man, sees his patients in a small compartment separated from the vending area by a screen. He diagnoses their condition by feeling their pulses and examining their tongue, then prescribes the herbs for the treatment. There is no fee for seeing the doctor, but you are expected to undergo an extended course of treatment because herbs don't produce immediate results.

Elderly Asians prefer to go to a Chinese doctor for their health problems. They believe that Chinese medicine is best for degenerative diseases. In Asia, practitioners of Chinese and traditional medicine receive a lot of respect and trust and aren't required to comply with the government's regulations when treating patients. It isn't uncommon to see ads by herbalists in Chợ Lớn with extravagant medicinal claims. In the States, such ads are prohibited, but herbalists are allowed to practice. In Chinatowns, they are in great demand probably because of the popularity of the health food industry, which is chiefly based on herbs, and because of the side effects of Western drugs. If herbalists print this statement on the bottle of their product—"this product is not intended to diagnose, treat, cure, or prevent any disease"—the FDA leaves them alone.

Chinatown is a model of the successful transplantation of immigrants' native culture into the U.S. Due to its economic self-sufficiency, large population, and isolation, Chinatown's residents can live their lives the Chinese way without interference from the mainstream culture. Many Chinese immigrants, and even native-born adults, don't even need to acquire English language skills because they probably never leave their ghettos to do business with the outside world.

I don't know what goes on in the Chinese American family. But I guess "the Chinese way" isn't always the preferable norm. Besides the old who stick to their native roots, there are the young who love the American way. Chinese American writers such as Jade Snow Wong, Louis Chu, Diana Chang, and Maxine Hong Kingston, among others, have dramatized the conflict between the young and old generations in their fiction, and I suspect in real life, the tension could be greater.

***

November 19th, midnight

I want to take advantage of my short stay to see New York as much as I can. A Chinese American friend suggests Harlem. I happened to walk by this place the day before yesterday, but it looked quiet, drab, and uninteresting. But this friend insists that to enjoy Harlem, I should see it at late night when it's at its busiest and liveliest.

I get off the subway at 125th Street a little before midnight and am deafened by a torrent of horns, trumpets, and whistles. A band is blaring. The audience claps, sings, and dances to the piece being performed.

Having little interest in loud music, I watch the crowd briefly and walk on. Something catches my attention. A group of young men dressed quaintly, wearing hats and sunglasses, are having their pictures taken. I'm struck by the way some Black folks live their lives. They just want to have fun, to be natural and spontaneous, not caring about proprieties and all the artificial stuff that would be strictly observed in Asian culture.

The merry-making that these young people indulge in suggests to me that it's part of African American culture, one that's characterized by letting go and "living natural"; it also indicates to me that by having fun, by enjoying themselves, most Americans take for granted what their country offers its citizens—peace, security, affluence. It's therefore natural for Americans to celebrate because they have everything they want in America. I can't help thinking of my children who don't have a chance to celebrate their birthday and right now may not have enough food to eat.

***

Having wrapped up my trip today (November 22nd), I'm now on my bus back to Austin. Because there is nothing more for me to see and the trip leaves me almost exhausted, I close my eyes and try to get some sleep. The smooth motion of the express Greyhound coach, rather than sending me to sleep, keeps me awake. The same old feeling of sorrow and guilt that was kept at bay during my travel now returns and assaults me relentlessly, more so than when it first started when all communication with home was cut off. It seems I can't afford to have a moment of joy on my own. The so-called "fun time" I had in Chinatown in New York two days ago, for example, was only a rare distraction, not a relief, from my long suffering. The same thing happened when, after passing my Ph.D. comprehensive exam, I tried to treat myself to a meal at a restaurant. After I ate a couple of bites, tears started gushing out of my eyes, so I had to leave the restaurant in a hurry, not finishing my meal. I just can't enjoy myself when my loved ones are hungry at home. It's a crime against those you say you love.

I get back to Austin on Thanksgiving Day when most students have gone home and the streets are almost deserted. The house in which I live is also empty with my two housemates gone for the holiday.

After taking my suitcase to the house, I go to the post office to check my mail. There is no mail from home, but I get such shocking news from Mrs.

Jenkins: Frances is dead. She killed herself by shutting herself up in her car in the garage and leaving the engine running. Mrs. Jenkins says that it happened right after I left Boston. I wish I had stopped by to see both Frances and her parents to say goodbye to them before going to New Haven or had left my forwarding address with them. I was touched by Frances' kindness and felt I was close to her though my visit with her parents in Boston was so short and I saw her only once. I thought of her a few times after I left Boston and planned to call her when I got back to Texas. She was very kind to me, and deep down in my heart I felt I needed this sister-figure to help me get over these hard times in America.

Frances' suicide shocks and puzzles me. I can't imagine how a woman in her prime, so pleasant and so gentle, could take her own life in such a violent way. In her letter, Mrs. Jenkins says she has no clue to her daughter's death because no suicide note is found, and she looked fine the evening before. But the horror and the violence of her self-destruction tells me that she must have consciously planned and then fearlessly performed it for a very important personal reason that nobody knew but herself. Much experimental research has been done on the subject of suicide, but it's in literature that the case of Frances is most relevant. In *The Sound and the Fury*, Quentin Compson keeps to himself his meticulous plan to drown himself in the Charles River. "*Nobody knows what I know*," he tells Mr. Compson when the latter challenges him to reveal it (emphasis added). Quentin jealously guards his secret—his incestuous thought about his sister Caddy—because nobody can understand him and commiserate with him even if he reveals it. Camus, whose death in a car accident was suspected to be a suicide, defends the withholding of information of the most private order by the individual who contemplates self-murder by attributing it to the problem of the human heart. "An act like this," he writes, "is prepared *within the silence of the heart*, as is a great work of art" (emphasis added).

Camus' view of suicide suggests that self-killing isn't an ordinary way of dying. The process of taking one's life by going through a meticulous ritual and by fearlessly inflicting on oneself such great pain, as in Frances' case, means that the subject attaches an important meaning to his or her self-destruction. Suicide, as Camus might put it, is a way of asserting oneself through one's death. In this respect, there is a similarity between suicide in modern Western culture and the Samurai's ceremonious hara-kiri. The subject uses suicide to assert his or her identity, the difference being the Japanese warrior killing himself to uphold a social and cultural value and the Western person taking his or her life for an ambiguous personal goal. By inflicting utmost pain on one's physical body, one wishes to inflict pain, sorrow, and guilt on one's enemy and the audience to teach them a lesson. In the words of Karl Menninger, suicide is a way "to retain one's omnipotence, not a real death."

These above thoughts are triggered as much by the death of Frances as by my quasi-suicidal experience after the fall of South Vietnam and the temporary loss of my family. In the past, I saw many dead people, but the thought of my own death never occurred to me. The death of my dear little sister, for example, shook me tremendously, but I didn't learn from it that someday I would be undergoing the same throes as she was. Piles of Việt Minh corpses with blood-caked faces and eyes open that I saw at an abandoned shed on my way to Chơn Phước school in Đồng Hới horrified me, but perhaps because I was young and immature, the scene did not reveal to me that the idea of death was so complex. Nor did the violent, tragic deaths I witnessed during the Tết offensive haunt me very long. I had so much work to do for the living—myself and my family—that the thought of death was irrelevant to me. It was only eight months ago, when what I had built for my future crumbled, that I suddenly had a fascination with suicide. It was at first a death wish materialized into a blind impulse to jump into the on-going traffic on Guadalupe Street. But in hindsight, it was not a suicidal act as in the case of Frances and as defined by Camus because I did not do it in my full consciousness and after a long preparation. It was an unconscious reaction to an unbearable, desperate situation, not a compelling desire to assert my identity, my "omnipotence," as is popularized in Western literature and society.

When I was pulled out of the traffic on Guadalupe Street amid yelling and deafening car horns, I felt like I was waking from a daze. I was horrified and frightened to think of what would have happened had I gotten killed on that day. I was not afraid to die, but I had no right to cause more misery and grief to my family by risking my life in such a foolish way. I bury myself in work to prevent relapsing into my suicidal behavior. But I feel just like an ostrich that hides its head in the sand upon seeing danger rather than fleeing away from it. We cannot solve a problem by just pretending it doesn't exist or seeking diversion from it somewhere. But even if we're willing to face it, we can also be defeated by its magnitude. This Catch-22 situation is what I face now. I try to keep myself alive in hopes for a chance—no matter how remote it is—to reunite with my family, but such an endless wait has proved futile as time passes. Overwork, desperation, and sadness take a toll on my health. I have nightmares again. Every morning, I wake up with a sensation of fatigue and ache all over my body. At thirty-eight not only do I feel old, but, for the first time, become acutely aware of my mortality. There lurks in the back of my mind the fear that the apparent weakening of my body, which I would have brushed off as an indisposition a few months ago, could be a sign of my inability to see my family again in this lifetime.

Age does not influence much the way we perceive human mortality. I know some people with advanced age whose joy of living is as great as or greater than those in their twenties. We are conscious of our mortality when we confront unsuccessfully the tyranny of our destiny, when we learn that despite our efforts, we are no match for many obstacles in life, when we've lost our ability to hope and dream, when we can no longer live up to others' (in my case my loved ones') expectations and ours. Our sense of mortality is therefore a psychological state of being generated by our realization about the terrible burden of life and our inability to shoulder it. When crushed by the force of circumstances, which is usually the case of those with suicidal behavior, like Shakespeare's tragic heroes, we will be left with no other alternative than opting out of the fight through self-destruction.

***

It has been a year since the fall of South Vietnam and Vietnamese students, who would have celebrated their successful study program here before getting on the plane and going home, attend their graduation with a heavy heart. I am happy for my young friends who can now enter the American workforce and succeed. But their transition to American life is not always smooth. The shock of losing their country is still fresh in their mind, let alone their feeling of being unprepared for permanently living in America. To avoid loneliness, they get married before they relocate for their job, but soon their marriage gets rocky. "That's the American way of life," a young friend, who is in a divorce settlement, bitterly comments.

My older colleagues fare even worse. My friend Hồng tells me her gay husband has disappeared. She does not want to seek a divorce from him because she is a Catholic. Nor can she return to Vietnam to live with her parents because the communist regime would not accept Vietnamese Americans. Thi, an officer in the former Republic of Vietnam army and a graduate student in engineering at UT, who has a wife and children in Vietnam, lives with a refugee woman who also has a husband stranded back home. I guess Thi and this woman live together because they think that they have no hope of seeing their family again in this life. They simply cannot bear their loneliness. I sympathize with them but feel that they act recklessly and selfishly. With time they will have children and their status will be legal. What if some time in their lifetime the new regime allows their own family to travel to the States to reunify with them? How would they deal with this dilemma legally and morally?

Refugees sponsored by churches and American families in Austin begin to arrive. Many have a sad story to tell. It seems in this colossal disaster of biblical proportions, only women are victims. Two attractive girls I help register for school in Travis County arrive here from Songkla refugee camp in Thailand. They had escaped from Vietnam, and disaster befell when they were trying to cross the Vietnam-Cambodia border. Women in their group were raped by the Khmer Rouge. The girls want to be excused from school. I explain to them that in the States they are required by law to attend school because they belong in the school age group. Then in tears, the older girl tells me her sister is pregnant and begs that she be allowed to stay home. The school district turns her down.

As I get to know the girls better, the older one confides to me that her sister resists their parents' attempt to take her to an abortion clinic. To imagine a Khmer Rouge pirate being their grandchild's father is more than they could bear. Fortunately, now that the girl lives in America, she cannot be forced to do anything against her will. As we talk, I see a flash of happiness on the teenager's innocent pretty face—the happiness of being an expectant mother, of carrying her baby in her own body—despite the most horrible experience she has experienced!

"SOLVEIG'S SONG"

Things calm down after a year of nightmare and terror following the fall of Huế and another year of grief and suffering. Now and then, I hear from home via France where mail from Vietnam arrives before it is forwarded by friends or charity organizations to stranded students like me in the United States. It is a great relief to know that my family is safe and that Nga occasionally—not always—receives the money I send through illegal channels. (Because the U.S. government has cut off all communications with the South, now annexed to the victorious North, former South Vietnamese nationals living in the U.S. give cash to the new regime's sympathizers who alone are allowed to visit the country, but then there is no guarantee that their money will reach their family or be given in full amount.) The sense of relief, which is no other than the pretension that I am doing enough for my family, makes me feel comfortable for the first time when seeking amusements and entertainments. Two years ago, a single thought of trying to enjoy myself would have made me cringe and suffer for hours. Now, I do not shut myself in my room after getting back from school but occasionally go to see some movies. As I am getting out of myself, I start going to some parties. My young Vietnamese friends, who left me alone before because of my penchant for solitude, now occasionally come to take me out for dinner. Being around with these people is a pleasure and a great comfort to me. Their situation is no better than mine, and yet they do not seem to let it interfere much with their living. This makes me feel better.

I am experiencing a sort of rejuvenation. I feel as if I have recovered from a lengthy illness. The more extended a sickness has been and the younger your body is, the quicker and surer its recovery becomes. Though I am not young anymore (my thirty-ninth birthday is less than six months away), I am amazed at my getting back on my feet so soon. I can sit here and look back at what happened to me with such a detachment, as if it was somebody else's experience. I still think of my family, but this does not happen as constantly as it did a year ago. There develops in me a habit to care more about myself than about my loved ones. Occasionally, I'm filled with a *joie de vivre* that has been unknown to me since I came to the States. Is this "rejuvenation" a sign of my complete health recovery, or does it mean that over the past two years, I have punished myself enough by wallowing in sorrow and now I need a respite to live? I do not know if the joy of living I occasionally experience is prompted by my moral weakness which causes me to divert my mind from my loved ones suffering at home or by my unconscious longing to be free of the terrible burden of responsibility as a family man when I can no longer handle it. I know some people in Austin whose condition two years ago was worse than mine, but they are doing better now. "We've suffered enough," they say. "Let bygones be bygones. Things will fall into place in the end."

It has been two years now since the fall of South Vietnam. Most Vietnamese students I know are resigned to what has befallen them. They accept their new status as refugees and start looking for jobs. Some get married and start a family, planning to live here permanently. Older students, especially those with U.S. government scholarships immediately cut off after the fall of Saigon, have real difficulty in making the transition. They either quit school and do menial jobs to support themselves and their family at home or stay in school but switch to fields that can help them find employment, such as business, sciences, and electronics. The transition is quite smooth for those with a previous background in math or science. Not all former U.S. government scholarship recipients are so lucky. Feeling too old to start over again or not qualified to learn new skills, these scholars or former South Vietnam government officials choose careers they had never thought they would choose in their life, such as selling cars, homes, or life insurance.

I consider myself luckier than these former Vietnamese nationals. In middle age and incapable of changing my career goals, I stay on to get my terminal degree and upon graduation, get an instructorship appointment at the UT English department. My salary is ten times greater than my Fulbright scholarship. I live a comfortable life like many educated Americans, commute to and from work in a used car (I never owned one before), enjoy teaching (students say I have great enthusiasm for literature, which makes them like my classes), doing scholarly research (my passion for literature comes back unawares), and much more. With all the privileges I am entitled to as an American Ph.D. I feel like a full-fledged American!

After leaving the library today, I take a leisurely stroll on the Drag on Guadalupe Street. This area is like a fair on Saturday afternoons with many activities that students do not want to pass up. They come here to relax and have fun after a week's hard work. Vendors, most of them married students, try to supplement their family income by selling their original work, such as paintings, handicrafts, bric-à-bracs, etc. Food stands and restaurants that serve American and exotic foods at reasonable prices are one block away. Added to the cultural richness represented on the UT campus is a dance performance by some Hare Krishna members, which is colorful and exotic but does not seem to attract much attention, probably because of their quaint attire and message. Nearby in front of the Co-Op Bookstore, a couple is performing "Solveig's Song," a piece by Edvard Grieg. The woman sings the song to the man's violin accompaniment. While obviously the two artists try to make some money probably for their living (scattered on the mat in front of them are some one-dollar bills, apparently rewards for their performance), there is no indication that they make their art a profane practice at all. The woman is a soprano who executes so well her role as Solveig, a central character in Henrik Ibsen's *Peer Gynt* on which Grieg based his famous piece. Solveig sings to express her sorrow and to remember her faithless lover Peer Gynt forever.

Hearing the song reminds me of the condition of women dramatized in important world literature. One can't help thinking of Dido in Virgil's *Aeneas*. Failing to capture her lover's attention, Dido burns the things that belonged to Aeneas before killing herself, hoping to take memories of him to the grave. In "Truyện cho những tình nhân" ["A story for Lovers"] Huế writer Nhã Ca talks about her heroine Diễm, who during the 1968 Tết offensive, gets caught in a Vietcong-controlled area and who keeps a journal to communicate with her missing fiancé. In her escape to a government-controlled area, she gets blown up by a Vietcong mine. When recovering her remains, people find an engagement ring in her entrails. Being denied the opportunity to represent her sorrow and suffering through speech, Diễm resorts to writing.

The long, uninterrupted plaintive voice that helps the soprano articulate Solveig's endless great sorrow brings me back to my present condition. Just when I am overcome by a great joy and gratefulness to be in America, having completely forgotten who I *am* and what I have been through just recently, I am caught off guard by an acute pain that shoots through my body and clutches at my heart. I am awake with a moan because the pain that I thought had gone away since I have not felt it for quite a while now returns and strikes me unrelentingly. It is the same old pain, but it now takes on a more complex nature. It has to do with the shame I feel upon realizing that I'm an involuntary exile, not an active participant in the American mainstream. It comes from my guilty feeling about forgetting my family, especially my little ones, who are hungry at home while I'm an instructor at this prestigious university pampering myself with comfortable living.

As soon as I have recovered a little from the attack, I discover to my amazement that the pain strikes me the moment I hear the song. The attack would have occurred sooner or later because chances are that my sorrow, latent but always keen, if held in check too long, will gush out even more violently. The music only makes the pain come back faster.

Like many who were born in the peaceful pre-war period, I grew up with vocal music since I was a child. First, songs are what every Vietnamese infant is unconsciously exposed to while snuggling in its cradle, and I was no exception. When I heard my mother sing nursery rhymes, which are often sad, to lull my baby sister, instantly I could recite some lines. My mother said that she used to sing the same rhymes to rock me to sleep, so does it mean that I might have heard in my crib and unconsciously committed to memory? She had a lilting voice that was unmistakably Bình Định—thick and slow, but sprightly and cadenced—that could make a happy child fall asleep fast, whereas my father's way of reciting lyrical poems, which was always prolonged and melancholy, guided me away from the real world—his life—marked by sorrow and wistfulness to a dreamland that exists only in his poetry. Since I spent a great part of my childhood with Father, and it was his sad recitation of T'ang poetry that lulled me to sleep every night, this sort of music was my main nourishment because I grew up with it and his love. More importantly, my long immersion in it created in me a passion for literature, especially poetry, a deep attachment to Vietnam, in particular Father's native land, and an incorrigible infatuation with the fantastic. Today these elements are still essentials of my nature.

My love of music and lyrical poetry became dormant after I started my family. My father, who lived with me after I got married, never recited his poetry again. I had thus lost my paradise but was not aware of it because I was too busy to think about it. Three years of burying myself in study for my Fulbright Program and subsequently another two years of living in a nightmare after 1975 were certainly not a suitable time for music and entertainment.

My love of music is reviving today because of my brief exposure to the two musicians' performance of "Solveig's Song" on the Drag. I am amazed that the song could hold me under its spell so long. It follows me as I walk back to my apartment. It is now gone, but I still hear and feel all its reverberation and simultaneously a tidal wave of immense sadness in my soul. I am amazed at the magic of the song. Judging the rapture as evidenced on the audience's facial expression, I guess the song must have provoked their different reactions depending on their emotional condition when they're exposed to it. No writer describes better the power of the music of sorrow than Marcel Proust. In *Swann in Love*, the *petite phrase* (little phrase) in Vinteuil's sonata makes Swann writhe in pain because it makes him remember Odette who has betrayed him. "Solveig's Song" reawakens the sorrow I have unsuccessfully repressed by engaging myself in self-indulgence or trying to sleep away the painful reality. The song's lyrics explains how Solveig misses Peer and wants him to come back. In her letters, my wife Nga also says everything is fine at home, but the tone of her writing strikes me as desperate. Reunion for us, as things stand now, is unthinkable. Though she works twice that hard by substituting for my role as a breadwinner, she takes time to write me unusually long letters. She explains that doing so makes her feel better. The chatty, quasi-cheerful style she uses in her letters to bluff me into thinking that things are going well at home fails to convince me. She knows that she cannot fool me, so she asks me to forgive her, but I know she cries a lot after that.

Not only does the female artist on the Drag make Solveig' sorrow real with her voice, but she also helps me understand that in life, in literature, and in art, nothing captures human feelings better than the human voice. I can understand Solveig's desperate love for her sweetheart by listening only to the artist's soprano. The long, sad highest notes she sings represent Solveig's greatest sorrow over her missing unfaithful sweetheart. Likewise, between the lines of Nga's casual writing, I can hear her voice describing the hardships the family is experiencing at home, see her tears as she is writing me, and so on. Of the many ways to express sad feelings and emotions, voice is perhaps the most effective one because it comes from our heart and it strikes the chord of our heart.

"Solveig's Song" takes me out of my present comfortable life. It brings me back to the reality of a person who has lost his family, who will soon become a permanent exile in the West. I am not different from the truant unfaithful lover in Ibsen's *Peer Gint* that Solveig talks about in her song. By making me shed tears of remorse, "Solveig's Song" makes me become *me* again. I am now a man who still has a family to remember, to love, and to live for. Hearing the song, I can perceive Nga's sorrow and hear her tearful voice. "Solveig's Song" is perhaps the most important piece of vocal classical music that has ever been created to depict the sorrow of the human heart in art and in life.

MY FATHER'S DEATH

In September 1980, my family traveled to the U.S. to reunify with me. My father, who had experienced so much transmigration in his lifetime (leaving his native place in Quảng Bình to seek fortune in Dalat where he and his bride had made their home and I was their firstborn), did not want, as he told his tearful daughter-in-law, to deposit his bones in a foreign land. When learning that I was applying for the family to come to the U.S. (after all my attempts to repatriate had failed), the old man repeatedly urged his daughter-in-law to seize the opportunity immediately. The day of their departure, Nga reports, Father left home early, saying that he was going to Đà Nẵng to visit my brother's family, but in fact, according to Nga, he left home because he could not bear seeing his grandchildren leave him for good. But when Nga and the children were about to leave, the old man returned and broke down. After tearfully bidding farewell to my father, Nga took the children to the railroad station, but as soon as the family got there, she frightfully discovered that Hùng was missing. The boy had leaped out to return home to be with his grandfather. Luckily, the boy listened to the old man and barely made it back for the train.

It's taken two years since our reunion before I can now think of my father! Work and family preoccupied me so much that the past and things and people connected with it had little or no room in my mind. I have been sick for two days, and today for the first time, I remember Father after I took a strong dose of Tylenol for my fever and fell asleep. *In his heavy slumber, he dreams that he is living in Trung Quán, a small village in Quảng Bình, where they arrive after their evacuation from Văn La, their home village, on hearing news about the landing of French troops at Port Đồng Hới. To provide food and lodging for him and his brother, their father takes a trip every fortnight to distant villages to tend his patients. After he is gone, his boy falls ill and runs a very high fever. Someone comes to tell him not to expect his father to return because he is gone for good. He breaks down in tears, completely awake.* Nga is sitting on my bed, crying. I see a Western Union telegram in her hand. "Ba has—," she sobs. I know what happened. My father's death was announced in my sleep through a dream, except that the event was distorted: I was brought back to my boyhood to relive the happiness of having a father and the sorrow of losing him. The person who told me about the sad news in my sleep was my wife, but she did not share it with me. She withheld the news because she feared that it would hurt me. But she could not keep it from me forever.

I cannot cry. I just stare in front of me. My mind is blank, totally blank, but I am aware that Father is dead, save that I have no reaction to the terrible news, do not feel overcome with sadness or anything. That *is* me in my full consciousness when struck by the saddest news I have ever received in my entire life. It is only when I am in a dream, when I am taken over by the unconscious, that I can connect with my past and the man I deeply love, be my real self, and cry over his death.

I do not know of anyone who is so unfortunate, who cannot shed a tear at his father's death, cannot go home to attend his funeral, cannot even tell his school his father has died (it would be embarrassing, even shameful, to be asked why he is not going home for his father's funeral). I go to work every day, give class lectures, but my mind is blank. This lasts several days, and then after that I start feeling the greatest loss ever in my life.

Three weeks later (communication with Vietnam is possible only via a third country, so it sometimes takes longer to reach relatives in the United States), I get a letter from my brother. He said that the day after my father was dressed for burial, he opened his eyes and asked for me. My brother did not say what he had told Father about me (I did not have the courage to ask him), and when he and his family came to the States, I never tried to find out from him about Father's last moments. It has been fifteen years since his death now, and still I cannot bring myself to listen to his last words that my brother had recorded on a cassette tape. Once I saw my father's belongings—a small bell for him to call my brother or his family (my brother tells me he needed to use it because he was bedridden), a crumpled felt hat that I had seen him wear whenever he went out to buy candies for his grandchildren, some clothes of his. Because Nga fears that I will break down if I see these mementos, she hides them away from me.

It is said that time is the best cure for psychic wounds. But in my case, my grief increases with the passage of time. I stay quite calm at school and in class, but after work would go up to my office, close the door, and cry quietly. I can fool others with my affectation of calm, but I cannot fool myself. The sorrow that I repressed when I was in front of people comes back and strikes me down vigorously when I am alone.

Because my health takes a toll when I perform that sort of double standard, Nga suggests that I go somewhere for a change. At the invitation of Kathy Parrington, a colleague from Louisiana State University, who takes her students on an international tour and who needs me to translate for her class, I join her and her group on their trip to Paris. When not accompanying them, I spend some time exploring the city. At these moments when I am all by myself, my "social" self breaks down. For the first time, I become acutely aware of my father's death and my *condition* as an orphan in my late middle age! I visit some bookstores in Paris, hoping my exposure to this intellectual ambience will alleviate my depression. But it does not always work. Today, when happening to browse a new edition of *Larousse Dictionary*, once Father's favorite reference material, at a bookstore on the Rue de Seine, I am seized with a fit of intense grief. I leave the bookstore in a hurry to hide tears rolling down my face!

I want to cry as much as I can. As if silent tears are not enough, sobs erupt from my long pent-up chest: *"Ba! Ba!"* I cry on my way back to my hotel. More than ever I feel the need for him though I know I do not have him anymore. When living at home with him, though I had already started my family and life back then when it was safe, I still saw Father as a mark of continued security and protection. Married with three young children, I still lived in an extended childhood, took for granted my father's presence in the family, and never imagined the possibility of losing him someday. Since that fateful date of March 26th, 1975, though I knew I would never see Father again in my lifetime and that telegram would come anytime, I was—and still *am* in my sleep—unprepared for the news. It is difficult to accept the death of a loved one who is still vitally alive in you. Even the dead sometimes do not accept their death because of their continued love of the living. Didn't Father revive for a short moment and ask for me after he had died the day before?

I love and miss my father after his death more than when he was living. What I had difficulty remembering about him when I was living with him *now* surges back to life, dominates my thinking, even haunts me. I can easily picture Father in those years of the Indochina war taking me and my brother from village to village in search of a new home after ours was destroyed by the Việt Minh in their "scorch-earth strategy." In his old faded black silk tunic, he looks thin and fragile but strongly determined to see to it that his children are safe. The magic lantern turns, and in the next scene I see him return from a long business trip (he used to be away for days to see patients in remote villages) with a string of mackerel in his hand and that evening, my brother and I would have a sumptuous feast. These moments of the past unfold in my mind like the episodes of a silent film in which I am both a viewer and a character. The images in the film are silent, but they are silent for a different reason—they represent the hardest, the most painful period of my entire childhood where mute endurance was our only course of action in the face of adversity. Only when I go down in time to my early childhood, my happiest time ever, does the film's soundtrack come on. *It is the voice of a middle-aged man who recites a Tu Fu poem to lull his seven-year-old son to sleep in his lap. Floating with the waves of his father's soothing tune and immersing himself in the bliss of happy childhood, the boy falls asleep fast.* That is the only time I hear my father's voice. At other times, his images just flit by in my mind's eye, fast, hurriedly, and without interruption as if my memory is running out of time.

In the short span of remembrance, my father's images during my thirty years of living with him, which were so vibrant with life, now become silent, sparse, and strange because of the absence of his voice. Only in my dreams can I occasionally hear Father, but the language he speaks from the grave is so vague, inchoate, and unfamiliar that I can hardly catch its meaning. Father has lost the power of speech, he belongs to a different world, and I can only communicate with him through distant memories. We are condemned to living in separate worlds, which with time will eventually sever us from each other permanently. I will also forget him completely. That is why in my dreams he looks sad, is often silent, and vanishes quickly. We can never recapture the past, regain our paradise in their entirety. During a dream, I always wake up and cry out tearfully, *"O Ba!"* when our reunion ends abruptly. When consciousness is not yet completely restored in me because I am not fully awake, it does *not* occur to me that my father is dead. I feel like a little child who cries because he is taken away from his parents. As I wake up, I realize I am not a sobbing child of years gone by, but it is *me in real life*. And yet I continue to sob like a child, my awareness of the loss of my father becoming more vivid than when I was in the dream. Tears gush out of my eyes. I lie in bed for a while to grieve over the greatest loss I have ever suffered in life. This state of mind does not last, however. As soon as consciousness takes over and I am fully awake, my father's image as well as my awareness of his loss fades. My tears run dry. No longer can I cry, but I feel more sorrowful than ever.

My brother brings some of Father's belongings, among them his neatly handwritten manuscript of a book of traditional medicine and translations of classical Chinese and Vietnamese poets, as well as his own poetry (Father had been hard at work on these projects for a long time before I left the country, feeling more than ever a desire, as he had always said, to pass on his fortune to his grandchildren before his death). While seeing other items of his belongings brings me sorrow and remorse, his translated and creative work bursts with life when I read and relish it in the solitude of my exile. A fragrance wafts softly from the pages of my father's book of poems into my nostrils. (When I was a child, before writing his poems in Chinese characters, he had me grind an ink stick mixed with a small amount of water against his inkstone until it produced a sweet-smelling thick fresh ink). *His words are not words, but they are full of scents and sounds and images of yesteryear.* Suddenly, I experience an epiphany of sorts: through Father's writing, I am brought back to my heavenly past. He is *not* dead, my family is intact, our life is simple but happy, and we are all safe and secure.

ANCESTRAL DEBT

November 22nd, 1998

My dear Ty Anh,

*B**ecause now I have little hope of telling you in person my last wishes, I'm writing this letter and will tell your brother to give it and all my writings to you when he and his family travel to America. I must write this "will" immediately as I feel I don't have much time left. Being a physician, I know my own condition better than anyone. My mind is sound, but my health is failing. My left eye goes blind completely. Luckily, I've finished a pamphlet on traditional medicine, and I hope my grandchildren will find it useful when they become doctors. But the letter I'm writing now is for you, my eldest son and our Trần family's male heir. Son, just as a seriously wounded bird's dolorous cry may deter the hunter from killing his game, so your dying father's message deserves your attention because he has cherished it for such a long time, and it comes from the bottom of his heart.*

It concerns the tomb site of your grandmother and your uncles Toán and Giáo. As you know, because we didn't have our own cemetery in Quảng Bình, I don't know where Grandfather was buried. He died when I was three years old, and Grandmother after his death worked hard to raise me and my brothers and therefore had no time to take us to his burial place for a visit. Besides, she did not live long enough to teach me my responsibility to our dead. But I remember Aunt Em, my half-sister, told me where Grandmother and your two uncles were buried. She and your uncle Giáo died in the same year. Your uncle Toán had died a year earlier. I had lost all my family when I was barely thirteen, old enough to understand the greatest sorrow of losing all my loved ones and becoming an orphan, but too young to cope with the tragedy and its consequences by himself.

To the best of my memory, Grandmother's tomb was in the backyard of our Văn La home. In 1947, when I took you home, you were too young to be told about Grandmother's death—what caused it, what made her so unfortunate, what happened to me after she died; why she, the daughter of the powerful province chief of Bình Định, left home to come here and become my mother; why she died so young. Because Grandmother's life and death was so tragic, telling you that the tomb in our backyard was Grandma's did not suit a child like you. When you got old enough, we left Quảng Bình to go south, so I didn't have a chance to instruct you to take care of it after I'm gone. Now that the war is over and the country has been reunified, when the new regime relaxes its policy toward overseas Vietnamese, I want you to apply to return home to find Grandmother's tomb, renovate it, and burn some incense to warm her spirit.

In my whole life, I've always been dedicated to the memory of Grandmother, Grandfather, and our ancestors. Before the first Indochina war, I had left Dalat to return to Quảng Bình just to take better care of their tombs. I consider leaving Quảng Bình after the Geneva Accords and failing to care for our ancestors' spirits a grave violation of Confucius' most important ethical code. For this reason, after your departure to America and before the unification of the country, when realizing that I couldn't go home again in this lifetime, I intended to build some wind tombs in Huế to commemorate our ancestors and Grandmother. I believed that would comfort their spirits because at least they would have a temporary home to return to for our reunion. Unfortunately, due to my poor health and old age, my dream didn't come true.

Right after the unification of the country, I found out about the fate of our ancestors' tombs. A distant nephew of mine from Quảng Bình came to see me in Huế and reported that most burying grounds in Văn La were leveled to the ground or blown up by U.S. bombing, so there is no hope of finding any that might belong to our relatives. My nephew went to our former ancestral home but found no trace of Grandmother's tomb. It looks like, Ty Anh, we'll have to build another burial ground for our dead. It's better to build one in Quảng Bình because it was their native land. It's better to erect empty tombs to remember them than to forget them and let them roam the strange land endlessly.

When Nga and the children came to America to live with you, I gave her a copy of our "Trần Family's History." It contains only a short biography of each of our main ancestors, along with their birth and death dates. Because they had died long before I was born, I know them only by hearsay and can't tell you much about them. All I can do is ask you to remember these important dates as a mark of appreciation for their starting and maintaining our lineage. But my mother, your grandmother, was the person I knew best and the reason I'm writing you this letter. Read on carefully to understand why Grandmother was most important to me; why she deserves our love, dedication, and faithful remembrance. For the last thirty years, I've always felt guilty for not staying in Quảng Bình to care for Grandmother's tomb and for not returning immediately after the unification of the country to see if it's still there. It's too late for me to do anything for Grandmother, so I want you to replace me after I'm gone.

Grandfather met Grandmother in Bình Định. He had retired from his post as tutor to King Hiệp Hòa in the Imperial Court in Huế. On his way home in Quảng Bình, he stopped by Bình Định to visit the province chief, his friend and colleague, and at the latter's request agreed to stay and teach his children for a while. Seeing that his friend was a widower, the province chief wanted to marry his eighteen-year-old daughter to him. Though it was a prearranged marriage, you couldn't rule out the fact that it was her admiration for Grandfather's scholarship that influenced Grandmother to marry him, a man twice her age. Shortly after her wedding, Grandmother gave up her comfortable life as the only daughter of a high-ranking mandarin to join her husband in his journey to Quảng Bình. I think had Grandmother not loved and admired Grandfather (who was her tutor during his visit at her residence), she would not have left home to come to a strange place.

Then tragedy befell their family. Ten years after they got married, Grandfather died. Life was extremely difficult for Grandmother, who became a widow at twenty-eight and who had to care for her three children, ages nine, three, and one, all by herself! She did menial jobs—gleaning grains in the rice field, hiring herself out as a seamstress or a maid at wealthy people's homes— to raise me and my two brothers. This went on for seven years. Things appeared to be paying off for Grandmother when your elder uncle Toán at sixteen took and passed the entrance exam at the Imperial Academy in Huế. He was also a virtuoso who could play a variety of instruments by just observing professional musicians play them once. Grandmother was so happy because her sacrifices finally were worth it. But misfortune didn't spare Grandmother and my family. In the evening of August 16th, 1906, my brother went to see a flood when he accidentally fell off a bridge. He was swept away by the flood before his playmates' cold eyes! His life was cut short at age sixteen, one month before he was to leave home to attend the Imperial Academy.

There is a line break in my father's letter. He might have paused momentarily to contain strong emotions when writing about his family's tragedy. "*Imagine my mother's great shock and grief at the loss of my brother,*" Father continues, but suddenly there is a change in his use of personal pronouns. He uses the neutral first-person pronoun *Ta* (I) to refer to himself in lieu of the emotionally charged *Ba* (Daddy). He says "my mother," "my brother" throughout as if Grandmother and Uncle Toán were his own people, and I am *not* privy to his family's sad story. Maybe he would rather see his misfortune as a personal matter of his own. This made him a proud but very lonely person.

Perhaps because of the urgency of the matter, he breaks his rule by divulging his secret to me. He writes:

At twelve, I was old enough to understand what it meant to lose a dear brother. But compared to my mother's grief and suffering, mine was nothing because my brother had been her hope and her pride, the reason she had taken upon herself so much self-sacrifice, which now came to nothing.

My mother continued to toil to raise me and my eight-year-old brother. But consumed by both hardship and grief, she fell ill and couldn't work anymore. She sent me to your Uncle Bảo for help, and you know what? He gave me the cold shoulder! My mother went back to work and her health deteriorated fast. Two months later, the greatest misfortune happened to me and my younger brother: Grandmother contracted dysentery from which she never recovered. She died at age thirty-five.

That is the longest letter my father has ever written me. His handwriting, which used to be neat, balanced, and graceful, now becomes convoluted, misshapen, and spidery. (Based on the date of his letter, he must have written it two months before his death.) I find it enclosed in his updated "Trần Family's History" that my brother gave me when he came to the States. Because the last page is missing (my father might have forgotten to attach the pages together, might have forgotten to finish the letter, or could not finish it because remembering his past was too painful for him or because he went completely blind before finishing the letter) and the narrative is interrupted, I do not know what became of him and Uncle Giáo after Grandmother's death. When living at home, I sometimes heard him say that Uncle Bảo took him in but made him work like a servant. As for Uncle Giáo, my father says in our "Trần Family's History" that he died at age nine, five months after Grandmother's passing away, but gives no specific information about the cause of his death. Even in this biographical account, scarcely does he talk about this youngest uncle of mine who must have been very close to him. I remember my father once told me Uncle Giáo had died of "a strange disease," but he stopped short of elaborating. Talking about misfortune in his family would make him suffer. His family's story was so sad that he did not want to share it with anyone, including me, his male heir.

Before my father died in 1989 at age ninety-two, he had compiled in longhand two copies of our ancestry records. The copy Nga gave me when she and the children came to the States in 1980 has detailed information not only about our ancestors' birth and death dates but the location of their tombs. I think my father gave me that copy because he wanted me to replace him in caring for our ancestors' well-being after his death. The task is very important because it involves not only worshipping them but tending to their tombs. The other copy that my brother brought to the States after my father's death is less detailed and much shorter, but in it, he adds his eulogies on Grandfather, Grandmother, and Uncle Toán, as well as this long letter addressed to me. I do not know why he had my brother keep it until his death instead of mailing it to me. Maybe he thought I would not need to be told about my obligations to him and our ancestors. Maybe he wanted my brother to have a chance to read and understand what he wrote and cooperate with me in fulfilling his wishes. Unfortunately, due to my hectic teaching schedule and the impossibility of realizing his request then, I did not pay attention to what he said in his letter until ten years later after I returned to Vietnam to visit my father's tomb and start working on my memoir. As I am writing about my past and my father, the information he provides in his work and in his unfinished letter is very valuable to me. It corroborates my memory of him and makes me understand him better. It also makes me aware of the urgency of his last wishes.

"So, you know now that I was the most unfortunate child in the world then," my father writes at the end of his tribute to Grandmother, but obviously he addresses us. *"I lost all my family—Grandmother, Uncle Toán, and Uncle Giáo. Three deaths in the family in less than two years! Aunt Em took me in for a few months, but because she couldn't afford to send me to school, she sent me to Uncle Bảo, my half-brother, Grandfather's eldest son from his previous marriage."* He does not say in his writing how Uncle Bảo had treated him, how long he had stayed with him, and why he had run away from his brother's home. When he was living, Father forbade us to share our family's story with anyone. Though he never told me why, I think this must have something to do with *noblesse oblige* as we came from a family with a long line of mandarins. I remember once hearing him say that Uncle Bảo made him work like a servant instead of sending him to school. Two years later, at fifteen, my father ran away from his brother's home, arrived in Huế, and found one of Grandfather's former students who helped him get accepted for the Imperial Academy. He stayed in Huế for five years until he graduated, then returned home to mourn his mother and his two brothers. He was mourning them for three straight years devoutly, faithfully, without fail. He did so for three long years in seclusion in accordance with Confucius' teaching of filial piety to scholars about their duty toward their deceased parents. I was amazed when hearing this story because he was then just twenty-two years old!

Then at the end of the mourning period, perhaps in response to the call of wanderlust, instead of accepting his appointment as a new mandarin in his hometown, one day in the summer of 1910 at twenty-three, he set out on a long trip that took him to Dalat, a mountain resort city in the Central Highlands founded by the French. It was here that he founded a private bilingual

(French and Vietnamese) school and married my mother, a widow twelve years younger than he was. I do not know why he went to that strange, far region when he was so attached to his ancestral land, particularly his mother's grave. Maybe his departure was prompted by his anger with Uncle Bảo. He could not get over Grandmother's death which he said could have been avoided had Uncle Bảo not taken all the property that rightly belonged to her and her children. Nor could he forgive his brother for treating him so badly after Grandmother's death. Maybe Uncle Bảo had abused his power as the family's oldest male heir by interfering too much in his brother's matrimonial matter, thus causing the young handsome Imperial Academy graduate to protest by fleeing home.

When he was living, I could not find out the truth as my father was tight-lipped about anything related to his private life. Nor did he ever tell me when he had met and wed my mother. As I remember, in Huế he had a couple of close friends who occasionally came to our home to visit him, but even at his merriest moments, hardly did he say a word about his emotional life. So, there is no way to find out when he met and married my mother. There is in the family album Nga brought with her to the States an old *carte postale* photo featuring my father looking very chic in his expensive semi-formal outfit. *"Chère ma sœur,"* he addresses Aunt Em, his only living half-sister in his very neat handwriting in French. *"I'm sending my current photograph to visit you. I just want to let you know that since my arrival here I've always been blessed by the new land's spirits."* The postcard was dated *"le 4 Juillet 1933"* but apparently was never sent. My father looks quite dignified, just like a newly appointed mandarin full of confidence standing with one arm akimbo and the other resting on a wooden stand. But there is a sad, wistful look on his handsome face. There is no shadow of a smile, nor a hint of satisfaction despite his career success. Though I do not know when my father met and married my mother, I do not think his broodiness in the photograph had anything to do with their marital conflict which happened several years after I was born. His sorrow, it is easy to guess, stems from his inability to get over the tragic ordeal he had experienced in Quảng Bình.

I remember when at home I often heard him talk affectionately about Aunt Em, who he said had taken him in for a short while immediately after Grandmother's death and had been very kind to him. "I don't know how I could live without my sister after Grandmother's passing," he said. Because Aunt Em was childless, he wanted me to light incense on her altar occasionally "to warm my unfortunate sister's spirit." I can see how my father was grateful and attached to his sister, and yet I cannot help comparing the casual tone of his postcard with the pathos and emotional intensity of his words in his tribute to Grandmother and in his last letter to me. This was very unusual for my father, who, perhaps because of the training he had received at the Imperial Academy, regarded emotionalism as inappropriate for a Confucian scholar and mandarin.

Having lived with my father for twenty-five years before I left home to come to the States, I had always seen him diligently playing his role as a Confucian father, loving us and making a lot of sacrifices for us, but often abstaining from openly showing his affection to us. But I remember every year on the anniversary of the death of Grandmother, my father got very emotional. His great filial piety toward her was shown in his meticulous performance of the commemorative ceremony. After we placed the food and fruits on her altar, my father lit three incense sticks and put them in the burner. Then raising his clasped hands to his forehead to show profound respect for Grandmother, he said his greetings to her, invited her to accept our food offerings, and asked her to bless her offspring. Next, he prostrated himself several times during the ceremony. He addressed Grandmother as if she was still living and he was performing his filial duty toward her. On more than one occasion, I saw tears in his eyes. Having participated in these rituals to honor Grandmother for a long time, I came to understand the meaning of filial piety as shown in Father's devotion to Grandmother and other deceased ancestors. Over time, I came to love Grandmother as much as I loved him.

Due to his Confucian background and my strict upbringing, we communicated better in writing than in speech. Growing up in the strait-laced Confucian culture, I was supposed to take and carry out my father's orders dutifully, not to ask him any questions. After I left home, because my father wrote me regularly, I came to know him better every day. In his letters, he appears more relaxed and at ease than usual, affectionately calling me by my childhood name. After 1975, he stopped corresponding with me in person, but once in a while I found a short cryptic message enclosed in Nga's mail in which my father told me "to stay put where you are to complete your education" which I would interpret as *"do not come home at this time."* After my family left Vietnam to reunite with me in the States, I only heard about him through my brother. I did not know that after realizing that he could no longer wait for our reunion, he immediately set about working, despite his deteriorating health, on two projects that were more important to him than anything: a book manuscript on traditional medicine and a biography of the founders of the Trần clan. Nor did I know that, after finishing these projects, my father went blind and had to communicate with me through my brother. He paid a very dear price for trying to make his eldest son, who was pursuing his vacuous dreams in America, aware of the importance of his ancestry. By reading what my father wrote, I came to understand him and what he had been through better. Because my life was intertwined with his, understanding him is understanding myself. It is easier for me to understand his message and the urgency of his request.

"It began with my anguished desire to return to Quảng Bình to care for our ancestors' tombs," my father explains. *"Your mother supported my plan. As you were in school, I took your brother to Quảng Bình first. The following summer, your mother sent you to Quảng Bình to stay with us until January 1945, eight months before the August Revolution."* He had just built a shrine where I saw him worship our ancestors and mourn Grandmother, Uncle Toán, and Uncle Giáo. He set a common date to commemorate their death anniversary, saying that it would be like a family reunion to him, because he and his loved ones could be together for a while. Being home did not seem to make him happy because all the people he loved were dead. He was an extremely doting parent, but I often found him brooding and taciturn. He often recited T'ang poetry and his own poems when he lulled us to sleep in his lap, but his voice was so sad that I would have cried had I not fallen asleep so fast.

"I found Grandmother's tomb. With difficulty, I found your two uncles' tombs in a parallel position. I remember it was Aunt Em's idea that they be together after death so they could be close to each other. But I had no luck with the rest of our deceased. Uncle Bảo had died before I came home, so I couldn't ask him. When he was living, I was too young to know the importance of our ancestors' tombs. Even if I were old enough, I wouldn't dare ask him." He gave up his successful career in Dalat to return here to fulfill his filial piety, but it did not pay off. While ordinary folks in his village were paying their visit to their family cemeteries during the Ancestors' Appreciation Day, my father, an Imperial Academy alum and the grandson of a former Bình Định province chief and the son of King Hiệp Hoà's teacher, could not hold a memorial for his forebears for lack of a family cemetery of his own! He faced the same reality he had encountered twenty years earlier after his return as a graduate from the Imperial Academy: nobody in the village could help him find his ancestors' burial ground. Being back in his birthplace made him miss his departed loved ones even more.

Early in 1945, my mother came to visit us, but she stayed only a couple of days. I also had to return to Dalat for school. *"I knew immediately that our rustic place didn't suit your mother,"* my father writes. *"But I didn't realize that her departing marked the end of our ten years' union. I had found a relative to entrust him with taking care of our shrine so I could return to Dalat when the war broke out and I lost contact with your mother. Rumor had it that there was a massacre of civilians in Dalat by the French in retaliation for their alleged support for the Việt Minh. I was so worried that I took your* brother to Quảng Ngãi, left him at your cousin Kỳ's home, and went on to Dalat. Luckily, I found the family in Phan Rang.

"I had successfully persuaded your mother to return to Quảng Bình," my father continues. "The French hadn't landed here yet. She urged me to take you to Quảng Bình first and she would join us later after selling the property in Dalat. As you may remember, we left a week later. By the time we arrived in Quảng Bình, the war had spread to Đồng Hới. As you know, we left our Văn La home and later moved around several times before getting settled down in Đồng Hới so you and your brother could attend school."

My father's taking us to the city for our education did not pay off either. As the French were losing the war, Đồng Hới became as unsafe as Trung Quán we had fled a few years earlier. Fighting now reached its suburbs and assassinations of local government officials by Việt Minh commandos took place almost every day. With the surrender of the French forces at Điện Biên Phủ and the convening of the Geneva Conference, prospects of a communist victory and its terrifying consequences haunted every resident's mind. Most people considered leaving.

Father made a decision that was to affect all our family for the rest of our life: leaving Đồng Hới after the Geneva Accords. *"You might not know that I didn't want to leave at first,"* my father writes. *"The idea of abandoning my native land and our ancestors' tombs was just too painful for me. I was sixty then, too old to start a new life in a strange place. It was better to live, die, and be buried with my loved ones here. I didn't want—still don't want now—to deposit my bones in this strange place* (until his death he still saw Huế, my adopted land and my children's native country, as a strange place). *But because of your education—."* A pang of guilt shoots through me. Father did not complete his sentence. He did not want to make me feel that because of us he had left his native land and had been subject to all the hardships beyond his endurance in a new place. For nine years after our arrival in Huế and before I got married, he had kept his personal thinking to himself, had never said a word about his native Quảng Bình or our ancestors. He only expressed his feelings of exile, homesickness, alienation, and loneliness in his poetry which I find so sad. He did not want us to feel guilty about being the cause of his leaving Quảng Bình and being undutiful to our ancestors. Our education was always his top priority in life.

Father continued to live with us after I got married, but he turned the last twenty years of his life into his most active period ever. While he was excited about the growth of his clan and his offspring's future in his new land, he continued to be brooding and taciturn as if he was preoccupied with something very important. When Nga and the children came to the States to live with me, she reported that no sooner had I left the country than Father set out to work on a book project about his experience in treating his patients that he said would be useful for his grandchildren when they become physicians like their grandpa. He also continued his translation of T'ang and Sino-Vietnamese poetry. His most urgent project that he finished on the eve of Nga's leaving Vietnam was transcribing our Trần family's genealogy records, a big volume started by my great-great-grandfather and passed down to my father, from Sino-Vietnamese into Vietnamese. There is in this beautiful handwritten manuscript a very moving eulogy on Grandmother along with her biography prepared by my father based on his memory of her as a thirteen-year-old. I am particularly struck by the way he shows his filial piety to Grandmother. He vividly describes all the sacrifices she made for him and his brothers after she became a widow at age twenty-eight. I do not know how he could manage to get such specific information about Grandmother, such as her family background. I suspect she might have told him in person, or he might have heard her story from someone who knew her well, or he just filled in the narrative gaps with his imagination. I have no way to verify all this. All I know is the past was very important to him and he had to recreate it even by reinventing it. But I am struck by the touching sincerity of his voice. In his writing he addresses Grandmother as if she was alive, as if he was writing a letter to a very important person who is present, not a eulogy. Though Grandmother had been dead for a long time, Father still loved and missed her. Respected her, too. He often interspersed his writing with the phrase *"Esteemed, Beloved Mother."* At the end of each piece of writing, he puts *"Your undutiful son."* I feel that by telling her story and repeating such phrases, he wants not only to show his love and gratitude to Grandmother but to comfort himself with the fantasy that he still *has* a mother to love, appreciate, and admire.

Because Grandmother was especially important to Father and he feared he could not fulfill his filial duty to her and our ancestors, he appealed to me, his male heir, to do it for his sake. *"Son, can I count on you to do it for Ba?"* (though he was trained in the Confucian tradition, he used this Westernized term *Ba* to refer to himself when speaking with us). *"It's too late for me to do anything for Grandmother and our ancestors."* Though he wrote these words ten years before his death, I take this as his deathbed wish because he stopped writing me after he became blind. These words, which my father had written before he went totally blind, release in me a plethora of images and meanings compressed, hidden, secret but familiar, poignant, and endearing. Father is speaking again to me after ten years of silence! I hear him again, hear his life story, hear his deathbed message.

Since our arrival and eventual settling in Huế until his death, he had always dreamed about returning to Quảng Bình to care for our ancestors' tombs and to die in his homeland, except that he did not know how he could do it. The unification of the country in 1975, which could have been a wonderful opportunity for him to realize his dream, worked against his wishes: Father could not go back to Quảng Bình to visit his ancestors' tombs because of old age and illness. Nor could I get a visa to go home because of my affiliation with the old regime, as well as my suspicious status (Nga says the university's new administration told her that I was working for the U.S. government because I studied under a Fulbright scholarship). Because he feared police might read his writing and I and my family could get in trouble, he couched his warning me not to take the risk to return at this time in a pro-regime language and did not reveal my whereabouts. *"Son,"* he writes, *"who wouldn't want you to return to visit the country and our ancestors' tombs now that the South has been totally liberated and everybody at home is celebrating this historic event? But I understand that you can't make such a trip at this time because you're still in school besides working hard to support your family."*

In his letter addressed to me, there strikes a note of heartbreaking urgency. *"My dear Ty Anh, I'm getting very old, frequently fall sick, and now blind in one eye. I've been waiting for our reunion these years so you could accompany me back to our ancestral land. It would be my greatest joy when that day comes. But like a ripe fruit that will fall from its tree any time, I don't think I can wait for you that long. Hence, take these as my last words to all my children, especially you, my most dutiful son: Always be faithful to your ancestors' memory. Please Father, Mother, and my ancestors, understand and forgive me for failing to fulfill my filial duty to you in this lifetime."*

Those are my father's last words to me found in the stack of his writing my brother brought to me. I do not know why Father never mailed me that unfinished letter but put it in the folder of his manuscripts. His handwriting, neat and easy to read in the earlier section of the letter, suddenly gets irregular, crooked, and spidery. As the letter comes to an end, the words are jerky and zigzag across the page and punctuation marks are put in wrong places. My brother says that he saw him work hard and long on this letter, beside other projects. He worked until he went completely blind and had to stop for good only two months before his death. I can imagine the great length of time he must have taken to do it as he could barely see with one eye and his health was failing. Though I cannot find the missing page of his letter, I know what he would say in it: he would reiterate the same thing I have read thus far, except that the tone of his writing would be very urgent as he knew he could no longer wait for me and had to say it all now or never. Each misshapen, twisted word he managed to put down in the entire letter speaks of his utmost effort to convey to me something he knew was unrealistic, but he was so passionate about—my *return* home to find and look after my ancestors' burial ground.

Each word in Father's letter, in its turn, evokes in me guilt, remorse, sorrow. Could I have been spared all this trouble had we never left Quảng Bình, or had stayed on with Father and my family instead of leaving home? Even if I had returned home before the change of regime to care for him until he died, would that make him happy? I do not know. But I know that he would rather refrain from visiting ancestors' tombs than see me perish in a re-education camp because of my American education. In his delirious moments shortly before his death, he felt the urgency of the call of duty to our ancestors. But when he was fully conscious, he gave up his wish and did not want to put me in danger. He blamed what he called *"cruel fate"* for his failure to accomplish his filial piety, and desperately asked me and my brothers for help though he knew it was wishful thinking. Whereas my father blamed fate for his many missed opportunities in life because he could not act differently, I acted blindly and selfishly, unwilling to consider the fact that what I did could hurt my loved ones. For example, it was me who wanted to accept the Fulbright scholarship, and I dismissed a colleague's warning about my father's old age and frequent ailments, about Nga's inability to keep the family by herself. I ignored the prick of my conscience. I chose to leave my loved ones in harm's way, not thinking about the possibility that I might not be able to see them again.

I found my wife and my children, but I lost my father eternally. When I left home for my studies in the States, I did not bring anything from him that could help me remember him. There was no need for that because until the eve of the fall of Huế, returning home for me was a sure thing. My remembrance of him as *a living human being* stopped at the moment I bid farewell to him and my family at Phú Bài Airport and turned around to get onto the airplane. To create Father's image after I left him and particularly in his last years, I contemplate what Nga and my brother brought to the States—pictures of him taken with his grandchildren, his writings, samples of his belongings, particularly the little bell, and the last letter he wrote me but never finished—and imagine what his life was like during my long absence. Every word Father writes is *an image, a sign, a voice*. I see and hear him again. *Father is old and sick. His voice is weak. He's also blind. He has been bedridden for a while and now is relying on a little brass bell to communicate with my brother. And the old felt hat? When living with him at home, I used to see him wear this thing when going out to buy candies for my children.* Nga's niece, who recently came to the States tells me that after my family's departure, Father often wore that hat when he went to visit Nga's relatives' children to find *reminiscences of his beloved daughter-in-law and grandchildren that he missed so much. Things belonging to a loved one who is dead, when seen again after a long time, can be heartbreaking because they would make you vividly remember him or her. Father has been ill for a long time when he suddenly gets better, sits up, asks my brother to give him pen and paper. Before he goes blind completely, he strives to write me his last letter. No one knows why it is inserted in the manuscript of his genealogy records instead of being sent to me. It is the longest, most poignantly eloquent letter Father has ever written me. He dies on the evening of January 27th, 1989, two months after writing the letter. The following morning, he briefly opens his eyes, asking for me by my childhood name: "Ty Anh? Ty Anh?"*

A pang of grief and remorse rips through me. *I am home right on time when Father wakes up from his long sleep and asks for me. I am right by his deathbed, listening to his last words.* Every word in his letter is the sound of Father's voice which was thin, feeble, and inaudible, but now it gets clearer, more distinct to me than ever. I absorb every sound of it, every nuance of his heavy Quảng Bình accent I have missed so much these twenty-five years. His voice is a whisper, but I catch every word he says and what it means—silent, noiseless but resounding in me like my own voice speaking to myself. *Son, these are Ba's last words. Just as a seriously injured bird sings more beautifully than ever before it dies, so I hope what I am going to say to you will make sense because I am in my last moments. Return to your ancestral land and light a stick of incense to warm your ancestors' and Grandmother's spirits. Their tombs were blown up by American bombing in the last war, so they have no place to return to but continue roaming the earth. They need to rest, which can be done only if you return and erect a memorial to honor their memory and to give them a lasting repose.*

As soon as the war ended, the Americans came back to search for their missing soldiers. Their remains were found and repatriated to their homeland. Our ancestors are not fortunate. Their tombs were gone, and so were their bones. Show them your gratitude by remembering them and teaching my American grandchildren to know who their ancestors and great-grandmother were. Take them to our former ancestral home in Văn La, if it still exists, for a visit. Teach them to love their ancestors. Tell them that their roots are here, not in America!

Carefully read my genealogy book. It is our family treasure as it marks the existence of our lineage. Keep it in a safe place. Do you remember that before we emigrated to Huế, we happened to discover that rats had gnawed several pages of the book? It was a bad omen as it turned out that we had to leave our ancestral home and land permanently, that our ancestors' tombs were destroyed by war, and that they have been condemned to roam the earth searching for their lost home since then. Return to hold a requiem for their souls. Build a memorial for them so they can come back to rest. Do not let them be vagrant ghosts.

Father's breathing gets thinner and thinner. *Do not worry about me. I will not be alone after I die.* A feeble sparkle of joy comes into his eyes. *Grandfather Grandmother Uncle Toán Uncle Giáo are here to welcome me take me home. It is going to be a big family reunion.* Father mutters, closing his eyes. Until his death, Father did not relinquish his search for home where he could reunite with his loved ones.

I am exhausted. The burden is too heavy. It is literally impossible. Father was morally and spiritually better equipped than I to carry out the mandate, but he had to give up. How can I, an elderly ailing exile, assume this task one hundred times harder than Father's? Would I be able to return in my lifetime? Would I be spared scorn and alienation from my people at home because I am not like them? How could I instruct my children and grandchildren their obligations to our dead when such a notion is alien to their American mind? Would they accept what Father calls *"their roots,"* that is, his past and my past, when these are but the sum of tragedy, misfortune, suffering, and sorrow, which is our fate and has nothing to do with their American identity? I shudder to think of my pathetic condition as a permanent exile who, until the end of my life, cannot even entertain a fantasy about home, let alone returning home to live and to die, or better yet, being remembered by my American children and grandchildren who do not share with me the same roots.

My brother says that Father told him he wanted to be buried in Văn La after his death. To him, to die in the strange land (all his life he considered any place other than Quảng Bình not his homeland) is to become a vagrant ghost. After a person is dead, his or her new ghost must seek ways to return to its ancestral home as the deceased person is deprived of his or her former place of residence. I remember after the Tết offensive, after his recovery from a grave illness, Father expressed to me his desire to build a small cemetery with wind tombs in place of our ancestors' lost ones in Quảng Bình. He and members of our Trần clan would also be buried here. His plan was designed to prevent him and all his offspring from becoming wandering ghosts in the land of his exile. It never materialized.

Father's message frightens me. To carry it out, we should reverse or change the course of History. But can we do it? There were a lot of things we should have or should not have done. We should not have left Quảng Bình, I should not have left Huế and Father, I should have sought to return home immediately after the country's reunification, etc., etc. But could I have done differently? Could I undo such things? And finally, could I ameliorate the situation, the cause of which was the inexorable force of circumstances over which we had no control? *"Định mệnh trớ trêu!"* (How ironic fate is). Father says this in his last letter, stupefied by the futility of his efforts to fulfill his duties toward his deceased people. It makes no sense that an old man like him could not die and be buried in his ancestral land as he wished. Nor can I understand why I could not return home to see Father in his last moments now that the war is over and the country has been reunified. There were tons of absurd things happening to Father and to me that even now I do not understand why they happened. If I could formulate a tentative response, then it would be like this: if fate is a blind force that controls the destiny of a people, then nowhere has it been more inexorable than in Vietnam. Every Vietnamese is inescapably subject to its cruel rule, and my family is no exception.

EXILE'S RETURN (I)

In June 1995, six months after the official normalization of relationships between the two countries, Nga and I secure a visa from the Embassy of the Socialist Republic of Vietnam to return home. Our children do not join us because they are in school and because Vietnam no longer appeals to them. Since during the war, North Vietnam saw the U.S. as its mortal enemy, I thought this epoch-making event would never take place, and thus it would be difficult for me to reunite with my family in my lifetime. The French involvement in the last Indochina war was on a lesser scale than the American one, and yet after the conflict it took three decades for many Vietnamese nationals living in France to get their family members out of Vietnam. Therefore, Vietnamese living overseas welcome the great news, which they believe will make it easier for them to get a visa to return to Vietnam to see their loved ones and hopefully get them out of the country eventually.

Though my family was fortunate to leave Vietnam in 1980 thanks to the intervention of the U.S. government and the approval of the Vietnamese government, I have been anxiously awaiting this momentous event since 1992, when news about a rapprochement between the U.S. and Vietnam was in the air. It is not that I want to return to Vietnam to realize my old dream. It is too late now to do anything about it unless I could be riding on, say, a "time machine" like the one in H. G. Wells' novel *The Time Machine*. I want to go back to Vietnam for one single purpose: to see my father's tomb and to satisfy his most cherished wish, namely, gathering our ancestors' scattered tombs in Quảng Bình in one place. Because I have no living family members and relatives in Vietnam, my trip will be like a visit to the dead.

In June 1995, six months after the official normalization of relations between the two countries, Nga and I secure a visa from the Embassy of the Socialist Republic of Vietnam in Washington, D.C., and board a China Airline flight which takes us to Hồ Chí Minh City, formerly Saigon, the capital of the Republic of Vietnam before 1975. With mixed feelings, I am returning to a country that twenty years ago was so dear and so familiar in my heart. As we are transferred in Hong Kong to a Vietnam Airline plane toward our destination, I feel a tight knot in my stomach. It is that same touch of pleasure and excitement that came upon me every time I returned to Dalat from Quảng Bình as a child or to Huế for the New Year holidays from my teaching post in

Nha Trang to visit my father. But today, no sooner do I feel that thrill of homecoming than I am plunged into a fit of depression. I was coming home now, but what an irony! My father is dead, our home was seized after the departure of my family, and we are to register upon our arrival as tourists and stay at a hotel like foreigners! Do you call home such a place? No, it is rather a strange land where you are hardly recognized or accepted. Twenty-three years of exile is long enough to show the effect of time on human memory, let alone the fact that I have no living relatives there. Chances are that I could be alienated by my own people in my own country not only because of my outlandish manners I have unconsciously acquired after so many years of living and working in America but also because of my timidity and self-consciousness that some people might see as a sign of unfriendliness and arrogance.

Right on this plane, I already perceive a constraint between me and my fellow passengers and between me and the crew. The elderly couple sitting next to us look morose and never speak to us during the entire flight. Maybe they are nervous or apprehensive over their visit, or maybe, like me, they do not feel comfortable talking to strangers. Except for the captain who occasionally makes announcements in English with a heavy Vietnamese accent, the flight attendants are unusually quiet. In their pink *ao dai*, they are very attractive but look cold. They go about their chores in a serious manner, hardly paying attention to us. Out of curiosity, I try to know what dialect a young woman who serves food and refreshments to us speaks by asking for a blanket for my shivering wife. To my disappointment and amazement, she does not say a word to me, though she quickly responds to my request. All this forebodes the ordeal I will be experiencing on my trip home. It is caused by the lack of regular communication between people of the same origin that has existed for a very long time. It has a lot to do with the nation's long history of division and disunity: the costliest civil war, the irremediable reconciliation between Northern and Southern Vietnamese, and the suspicion and resentment of some Vietnamese at home toward returning overseas Vietnamese who they think are rich and too Americanized.

A female voice announces over the intercom that the plane is landing at Tân Sơn Nhất Airport and reminds us of safety measures and customs procedures. The flight attendant must have come to the South from her North after 1975, for her heavy northern accent is so much different from the accent of those who came to the South in 1954, which is usually much lighter due to their long resettlement in southern regions. The announcement wakes me from my train of random thought, bringing me back to reality: I am back in Vietnam now; my native land which for the last twenty-three years—and just a short while earlier during my daydream—was so close and so dear to me but now suddenly becomes a strange place that could pose a lot of risks to someone who was affiliated with the defunct South Vietnamese government. Because I came to the U.S. with a government visa, police may hold me at the airport, or worse, they may detain me for interrogation. While envisioning potential problems I may soon encounter, as the plane is taxiing down the runway, I cannot help looking out the window to catch my first glance at former Saigon. Moving fast in my direction are the things and objects I can instantly recognize—the same lush grass field with scattered white spots that my mind can immediately recognize as cranes, the same overcast sodden sky that one would usually find in Saigon in summer almost every late afternoon. Almost intact along the runway are abandoned moss-grown bunkers once used by the former army of the Republic of Vietnam to protect the airport. Twenty-three years ago, during the takeoff of a Trans World Airlines flight that took me to the States, I concentrated hard on these images and tried to commit them to memory, vaguely feeling that would be the last time I saw them. Things bravely stood the test of time, and I cannot help thinking of so many losses and tragedies my people in the South had suffered in the war. How fragile we all were in the face of brutal history! Even survivors could not remain in one piece. They survived, but their lives were crippled, their hearts broken, their dreams shattered. Only insentient things stand the test of time and the brutality of history.

After getting out of the plane, we board a bus that takes us to the customs area. The comfort I felt upon recognizing familiar things during the plane's touchdown is replaced by a sensation of anxiety and apprehension as we are rushed along a long corridor in the airport building. Our eyes occasionally meet armed patrol officers in moss green uniforms (former South Vietnamese police uniforms were white) who shot at us with their cold, piercing glances. The police who process us are a man and a woman. They look young but very austere. The man motions us to come forward with a nod and throws at us a cold look before accepting our passport and visa. The woman clicks on her computer, apparently verifying our personal information. The man greets me by curtly stating my name, which I instantly understand as a question about my identity, so I answer, "Yes." I notice he has a northern accent. The woman does not speak, but I guess she could be from the North as well.

We run into trouble when proceeding to the next station. A policewoman tries to make Nga pay a fine for not declaring her ring (which we do not think is very valuable) in the customs form. Knowing what the customs officer wants, Nga gives her a $10 bill and says, "Please accept my little gift." The woman relents and lets Nga go. But I am not that lucky. The customs official who inspects my bags greets me warmly but complains in a suspiciously friendly way that he has been working so hard that he has no time for a cup of coffee. Because I fail to understand his cue, or perhaps I am too shocked to act accordingly, he sends me to a room in the back to "work" (*làm việc*) with an older police officer who speaks with a southern accent. He tells me I am stopped because they find books, which he calls "cultural materials," in my luggage. Immediately Nga produces another $10 dollars to bribe the man. In his most genuine, good-natured South Vietnamese demeanor, he thanks us profusely and wishes us "a pleasant visit to your home country." The man's honesty makes me feel better.

I do not know what will be in store in the days ahead of our visit, but I feel much better now that the hassle is over. I can see excitement and joy on everybody's face as they hurry toward the gate with bundles of luggage to meet their awaiting relatives. I also feel I am home, though I no longer have a home here. Is this the feeling we experience when our endearing past returns and transcends the present? I completely forget what we went through in the customs clearance area. I am as excited as when I returned home in Dalat from a long trip with my father and my brother.

Outside is a huge crowd waiting for their relatives returning from *Mỹ quốc* (America: the Beautiful Country). Vietnamese at home use this term to proudly refer to where their relatives are returning from. The feelings of frustration, anxiety, isolation, even anger that overwhelmed me when I went through the headachy customs line disappears the moment I exit the airport building. My head swirling, my feet wobbling, I am sucked into the ecstatic crowd, feeling as though I am a long-lost relative who is welcomed home by *my* own people. My American identity is lost. I am now one hundred percent Vietnamese!

We are met by *chị* Thúy, Nga's older sister, who saw me off at this same airport twenty-three years ago. *Anh* Đắc, Nga's oldest brother, also came a long way from Huế to greet us. It is the first time that I meet *anh* (eldest brother) Đắc who had gone north with the Việt Minh under the Geneva Accords before I married his sister. He looks excited when meeting me, telling me he is proud to have me as a member of his family, acting like he was my oldest brother. Never have I been given such a kind treatment. I am also happy that Nga, who has not been back since our reunion in the States, can see her relatives again tonight. *Anh* Đắc is extremely attached to Nga. He returned to Huế immediately after the fall of South Vietnam to protect his sister who he suspected might have trouble with the new regime because of my being in the States. He also urged Nga to leave the country to reunite with me as soon as she got her visa.

I leave Nga and her relatives alone so I can explore for a while—and in doing so hope to rediscover the familiar, loving city I have not been back to since my departure to the U.S. Forgetting completely that it has become a different place now, I relish the familiar air I breathed back then. On our way to Chợ Lớn where *chị* Thúy lives, the streets even at these late hours are swamped with motorcycles roaring in our and the opposite direction, honking for a space in the traffic. The lack of space gives me a sense of closeness and belonging that I missed for so long. There arises in me a feeling of déjà vu acute enough to cause a spasm in my stomach. I can also recognize in my mind's eye old houses and buildings of years past, just as I could recognize earlier today the lush rice field at the airport. For me, they represent the past I return here to find, the past that withstands the onslaught of history as well as the ravage of time, the past that stays intact so much so that it becomes an enduring present.

When we arrive at *chị* Thúy's home, I still relish that marvelous sensation. It is Nga who notices that transformation in me. "Why, you look happy," she says, perhaps recalling that she often found me gloomy and depressed before and during the trip. In fact, at the bottom of my heart I know that it is but a euphoric feeling, momentary but necessary for my emotional survival. We go to bed late after Nga's family reunion, but maybe because of that transformation taking place in me or maybe because of the change in the time zone, I do not wake up until noon the next day.

Lâm, Nga's nephew, takes me on his motorcycle to downtown Saigon. Unlike many downtowns in the U.S. which are solely used for business operations, downtown Saigon is the hub of the city's commerce and the residential area of the wealthy. Whereas the city's suburbs are crowded and populated with slums, "central" Saigon, as commonly called, except for the never-ending flow of Honda motorcycles through its major one-way streets, is every Vietnamese citizen's dream world with attractive European-styled villas, high-rise buildings, luxury shopping malls, fascinating bookstores, and many other first-class facilities. That is why, as Lâm tells me, wealthy and powerful cadres from Hanoi have moved to Saigon to enjoy the best that Vietnam's most modern city can offer. Lâm says that when he gets bored or depressed, a whisk through this section of Saigon on his motorbike would perk him up. When living in Saigon years ago, I did a similar thing: taking a bus that would let me off here and spending the late afternoon doing window shopping, stopping by the birds' section of the flea market on Hàm Nghi Street to enjoy the rare sounds of nature in the noisy city, and finishing the day in Xuân Thu *Librairie*, the famous French bookstore on Tự Do Street (now renamed Đồng Khởi), browsing its fascinating collections of foreign literature.

Hardly can I recognize Saigon at first. It is decked with flags, banners, and posters that praise the Communist Party and brag about its so-called accomplishments in many fields. A huge portrait of Hồ Chí Minh is displayed on top of the biggest building at Bến Thành Market Square with a banner carrying a mantra-like slogan: "*Chủ tịch Hồ Chí Minh sống mãi trong lòng chúng ta*" ("President Hồ Chí Minh lives forever in our hearts"). While people seem to go about their business with indifference, it takes me a while to get over my initial shock of seeing such a sea change in the former capital of South Vietnam. Because I left Vietnam quite a while before the march of North Vietnamese troops into Saigon and am back just shortly, I am not accustomed to all these flags, banners, soldiers, and policemen in moss green and yellow uniforms, and all that stuff. The communist presence in this city means that all is over for me. My erstwhile dreams and hopes are long gone, I cannot settle here anymore, and soon I will have to go back to America and continue to be an exile.

Trying to overcome my emotions about the appearance of the city, I cajole myself into believing that nothing is permanent and all is superficial and subject to change. I walk down the two main streets I often frequented in the past, namely, Lê Lợi and Nguyễn Huệ, hoping to find the past in the pedestrians. I follow, watch, and scrutinize them for any trace of the years gone by, but find nothing. They all are in a hurry, intent on their business, and do not have the leisurely gait of folks I often observed in the past on the same streets. I do not know where they are heading, but I know my former favorite places—the bookstores and the curio shops—must not be in their minds. They are not the people I envisioned in my fantasy after my arrival last night. In broad daylight, the phantoms of the past disappeared, giving way to *real* people and their *real* world. Suddenly, I feel sorry for myself. I came a long way to search for an unreal world of the past only to be confronted with a real world with real characters.

To redeem myself, I visit the former French bookstore on the most cultural street of former Saigon. Hardly can I recognize it at first. Not only is it now state-owned and has a new name, but the titles on display show the Communist Party's attempt to abolish entirely what is called "the remnants of the Saigon regime's decadent culture." I cannot find any titles on European, American, and South Vietnamese literature, only a large quantity of materials on socialist literature, Marxism, and surprisingly, a considerable number of titles on business, marketing, computer science, and English textbooks. Perhaps because the defeated South is not ready to accept Marxist-Leninist ideology, the new regime exposes its people to the necessity of learning to live in the real world of technology and business. Conversational English is taught everywhere—in public schools, in language training centers, even in private residences. Everyone gets geared up for doing business with the U.S. and the English-speaking world.

There is a twitch in my heart when, in my despair, I look out at the formerly most elegant street and seem to perceive the shades of an evening so familiar to me. I saw many evenings like this before but never paid attention to them. My heart aches with a common and pleasurable sensation, the same one I felt when my father and I were returning home to Dalat after our long trip to his native village in the north. But no sooner do I try to savor the sensation, and no sooner does it awaken in me nascent memories of an idyllic past than this past is gone. My past must be lingering around here, but it is too feeble to greet me. Heavenly but ethereal because it is made of fragile memories, mine is swept off by a cold and brutal present. This bookstore that I thought would be my refuge from reality is only an extension of the world I encountered this afternoon.

The next morning, I join Nga and her sister on a sightseeing tour in the suburbs of Saigon. I do so to please them, not because I want it. I would rather visit places I often frequented in the past by myself than with anyone. On our way home, at *chị* Thúy's signal, the driver stops at a lunatic asylum and a nursing home. I do not know if she wants to provide us an all-around view of present-day Saigon, or if she desires to torment her "fat American" relatives by bringing them here to see for themselves the inmates' indescribable misery. If this is *chị* Thúy's intent, as Nga suspects, then I can understand why her sister acts that way. While she, and perhaps many others, love to see their relatives return for a visit, deep down she might hold a grudge against us. We are not different from them, but we are very fortunate to live in America and have a good life. I had an inkling of this when enduring our ordeal at the airport last night. I feel the police are rough on us not only because we are not their people, but because they thought we were rich.

The nursing home is one of the most depressing places I have ever been to. It does not look like a nursing home. I see not only the elderly but also young and old inmates. When they get in line to receive our food donation, I notice that many of them look sick and hungry. Our driver whispers to us that an old lady with a dignified look was the owner of *Thương xá Tax*, the biggest department store in Saigon before 1975. To help her children buy their way out of Vietnam, she sold her property and moved out to live by herself while waiting for her reunion with them. Never hearing from her family again and running out of resources, she got sick and was taken to this public nursing home by a Samaritan. When Nga gives her an envelope with some money in it and tries to comfort her, her face turns hardened as though she is not accustomed to receiving charity, but I see tears in her eyes when Nga holds her hand fast and whispers to her, "I love you very much, *Má* (Mammy)."

There is such a heart-wrenching scene at this so-called nursing home. The patients include those who were completely incapacitated and the elderly who can move around a bit on their wooden beds. There is in the middle of each bed a hole through which, we are told, the inmates urinate and defecate into a container underneath. There is a bad odor because human waste is not disposed of properly. A staff member tells us these folks have no relatives nor income. When Nga gives money to an elderly man, he is so shaken he can hardly hold the bill in his hand!

Our next stop is a lunatic asylum. I am shaken with horror when seeing it with my own eyes. The so-called lunatic ward is about a 35 square meters room with around two hundred men, young and old, some totally naked, all standing as there is virtually no room for them to sit or lie down. Their vacant eyes sadly stare at us or at something only God knows. The room where they are standing must have just been sprayed earlier as the floor is wet. Some questions instantly arise in me. Might the inmates have been rounded up here for being sprayed too? They will have to sleep sometimes because even the very sick cannot avoid this, but how can they do it when there is not enough space for them even to sit down? The scene strikes me as horrible but surreal. I cannot imagine it exists right here, in this city which not long ago was known as the Pearl of the Far East. What amazes me is in the crowd, there are some who not only are handsome, but their faces shine with intelligence. I suspect that before they got here, they must have had a successful career and must have led a happy life. Like other inmates in the room, except for their sad, vacant eyes, which indicates somehow the existence of a feeble consciousness, they do not seem troubled by anything, even their total nakedness. Maybe they are very sick, or maybe it has got to the point where nothing matters to them anymore.

At another ward there are fewer inmates, but they are all chained and naked. *Chị* Thúy says that they are kept in isolation because, according to our guide, they are very violent. But I see that they look gentle, even sad and pensive, as if they were thinking of their good old days in the past. Or maybe they are not insane now.

Outside the building, I see two young men with their legs chained to a tree. One of them is wolfing down his food while gesticulating and rambling senselessly. We learn that they are put outside and chained because they are extremely dangerous. Near to him is a man much older who seems less violent but is madder. He urinates into his metal bowl, declares it is beer, and drinks his urine with relish before our eyes!

Two young Buddhist nuns are diligently caring for these sick inmates. I am mesmerized by their way of caring for them. Their faces and their gray robes are tainted with the patients' spit, and yet this does not seem to bother them at all. Nor do they seem afraid of the inmates' dangerous behavior. They are doing their job with such serenity and tenderness, not with a slight sense of resignation or affectation. Had they not been inspired by strong religious convictions, they would not have been here doing things beyond our comprehension.

I feel bad about misunderstanding *chị* Thúy's intention. As a devout Buddhist who strongly believes that one can redeem one's present and future human lot by inculcating in us the virtue of compassion for all suffering sentient beings, she might have wanted to help us improve our karma. This is the purpose of the visit she has planned for us today. I could not agree with her more and am very grateful to her. I ought to try to rekindle my compassion which has become almost extinct due to my long residence in one of the most materialistic countries in the world.

These horrid, heartbreaking scenes will continue to haunt me because they are linked to my people's tragic history, which was also a period of my painful past. When I lived in my father's small hometown in Quảng Bình, I witnessed many instances of human agony that still today remain sharp in my memory. If I close my eyes, I can still see the most horrified look on the face of my neighbor, a beautiful young woman, dragged off her house onto a military truck by the *Légionnaires* so famous for their savagery and brutality; I still think of her every now and then, can still hear her piercing shriek, and feel pained although it happened fifty years ago. Likewise, I am no stranger to scenes of insanity so common in the war, though they were of various kinds. I knew one old woman who received news of the death of her two sons—one serving in the South Vietnamese army and the other fighting for the Vietcong—on the same day! Could she stay sane in the face of such a great tragedy? The suffering borne by the people I knew in the past and the horror reflected in the inmates' stares today in that airtight suffocating chamber derive from the same origin: the intervention of world powers in my country's politics which has caused the two longest, most devastating wars in its modern history. The ghosts of those who were long dead or those I see live today at this lunatic asylum all belong to a past that, to my horror, permanently exists in me. To try to banish it from my memory is to renounce my native country and my identity. Thanks to this trip home and through these inmates' suffering, I discover this painful past of mine today—one that in America I tried to ignore because I was afraid that it would hamper my search for the far-flung paradisiacal past of my childhood. Since soon I will be going to Quảng Bình to visit my father's native land, I am sure I will be encountering the resurrected ghosts of people who were both victims and witnesses of my native country's most brutal history.

IN SEARCH OF LOST TIME (I)

We are on Highway 1 en route to Đồng Hới in a rental Toyota van (Japanese-made cars are very popular in Vietnam because they have good mileage and do not need extra maintenance), accompanied by *chị* Thúy and Hương, Nga's niece. On our way, we stop by a temple to pick up a monk who will be officiating prayer ceremonies at our ancestors' wind tombs built by my brother in Quảng Bình. To allow us to enjoy the cool weather before it gets very hot at midday, Duy, our driver, rolls down the windows and, perhaps because he knows we are *Việt kiều* and Southerners, plays some very good music by South Vietnamese songwriters currently banned by the new regime. Judging by his young age (he should have been in school rather than in the workforce), his use of the Saigon dialect, and his love of this "decadent" music, I suspect Duy must come from a southern Vietnamese family not faring well economically.

As our car rolls smoothly along the highway, a waft of cool air blows in the car. I close my eyes and relish the felicitous, familiar sensation I felt some forty years ago when traveling by train at night with my father from Dalat to.Quảng Bình. The south breeze (which I am sure it must be as we are heading north) in a tropical region like southern Vietnam's countryside in the early morning is a rare bliss. It cools you down after a stuffy night in the big city, invigorates you with a fragrance of vegetation and freshly plowed-up soil ready for a new crop, and makes you doze off while allowing you to remain conscious of the pleasurable sensation of being in touch with the healing power of nature in your native land. In the twilight of the early hours and the serenity of the earth, our car glides effortlessly and smoothly, taking me back to a certain time in a distant, unhistorical past that we were born to before we lost our innocence because of our experience with suffering and sorrow. In my semi-consciousness, I float, seem to grow wings, and fly. I feel like H. G. Wells' character in *The Time Machine,* save that the ancient worlds, times, and peoples he encountered are those he cannot relate to, while in my dream journey today, I recover many happy moments of my childhood, find again my loved ones' endearing faces, hear again the voices and sounds of yesteryear. This is my country with my people, my past. It protects me against the tyranny of history and time. It revitalizes me, it cures my afflicted body and soul. I belong to it, rather than it belongs to me.

Being a keen admirer of nature, a few times I got on a Greyhound bus to travel across America to see for myself what nature is like in a country known in Asia as *Mỹ quốc* (the Beautiful Country). Yes, there is no doubt that America is the most beautiful country I have ever known. But inside the streamlined, airtight coach and through its glass window, the American landscape appears to me just like a silent movie that keeps stretching in one direction endlessly, uniformly, tediously. Completely sealed off from the outside world and with the coach noiselessly gliding on the smooth surface of the road, the sleepy passenger feels like he is traveling through outer space rather than on earth. Silence is observed in America as a rule of law. Not only on the bus where everybody seems to fall asleep except the driver who periodically makes an announcement, but also in bus stations where the bus stops for passengers to buy food and refreshments. They are as silent as ghosts. When traveling in this condition, I missed the unruly, boisterous sights which were common at home upon the arrival of a bus or a train. Passengers struggling to get off while yelling at their small companions to make sure they would not be left behind, peddlers shouting their wares at the top of their voices, horns repeatedly blowing to signal the resumption of the journey, all signify that the Vietnamese world is small but full of life and energy. It is important for me to return to it for comfort, the American world being too vast, too cold for a wearied, anguished soul like mine.

Duy plays some music very popular in the South before 1975 and softly sings to its tune. Before I left home for the States, I had never paid attention to it because I had no time for enjoyment and because, being a Western classical music enthusiast, I found Vietnamese music in general too maudlin. But hearing it again in this homebound journey mesmerizes me. Because the past is gone, whatever remains and can help me remember it becomes important to me. Such things as the music provided by Duy, my contact with the air and the soil of my native country help me in the wee hours of my first day of being home relive a past long lost or forgotten. In our small world here, I can imagine a capsule of the former Republic of Vietnam to which I would have returned to realize my dream. This world that I live in tonight is small, fragile, and transient as it exists only in my imagination, but it is safe and secure and is the object of my search.

Duy slows down as his car is climbing a steep winding pass. It is still dark. A sleepy voice asks the driver where we are now. *"Đèo Rù Rì"* (Rù Rì Pass) comes the reply. The music has stopped. All is quiet in the dark, still night save the steady cushiony motion of the vehicle which feels like that of a train. The voices are light, faint, almost indistinguishable like the sounds that arise out of the sleeper's unconscious. The car continually lurches into darkness, plunging him into his distant past and the depths of the country's history.

During the Indochina war, his father risks his life by coming to the South amid heavy fighting to search for his family. It is here that the ten-year-old boy takes a night train with his father to return to Quảng Bình after tearfully saying goodbye to his mother. French air raids against the Việt Minh are so frequent at this place that trains can only run in the nighttime. Still, they occasionally get hit and civilian casualties are very high. With time the Pass becomes known as "the region of death" as it is reported that ghostly apparitions are often seen here. The bloodiest conquest of Champa, which marks the beginning of Vietnam's brutal policy of expansionism, originally takes place at *Đèo Rù Rì*. The battle cry of the victorious army, the galloping hooves in their final assault on Đồ Bàn imperial palace, Champa's last defense line, he still can hear in his sleep. Against a backdrop of smoke and torn flags loom large images of death and destruction. The fall of Champa's capital is reminiscent of the sack of Troy: the palace looted, prisoners slaughtered, infants snatched from their mothers' arms and thrown from the walls, women taken to the north to become slaves in the victors' households. Mỵ Ê, the Cham empress, is ordered to play her flute to entertain King Lý Thánh Tôn and his generals. When she is forced to serve wine to the Vietnamese monarch on his ship, Mỵ Ê jumps into the river and drowns herself. Mỵ Ê's heartbreaking story makes its way into Vietnam's folklore as a celebration of female chastity and a condemnation of male cruelty. Since the capture of Cham ladies-in-waiting from whom Vietnamese courtesans learned their doleful art, a trace of disconsolateness has crept into Vietnam's traditional music. Songs from Huế are sad, dolorous, mournful like a young widow's sobs and moans. They express sorrows, herald tragic things.

The destruction of the kingdom of Champa revisits the old imperial city and haunts the people of Huế. The Chams are back, and their revenge wrought on their victors' offspring right where their empress was humiliated is ten times greater than the Vietnamese conquest of their country in 1471. The spring 1968 offensive leaves the old imperial city in ruin. It has been raining on end, cold and dreary when it should have been pleasant at this time of the year. In the cold, dark night at their captors' gunpoint, captured South Vietnamese soldiers on leave for Tết, local government officials, students, and civilians are marched to their shallow graves. In darkness and the cold rain, they lean on one another, plodding their long weary way to death. Cold, shivering, and hungry, they are forced to plod to their appointed mass grave. It is cold, dreary, gloomy, and overcast several more weeks until the victims' bodies are accidentally found by their relatives. Freezing weather temperature keeps the exposed corpses from decomposition, but the endless cold rain makes life miserable. Many people are believed to be dead because they are still missing, so the old imperial city is ablaze at night with candlelights and incense burned to console their vagrant ghosts. One can hear the long, heart-wrenching, high-pitched ululations all night, and cannot tell if it is the women mourning the loss of their men, the ghosts grieving at their wrongful untimely deaths, or the wind howling in the freezing cold wind and rain, which is unusual this time of the year, so unusual that Huế people are convinced that *Trời Đất* (Heaven and Earth) are in mourning. The wailing is intermittent, inaudible at times because of the weeper's exhaustion, because of the recurrent wind, or because the wailing comes from the faraway region of the dead, but all night it never ceases. It does not cease until dawn when the mourning is overtaken by noises of the day, or perhaps because ghosts are said to retreat at the approach of the day. *The dead*, Father said, *are very lonely*. Like the exiles, they are lonely and attached to their loved ones from whom they are severed eternally. Because their death was wrongful and untimely (many of them met their fate in the brutal protracted war before they could fulfill their destiny), they are condemned to roaming our land eternally and inconsolably. Only through our remembering can we alleviate their grief. Would not these feeble glows in the dark mean that the dead are still clinging to their former land, that they are desperately searching for a home beyond their graves, and that they are striving to keep alive our memory of them? But how can they succeed when they (the dead) are no longer important to us, when because of our preoccupation with the living, we would rather forget than remember them? Father said these are *"cô hồn"* (hungry lonely souls) because nobody cares to remember them, think about them, offer them food, light incense for them. Because of its connection to a long history of territorial conquests, internal conflicts, and resistances to foreign invasions, Vietnam witnessed many tragic wrongful deaths that until today are still unacknowledged, unrecognized, or forgotten. Mourning, if it exists, is conducted in secrecy within the household because public commemoration for those who died on the wrong side is forbidden by the victors.

Appearing among the dead are victims of the recent massacre and past wars, including North Vietnamese soldiers sent to the South to fight the war and killed in action (among them Vietcong commandos in the trenches at the police station near Trường Tiền Bridge in Huế). The dead do not appear with their own groups but mingle with one another as if closeness and mutual sympathy could mitigate their pain of loneliness, as if only the dead, that is, those who share the same fate, could understand each other, or as if separateness, a mark of distinction among the living, did not concern them. They all plod in a steady stupor, their faces gaunt and completely drained of color, their eyes shut, their mouths twisted and crooked as if torn, consumed by anguish and agony, not by anger and hatred as when they were living. Everyone is in deep sorrow, including those who took part in the Tết offensive's massacre and those who lost their lives in the spring 1975 assault. Everyone suffers beyond measure. Everyone—victims and victimizers, friends and foes, who died of wrongful deaths—met their fate due to a certain mysterious curse called down on them, on their country and people, for the sins committed by their distant forebears in a distant past. The dead suffer immensely. They will not rest in peace until their remains are found, repatriated, and properly buried at their ancestral burial sites and until requiems for their souls are held and assured of a passage into a better new world.

The pitch-black Rù Rì Pass is punctuated by flickering ghost lights in the distant dense foliage of the southern jungle. After their massacre, the people of the former kingdom of Champa became *Ma Hời* (Chàm ghosts) who are condemned to roaming this very land that used to be theirs in the past. *Ma Hời* are not forgetting their land, nor are they forgetting to use their supernatural powers for vengeance, which is often terrible. They patrol the Rù Rì Pass in the dark of night and cause many deadly accidents. In the dead of night, they walk the tortuous pass which rightfully belonged to them. They roam only in the dead of night because they are ghosts and fear sunlight. They call down curses on the Vietnamese people for the wrongs committed by their progenitors.

They had fought their last battle here before their government fell. They had fought heroically but desperately all the way from abandoned strategic posts in the Central Highlands. As soon as they got to Route 7B, they were ambushed and slaughtered like animals. Their dependents (spouses, young children) and civilians who were evacuated with them also suffered the same fate. The most chaotic retreat became known as "the convoy of tears," and Route 7B was named the Death Road by survivors of the retreat. The government fell too quickly afterward to have time for recovering, repatriating, and burying the dead properly. Like the Ma Hời, *they become ghosts condemned to wandering on this former battlefield every night. Every night since the end of the war, they are condemned to doing the same thing. Before daybreak, they reassemble from their roaming to perform the last rituals—saluting the tattered South Vietnamese flag, the soldiers firing their soundless rifles, everyone (the soldiers, their spouses, their young children) in tears mutely chanting the South Vietnamese anthem beside charred armored cars. Then they vanish. They vanish into emptiness or somewhere at the approach of dawn only to reappear to resume their routine activities the next day at dusk, like people and things in a silent film programmed to play and stop at a certain time every night on a giant screen, which is the Rù Rì Pass. (There is no way to know the origin of the Pass' name, but the phrase "rù rì," which means "whisper, muster, murmur," explains why the dead assemble here. They assemble here to silently tell and retell every day their tragic stories to the deaf ears of their imaginary audience, who are us, the living, and their relatives. They want to talk about it, but they cannot go beyond a whisper.) They perform their role with such diligence and faultlessness as if they were automatons or playthings of a mysterious force that still manipulates its victims after death. There is on their ageless faces an expression of unappeasable agony and grief that lost souls commonly share. For the dead, no suffering is greater than being neglected by us, the living, their relatives. The dead are free of time but not of memory. Their nightly rehearsal of past activities, their inseparableness from those that once belonged to them (broken weapons, charred armored cars, torn flags) means that for them, living with the past—not remembering it—is their only way to cope with the living's neglect and oblivion. Their loneliness is heightened by the darkness of the immense jungle and the freezing cold rain. Cut off from Time, they are condemned to silently playing repeatedly that game of History—not one in progress, not one in the making—but one that is non-existent, terminated, superannuated, antiquarian, ridiculous (broken weapons, charred armored cars, torn flags) found only in the victorious regime's war museums purported to show the defeated side's "illegitimacy." How long will the phantoms be playing this game of History when History will be forgotten by their survivors? Will they be, say, in another fifty years in the mind of the next generation of Vietnamese who hardly know the country's contemporary history, the war, the dead, the heroes? They (the phantoms, the dead) will be pushed into the abyss of darkness, the beginning of Time, the fathomless past, confounded with the ghosts of ancient warriors, all lost in the infinity of Time or No-Time. History, if it ever existed, is lost in the emptiness of the No-World and No-Time. Can we visualize, recreate the famous Southward March (Nam Tiến) as it took place that destroyed the Champa kingdom with bits of sparse references in history books? Even an earthshaking event in the nation's modern history, such as the death of South Vietnam, is fading in the memory of witnesses and survivors and will not be heard of after this generation. Our memory is too feeble for the past which was so long and so vast that everything in it is lost, lost in emptiness, does not seem to ever exist. History (the dead, the phantoms, things that are dear to them and inseparable from them, i.e., rusty guns, charred armored vehicles, torn flags, nightly parades) flashes into the mind of a returning exile tonight only to resink quickly into the bottomless pit of No-History, No-World, No-Time. Halfawakened, he hears the silent night, the dead years, the noiseless sounds of the phantoms' parade, sees their silent enacting of the so-called game of History for another short while before everything dies out. Exhausted, he laboriously wakes up to the steady buzz of the car engine slowly descending the Pass, leaving behind the forgotten participants of History and their sorrows. Out of the depths of the jungle comes the soft crying of myriad insects, the gentle falling of the rain which he has heard since when he does not remember, maybe very far and remote in Time, maybe since the beginning of Time. He hears again the insects, the rain, the stirring of the earth. Daylight. Things are back in time.*

I awaken to the tune of a familiar song about Vietnam's countryside coming from Duy's hi-fi player. We have just finished the last leg of the Rù Rì Pass and are heading toward Mũi Né, Central Vietnam's famous seacoast, with row after row of lush rice fields dotted with tiny thatched-roof huts. Sunrise at sea is breathtaking after a long night's drive. Boats returning from their night-long fishing trips in the horizon are silhouetted against a morning sky resplendent with vibrant sunlight. A vast range of misty mountains backdrops the mysterious, gloomy Pass we just covered. With the night, my dreamy world, and the ghosts of the past behind me, I am entering a new world full of life.

Life in the country begins in earnest very early in the morning. At 5:30 a.m in this tropical region, the peasants already begin their day. In small groups scattered along Highway 1, they are heading to their rice fields in an unusually leisurely manner, accompanied by their slow-moving water buffalos, the peasants' most essential companions. About half an hour later, the peaceful scene becomes vibrant with children on their way to school. They wear white shirts and blue pants, some with a red scarf across their collar, a mark of their academic achievement and their being *"cháu ngoan Bác Hồ"* (Uncle Hồ's exemplary children). They wear plastic sandals, not shoes, and some are barefooted. Because children in the country are poor and ought to help their parents in the rice field after school, shoes and good clothes are usually inaccessible to them. They look small for their age, probably because of hardship and poor nutrition. But there exudes from them a flow of liveliness and joyfulness, which is typical of young children.

There is a spasm in my stomach. The pain seems to come from a faraway region and time. *He is one these children, afoot to school which meets only one half-day a day. Class is always interrupted by French air raids, by the arrest or killing of the teacher by the Việt Minh who suspect him of collaborating with the French, or simply by the teacher's quitting the job and fleeing to the city for safety. Materially, he is the same as other children in the country. But while their family is intact, his is a broken one. He has light moments, though, when in the company of boys his age, they play on their way to school. Children are carefree, insouciant, and playful even in the worst of times.* The spasm, painful but blissful, is caused by my realization that I *am* among these schoolchildren, my face among their faces, my destiny among their destinies. I am not lost, never was lost. No other place suffered greater devastation than the country, a free-fire zone, during the war, and yet no place could demonstrate better the ability to overcome destruction and death and the will to live than the country. This power the peasants owe to the earth which has sustained them and to which they have been tied since time immemorial. As for me, I find myself inseparable from this earth which, like an umbilical cord, still connects me to my roots, my past, and is the driving force of my life of exile.

***

We arrive in Hội An on a hot summer afternoon and immediately come to visit my father's tomb at Long Tuyền Temple's cemetery. I could not get home for Father's funeral, so this is the first time I see his resting place. Finding Father's tombstone, Nga (she is excellent in locating the tombs of her loved ones even in a big cemetery) bursts into tearful sobs. I am amazed at my quasi-indifference to the tomb of the most important, most beloved person in my whole life. I do not slump and break down in tears as I thought I would. I manage to shed some tears, but by the time we wrap up the short visit, my eyes are already dried out. Am I the same person who, a few years ago, on a street in Paris, which is so far removed in distance from where his father is lying now, could not hold back his tears and sobs when remembering him? Am I still the same man, my father's son, who while he was in the States, would wake up suddenly from his sleep, crying inconsolably like a child just because his father went out of his dream and was no longer with him? The impact of the dream was so strong that, though awake and fully conscious, I could still feel for another while that my father *was* real, in the flesh, not a phantom.

There is a reason for my failure to visualize my father as he would appear in my sleep and dreams before I get here. As Proust has pointed out, our past does not go away but is hidden in the "lowest depths" of our soul. To recapture it, we must unearth this subterranean region for it to reappear. In Proust's fiction, Marcel regains his paradise by digging up his long-lost trove of memories and recreating favorite scenes and events connected with those memories. He performs his role in his most earnest and pious manner, like a fervent seeker of truth, like a devout pilgrim in search of spiritual salvation. I am not so fortunate. Being a stranger in a strange land, I do not have a home nor anything to search for. What depresses me is instead of my father and my happy past as I would see in my sleep and dreams when I lived in the States, I am now confronted with this weed-grown solitary elevated structure, which is my father's burial site. Because I depend too much on my happy memories of my father to survive emotionally, it is not easy to accept his loss immediately, any more than face the fact that he now is lying permanently under the cold earth. Is this my father, the purpose of my trip home, the object of my search? This reality is so brutal that it destroys my sensibility, my nascent memories of my father, my childhood, my paradise.

We arrive in Huế late in the evening. We decide to stay here for Nga to visit her folks for a few days. I also need to spend some time exploring the city with which I was emotionally involved for a very long time. Huế has changed completely. It is hot, noisy, and very crowded. Most stores and shops fly the communist flag although today is not a holiday. The movie theater that showed the film *Chúng tôi muốn sống*, which aroused my nostalgia for my father's native land in my second year of our resettlement in Huế, is not there anymore (can it be the same theater but with a new name?). There are more motorcycles on the street than bicycles and pedestrians. Everybody is in a rush, all looking tense and grim, just like people in Saigon. Preoccupation with speed and expediency seems on everyone's mind. Huế is no longer the old imperial city, quiet, tranquil, and nonchalant, which once was the cause of my foolish fantasy about my first love. Though Huế changed much after the Tết offensive and before my leaving for the States, roughly it followed the same life patterns I had seen in the early years of my arrival from Đồng Hới. Now only twenty years after the communist takeover, the city has changed beyond recognition.

At Nga's suggestion, I accompany her to our former neighborhood to take a look at our former home on Võ Thị Sáu Street (it was called Nguyễn Thị Giang Road before the regime change). We cannot find any "reference point" that can help us locate the place I knew so well that I could walk blindfolded for a short while. All the streets have new names, some leveled out to have space for new home construction. Big, expensive residences pop up everywhere, making it very difficult for us to identify our former small house. With the assistance of a kind resident in the neighborhood, we finally reach our former address, but we find a two-storied house instead of our small home. There is nothing left—not even an insignificant thing like a small alley or a utility pole—that can evoke in me a place where I had spent my entire youth and the early years of my middle age with my loved ones before I left home. Everything is gone. My mind is blank. My memory stops functioning. I feel not only shocked, but lost and depressed.

I tell Nga I have had enough of the city and want to stay in a small hotel in Vỹ Dạ near her parents' ancestral home. Because Vỹ Dạ is where I met and married Nga and where her close relatives live, I can easily relate to it and hope I can start to search for my past there.

From the terrace on the top floor of our rural hotel, I get a panoramic view of the city's suburbs. Suddenly, a flood of old memories springs forth in me.

It is here that Nga had a miscarriage and my father taught me to bury my unborn baby, which was a female fetus, according to my father's astrological calculation. It was a late, cold, dreary afternoon in November thirty years ago, and it was the first time as a father, I was burying my baby. My father instructed me to lay the small coffin underground, burned incense, and began to pray for her soul. I mourned my child's death and feared my father's sadness. He must be very upset because the loss of his baby granddaughter had foiled his plan to establish a *Yin-Yang* balance in his Trần clan which he thought was too male-dominated. It has been thirty years now, and the image of Father in his black tunic, frail, stoic, grief-stricken, praying with all his heart and soul to our ancestors for accepting his grandchild's spirit is still vivid in me. *He is in his late twenties, married for two years, standing beside his father, nervously and awkwardly performing the burial ritual according to the old man's instructions. For the first time, he is assuming the grave moral responsibility of being a family man. He feels he is very closely related to the unborn child, his heart heavy with sorrow at her loss. He is worried about his wife who is bedridden after her miscarriage, with limited healthcare resources in this rural area. Looking very sick and pale, she still gives him a smile when he returned from his teaching post in the south to see her.* All these scenes arise in my mind now, but what stands out most clearly is Father's image, frail, stoic, sad in his black tunic, murmuring his prayer for his grandchild's soul and his daughter-in-law's safety. Thirty years after that dreary, cold, overcast late afternoon of November, I am back at this same place, my father and I stand at this cemetery mourning my child's death, him looking grave and doleful, intensely praying for his unborn grandchild's peaceful passing into the land of ancestors and for his daughter-in-law's quick recovery. The scene switches to Trung Quán. On a cold, wet, gloomy, and overcast day in November, we are ordered by the Việt Minh to leave Văn La, my father's native village, as the French are landing at Đồng Hới Port. We walk 10 kilometers and arrive at Trung Quán at nightfall. That night for supper, each of us is given by the local authorities a bowl of plain rice gruel. Father does not eat, but he gives his ration to us. It breaks my heart to see him fix on us such a gentle, affectionate look as my brother and I devour the food he gives. My memory leaps back to the scene of my permanent departure from Huế. It is a hot, stuffy, but overcast afternoon in late August when I leave home to study in the States. Father is silent and stoic as usual. But never have I seen him look so sad. Suddenly, I have a feeling that this will be the last time I see him.

    By the time my remembrance has run its course, I am exhausted. The cataleptic state I was in, which encapsulated nearly forty years of living under my father's protection into ten minutes of remembering, drains all my energy. I cannot indulge in it anymore. But just like a shaman who faints at the end of his séance and yet is still beside himself with ecstasy, I find my use of memory today an overwhelming experience. For the first time since my leaving home and becoming an exile and for the first time since my return, I have been reunified with Father for so long (ten minutes of remembering him, thinking of him, continuously being by his side)! I am sapped, worn out, but happy and grateful.

Home is where one should return to recover one's lost time. I should reconnect with the old earth to replenish myself because my lengthy stay in America has depleted my memory and imagination. Returning to Huế is returning home because I had lived in Huế since my adolescence with my father and later with my own family until I left Vietnam. In my mind, *whatever is associated with my loved ones, especially Father or his image, is home.* Maybe that is why, as soon as I set foot in the suburbs (not the noisy city which is unsuitable for my meditation on the past), I plunged into a sea of remembrance. Though harrowing experiences like my semi-slavery at Mr. Huy's house and the horrors of the Tết offensive are fresh in my mind, I hardly dwell on them. Rather, only impressions of rarefied moments accompanied by tender feelings surge in me. Remembrance of Father and my loved ones, or anyone or anything that was dear and important to me, can be very painful, but it gives me great pleasure. To be called a *"moment bienheureux,"* as Proust might put it, a past event did not have to be always joyful. Sorrow assuaged by the passage of time and filtered through memory can be a source of joy, *the joy of sorrow.* I shed tears of joy when I come back to Huế and remember my late father, feeling like I am home to be reunified with him. Through this unique moment that occurs today, I can revisit him, appreciate what he did for my sake, and silently from the bottom of my heart express to him my gratefulness and love. Energized by the old earth, my unconscious, which when living in the States I would repress to comply with my social self's requirements and which emerged only in my disturbed sleep and oft-interrupted daydreams, springs into life, revealing, as it were, an unchanged world of the past that belonged to me. This world becomes dearer and more important to me now than it was in the past. In the twinkling of an eye I am back to where I was twenty-three years ago—and even further in that faraway region of my early years should I wish to continue the journey. *His wife wakes up their three children to take them to the airport to see him off. He is leaving for the U.S. on a graduate scholarship. It breaks his heart to leave his old father, his young pregnant wife, and his three small boys, while Huế is facing another communist offensive. But he cannot pass up the scholarship because it will improve his future when he completes his study program and returns home. His youngest boy is all awake, excited about taking a ride with the family. On the way to the airport, he talks continuously, pointing to this and that on the* highway, not knowing that his Pa is leaving home (and their separation, because of the fall of Saigon, lasts eight years, not two years as scheduled). But as soon as everybody gets out of the car and gets in the waiting room, the little boy stops talking and asking questions, looking so sad as if he knew something wrong was going to happen. Everybody is quiet, in deep sorrow. His wife wipes off a tear, his older boys are no longer playful, his father looks frailer and thinner than ever. Suddenly, he has a premonition that his return home will not take place as planned, and today might be the last time he sees his father.* Yes, I did pay a very dear price for abandoning my family to pursue my foolish dream. I had not seen Nga and the children for eight years, they were in terrible shape when they came to live with me, I lost my father forever, I have not been back to visit his tomb to atone for my sins against his soul until today. It is strange, though, that today is the first time since my departure from home that I can evoke better than ever my heartrending parting scene on that afternoon of late August 1972. Every gesture my loved ones showed on that day had a significance that I did not understand until today, twenty-three years later. The past is not dead: memories are formed when a life event occurs; the longer memories are kept in the dark world of the unconscious, the sharper and livelier the past becomes when it is resurrected. Nothing escapes my memory of that afternoon in late August 1972 when I was about to leave home for America. It breaks my heart to see my children, even my four-year-old (now a handsome young man), act so mature by trying to keep quiet until I board the plane. I suspect that Nga must have forbidden them to make a scene in front of me. When I kiss the children and turn around to head to the plane, they start crying when Hùng, our eight-year-old son, gives his younger siblings a stern look. Nga tries to smile, but I can see tears in her eyes. My father maintains his composure but looks so sad.

Whereas the sorrow I experienced in the States consumed me, gnawed at my heart, caused me despair and depression, today the same sorrow of being back home and getting a glimpse of my past gives me an exalted sensation. It is not an ordinary sorrow. It is the joy of sorrow felt by an exile who finally can contact his native earth, his past, and his home. It gives me knots in the bowels, but it excites me and elevates my soul. "*Sống gửi, thác về*" (To live is to stay here temporarily, to die is to return home permanently), my father taught me. Resurrection is an alien concept in our culture, but death is as much celebrated as life. My father did not die, he just returned to our native earth. Being home to connect with the old earth thus means being reunited with Father.

Taking advantage of having the good fortune to evoke such privileged moments, I venture further into my search for the more distant past. It is ridiculous for a man in his sixties to "rejuvenate" himself in this return home by trying to relive his high school years in Huế. But it is an important part of my quest because I fear that I might not have the opportunity to do it again. Of myriad remembrances, the most vivid one that comes across my mind is my first love I carried from Đồng Hới to Huế. The remote, murky past is screened by my memory for the most privileged moment of my youth. Trang becomes alive again. My heart beats fast. Things seem unchanged since I saw her last. *Trang strolls hand in hand with four or five girls her age on Trần Hưng Đạo Street in Huế. They all smile, seeming to enjoy their New Year's outing. Trang doesn't seem to see me.* The vision lasts less than thirty seconds. Trang had never left Đồng Hới to come to Huế, but the fantasy I had on that new year's day of Tết 1954 had rankled in my mind until I married Nga. When I came to the States for graduate study and during my exile, I did not think of Trang until today twenty-six years later. It is the same vision, short like a flash of lightning but powerful. It torments me for another while after it is gone.

Because Huế is where I spent my late adolescence and lived until my early middle age and permanent departure to the States, it plays an important part in my quest of the past like Dalat and Quảng Bình. In a sense, Huế is perhaps more important to me because it is here that my father lived with me for almost twenty years, had watched Nga and me raise his four precious grandsons. I must try to evoke the period when I lived at home with my father, my young wife, and my little ones to prove that living with my family was more important than pursuing my empty, foolish dreams in America. Though it is a vision, it is my best family reunion ever because all my loved ones are present now in my mind and because it takes place right here in my homeland.

As we prepare to leave Huế for the remainder of our trip, I am filled with a deep, inconsolable grief. I feel that I might not experience these happy visions ever again, that I will have to leave behind the past I just recreated here. For lack of sustenance, this past will sink back into the abysmal emptiness of time like the past of the unknown deceased soldiers of the defunct South Vietnamese army I saw in a vision on the Rù Rì Pass. I have now come to discover these verities about the quest for lost time. It should be conducted right in my native place, not in a foreign land. Because my quest has left me exhausted, I should turn to my native land for replenishment. Like a plant starting to grow vigorously when transferred back to its native soil, my memory is at its best when used in my homeland. When I lived in America, I rarely had success in evoking the past. It always appeared in fleeting, fragmented instances that vanished quickly. Here, by contrast, a least single thought could trigger a torrent of associations and remembrances. They come out from all the cracks of my being, swamp me with their presence, demand my recognition. I am too dazed to recognize them all, but I am intensely conscious of their overwhelming presence.

The blissful state I have been in since this morning saddens and worries me. Would I be able to keep it with me until the end of my trip and even back to America? Would my search which has brought me halfway around the globe here be fruitless? Thus far, as I have said, it is my contact with my native land that has been instrumental in helping me revive my past. Does that mean that it—my past—will be lost again if I do not come back? I can carry memories with me whenever I go because they reside in me, but the phantoms of the past—not my remembrance of them—are to stay where they are because they belong to this earth and are inextricably bound to it.

I must catch up a lot on this trip home. The trip is not solely intended for a search for lost time, but also for personal and family business: I want to try again to find my sister's grave in Dalat. I did try once in 1960, but perhaps because my visit was short or because I was not old and responsible enough as the head of our clan, I did not pursue my search to the end. Never did I feel compelled to carry out my late father's wish more urgently than I do now. Anything can happen to a person my age. I must try to find Như Cầm's grave on this trip or never.

Thảo, Nga's younger sister, says that because my problem is beyond human capability, I should seek supernatural beings' advice. At her recommendation, I go to see Miss Thu, Thảo's favorite spiritual advisor. Thảo believes that Miss Thu can pinpoint my sister's lost grave by consulting her deities. I do not believe in superstition but decide it will not hurt to try our luck this time.

Miss Thu is in her early fifties, a very thin woman with a pale face and piercing ogling eyes. She strikes me as an unearthly being or this being was inhabiting her. Miss Thu takes me into her little shrine, and after performing her divination rituals she closes her eyes for a moment as though she was having a séance with supernatural beings. In the end, she opens her eyes and speaks to me in a voice that seems to be coming from another world, with a totally strange accent that I have never heard before. *"How sad your fate is, son,"* the spiritual advisor incants in her calm, deep trance. *"Misfortune often befalls you,"* she continues, *"and that's because of your previous bad karma."* I do not understand what she is talking about because she is not responding to my question, which is about the whereabouts of Như Cầm's grave. Nor do I comprehend why she calls me "son" when she looks so young. Some supernatural being must be speaking to me through Miss Thu. When the séance is about to end, Miss Thu stops talking and closes her eyes again. But before long, she opens her mouth, giving me her most cryptic counsel again with motherly affection: *"Dear, if something turns up when you get back there, don't pass it up. The most important thing is you should take better care of your health.*" And the séance ceases. It lasts only five minutes, including the ceremony. Miss Thu now becomes a normal being, exchanging her greetings with Thảo in her Huế dialect and accent in a very respectful manner, her eerie facial expressions totally disappearing. She does not seem to remember what has happened.

I find my séance with Miss Thu intriguing but troubling. Did an unearthly being speak through her or did she fake it? Why didn't she answer my query directly (she could have done it easily by talking about things that only fortune tellers know), but instead confuse me with her cryptic words about my fate? I know people in her practice—and most service providers today—tend to cater to their clientele's needs by always staying alert to their questions, but why did Miss Thu leave me alone in her trance and address me in such an affectionate maternal voice? Lastly, what did she mean by telling me to take whatever opportunity that comes my way when I "get back *there*"? How did she seem to know I am *not* from here? And this worries me most—is there any connection between what she calls my "sad fate," my health condition, and the upcoming opportunity? What is this opportunity and why is it important to me? Does Miss Thu, or rather a certain supernatural being through its medium, mean to suggest that a disaster—a grave accident or a major illness that, if not treated, *will* turn fatal—*will* happen but from which I *will* be saved should I accept an opportunity that accidentally turns up? Miss Thu's saying could trigger more lugubrious and scary interpretations, but I am comforted by the fact that psychics are inaccurate and untrustworthy because they don't use logic in their predictions.

Still influenced by the corrupt form of the Taoist tradition (when I was a child, I would get out at night of our mountain home in Dalat to summon down the deities after reading supernatural stories in my father's library), I tend to half believe Miss Thu's divination today. She is quite right about what I have been through this far; there have been more downs than ups in my life. But being a human, she does not know everything. Who knows, with my prayer, I will be able to find my sister's grave and fulfill my father's last wish, among other things. I feel better and brush off any lingering apprehension about Miss Thu's reading of my fate.

Quảng Bình is the last leg of our trip. When we get close to Quảng Trị, where bloody battles in the summer of 1972 turned the city into a ghost town, Route 1 in this area is so congested that our car can hardly move. The city's market is a sea of buyers and sellers. Pocket meetings are held even on street pavements. When Vinh, our new driver, is trying to inch through the market, honking incessantly, a dog starts running across the street and gets caught under his car. I can hear the animal's piercing heartbreaking cry when it is crushed by the three-ton vehicle. It must be a stray dog because nobody gives Vinh trouble and he himself does not seem to care. *Chị* Thúy mumbles *"A Di Đà Phật"* (Amitabha) to pray for the animal's spirit. According to Vinh, because the market meets in the wrong place, often a lot of animals and even humans have been hit by cars on Route 1. "But don't you worry, Auntie," Vinh gets sarcastic. "I'm sure people here know how to deal with the dead animal. It'll somehow end up in their stomach today." Something painfully familiar leaps to my mind. One day in 1947 in Trung Quán village, Quảng Bình, I saw our landlord drag his old dog to the river where he strangled the animal by putting him in a rice bag, fastening it with strong ropes, and plunging it in the river. There was some quake along with bubbles coming out as my landlord tried to hold the bag under the water. Later that day, he and his family had a big feast. I could not imagine why people could use such a barbaric technique to kill and eat the animal that was loyal to them for so many years. That technique of killing a live animal, I later learned, was used by both sides in the war to exterminate their enemy and opponents in the 1950s and in later periods. It was clean, cheap, and effective.

We stop for lunch in Đông Hà. In 1972, it was a free-fire zone because it was near Khe Sanh where U.S. Marines fought their bloodiest battles against the NVA. Now Đông Hà is a boom town with new luxury homes, busy business stores, and a big marketplace. Despite its prosperity, Đông Hà's growth does not follow a normal pattern. Old buildings with signs of war damage are interspersed with new residences that are expensive but look gaudy and unappealing. Stores are stacked up with piles of goods. There is a huge concentration of population in this small area. The growth is incredibly fast, but it is more like metastatic growth. Vinh says because Đông Hà is connected to Laos via Route 9A, smuggling is a thriving business here. While we are eating lunch, a woman comes over and offers to pay him if he could deliver for her a bag at a certain address in Đông Hới. Not wanting to get in trouble, Vinh refuses the woman's offer.

We arrive at Bến Hải, the former DMZ, a little after noon. We get out of our car to see what it looks like that made it so famous before 1975. It is not bigger than a bayou with shallow, turbid water. It was a demarcation line dividing Vietnam into the South and the North. During the war, there was not a single battle here, only the war of words between the communist and nationalist regimes. In the final days of the war, North Vietnamese troops did not even cross the border to occupy the South; their invasion started and ended elsewhere. It is amazing that such an insignificant, peaceful rivulet had captured the attention of the world, as well the imagination of many South Vietnamese artists and writers. They saw it as a symbol of national division and disunity which started as early as the 17th century. Vietnam back then had been plunged into the hundred years' civil war which also ended with the partition of the country at a different river, the Gianh, at the 16th parallel. Bến Hải, nevertheless, did not find its way into North Vietnamese writers' creative imagination. Such a theme, deemed decadent and unsuitable for socialist realism, is taboo in North Vietnamese literature.

IN SEARCH OF LOST TIME (II)

A spasm seizes me when we pass through the remaining part of Quảng Trị (once belonging to North Vietnam) and the beginning of Quảng Bình. I find the land and the environment intriguing, familiar, and unfamiliar. I cannot recognize anything here, and yet I find it astonishingly intimate. I am breathing the same air I was breathing when my father and I traveled on an express train to his native place. Though I do not remember in the least these hawthorn bushes, bamboo trees, and tall poplars, they appear very close to me: *we* breathe the same air, are nourished by the same land. And suddenly, images of a past so real, so pleasurable, from nowhere pop up in my mind, not appearing in a sequence and in an orderly manner but competing with one another to gain my attention and recognition, as if they have missed me so much that they can hardly wait to see me home. *To be in one's father's land is to be home.* These images are parading across my mind, unhurriedly and recurrently, like things on a magic lantern, as if to allow me to observe and remember them better so that I can recapture my past with more ease later in this important journey. While our vehicle rolls on toward Đồng Hới, I feel I am traveling backward, closer and closer to my past. Time, which has brought me sorrow and suffering, is suspended, halts, stops.

Rather than staying in a hotel in Đồng Hới like foreign tourists, I pass the night in my father's former home at Văn La village, now occupied by a relative. I want to make the most of my short visit here, trying to get as much work done as I can in a few days' time before returning to the States for the new semester. But I also want to pass the night here for a reason personal yet very important to me: I want to resume my quest of the past interrupted by the hustle and bustle I encountered in Hồ Chí Minh City and Huế. I want to sleep here in this old house that used to be home to me, my father, and my brother, to hopefully recapture my happy childhood I caught a glimpse of this afternoon when I set foot on my father's land.

A rumble of thunder awakens me in the middle of the night. Because it is not so loud, it must be coming from the faraway Đầu Mâu mountain or from the sea, signaling that a storm is brewing. Suddenly, a saying (I do not remember when and where I first heard it, but it was very popular when I lived here) comes to mind: *"Chớp bể mưa nguồn"* (Lightning at the sea signals torrential rain in the mountain). The little phrase, packed with endearing connotations of a past long gone that my English translation fails to render, releases a plethora of poignantly familiar images and sounds, sending a sudden spasm of sadness through my body. I came across this quote of folk weather forecast in my childhood reading about rains and floods in the north in the fiction of the Tự Lực Văn Đoàn literary school. In my unconscious mind, words become sounds and evoke memories. The sounds I hear now must be the same ones I heard in my childhood reading and in the past because they render my nostalgia acute and immense. I had heard this thunder before, both at night in my sleep and during the day when I lived in the country with my father. Its frequent reverberation would fill me with overwhelming feelings of fear and anxiety as I looked at the gray sky and knew that heavy rains and sometimes floods would occur afterward. (My father said his older brother had drowned in a major flood and he never got over it). But there were times when cuddling myself in my warm bed at night, I found the distant rumbling pleasurable because I knew my father was beside me and he would protect me from danger. After a while, the rumble became magic sounds. I have carried them within me as a metaphor for my father, my childhood, and my country since I went into exile.

Tonight, I relive my short, happy childhood in Quảng Bình when hearing these magic sounds again after half a century of being uprooted from my father's land. As I drift into sleep, the painful spasm vanishes, and I become the happy child I was in the distant past. In my half-awakened state, when consciousness is not totally suspended but not strong enough to drag me back to the present, these magic sounds release their formidable power: they bring back the dreamland of my childhood, free me from the sorrow and burden of old age. Early in the morning, I am awakened again by other magic sounds of years past—the gentle patting of raindrops on the windowpanes. In the absolute stillness and serenity of the wee hours in the country, the regular, clear, rhythmical taps accompanied by the soft cry of crickets outside reverberate in the depths of my soul like the notes of a folksong. I lie still, body and mind afloat in the stream of sounds, feeling like returning to a period so distant in time but so near, so cozy, so delightful.

In the States, I occasionally heard sounds connected with my past but would not characterize them as magic. They stirred more sorrow and regret than joy and happiness because I, the subject, was not rooted in and sustained by the native land. The echoes of the past triggered my memories of the native land and made me remember it intensely, but at the same time they caused me sorrow and homesickness. Here is what I put in my journal about my impressions of a shower in the Texas Hill Country:

It [the shower] comes crashing down from the sky. Its cascade catches me off guard, plunging me into a stream of familiar sensations of exhilaration and joy I have not experienced for a very long time, perhaps since my arrival in the United States. The sound of the downpour transforms the place where I have lived for almost thirty years and yet still feel like a stranger into an instant home. Home! This is exactly how it rained in Saigon thirty years ago: it came suddenly without warning, it drowned out the city in its cascading noise, and then it stopped as quickly as it came, without warning. Whereas in Huế it would drizzle for days on end, in Saigon a downpour would not last longer than ten minutes, just long enough to cool you down a bit on a hot summer day, but not too long to make you feel depressed. This is exactly how I feel today about the rain thirty years later also on a summer day in Texas. It arouses in me the pleasure of experiencing something dear and familiar connected with home. It brings out at the same time an unrelenting longing for something unattainable, a profound sadness upon realizing that this precious thing that I catch a glimpse of today will not last. The rain will end. With its passing, my sorrow of exile will return, perhaps will get more intense. Memory plays a significant role in resurrecting the past but cannot sustain it forever. The search for paradise is not simply a mechanical-like remembering process. Because it is an extremely exhaustive endeavor, it should be conducted in the exile's native land where his past resides and where he can get replenished and strengthened when he runs out of energy during his search.

My short visit to my father's birthplace ends with my paying respects to my ancestors' tombs on a remote hilltop. On our way, I drop in to see a relative who lives near my former ancestral home in Tráng Thiệp village. I hit upon a small brook and feel the urge to dip my hand in its clear water. It is a very hot summer day, and yet the water is chilly. Suddenly, there is a squeeze on my heart. Immediately, a poignant, familiar scene with clear, sharp edges resurges in my mind. *A man in his late fifties takes his nine-year-old son on a visit to his ancestral graveyard in a neighboring village. They pass a shallow stream, and the boy stops and dips his hand in the water to catch the minnows. "Don't touch the water, son," says the man. "It'll make you sick." Then he continues, explaining to the boy that people in this village are not well because they drink water from this source, which is always chilly even in summer. The boy is not listening to his father because he does not understand what he is saying and because he is busy chasing the minnows. The incident was so insignificant* that I did not recall any detail of it until today as I set foot on this place almost fifty years later and dip my hand in the water of perhaps this same brook. *Despite his father's scolding, the boy hangs back to play along the way. He particularly likes to catch butterflies, small fish, and the like. He tries to catch with his bare hands the minnows darting about in the stream. The water is so cold that his fingers are numb and tingling.* Fifty years later, I still vividly remember that day in that far past. My father wore a faded black tunic and white pants. He carried in his hand a bundle of joss sticks that he would light on our ancestors' tombs. On that day, I wore a white tee shirt and blue shorts. Father always made sure that I wore a felt hat (it was a blue marine one) when going out because summer in Quảng Bình was very hot. Maybe because my mother was not living with us, my father rarely smiled, spoke little, kept to himself most of the time. But he took excellent care of me and my brother.

In the afternoon, I stroll around the place where my guide says my ancestral home was to get another "feel" of the past. I cannot recall anything here at all. In place of my little ancestral thatched-roof home is a big brick house with additions to it obviously to accommodate more than a family. The premises are all concrete. Even if things did not change, I would not be able to tell what they were like fifty years ago. The entire scene leaves me disappointed, so I ask my guide to take me back to the hotel. But as soon as I turn around, I am struck by something. No sooner do I recognize it—two pots of coleuses on each side of the front gate—than a thrill runs through me. The physical world of my past is no more, but the coleuses are still here. To be sure, they are not exactly those I saw in the past from a scientist's point of view, but can I just say that they are the same coleuses I lived with for a while, and they have withered, died, and grown back again and again these last fifty years in this land of my ancestors? For if these plants did not belong to—and represent—my ancestral home and my childhood, the object of my quest, then how can I explain the quivering that shoots through my body when I accidentally see them today? To avoid the destructive force of history and time, the soul of my past lies hidden in a world of insignificant, commonplace objects, awaiting my return for its resurrection. Despite so much violence done to my ancestral land, it is still able to produce these coleuses that represent the persistence of the past. Instantly, these plants call to mind a sunny, hot region, which was my ancestral village in Quảng Bình. This is the first time since I left Văn La that I come to understand why, as a child, I felt a strong attachment to the coleuses, already missed them as though I had not seen something very dear to me for a long time. I loved these plants because of their representation—the hot, sunny country of my father. *I was carrying within me its image and with it my happy late childhood and adolescence since my departing from Quảng Bình*. Even when living as an exile in America, I felt knots in my stomach every time I happened to spot these plants in a nursery. They poignantly evoked in me my father's hot, sunny small village, which, with time, had become a metaphor for Vietnam, my long-lost native home country. The small ephemeral pleasure derived from seeing a symbol of home in your exile is nothing compared to the thrill of being home and sucking the raw life force in the earth that has nurtured and safeguarded your past.

The absolute stillness of the hot summer afternoon is punctuated by a solitary cock-a-doodle-doo as I make for the village's entrance. The cicadas from the trees in front of me respond to the rooster's reveille by letting out some isolated notes, as if to gently wake nature from its siesta, then turn their solitary overture into tidal waves of sounds that increase in intensity with the participation of myriad tiny musicians from farther groves of trees. They come out to sing in early and late summer afternoons, their sad music (in Vietnam, they are known as *ve sầu* (mourning cicadas), coming down on me wave after wave, reaching the innermost recesses of my soul. My melancholy is as boundless as the space that surrounds me. It gives me joy to hear again the sounds of years past, and yet it is so sad to realize that this *is* a strange land, the cicadas are not singing for me anymore, and that such memories of the past, though sweet, only make me poignantly aware of my condition. Even when I was a young child living in Quảng Bình, I found the cry of the cicadas sad. I felt a pervasive melancholy when hearing their singing on summer days—a melancholy that was vague, indistinct, unfounded, but overwhelming. In my adolescence, as I became more mature, I came to understand better the meaning of this sad music. It was related to the end of my pleasant summertime, to my farewell to Trang when she returned to Hanoi for school. My disappointed first love and permanent separation from my sweetheart also took place at the end of a summer.

That is the best I can manage to describe my life on a sunny, hot day in our ancestral country fifty years ago. What my memory fails to supply, I fill in with my imagination. The information may be inaccurate, unreal, to be sure, but the picture of my father, myself, my country, and our visit to our ancestors' burial site is sharp, so sharp that it makes me cry when I know that *is* my past, my paradise, and nothing else. Time has no impact at all on my past. Instantly, I become again that nine-year-old boy playing with the same minnows on this same brook with the same water with its unchanging temperature, except that that child now is a sixty-year-old man who loves his father and understands the meaning of his teaching better than ever. The vision of this moment of truth expands into the burial ground of the boy's ancestors. Again, he sets out to chase grasshoppers, plugs out wild nuts or the like, too young, too innocent, too excited to pay attention to the ritual the man (the boy's father) is performing in honor of their ancestors and whose role the boy (the man's male heir) will be expected to play after his passing. I share this moment of truth with Pip in Charles Dickens' *Great Expectations* when today, on this windswept hilltop of my childhood, I cry like Pip, who returns as an adult and feels like a child and weeps on perceiving "the identity of things"—the same marsh country of his past, the presence of his loved ones in the parish's churchyard.

The war destroyed almost everything when it came. But like Pip's marsh country and churchyard, nature and my ancestral land remain intact. Today, I see the same coleus plants I saw fifty years ago. I hear the same cicadas crying in the trees I heard before the first Indochina war. What makes my situation differ from Pip's is that I cannot find my ancestors' tombs which were destroyed after a heavy U.S. airstrike. Nevertheless, like my father who was able to invoke Grandmother although she had been dead for a very long time, I can perceive my ancestors' continued existence in my ancestral land where they had lived and died. An epitome of absolute immutability, the native land provides our past a powerful protection against the assault of time and the brutality of war. My childhood paradise is not lost. It has been there safe and unchanged until I return to recover it.

I spend two days at the home of a distant cousin in Lương Yến, a small village on the outskirts of Đồng Hới. After our successful flight from Trung Quán, we arrived and stayed here while waiting for our safe passage to the city. Knowing the purpose of my visit, my cousin Tân leaves me alone so I can roam the place as much as I please.

A familiar tune is played on Tân's radio. It's "Du kích sông Thao" ["River Thao Militiamen"] performed by the virtuoso soprano Lê Dung. I first heard the song in Lương Yến shortly before my father took us to Đồng Hới to start over our new life. Composed by Đỗ Nhuận in 1947 at the height of the resistance against the French, the song, which describes the guerrillas' activities on River Thao, mesmerized every Vietnamese. It also mesmerized me, a thirteen-year-old boy, and made me love Vietnam so. It reminded me of students at Lycée Yersin, a French high school in Dalat, among whom I could recognize my half-brother, who gave up their study and enlisted in the army to fight the French. On that day of August 1945, we children saw them off at Dalat Railway Station, electrified by their way of showing patriotism. Before boarding the train that would carry them, we were told, to the front, they executed their intricate formations with incredible precision, shouting anti-French slogans and chanting patriotic songs which were as powerful as "Du kích sông Thao." There were tears in everybody's eyes. We were all spellbound. How I wanted to emulate these brothers and sisters!

Lê Dung's singing also evokes snapshots of my short stay in Lương Yến. While awaiting a safe passage to Đồng Hới, the only area that was not under Việt Minh control, I met Tiến, a member of the local guerrilla band, who very much reminded me of our patriotic sisters and brothers at Dalat Railway Station. An educated young man, Tiến truly loved Vietnam and fought for his country's independence and freedom. Though he seemed to know of our plan to flee to the city, he did not try to interfere but encouraged me, in his words, "to pursue a good education in order to serve our country better in the future." Where could I get a good education if not in the city, which was under the government's control? It was obvious that Tiến wanted me, his little friend, to move to a better place for my future, for he could have stopped our plan, or worse, could have notified the Việt Minh and we could have been punished for attempting to flee them.

I saw Tiến only a couple of times when he was off from fighting. But when he came, he brought me great pleasure. He taught me to draw people and things in quite simple lines, which was later to become my chief hobby. I remember best his musical talent. Once in a meeting with his group, I heard him sing patriotic songs to the accompaniment of his harmonica. Tiến was at his best when he performed "Du kích sông Thao." His great love for Vietnam, his flawless execution style, and his tenor voice, which fitted this song, contributed to making his performance a great success. We were moved to tears as Tiến's solo ended.

My association with Tiến, his taking me to the meeting with his group, and even my patriotic feelings, all become alive today as I hear Lê Dung's performance of Đỗ Nhuận's masterpiece. The contemporary best-known, best-loved Vietnamese soprano leads me to my past and I hear again "Du kích sông Thao" sung by Tiến on that day fifty years ago at Lương Yến on the eve of our leaving for Đồng Hới. A wave of flashbacks rises before my eyes, each image throbbing with life. Just as Lê Dung's and Tiến's voice blends into a harmonious whole, the past comes to life, mingling with the present. The song animates the past, bringing it to the present, turning it into a kind of timeless present, or a continuous past-in-present. It exteriorizes, brings to surface my ever-existing unconscious longing for home which has been smoldering in my heart since my leaving Đồng Hới. I do not need to use memory to recreate the past. Transported on the wings of music, the past comes in full swing, uninterruptedly and continuously before my eyes. It really comes to life along with the tune and patriotic emotions that overwhelm me now but that I hardly felt or heeded then. Who's singing now? Lê Dung or my lost friend Tiến? Whose singing awakens my longing for home, my love of the past, my joy of finding it, my sorrow of losing it?

The song begins with the speaker addressing Hồng Hà River which was frequently used to transport the militia to the front during the resistance against the French. Because the river has been part of the peasant soldiers' lives since they were born, it is like their trustful and loyal companion with whom they can share their thoughts and feelings. To the Vietnamese, things that have been in existence since time immemorial and have nurtured and sustained them like the land, mountains, and rivers are not only important but sacred. Protecting those means protecting their country.

At the beginning of the song, the speaker reminisces about living in the peaceful country before the enemy's invasion. As Lê Dung uses her soprano to render the speaker's exalted state of mind, I am elevated to the heavenly sphere of pure bliss of my childhood. As the vocalist switches to a contralto to bemoan the fate of the speaker's country, I am brought back to my exile and my sorrow. My heart grows heavy when the vocalist laments the peasant soldier's homelessness, and their feeling of being lost souls who dream of going home. We thus share a similar dream, the young soldiers in Đỗ Nhuận's song and I, an old expatriate returning from America. Homesickness brings me back to my native land, but the music connects me with the known and unknown phantoms of the past and, through them, my lost paradise. My heart rows heavy when the vocalist laments the peasant soldiers' homeland and their being the lost souls who dream of going home. I am also a lost soul who is going home but cannot find home.

Though classified as a military song, "Du kích sông Thao" is composed in the vein of an elegy. It is not meant to raise one's martial spirit because its allegro movement is so short. Rather, its predominantly slow prolonged tempo is suitable for expressing sorrows deeply stored away in the human soul that only exiles feel and can never get over. Their sadness is long and immense like my sorrow, like the vast space (this river, this war-torn country) the speaker is addressing, like time (not chronological time, but memory time, which is immobile, thick, dense) that coalesces with space. The artist's singing and the sad lyric penetrate every cell of my body, soak the density and vastness of space and time, and turn into drops of sadness as they touch the leaves and branches of the trees in front of my ancestors' country home. My heart and the vast space around me throb with waves of melancholy music and glittering images of the past. The song brings back my past, but the pleasurable moment it evokes is so short that I am filled with feelings of loneliness and loss. Also, because I evoke the past as an old man, I cannot avoid the age-related fatigue that prevents me from feeling and seeing like a child—a prerequisite for regaining my paradise. Watching the past is like watching its images unfurling across a magic lantern. Simple and homely as the images are, they do not have the vitality and exuberance of living time to counteract my pain of exile and the feebleness of my memory. No sooner does the past—childhood, home, paradise—appear at my reach than it vanishes into emptiness, leaving me with inconsolable grief.

I end my brief visit to Quảng Bình by trying to find our old home in Đồng Hới under Tân's guidance. It is a new city, totally rebuilt after the war on an entirely new map with roads and streets entirely repositioned. Our former home cannot be found anywhere, or it might have disappeared after a U.S. air strike. I accidently hit upon my former Chơn Phước School, which now has a new name, but cannot determine where it was situated in the past; the only point of reference that is available to me is the sea, but the new school, unlike the old one, does not face the ocean. Getting around in Đồng Hới now is like groping along in a labyrinth because you have no sense of direction.

During the war, Quảng Bình suffered the most damage from U.S. bombing. Đồng Hới, which was less than fifty miles from the DMZ, was razed almost to the ground. The rise of the city from the ashes into a boom town in just twenty years is a miracle. But rebuilding does not mean completely doing away with the old town's original architecture and directions. The Vietnamese are less interested in preserving historic sites and cultural monuments than in building a completely new city in place of the old, broken-down one. Even war vestiges, which I suspect should be many, might have been destroyed or taken to a war museum. Probably too passionate about implementing Hồ's teaching—"We'll build a new Vietnam ten times more beautiful after our victory over the Americans"—the Vietnamese have eradicated things that would remind them of the war, not realizing that war can also be prevented if there is something to remind one that it should not be waged in the first place.

On our way back to the hotel, we pass a market square on the bank of Nhật Lệ river. According to Tân, this used to be Đồng Hới port where a French navy ship was docked to pick up refugees who wished to go south after the 1954 Geneva Accords. A reminiscence flashes across my mind. Forty-one years ago, it was here that we were evacuated from Đồng Hới to Đà Nẵng. I have not thought about Trang for a long time, but today, the old wharf rekindles my memory of her as it marked the day when I left Đồng Hới and lost her eternally. When I ask Tân, who knew Trang well, about her, he says that she stayed with her family in Đồng Hới, got married shortly after my leaving and after her Việt Minh brother's return, and had a daughter who now lives in her parents' home. Trang and her husband were killed in one of the heaviest bombings by U.S. warplanes in 1965. Tân says Trang was pregnant, and though she suffered a minor injury, she lost a lot of blood and died due to lack of emergency care. He suggests that I stop by her daughter's home to light an incense stick for her. Forty-odd years have passed, and I do not remember what Trang looked like when I first knew her. But when Tân introduces Hiền, a pretty woman in her early thirties, and her little girl as Trang's daughter and granddaughter, I suddenly feel that they *are* close to me. An unconscious impulse must have brought me back to a very short period of the past during which I had been in love with Trang, for I did not intend to look for her in this visit, have not thought about her for a very long time, have almost forgotten her.

On the family altar, there is a blurry black-and-white cellophane framed photo of a smiling, handsome man in his thirties and a woman who looks like Hiền but much younger. The woman in the photo has beautiful eyes with a quizzical look which reminds me of Trang when I first saw her at her parents' house, except that she looks so sad in the picture. The couple wears coarse cloth uniform clothes with a gold star on the lapel of their shirt. Tân says that Trang and her husband were members of the Communist Party. I mumble a few words to Hiền, telling her I am sorry about her mother, then light incense on her altar. I perform the ritual perfunctorily, not knowing if I do it sincerely or out of courtesy to Trang's daughter. My mind reels when facing Trang on the altar. I close my eyes, trying to invoke from my memory the girl who haunted me for a long time, but only see her jumbled images flickering through my mind. I open my eyes and give the joss sticks to Tân for him to put in the incense burner. There is shock on Hiền's face. I do not know if she is touched by a *Việt kiều*'s loyalty to her mother's memory, or if she sees constraint in my manner of expressing sympathy. Tân must have told Hiền about me, about my short but endearing relationship with her mother, and this might have touched her heart. Suddenly, I feel so sad. The war cut short the life of a woman in her prime before she could fulfill her destiny as a mother and wife. This thought and particularly seeing Hiền, who is Trang's replica, immediately bring back my childhood sweetheart whom I found unrelated to me when I first saw the photo. I see myself as an eighteen-year-old lad, back at the very place where my father took me to see the girl I had secretly loved and her parents for the first time forty-one years ago. She is so pretty, and on our subsequent dates, I notice that she speaks with a faint Hanoi lilting accent, which makes her speech very elegant and attractive. There are tears in her eyes when she feels that our union might not materialize. Suddenly, today in this same house, these forty-one past years crystallize into forty-one seconds during which I participate in the revival of my short past in a capsule drama that involves three existing generations—Trang's daughter and granddaughter and me, her admirer and would-be fiancé. Instantly, a wave of resurrections surges in my head: my father's escorting me to Trang's home on Đường Nhà Tằm street in the afternoon of a sunny day in June 1954, her mischievous twinkle cast at me as if to tease my timidity. My remembrance then lights on the scene of my family boarding the French Navy's "gaping maw ship" to go south and my permanent loss of Trang. I could recall more sweet memories of my sweetheart, but suddenly they fall apart, appear in jumbled fragments. I look again at Trang's photo, trying to search for a beautiful girl with rosy cheeks and shining eyes who would walk down my street with her garrulous little band of young girls every summer sunny afternoon, whose emergence in the far end of the street I would await with both excitement and trepidation. That girl who later held my hand in hers with tears in her eyes when she thought that our union would not materialize, who briefly appears in my mind today, is gone, gone forever with my unrecoverable happy adolescence and Đồng Hới, our hot, sunny, peaceful city by the sea. Gone is the place, the framework of my sweetheart and my first love. Through memory and fantasy, I could resuscitate a glimpse of my paradise, but because it lacks the support of *real* space—the peaceful sunny city by the sea where we lived, the street where our first and subsequent dates took place—the ephemeral paradise vanishes like a bubble. I take one last look at the photo on the altar, trying to scan the picture for my childhood sweetheart's face, trying hard to evoke Trang's image which mesmerized me when I first saw her after her return home from Hanoi for summer. No matter how hard I visualize, I see nothing save Trang's privation and hardship in Đồng Hới under the Việt Minh regime. Nor can I separate her from her husband in the photo. His forbidding presence scares me. I feel jealous of Trang and her husband when I imagine how happy their life would have been if they had been still together now. Then I feel angry with Trang for betraying me. She got married shortly after my leaving! Did she ever love me as she swore? She forgot me so soon. So soon for a girl who cried when she suspected our union would not materialize. I should not have been that loyal to her. It was not worth it!

But I cannot forget Trang's sad look in the photo which seems directed at me. It is gentle but it strikes me as full of reproach. Why does Trang look so sad beside her happy-looking husband? Was her marriage a happy one? Tân says that Trang got married shortly after her communist brother's return. Because he did not allow his family to go south, could he also have had a say in his young sister's hurried marriage? Could he also have chosen her husband for her? Tân says that Trang's husband was the son of her brother's close comrade. Even if I had not left Đồng Hới after the partition of the country, there was no guarantee that our planned union would have worked out. Her brother would object to our marriage because of our disloyalty to the Việt Minh. In addition, at that time I was too young to understand the meaning of my father's teaching that human relationships, no matter how close they are, might be subject to change. Trang failed me because I had abandoned her, or maybe she might have found her right man. But the change in me is tremendous. I am *not* the person I was; my way of thinking and feeling is not the same; I have become selfish, pompous, arrogant. I am shocked by the change in me rather than by the passage of time and its effects on me. Maybe a person my age does not value childhood memories as much as when he was young. Or maybe we can regain our paradise from different avenues, not just through the resurrection of a foolish, childish love. When I look at Trang's photo, I feel pity for an ordinary person who happened to be so unfortunate, rather than the great pain we would feel about the loss of someone we deeply loved for such a long time.

My mixed reaction to Trang is caused by my encounter with the photo. My faithful memory of my idyllic lover is shattered when I learn from Tân that her husband loved her and she was happy in her marriage. Suddenly, I feel that she appears to me like a stranger, like someone I scarcely know. Feeling jealous and a bit angry about the couple's happiness, particularly about Trang's apparent loyalty to her husband, I vent my negative feelings by looking down on my *dead* childhood sweetheart and her husband, by taking pity on their poverty, by offending the spirit of the woman I should have taken care of and protected.

Thus, my search for that short but happiest period of the past ends in failure with my accidental encounter with Trang's photo and what it transpires. Again, fate plays a trick on me. The photo first connects me to the girl I was madly in love with for a long time; it briefly resuscitates my best memories of her; then it severs me from her by making me aware of the great distance between us. All my dreams and fantasies I had about her end in smoke when I am brought into contact with the reality of her life and death. Trang is *not* my paradise, the object of my search, in this return. My mind buzzes with many questions: Did my father ever take me to Trang's home to see her? Was she ever my sweetheart? Did she ever love me? Finally, is the woman in the photo Trang? It has been so long (more than forty years since I left Đồng Hới and saw her last) that I have totally forgotten her. It is Tân who told me this woman was Trang and to me she looks like Hiền. But what if Tân did not tell me the truth and the woman was not Hiền's mother? My head buzzes with lots of questions: Did I ever know Trang? Did she exist as my lover, or was she a result of my erratic imagination, a chimera unconsciously formed in my mind to help me cope with the harsh realities of existence? I cannot say no to any of these questions because they were all truth to me. To say I was never in love with Trang is like to say I never left Đồng Hới to go south. The appearance of Trang and her band I saw on Trần Hưng Đạo Street in Huế was an illusion, but wasn't it because I had thought so much about Trang that she became an obsession in my mind? But why do I treat Trang's memory today with such unkindness and insolence as if I never knew her or she never existed? Is it because I thought Trang had failed me by hastily getting married although I knew it was not her fault? I feel awful when remembering the sad look on Trang's face in the photo. Isn't she reproaching me because I did not appreciate the importance of our first love and trampled on her feelings by leaving Đồng Hới without trying to see her and who now treats her memory so cruelly?

I end my visit to Quảng Bình with disappointment, sorrow, and remorse. My search for paradise through my first love is doomed for many reasons: my arrogant and selfish American ego revealed in my encounter with Trang's memory, the tragedy of her life, and my inability to forgive myself and my former sweetheart. I can no longer regain that paradise, that idyllic time in which I experienced for the first time both happiness and sorrow, joy and suffering, in my short relationship with Trang, any more than recover my ability to dream, fantasize, and suffer as when I was first in love. The heart is a strange thing. It is full of paradoxes and irrationalities. It is also very stubborn. It makes us desire to relive the past to relish it, not knowing or refusing to realize that reliving it can make us suffer. I had thought that Trang would be loyal to me, but today her apparent happiness of living with her husband as revealed in the photo on her altar makes me not only jealous of Trang's husband but angry with myself. Why was I so stupid when, after living in Huế for quite a while, I still fantasized about Trang by reenacting the scene of her promenade with her girlfriends on my street in Đồng Hới when she was happily married to her man at home? Today I committed a similar blunder by fantasizing my reunion with Trang and her family as if they were my loved ones! But this was but an ephemera. Before long, I went back to my blame game, and poor Trang became my victim.

I leave Trang's house, feeling bad about the accidental visit. On my way back to the hotel, as I hit the old port, the place that witnessed my permanent loss of Trang, a sea of sorrows rises in me. Again, I cannot help remembering my sweetheart who cried when she heard of my leaving her; nor can I forget her sad look in the photo on her altar that makes me suffer with tremendous remorse. Remembering Trang also brings back my most pleasant time at home when I awaited with excitement, trepidation, and anxiety the strolling near my street of Trang and her band of young girls whose white *ao dai* fluttered in the summer breeze like white butterflies. Suddenly, I raise my hand and instinctively touch my heart.

How long am I able to maintain that state of mind toward Trang? I do not know. But during the past twenty minutes of my visit at Trang's house, I have been transformed into a being with conflicting personalities and states of mind. No matter how powerful Trang's sad and reproachful look directed at me, it will not bring back again the girl I saw in a vision on Trần Hưng Đạo Street on that New Year's Day in Huế. Paradise, to be regained, must be in an absolute pure state, and the subject must be fervent and single-minded in his quest. I wish I had not visited Trang's house, had not been told about her condition, and had not seen the photo of Trang and her happy husband on their altar.

ILLNESS

Things returned to normal after we returned to the States and I resumed my academic duties at Schreiner University where I had taught since 1982 after my reunion with my family. In January 1998, I traveled to Washington, D.C. to read a paper at the Asian Studies Association annual meeting. Just a few minutes before I walked into the meeting room, a colleague, who knew me well and my desire to return to Vietnam to teach, told me about the U.S. Fulbright Scholar Program available for the first time this year after the normalization of the relations between Vietnam and the United States. While I was excited about a possible opportunity to make my dream come true, I had an eerie premonition that something wrong was going to happen.

In the fall of 1998, I received a sabbatical leave from my university. It came at a time when I wanted to apply for a Fulbright grant, so it seemed like a perfect divine arrangement. I went to a Kelsey Seybold clinic in Houston for a physical as part of the application requirements. After examining me, Dr. Nguyễn asked me to come back for further evaluation. A sigmoid exam and later a colonoscopy confirmed that I had colon cancer. The world came crashing down on me. Not only had my dream of going to Vietnam evaporated, but I was facing the likelihood of dying. While living in Washington, I had a friend who was undergoing chemotherapy for lung cancer. Just seeing him, who had changed from a robust person to a dying emaciated old man in a few months' time, filled me with horror. In his last moments, he became a skeleton with a huge skull and two sunken sockets that used to be his eyes. He remained unconscious most of the time, unable to recognize visitors and even his relatives who were attending him. But his continuous groans and convulsions despite strong doses of morphine he had received told me that, though unconscious, he was feeling the excruciating pain. He was like a living corpse being tortured to death, quaking and writhing with intermittent ear-splitting groans and screams. I did not want to be in a situation like his. Nga and my teenage children needed my support and care, and I was afraid of pain. Starting my academic career in the U.S. rather late, but with a great passion for professional and scholarly success, I wanted to live long enough to fulfill all my plans and expectations. I also wanted to have a productive retirement combining resting and writing, which is my favorite interest. After that, I wanted to return to Vietnam to live a few more years and die in the land where I was born and grew up.

My psychiatrist son Hùng made an appointment for my surgery at St. Luke's Hospital in Houston. The procedure started in mid-morning, and I did not wake until mid-afternoon. In my sleep, I heard a female voice calling out my name several times. Trying as hard as I could, I was unable to open my eyes. I fell to instinctively reciting mentally (it resounded in my head) the name of Kwan-yin, and in about five seconds, I opened my eyes and saw a nurse bending over me, still shouting out my name to my ears. Seeing me awake, she said I had been asleep longer than anticipated. I found it strange to be in this room, vaguely knowing what I had been through, my throat dry and burning, my head swirling. There was a smart pain in my belly, and I slowly began to realize that I had been brought in here for a procedure. The anesthetic I had received must have dulled my consciousness and sensitivity even after I woke. I had slept for seven straight hours, but it felt like it was a nap. Then I fell asleep again for how long I did not remember. When I opened my eyes, I saw Nga and Hùng in the patient room with me. The pain shot through my belly again, the attack growing more intense and frequent.

I was discharged from the hospital a week later. As soon as I felt better, another rigorous course of treatment began. Hùng took me to see Dr. Richard Pazdur, an excellent oncologist at the University of Texas MD Anderson Cancer Center in Houston, who put me on a six-month adjuvant therapy. The side effects were terrible: my hair was gone after two weeks, my face got ashen, and I often had a severe stomach pain. My life was a living hell when I went through chemotherapy. The dripping of the 5-FU into my system was like a slow injection of poison. My entire body was on fire. The heat was internal because it was generated by the burning of my organs by the toxic drug. My body from head to toe felt hot and dry as if it was roasted under a slow flame. But because I was not thirsty, drinking cool water did not help. Dr. Parduz wanted me to do some light exercise at home, but because I was too drowsy to do it on my own, Nga had me place my hands on her shoulders so she could lead me around the house. I walked behind her, my eyes shut, like a blind man or a somnambulist, asleep and awake, constantly feeling the dry, hot flame inside my body, constantly feeling nauseous. When I got too tired to continue, I lay down. My eyelids got heavy, but I could not fall asleep. My consciousness, if any, was the excruciating pain I felt after each chemo treatment and the morphine I was prescribed for the pain. Suddenly, I became fascinated with death. It would make me feel better because I would be off those killing drugs and the pain they caused. But it was not easy to die. Because I had to live for my loved ones, I was willing to endure pain and agony until the end. I did not know if I would be successful or not. What I knew was if the treatment failed, like my late friend in Washington, I would not have a quick and easy death.

My illness might have been predicted by the psychic in Huế when she alluded to my sad fate, but might she have equally predicted my possible death in her vague words that I did not understand? Curiously, Nga also had a vision of my fate the night after my surgery, but it was, as she said and I knew why, an auspicious one. She said in her dream, she had seen my father, who told her that I had been *home* with him for the night and that I had been told to return to my family in the States at daybreak. She went on to demonstrate her theory that my recovery was a sure thing: my surgery occurred around noon in Texas, which was around midnight in Vietnam (Vietnam time is 12 hours ahead of U.S. Central Time), meaning, according to her interpretation of the dream, I had originally reunited with my father and my ancestors in the other world in Vietnam but later was sent back to America. I would not have woken from my long sleep had I not been turned down by my people in the other world! There was a grain of truth in Nga's theory from a Buddhist perspective. But her belief, I think, stemmed more from her love of me, her desire for my recovery than from her religious conviction. Thus, she presented her argument with the following sequence of causal inference: had the Fulbright opportunity not turned up, I would not have taken a physical, which revealed my sickness, which led to my surgery and chemotherapy, which would certainly cure me shortly and I would return to Vietnam in no time. She would be at her most eloquent when I was in pain. *"You're going to be all right, darling. You're just cleansing your karma for better days ahead. Heaven, Buddhas, and our ancestors are protecting you. Trust me."*

My prognosis was good, and at the end of the treatment period, I returned to teaching. Everyone was thrilled to see me back on campus, and I could not thank them enough for their kindness and care during and after my sick leave. I was assigned a very light teaching load, so I had plenty of time to rest. I completed my application for the Fulbright lectureship I had not finished due to my illness. My English department again promised me another leave of absence should I receive the grant.

***

Despite my euphoria, I am not entirely out of danger. Dr. Pazdur says that since my illness was left untreated too long, I would have only a 60 percent chance of survival. I am scheduled to return to the hospital for routine check-ups and tests every three months. It depresses me to be a patient again. I marvel at the general congenial appearance of the patients in the waiting room. The American family support system seems very good as I see that most patients are accompanied by their relatives. They might have been taken here by someone in their family, whereas I drive 200 miles from where we live to the hospital. Luckily, throughout my ordeal, Nga is with me all the time.

We immigrants are poorly prepared for our new life in America, even more so for any disaster that strikes us. Because of the location of my job, we live in isolation and have no friends nor relatives near us. My recent illness caught us, particularly Nga, off guard as she is not familiar with American culture. I can see not only terror but helplessness on Nga's face when the doctor tells her of my illness. There is alarm in her voice even when she tries to comfort me and assure me of my recovery. There were a few times I wished I could be liberated as soon as possible from the horrible, unbearable side effects of the cancer drug they injected in my body. But I was abhorred immediately by my selfishness. Our children, except Hùng, are underage. And Nga, she was just reunited with me after a decade of separation. She seems to read my dark thoughts as, at such moments, she looks so helpless and pitiful. Were we at home when this happened, we would have access to a network of friends and relatives designed to provide support for a family when a disaster strikes. I do not know what Nga would do to keep our family together without me.

It is hard to die then, even if you want it. Family is a human bond that is most difficult to break off. It is where relationships are formed and become intertwined, so much so that with the passage of time, we grow—and feel—inseparable from one another as long as we live. No people are more acutely aware of this than Asian immigrants and refugees who realize the importance of family cohesion in coping with the unexpected in the new land. The absence or death of someone in the family, especially the breadwinner, can severely affect his dependents' emotional and material well-being. I am thankful that I have survived the greatest health crisis I have ever experienced to continue assisting Nga in raising our children until they come of age.

My other reason for rejoicing over my survival is I will have a chance to realize the rest of my important aspirations. I want to return to Vietnam again to continue where I left off since my last trip. One month was not long enough to recover those twenty-eight years I had lost since my coming to the States. One month was too short to retrieve from the dense past so many things related to me—my lost time, my old family, particularly my late father (had the communist takeover not happened or had it been delayed a few months in 1975, I would have returned home to see him before he died). It is important that I return to do it now before it is too late. More than ever I feel in me the need, the impulse, the call to complete the unfinished search. I must do it not only for me but for my children. They ought to know who their ancestors were and what and where their roots are.

EXILE'S RETURN (II): VIETNAM DIARY

In June 1999, my fondest dream materialized: I was notified by the U.S. State Department Fulbright Commission of my one-year appointment at Vietnam National University, Hồ Chí Minh City. My excitement about the news was mixed with apprehensiveness. For the first time, communist Vietnam accepted a former South Vietnamese national for teaching at one of its major state universities a "sensitive" subject like U.S. literature and culture. Had I returned home in 1975 or shortly afterward, I could have been sent to a re-education camp because of my living in the States, particularly my training in American studies! I could not figure out why they consented to let a Vietnamese Americanist return to work with their young people who, I suspect, must have been told since grade school about "crimes committed by the Americans and their lackeys." What concerned me was that teaching such a subject as American literature and culture would be impossible in a place that doesn't permit free expression and exchange of ideas in the classroom. Luckily, when contacting the State Department, I was told that academic freedom would be assured for every Fulbright lecturer. I accepted the grant offer and spent my remaining time in the U.S. preparing for the adventure.

***

Our return to Vietnam this time is not exciting as it was in 1995. The State Department official's assurance does not put me entirely at ease. There is no word from the U.S. Embassy in Hanoi that I will be protected during my tenure at the host institution. Perhaps my appointment is nothing extraordinary to them; perhaps there are so many things for them to do when the normalization of diplomatic relations resumed not long ago; or perhaps I am too paranoid about my safety. Regardless, I cannot get that nagging feeling of discomfort and anxiety off my mind. I am about to enter a world that I think would be more hostile than friendly to me because of my South Vietnamese origin and American training. My situation is unique compared with other Vietnamese Americans working in "unsuspicious" fields such as computer and business. I am expected to work closely with, according to the terms of my appointment, many colleagues who do not share the same background as me and many students who have not been exposed to any Western culture before except Marxism. It will be an adventure, a risk rather than a homecoming, to search for a happy past as I wished four years earlier.

Shortly after my arrival, I report to the English Department, College of Social Sciences and Humanities. On their English stationery, the Vietnamese refer to their college as the University of Social Sciences and Humanities. I find this both confusing and amusing. How can you explain the existence of more than one university—the University of Social Sciences and Humanities, the University of Natural Sciences, the University of Law, etc.—all under the aegis of Vietnam National University? A colleague and friend offers an interesting explanation: "Our institution is too big to be called a college. Besides, the university status makes us more prestigious!" The office of the English Department is too small to manage an enrollment of more than 10,000 students. The Dean (in the States we would call her department head or chairperson), the Associate Dean, their two assistants, and the staff squeeze up in a small room. I am able to recognize the dean, a gaunt, stern-looking woman in her fifties, thanks to the brass plaque with her full name and title on her desk. Apparently knowing who I am because of my outlandish appearance and manners, she casts at me a piercing glance, nodding her head. I greet her by her title, then introduce myself.

I hear Dean Hoàng's assistant politely call her *"Cô."* (This title, originally used for young unmarried women, can apply to older married ones who want to be considered young but are powerful enough to command respect or inspire fear from their subordinates.) According to one of my colleagues, Dean Hoàng was a police colonel. Speaking with a heavy North Vietnamese accent, she rapidly glosses over routine matters like school, students, and course assignments. She slows down, speaking clearly and emphatically when she lays out what she calls "state security rules" that all foreigners and *Việt kiều* are expected to follow. Because I am going to teach "a very sensitive subject" (meaning "because American writers are notoriously known for championing freedom and democracy"), she asks me to confer with one of her assistants who is in the meeting about selecting texts "suitable" for the students' level, which means students must not be exposed to stories that describe violence, sexual and political freedom, etc. Through inference, a technique I learned when growing up and living in a culture where your superiors (like the dean here) would indicate their desire not verbally but through implications or vague physical gestures, I can easily get at Dean Hoàng's message. So, in a nutshell, she wants me to do just like everyone else at her school—stay out of politics; watch my language in my lectures; do not criticize the regime in front of students; do not discuss "sensitive" issues with my audience, whether they are students or the faculty, etc. A funny thought occurs to me during my encounter with Dean Hoàng. What if a native-born American Fulbright scholar *were* in my place today instead of me! Since the dean's English (I later find out) is limited, she would not be able to communicate with my imagined American colleague and make him or her understand what she would want. Were her English good enough, she still would have difficulty getting herself across with her cryptic language. I guess that could be why I got the appointment rather than a native-born colleague!

My conference with Dean Hoàng gives me the impression that the U.S. and Vietnamese governments might have forced her university to implement the Fulbright lecture program in Vietnam, but her school and her department are not ready for it, or they are not familiar with the value of the program and its participants. For example, I am assigned a very heavy teaching load—five huge undergraduate classes—while at my university in the States as a full professor, I have never taught more than three courses per semester. There is no mention of my role in curriculum development or teacher training as listed in my Fulbright appointment package. I feel that I came a long way from America on a rare leave of absence just to become a substitute teacher at Dean Hoàng's English Department. That is the price I am paying for my being here to search for the past!

***

September 13th, 1999

First day of American Studies class. Shocked and frustrated because there is no English Department official around to introduce me to the class. At least over seventy students crammed into a small classroom with no air conditioning. They all rise to greet me. This is a tradition I last saw in my classes twenty-seven years ago before I left home, and it's still being observed in communist Vietnam! I thank them and ask them to sit down first in English and then in Vietnamese. For the first time since I left Vietnam, I use my native language in a class, so I feel odd and embarrassed. Had I been introduced by a college official, this could have been avoided. Using my method of beginning my first day of class in the States, I write on the blackboard (not the green one as in an American school) my full name in the Vietnamese order, my Fulbright scholar title. I don't put my home institution's name because I'm afraid that students would see it as showing off. Some students take notes, but many of them stare at me. Maybe they're curious about me and my outlandish manners. But the entire class is so quiet I can hear the whirring of the ceiling fans and my own voice speaking. I try to break the silence by interspersing my lecture with anecdotes about America (is this my way of letting my students know where I'm from? I don't know; all I know is the act occurs so quickly and spontaneously like a reflex without premeditation) and they burst out laughing. So, my students' previous silence means they have curiosity about their new teacher from America! There is no negative feeling about me or anything of that sort.

During the break, I learn more about my Vietnamese students' perception—and even knowledge—of me. I'm bombarded with questions about America, my family and my residence in America, when I left Vietnam, the reason of my "homecoming." Hearing the phrase almost moves me to tears. It means I'm home now and being accepted by these young people who hardly know me because they were born after I had left the country. I'm also touched to learn from my students that their English teachers have told them about me (did I need to be introduced to the class then as I griped earlier?). All my misperceptions, my misgivings of my Vietnamese students and my Vietnamese colleagues, which put me ill at ease before I came to this class this morning, are gone.

After the class, a student follows me to the building stairway. He greets me with profound respect and identifies himself as a double major in English and Economics. Graduates with both degrees have a good chance of finding jobs with foreign firms in Vietnam. They want applicants with training in commerce and related fields and with strong English language skills. It's sad that not many students study literature to teach or to do literary research.

The student wants to hear from me whether the Americans, as his government says, are "too aggressive" in Kosovo. Having just had a conference with Dean Hoàng, a former police colonel, I don't want to get in trouble, so I refuse to offer my comments on his query. My brother-in-law Hảo has told me to stay away from politics in my lectures and exchanges with students. Because I'm a *Việt kiều* returning from America, everything I say or do may be reported to the police.

Knowing that he can't get my response to his question, that student thanks me and leaves. Seeing his disappointment, I'm convinced that he isn't working for the police. Poor kid, he must have put a lot of trust in me whom he might think is not only knowledgeable but also, in my capacity as an American professor, unafraid to speak my mind freely for what I believe is truth, even if it might contradict the government's view. The event makes me feel awful. With my appointment at his prestigious institution, I thought I could serve as a role model for my students at home. It turns out that I have let them down because of my lack of moral courage and intellectual integrity. I try to find him a few times to make amends for my failing him, but because my classes are so big and I don't remember his face, I give up on the effort.

***

September 14th

First day of American literature class today. Another huge class. I sweat profusely because it's too warm, but I'm pleased to find out later students from other classes I didn't teach were sitting in my class today to hear me.

A few years ago, I saw on CNN an instructor from this college sweating in her class and I felt sorry for her. I thought she was perspiring because she was too active, rather than because the room had no air conditioning. Now I find myself in the same situation. I have great admiration for this teacher who returned from England with an MA degree in Linguistics to teach under these very difficult circumstances. She makes me feel bad because, unlike her, I don't understand the hardships my people suffer at home. My long stay in the States and the so-called American acculturation obviously make it difficult for me to sympathize with and relate to my people.

***

September 15th

At the suggestion of Tú, Nga's niece, Nga and I go to the Botanical Gardens to learn calisthenics. At daybreak, there is already a lively scene with people of different ages jogging, walking, playing badminton (a popular sport in Vietnam, for it can be played anywhere and isn't too strenuous), performing Tai-chi and various sorts of calisthenics. At the other side of the museum is another group mostly of women doing a kind of Chinese calisthenics called *Hương công* ("fragrant" energy training), so called because skilled practitioners claim that their body can produce a pleasant aroma when they perform this *chi* exercise. Their movements are very gentle and rhythmical. We join in and have practiced *Hương công* ever since. The people I see at the park, contrary to my belief, appear relaxed, caring more about their health and well-being than about politics. Before 1975, these things didn't exist. Could it be because, during the war, it wasn't safe to congregate in public?

The bust of the founder of the Botanical Gardens is said to be erected after 1975. He looks like Lenin.

We have settled nicely in a nice townhouse on Lê Thánh Tôn Street about ten minutes from the college, so I can walk to school to teach. We'll prepare an offering of fruits and rice to the local gods as required by tradition as soon as we can.

***

September 20th-23rd

Where we live there are many restaurants which serve good food at reasonable prices. As early as 5:00 p.m. most bars and open-air restaurants are stacked with people, most of them men. They come from different walks of life, but all seem to have a good time. They eat, drink, and talk noisily.

Southerners are well known for their lassitude to the point of irresponsibility. They're willing to spend all their fortune for fun. A Honda motorcycle driver tells me his friend, a pedicab driver, burned all his earnings in a gambling house instead of buying food for his family.

Northerners are different. They try to save every penny they can. Not only can they manage to live within their means, but they also know how to impress people and save face. My father used to tell me that he knew some families from Hanoi who never touched their fried fish dish during their meal. What he discovered was shocking: the mouth-watering dish was a wooden one! I've read in the fiction of Tự Lực Văn Đoàn authors that a former mandarin now reduced to poverty had his maid wash lots of dishes—to let everyone know that he was still wealthy.

Southerners I had a chance to chat with blamed the loss of their south to the communists on the former government's ingrained complacency and lack of foresight. The land in the south is so abundant and fertile that peasants, it is said, can get three crops a year compared with two in the north. The Mekong Delta is crisscrossed with canals with abundant fish, turtles, snakes—an important source of food at the peasants' fingertips.

Vietnamese historians and scholars who study Vietnam's famous Southward March offer an interesting theory about those happy-go-lucky Vietnamese Southerners. Their ancestors, who were originally from the north, early in the 16th century joined the Nguyễn lords' campaign in their conquest of Champa and in subsequent centuries in their annexation of part of Cambodia, now known as the Mekong Delta, to what was their Đại Việt (Great Imperial Việt). These soldiers and their families later settled down in the new land permanently. With the passage of time, they grew pampered by mother nature and lost their northern traits, that is, resilience, self-discipline, resourcefulness, and combativeness.

Fifty years ago, after the partition of Vietnam in July 1954, more than a million people left the north to resettle in the south, particularly in the Saigon area. Almost overnight, these refugees who had arrived as paupers became owners of Saigon's most elegant, prosperous business district on Lê Thánh Tôn Street and adjacent areas.

History repeats itself with an ironic twist in 1975. Fearing for their safety, these former Northerners fled Saigon before the communists' arrival. Lê Thánh Tôn Street changed hands again, and this time, its new occupiers were Northerners who came to the South after the communist victory. (Native Southerners call these new settlers "Northerners '75" to distinguish them from "Northerners '54," who arrived as refugees in 1954 after the partition of Vietnam.)

Lê Thánh Tôn Street, where we presently live, is a new prosperous Northern colony with most residents from Hanoi. Many of them are renting out their houses to foreigners. Our rent is higher because the neighborhood is relatively safe. Except for petty thefts, no serious crimes have been reported.

Our landlord, a Navy major originally from Hanoi, like most of his comrades-at-arms in the victorious army, according to our informant, was assigned a lot on which he built a townhouse which he rents to foreigners. Over the years he and his wife have made enough money to buy more land for further investment.

The assignment of land to northern migrants started after "the liberation of the South." Our Tai-chi partner told us that she should have selected a lot in the front street to build her residence and use it for some lucrative business. During our visit at her home, a local police officer came to remind her to pay her overdue membership. After he left, our Tai-chi partner told us that the local authorities usually harassed people in the neighborhood for money. As the government is corrupt, bribing government employees, especially the police, is a sure way for innocent people to stay out of trouble. Foreign nationals and *Việt kiều* are no exception. We pay a higher rent for our guaranteed security and freedom from the police hassle. These things aren't free in Vietnam.

***

September 26th

Today I'm invited to serve as an examiner for the Michigan Proficiency Test. It has been only four years since the normalization of relations between the U.S. and Vietnam, and yet all the major language tests administered by U.S. educational agencies are already in place in Vietnam. Many students take these tests as part of their endeavor to seek an opportunity to study in the U.S. Have the Vietnamese forgotten their mortal enemy, the "U.S. imperialists," that fast? I'm amazed at the candidates' understanding of, devotion to, and craze about America. A young man, when pressed for the reason of his interest in America, confesses that he doesn't know why he finds this country so irresistible to him and he has no trouble relating to it.

Most young candidates interviewed show a remarkable familiarity with American folk culture like jazz and MTV. The oldest applicant is a seventy-year-old woman who speaks English with an American accent. She says that she used to work for the former U.S. Military Assistance Command, Vietnam (MACV) in Saigon and now wants to travel to the U.S. to study for a college degree and to find her former American friends. (I wonder why she didn't apply to immigrate to America as a former MACV employee right after the normalization of relations between the two countries.) Another amazing applicant is a girl who says she's home from her one-year attendance at an American high school and now wishes to apply to Harvard. I'm impressed with her command of American English but shocked by her American mannerisms. A colleague later tells me that she's the daughter of a high-ranking government official in Hồ Chí Minh City. To prepare her for future study in the U.S., her parents had her take private English lessons since she was a child. It shocks me to learn that though the government propaganda still slams the "U.S. imperialists," the communist elite has already sent their children to their former enemy country to study. Suddenly, I'm carried away by a feeling of "patriotic" gusto. For the first time, I feel proud to be an American conducting a U.S. cultural mission in Vietnam, forgetting that all my life, I've always considered myself an exile in my new country!

An American man makes quite a scene today. He vociferously blasts the college for messing up his schedule. Some staff members say they're shocked to see an American get angry in public for the first time in their life. I'm also embarrassed to see what's happening. Because the two countries established their relationships not long ago and Vietnam is still leery of America, U.S. citizens who are here should avoid displaying any kind of behavior that reflects America's negative image during the war. Some people might think he's a madman because he talks angrily in his language which they don't understand!

***

September 28th

Have a private meeting today with Dr. Trần Xuân Thảo, Vietnam Fulbright Program Director from Hanoi, and Dean Hoàng at my request. I want a reduction of my teaching load and a clarification of my appointment. Dr. Thảo stresses my role as advisor to a future American Studies program at the college and trainer of the English Department's junior faculty. Dean Hoàng states that it's too late to change my schedule but promises to implement Dr. Thảo's recommendation next semester. I appreciate the Fulbright Program's prompt intervention. It will make it easier for future Fulbright appointees to work in Vietnam.

***

September 29th

Meet Dr. Nguyễn Văn Tài, the college's Vice-Rector. A remarkable man! He seems to sympathize with me, a South Vietnamese citizen who lives in exile. He expresses his regret that "a person of my caliber" must serve a foreign country rather than his native country. He criticizes corruption and the government's ineptitude, sharing with me his vision of a new Vietnam where freedom, democracy, and justice prevail. Knowing my experience in American Studies, he enlists my assistance in establishing during my tenure here a possible American Studies research center at his college. "There're a lot of things we can learn from America which rose from war and division to lasting peace and national unity," Dr. Tài says. I don't think the university leadership will accept Dr. Tài's ideas which are too bold at this time. Furthermore, based on Dean Hoàng's rough treatment of me and her insistence that I adhere to her policy in preparing my course syllabus, the idea of setting up an American Studies program on this campus is too daring and unrealistic.

***

September 30th

All classes are so big. The *lớp trưởng* (class heads) who take the attendance for me report only a couple of absences. The heat is unbearable in the classroom. I sweat profusely every time I enter a class. I also feel depressed. But seeing my students sit stoically throughout their class, their faces moist with sweat, patiently taking notes of my lectures, I feel ashamed of myself. My colleagues at this university have been in this state for years and they've never had any complaints.

***

October 2nd

A student reveals to me something very shocking today. He says that in my classes there were some plainclothesmen sitting in the back taking notes, but after a week they're all gone. He jokingly comments that they "drop out" because they don't understand English! I'm shocked and angry to learn of this, but very happy because this student—and perhaps many more, judging by their warm attitude toward me—is taking me into his confidence. This completely changes my erroneous perception of these young men and women I formed before my arrival here.

Regardless of whatever political system in which they grow up, young people are honest, sincere, tolerant, and idealistic. By contrast, adults are generally prone to mistrust, suspicion, and intolerance. A colleague takes me to the college's planning department where he introduces me to an unfriendly-looking man and asks him to allow me to use the Internet. The man is very rude; he just throws at me a cold look, not saying a word. He strikes me as a plainclothes *công an* (police officer; there are several of them in most public institutions such as this university, I'm told). Is it possible that he's suspicious of or hostile to a *Việt kiều* like me?

***

Evening of October 2nd

Parents here care more about their children than about politics. Special shows on TV1 channel such as "The Family and the Little Citizen" are designed to help parents raise their kids in a proper manner. Kids are also taught to respect and love their elders. Awards are given to these young winners.

Elderly people seem more privileged here than in America. Old age is celebrated on the "The International Day of the Elderly." We're asked to join our *Hương công* group's march to Lê Văn Tám Park to pay our respects to people over seventy.

Last week, we went to Lê Văn Tám Park to practice. I was amazed to see so many groups do various sorts of exercises at the former Mạc Đĩnh Chi cemetery. They look focused but relaxed.

***

October 3rd

Meet Prof. Lê Ngọc Trà from the College of Education. Dr. Trà, who received a doctorate in sciences from Moscow University in 1988, is a well-known literary critic and theorist. Currently, he's Director of the Center for International Education and Culture Exchange, Hồ Chí Minh City College of Education, and as such a fervent advocate of educational reforms and cultural exchange with the United States. He finds me at my English Department's reading room and invites me to give a lecture at his school. Because of my hectic teaching schedule, I decline his invitation but praise his interest in establishing an American Studies program in Hồ Chí Minh City. I'm a little confused by what has transpired since my arrival here: both the College of

Social Sciences and Humanities and Dr. Trà have expressed their desire to set up an American Studies center at their institution. Did they get the government's green light or is this their own idea? A colleague and friend at the English Department says that Saigon—most people I speak with use the term Saigon in lieu of Hồ Chí Minh City in their informal exchange—is more *"thoáng"* (relaxed) than hardcore Hanoi because of the people's relaxed manners and the city's long exposure to South Vietnamese culture and French influence. America seems to be attracting the people's greatest interest. A quick look at the commercial ads in public will suffice to prove the point. English spelling that I saw four years ago has changed from British English to American English, for example: "color" rather than "colour," "center" instead of "centre," and so on. Dean Hoàng's English Department is using some American teachers to teach spoken English. Americans are back, though not in a prominent role as they were before 1975.

I find it hard to decline Dr. Trà's invitation. He strikes me as sincere and very much committed to the project. I will probably commit some time to it should things turn out well.

***

October 4th

We do our grocery shopping every day at an open market near our place. Buyers can find most food items here. I see vendors kill live chickens, skin live frogs. To make a living, people must be cruel. I would do the same thing were I in their situation.

A rooster with his leg connected to his owner's vending area by a string catches my eyes. It reminds me of the Vietnamese people. For many centuries, they've been terrorized into silence and absolute obedience, ripped off everything, not daring stand up for their rights. Off the zoo is a canal with black stinking water. The canal banks crammed with tiny huts are where my people have lived since I left the country twenty-seven years ago. Like their predecessors I saw in 1972, they seem content with their lot.

Seeing the rooster brings back to me a short span of past time. I used to see him strut in our ancestral house's front yard in Văn La. He would cock his head at the slightest noise, then upon realizing that there was nothing suspicious, would close his eyes, puffing his throat as he let out a clear sonorous cock-a-doodle-do. I also heard him crow, usually at noon somewhere, in our backyard, but I didn't know where he was. Today, I suddenly hear him again, his cry coming out from the deepest recesses of my heart, achingly sweeter and clearer than it was in the past, reverberating all over my body and soul.

The sound of yesteryear isn't dead, it hibernates in your mind, and comes out when triggered by memories of things that represent the past.

***

October 11th

Attend the English Department meeting for the first time today. Feel odd to sit next to "Vietcong" school officials and hear live speeches punctuated with such phrases as "the Party and the Government." I'm proud, though, to be introduced by Dean Hoàng as "a doctor professor [sic] on assignment here from America." What does the audience think of me? How would I have been treated, had I returned, say, three years ago? The U.S. seems to have succeeded in establishing a foothold here. I've often heard an interesting cryptic expression since my arrival here: *"Mã quy,"* a phrase which originally means "The horses are back," but when the vowels and consonants in it are switched around, it will read *"Mỹ qua,"* meaning "Americans are back." The folks I sit next to seem reserved and cautious. But the general audience gives me a warm welcome.

***

October 12th

The student who told me there were cops in my classes was right. Class attendance is getting smaller. Maybe the police found me harmless, maybe they didn't understand my lectures and couldn't take notes, maybe it was too hot to sit through my class sessions, or maybe they've done their job and quit. Anyway, I feel relieved to know that their surveillance is over, and I have my classes back. It's good to be with my own students who seem to be developing trust and confidence in their *Việt kiều* teacher. Students, especially the girls, are warming with me. Some of them teasingly ask me to take them to America! The boys are still reserved. The boys originally from the North are cautious but very courteous.

***

October 14th

Kim Lan comes to our place to see us today. She's one of my most unfortunate students. Her mother died of cancer when she was thirteen, her grandfather died last week, and now her father suffers heart failure. An extremely devout Catholic, she says she intends to become a nun after her father's passing. Nga gives her some money. There must be many young people like Kim Lan in Vietnam. Some girls in my classes are pretty, but they look pale. I learn from a student that those who came from remote areas in the Mekong Delta are very poor. Because they have to save money to pay their tuition, they can't afford to buy enough food to eat. Some male students, we're told, work their way through college by hiring themselves out as motorbike drivers at night when they can't be seen.

From our house very late at night, I hear peddlers hawking for their goods, but don't know what they're selling. Feeble, anguished, and prolonged, their cries sound desperate, like their condition.

***

October 15th

Have a meeting with a delegation from Columbia and Duke at the Office of the College's Rector. Both the rector and the vice-rector are absent. They're represented by Dr. Trần Đình Lâm, Director of International Relations, and Dean Hoàng. The Americans say they want to help the college set up an American Studies program. The Vietnamese side's reaction isn't very warm. Later, a member of the delegation privately expresses to me his disappointment and dismay at the turnout of the meeting. He doesn't understand why the Vietnamese turned a cold shoulder to his team's offer, which he says is a gesture of good will, and this makes him upset. I only try to comfort him. If I tell him the truth, he wouldn't understand. As happened in the past during the U.S. involvement in the war, it all boils down to the U.S. failure to comprehend the Vietnamese and their culture and now their new political system. The American mindset is that an American Studies program is very important, and Vietnam would welcome the opportunity to have one in the country. These American officials today don't seem to realize that with the so-called "resistance against U.S. imperialism" slogan still fresh in their mind, the communists look askance at any offer by the U.S. The other reason is more important. In Vietnam, higher education institutions are placed under state control. Any effort to establish an American Studies program as offered by the Americans today without the government's prior approval will get the institution in big trouble.

***

October 20th

A group of students come to our house for a conference with me. Things go well until Phúc shows up late. She starts accusing me of not returning her homework she just turned in the day before. She also angrily scolds me for failing to give clear lectures. How shocking! She does this in front of her classmates and my wife! My students in the States were never that rude to me. I thought all Vietnamese students were well-mannered. Maybe Phúc doesn't like me because I'm a *Việt kiều*. Nga says that some students whose parents belonged to the victorious North might not want to have a citizen of former South Vietnam for their teacher. I'll have to check on her theory, but a student later tells me Phúc's father is a hardcore communist. From now on, I will have to be more careful in my relationship with students. Familiarity breeds contempt. I wouldn't have received that bad treatment hadn't I been easy-going and nice in class. I'll have to cancel my regular conferences with students and other American instructional strategies before it's too late. It's too hard for me and it's not worth it. To think of my colleagues here who have never met with students or corrected their homework assignments!

***

October 26th

Have finished grading all 240 themes required in four classes! Would they appreciate my so-called labor of love? What do students like Phúc care?

***

October 27th

I still feel bad about what happened yesterday, not because Phúc let me down, but because I let my anger with her defeat my purpose of coming here. Didn't I tell myself when applying for the Fulbright grant that I wanted to return to Vietnam not only to visit the country but to help the young people? Didn't I see that most of my students appreciate my teaching and have a great respect for me and Phúc is a rare exception?

***

October 28th

I come upon three kids on my way home from a newsstand on Lê Thánh Tôn. The oldest one holds her baby sister (or brother) in her lap in such an experienced manner that at first I thought she was the mother (Vietnamese women get married at a very young age). Her other sibling sits nearby. When I ask the oldest kid where her mother is, she mumbles something I don't understand. Maybe she says her mother is dead.

These young beggars sit on a veranda and look hungry. I give the little one some money. I can't walk away without doing something. I did try to ignore them and walk away at first, but something holds me back. I give them some more money, asking them if they're hungry and they say they are. I rush home and return with some food.

The little urchin is very clever. She's about 3- to 4-year-old but is so thin and small. When I give her money and food, her face lights up. Though so little, she already knows the power of money. Perhaps she has been rewarded many times for her successful begging.

I see the little kid holding out her plastic bowl to a passing Western tourist who gives her some change. There is a ring of joy and excitement in her shrill voice as she proudly gives her trophy to her sister. When I come closer to tell them not to go anywhere so I can bring them more food, this little urchin, who may have forgotten that a few minutes ago I gave them food and money, holds out her bowl to me again! She's so funny, but I like her very much.

***

October 30th

Meet with Dr. Lê, the College's *Hiệu trưởng* (Rector) to sound him out about my proposal of an American Studies program. (The use of *hiệu trưởng* to refer to the top administrator of this prestigious College of Social Sciences and Humanities puzzles me. Whereas a tenured academician with a doctoral degree is granted the coveted accolade *Giáo sư Tiến sĩ* (Professor-Doctor), the term *hiệu trưởng* applies to the head of a school at any level—primary, secondary, or college.) I didn't realize that Dr. Lê is involved in a similar but feasible project. He lets me see his blueprints for an international studies center which would include an American Studies program as well. He says doing so could increase the chance of his proposal getting approved because the concept of an independent American Studies program is too bold. He says that the political atmosphere here isn't "relaxed" as it is in Hanoi where overtures to American culture are gaining ground in the academe.

Unlike many northerners I know who strike me as uppity and overbearing, Dr. Lê is a very humble man. He says he's here in this position to *"làm ăn"* (make a living), but his heart and mind are on his native North. My condition doesn't differ much from his. I've been feeling like a stranger since I came to America. No place is like home. I'm grateful to be back. As I'm writing these lines, I don't feel I want to go back to the States anymore. I feel sorry for some students who told me they'd rather immigrate to America, though I don't blame them or criticize their motives.

***

November 1st

Have a meeting with Dean Hoàng and her staff and am notified that she approves my request for reducing my teaching load. Next term, I'll be teaching only one combined class. What a relief! I can now use my free time to visit many more places and to write my memoir.

***

November 4th-6th

Most central provinces are heavily flooded. TV clips are heartbreaking. Even the anchor cries. What can be more heart-wrenching than seeing naked young men diving into the flood water to recover their relatives' bodies?

TV says three sailors lost their lives while trying to rescue flood victims. A civilian also drowned while on a rescue mission done on his own.

A very moving scene: school children crying over their books damaged by the flood. They say they don't know what they're going to do when they have no books to study with. Vietnamese kids care so much for their education.

English Department meeting is held today, Nov. 5th. Ms. Hạnh begins by giving a report on two conferences she attended in Hanoi. This is the first time I see a Vietnamese colleague so genuinely interested in professional activities. Vietnam is getting more open to the West, especially its know-how. The English Department's plans are impressive. Next year, starting the third millennium, Ms. Hạnh says, several sections like Literature, Translation, and Cultural Studies will be added to the existing curriculum. The next speaker has the same name. She covers everything we need to know to run classes smoothly. She also recommends that all classes be conducted exclusively in English. Ms. Phương Thiện talks about the American Studies conference she attended in Hanoi in October 1999. According to her, there was a consensus that American Studies should be taught, but at this point Vietnam wants to concentrate only on American culture and literature, not American politics. Based on Ms. Phương Thiện's presentation, it appears that Vietnam wants America back, at least in the classroom. Dr. Phương Anh, Assistant Dean, holds a pessimistic view of Vietnam's higher education system. The recent TESOL conference hosted by Vietnam, she says, leaves much to be desired. Vietnam's role at the conference is insignificant with fewer presentations. Dr. Phương Anh stresses the need for professional associations and networking.

I'm amazed but delighted to discover that the faculty are critical of the administration, especially its management ability. I'm impressed by the relaxed atmosphere of an academic meeting in communist Vietnam. It doesn't begin with everybody saluting the communist flag and hailing Hồ, though there is a bust of him at the center of the meeting room. I hear my colleagues sitting in the back with me engage in private conversation rather than paying attention to Dean Hoàng's report. To my surprise, that doesn't seem to bother the dean.

***

November 20th

Teachers' Day. A very nice tradition of honoring teachers that I've seen for the first time. Vietnam today observes most holidays adopted by the United Nations, but this one is particularly Vietnamese. Though not invited (error on students' part?), I attend the English Department's Teachers' Day celebration at An Vi's insistence. At 7:30 in the morning, I already saw students at Nguyễn Thị Minh Khai High School (formerly Gia Long Girls High School; after the unification of Vietnam, single gender education is abolished) carrying flowers and gifts to the campus to present to their teachers. I'm touched to see eagerness on these students' faces. Scores of flower vendors try to accommodate students who don't bring flowers with them to school. What a splendid tradition!

The auditorium is packed. An organ blares loud music. A student in my class introduces the singers. Then student representatives give speeches thanking their teachers. This is followed by the students' presentation of flowers to the administration and the faculty present. Two big wreathes of roses are presented to Dean Hoàng and Ms. Thu, Assistant Dean in charge of ideology. Ms. Thu is a gentle, meek-looking woman, but she must have been selected among hardcore communist cadres for this important post.

I feel embarrassed because I wasn't invited and introduced by the event organizer. He doesn't seem to like me, perhaps because of my national origin! (I went to this event out of curiosity and because I wanted to gather information for my book project.) Perhaps Dean Hoàng notices my embarrassment, so when it's her turn to give a speech, she ceremoniously introduces me as "a guest of honor, a doctor professor [sic] from America in the Fulbright Program." I'm moved and feel better because of her warm introduction.

Students put on a skit called *Hội nghị Diên Hồng* (Diên Hồng Assembly). In 1284 in the face of the Mongol invasion of Vietnam, King Trần Thánh Tông convened an assembly of notables at Diên Hồng Palace to seek their advice about a viable course of action. Since then, the expression *Hội nghị Diên Hồng* has been used to refer to the necessity of calling for a national referendum when the nation is in danger. The students' presentation, despite its title, doesn't show the spirit of the Diên Hồng Assembly. Rather, it strikes me as an illustration of a nation striving to build itself on socialism. Performed in a heavy Bolshevik style, the piece, it seems to me, is a dedication to socialism or political correctness.

In the middle of the ceremony, An Vi asks me to go with her to what she calls "a special meeting." It is, I'm delighted to discover, a gathering of the junior English faculty to honor me on this special day. I'm presented two beautiful gifts. I feel better as this gesture compensates for my "loss of face" when I wasn't invited to today's teacher appreciation event.

In the afternoon, I attend a party organized by students of Class E1. The atmosphere is very cozy. I enjoy the party very much and completely forget what happened this morning. Diễm, a student in that class, conducts a couple of games in Vietnamese interspersed with her singing in her beautiful English. She later comes to sit by my side, and I have a chance to talk to her. She says she wants to pursue a master's degree in English teaching in the U.S. and would like to seek my advice about this matter. Thanh, a girl with a charming face, who was the MC at today's ceremony, also sits next to me. She has come to see us several times before and Nga likes her very much. She tells me she's from Phú Yên, close to my mother's native province.

Nga tells me when I return from the party that several students came to give us gifts and flowers. What a beautiful tradition!

Lying down in bed on this 20th November night, I feel bad for a while. Teachers' Day was celebrated nationwide today because teachers in Vietnam are very well respected. In traditional Vietnam on the social hierarchical scale *Quân, Sư, Phụ* (King, Teacher, Father) teacher comes second. At my school in the U.S., I also earned my students' respect. And yet here in my native country today, I suffered a loss of face. But remembering the warm treatment I've received from a group of students, particularly Lê Hải Anh, one of my best students, who came over today and presented me a small bouquet with a comforting note, I start feeling better. Did she do that because she noticed my embarrassing situation and felt sorry for me, or because she wanted to show her appreciation to "a great teacher" as she put in her note?

***

Sunday, November 21st

I'm watching a fascinating live TV broadcast this Sunday morning: Run for Children's Rights. TV says Vietnam is the first and only country that has signed the United Nations convention on children's rights!

The UNICEF representative gives a speech. The translator leaves out the UN rep's mention that Vietnam is one of the poorest countries with many children having no basic rights. But I'm moved to tears when a very young student in her speech asks her fellow students to think about young flood victims her age in central provinces.

I don't hear Vietnam's national anthem at the event. Does it mean because the regime has no trouble keeping the people in line, adherence to such formality is no longer a requirement?

***

November 24th

Ms. Phạm Thị Ly, Dr. Trà's assistant, picks me up and takes me to the College of Education to see her boss. As the idea of setting up an American Studies program is too daring now, we discuss various feasible options. Ms. Ly shows me a catalog of her institution, and I notice that American culture is featured, but it covers too much practical stuff like business English and social life. Prof. Trà asks me to review the American culture course description with a focus on important subjects such as U.S. intellectual history and literature. He says that this will stimulate scholarly interest in America, which is the principal purpose of his contemplated American Studies program at his university.

***

December 3rd -4th

I haven't kept my journal for over a week. I didn't feel good all week. On Monday, I had my blood/urine tests at the Medic. The results are fine. In the evening, I saw Dr. Nguyễn Chấn Hùng, who said he knew Dr. Pazdur, my oncologist in the States. He's a very nice man. He didn't charge me a fee for the visit.

Most of Dr. Hùng's patients are young women. Their faces are ashy pale in the waiting room's dim light. Based on my experience, this is a sign of advanced cancer or the side effects of cancer drugs. But I wonder why they don't have hair loss whereas my hair was gone after my first course of chemotherapy. They all look tired and sad but resigned. In the U.S. when coming for treatment at MD Anderson Cancer Center, I saw a lot of patients whose condition could be worse, but they didn't look as desperate as the patients I see at Dr. Hùng's office tonight. Cancer is a terrible disease for Vietnamese patients!

It has been a busy week. Grading midterms and reading students' journals takes all my time. I begin going to the faculty's lounge but find it hard to strike a conversation with the faculty. Should I try to break the ice first?

Thursday morning, I came to look for Mr. Tài in the faculty's lounge, but he wasn't there. He's from Huế. I met him last week, and we had a friendly talk about people we mutually knew in the past. Was he afraid that his relationship with me could get him in trouble? Am I right to think that no matter how hard I've tried to make friends with the Vietnamese, they seem to resist my efforts? Is it because of their anti-(Vietnamese) American sentiment or because they don't want to get in trouble for associating with *Việt kiều*? I feel the same way about my Vietnamese students. They don't seem to accept me wholeheartedly, though I've been here for over two months now.

***

December 6th

Today I bump into Bùi Thế Phiệt, a former classmate and friend from Huế, in the faculty's lounge. He's a martial arts master and teaches part-time in the French department. I'm shocked by his outspokenness. He says the country's problems have to do with the government's mistreating the dead on the former South Vietnamese side. *"Nghĩa tử là nghĩa tận"* (Don't take revenge on the dead), he says. I couldn't agree with him more. Why is memorial after memorial erected to honor the dead on the victorious side and the graves of the defeated leveled off? Why is the new regime still hostile and unfair to the defeated South Vietnamese? How much longer will it take for them to realize that twenty-five years is long enough for them to reconcile with their defeated enemy, who are also Vietnamese? It didn't take long for Americans in the North and the South to come to a reconciliation that resulted in making America a super world power today. The two Germanys were also unified without firing a shot or shedding a drop of blood. Why are they so paranoid about overseas Vietnamese?

On a positive note, I receive great news today. My CT scan is clean. *Chị* Thúy and Nga had a big scare this morning when the radiologist told them he found something abnormal in the scan and wanted Nga to sign her consent to let him inject some drug into my veins for another CT exam. It turned out to be clean. I recall I was shivering throughout the tests for fear of bad news. Poor Nga, she was sitting in a corner, looking meekly at me, not smiling as is her wont. Not smiling is her way of showing her worry, and looking timidly at me is another way of confirming the bad news.

***

December 10th

Attend Christmas party given by the U.S. Consul General in honor of Fulbright alumni. Dr. Thảo introduces me and Dr. Phạm Chung from New Mexico State University in glowing terms.

Most former Fulbrighters I meet strike me as very pleasant. Some confess that they miss their alma mater and share with me their fond memories of America. Had nothing happened to the South and had I been able to return home after finishing my studies, I would have felt the same thing about America. Do they understand my odd situation now? Or do they take the non-committal way I exchange my ideas with them a mark of vainglory? As far as I'm concerned, it's hard to act like an American in America; it's even harder to conduct myself like a *Việt kiều* in Vietnam. Regardless, I'm grateful that my Vietnamese colleagues are very nice, courteous, and gracious.

A colleague introduces me to Y Lan, a young writer, who speaks fluent English. I don't know if Ms. Lan has ever been to the U.S., but I think she's too much "Americanized." I find her blunt, direct, and indiscreet. She speaks only English in our conversation.

***

December 14th-16th

Nga joins a group of Buddhists on a trip to Quảng Ngãi to donate food and clothes to flood victims. Her niece Cẩm Vân comes over to cook for me. I feel lonely because Nga is away and the Phúc incident still bothers me.

***

December 17th

Attend a Christmas party given by the college. The food is delicious. The party is an eye opener for me. The Vietnamese know how to spend their money. They aren't country bumpkins as I thought but are experts in the art of decorum and etiquette.

***

December 21st

I've been so busy recently that I find no time to keep my journal regularly. Correcting—not just marking a few errors as I did in the States—all the 240 papers to help students improve their English isn't easy. I'm losing interest in teaching here. It becomes a chore. Phúc's ingratitude and insolence still hurt me.

***

Christmas Eve

There is no sign that Christmas is here in Saigon. I don't see the flying of the Vatican flag and the display of Christmas lights on private residences and public buildings as I usually did at this time of the year before I left the country. People conduct their business as usual, traffic is always heavy, and speakers blare revolutionary songs rather than Christmas carols. There are two big scrolls on the façade of the Nhà Thờ Đức Bà (Notre Dame Cathedral): *"Sáng danh Chúa cả trên Trời, Bình an cho người dưới thế"* (Glory to Almighty God in Heaven, Peace to men on Earth). Kim Lan tells me Catholics may worship now. "A few years ago," she says, "my older sister had to go to church in secret. You couldn't even see any praise of God in public. All ceremony was confined within the church."

Being back home at Christmas for the first time since 1972, I want to go out to see for myself what things are like in Hồ Chí Minh City at Christmas time. As soon as streetlights are on, the city is hit by a tsunami-like phenomenon. Torrents of cars, motorbikes, bicycles, pedicabs, and pedestrians pour out from everywhere—hidden alleys, adjacent streets, private residences—roaring in the direction of Nguyễn Huệ and Lê Lợi avenues, the two most beautiful thoroughfares of Saigon then and now. Everywhere is ablaze with multi-colored lighted ornaments. I'm particularly struck by motorbike riders. Despite the crammed traffic, they scurry around with remarkable ease. People don't seem to know where they're heading or for what purpose. Maybe they just get out for fun, or maybe they want to escape for a moment their cramped living quarters. Such a big public celebration like this one is an ideal opportunity for them. The heat, the terrible racket of the traffic, the suffocating gas exhaust from cars and motorbikes don't seem to bother them. "People are having fun," Nga comments. "They're not celebrating Christmas."

We pass by the Notre Dame Cathedral. It's quiet here. Maybe the Mass is held inside with fewer people in attendance than at the corner of Lê Lợi and Nguyễn Huệ.

***

December 30th

I take Nga to Lê Lợi and Nguyễn Huệ avenues to watch preparations for welcoming the new millennium. There is a huge stage at the corner of the city's main streets. Young students are practicing their parade. The girls look tired and resigned. I remember when I was in high school in the 1950s, we had to line up all day on Lê Lợi Street in Huế to await President Diệm's motorcade and felt the same way about involuntary participation in politically inspired events. In the States students participate in public events only on a voluntary basis.

***

January 3rd, 2000

Vietnam is celebrating the new millennium because it realizes that it can't save its people with patriotic slogans. To get out of its backwardness, Vietnam must earnestly implement its national policy of industrialization and modernization, which can be done only by relaxing control over the people and the press and by permitting democracy and freedom.

Vietnam has a long way to go despite its encouraging signs. Who knows, the pomp and extravaganza of the celebrations is but a sort of "blowing off steam" to appease those who have been repressed for so long.

Vietnam's Party Chief Lê Khả Phiêu recently stated that in the year 2000, Hồ Chí Minh City will be the first to arrive at the destination. There were rumors that the victorious North didn't want the vanquished South to be ahead of it. Now that Hanoi has achieved its goal and may have realized that former Saigon is more important commercially and culturally, the Party stops its discrimination against the South. HCMC leadership is excited about the Secretary General's statement, according to reporters. I feel sorry for the NLF. They must be disappointed that the South isn't getting what it's rightfully entitled to despite the enormous sacrifices they made during the war.

***

January 5th, 2000

Come across in *Tuổi Trẻ Daily* today a news report that students who haven't paid their tuition won't be allowed to take their finals. Many students are unable to pay their tuition. "My family's chief occupation is farming," the paper quotes one student as saying. "It isn't easy to have enough food to eat, any more than find a million *đồng* to pay my tuition right away." The reporter comments, "Tuition is a nightmare for students in their college years."

In Vietnam, students can't take a loan from a bank to pay for their education. Meanwhile, a student from Vietnam attending my institution in the States pays $17,000 for his tuition. His father is a very wealthy man. I remember that in November during his visit with us, Hải, our son Long's friend, cried when he talked about what he called "Vietnamese youth's misfortune." World computer gold medalists like Tiến, Hải said, would end up in poverty because opportunities to advance themselves in Vietnam are limited.

Since my coming here, I've seen numerous plays/oral narratives dramatizing Vietnam's resistance against Chinese invasions in the past. Whatever their purpose, their impact is positive. They incite patriotic feelings. But how can you reconcile patriotism with Marxist-Leninist ideology, nationalism with internationalism? Vietnam can't stay in the middle but should choose between the two. Meanwhile, the view of the man in the street is very clear: it's nationalism that counts. For example, one can see this in a recent rowdy public celebration of Vietnam's victory in an international sports competition in Hanoi or Hồ Chí Minh City.

***

January 6th

In her journal, a student expresses her frustration about what she calls "the invasion of Western TV full of violence and sex which is harmful to our traditional culture." I try to explain to her class that TV commercials and movies (which are, to my astonishment, are very popular in a country whose leadership five years ago still saw the U.S. as its mortal enemy) don't represent American culture. In the 1960s and mid-1970s, despite the presence of USIS offices in South Vietnam, we still held a similar erroneous view of American culture. Currently, there is in Hồ Chí Minh City a USIS office, but for security reasons, it's difficult to gain access to it. I can understand why Prof. Trà emphasizes the need to promote a serious understanding of American culture through a viable American Studies program at his university. The current USIS office can play a significant role in providing resources for Vietnamese researchers, when requested.

***

January 7th

The regime doesn't seem to hide its people's stark poverty. TV news reports and newspapers such as *Phụ Nữ*, *Thanh Niên*, and *Tuổi Trẻ* shamelessly cover stories of terminally ill women and children who can't afford to get medical treatment and appeal to readers' compassion on their behalf. What bothers me is in this city, there are many wealthy folks who can afford a 300,000 đồng ($30) meal ticket in the New Year celebration in luxury restaurants such as the Rex and Caravelle. It's also ironic that while many people are homeless and hungry, the city had the biggest New Year celebration ever!

***

January 8th-9th

A woman, who identifies herself over the phone as Hoàng Yến and speaks with a Huế accent, wants to discuss Vietnam War literature with me. We meet for a couple of hours today, and it's the most interesting encounter I've ever had since my arrival in this city.

It's rare to meet someone who is so interested in war literature and wants to study it impartially. Ms. Hoàng Yến, who often uses English in her exchange with me, criticizes Hanoi writers who, according to her, glorify the war as "a sacred war," ignoring the enormous sufferings and losses it has caused to the people in the South. She recognizes the value of writings by American combat veterans, but she says that the war is seen solely from an American perspective. I couldn't agree with her more. The last war is too important to be looked at solely from an American or socialist realist viewpoint. As I recall, when preparing for my course on Vietnamese literature at George Mason University in Virginia, I came across an enormous bulk of writings about the war by South Vietnamese authors. Their perception of the war is complex, honest, and candid. Unfortunately, because after the communist victory South Vietnamese literature was banned, young generations who were born or grew up after the war hardly know if this literature ever existed. American scholars also don't have a chance to get a balanced view of the war because virtually no South Vietnamese writings on the war have been translated into English.

Ms. Hoàng Yến suggests that I read Nguyễn Huy Thiệp and Phạm Thị Hoài who she says are among the very few who don't subscribe to prescribed conventions in their writing.

I enjoy very much my conversation with Ms. Hoàng Yến. Like my friend Bùi Thế Phiệt, she's honest, outspoken, and unafraid to speak out her mind even if it could get her in trouble. She's *not* from the Ministry of the Interior as I thought at first, but a very pleasant person and a serious scholar! Unfortunately, I forget to ask her to give me her address for possible future correspondence.

***

January 10ᵗʰ

Today is Vietnamese Youth's Day. Public celebrations of the ceremony are heavily politically oriented. Parades and skits broadcast live in commemoration of the so-called "sacrifice" of Trần Văn Ơn, a high school student killed by Saigon police in an anti-government demonstration in 1950. Vietnam controls its youth by mobilizing them for political goals. In the past, subtle propaganda techniques were widely used to manipulate and mobilize the public for war efforts. One of the most famous examples of North Vietnam's propaganda campaign against the Diệm regime's "atrocities" was this statement: "It wheeled a guillotine all over the south to execute our patriots." Many North Vietnamese brought food to the South soon after it was "liberated" to feed their relatives because they had been told by the government that their loved ones were starving. They were shocked to discover that the South was more prosperous than the North.

***

February 4ᵗʰ (29 Tết)

Vietnamese people celebrate Tết sumptuously. Nguyễn Huệ Avenue sparkles with beds of multicolored flowers on its pavements and is ablaze with multicolored lights at night. People pour into every street to watch Tết celebrations. Except for the flying of red flags with a gold star everywhere and the display of a giant scarlet banner across the front of HCM City People's Committee Building praising Hồ, one would think that this is South Vietnam's Saigon in its heyday.

Photographers are everywhere. They're after tourists, children accompanied by parents, and foreigners. One of them succeeds in persuading my son Kiến to have a picture taken before the statue of *Uncle Hồ and the Children*. He tells him that he's "a *Việt kiều* from America." Mightily impressed, Kiến points to me, asking: "What about that old guy? Where's he from?" "No, that uncle *is* from here," the photographer answers, shaking his head.

***

February 5ᵗʰ (lunar New Year's Day)

We leave for Tây Ninh very early in the morning at the invitation of Minh Thảo and Mỹ Hạnh, two students from the Mekong Delta. Because we get on the wrong bus, it takes several hours to arrive. We finally find Minh Thảo's home. Minh Thảo and Mỹ Hạnh are thrilled to see us. We're warmly welcomed by everyone. After we have lunch with Minh Thảo's family and friends, we're taken to Cao Đài Cathedral for a short visit. Mỹ Hạnh's mother is an excellent guide. We visit Tây Ninh's Holy See during its noon service. The service is conducted in a very solemn manner with participants at some point intoning their prayers after the priest, reminding me of a prayer ceremony in a Catholic church. Mỹ Hạnh and Minh Thảo explain to us the seating arrangements in the cathedral. Facing the Divine Eye (symbolizing God) over a globe are the elders robed in the color reflecting their adherence to syncretic aspects of Caodaism: yellow for Buddhism, blue for Taoism, and red for Roman Catholicism. After the elders are lay followers in white robes, with men sitting on the right and women on the left in symmetrical rows. Minh Thảo goes on to tell us about her religion's organization which reminds me of the Roman Catholic Church with different levels of hierarchy, including a pope, cardinals, archbishops, and priests. The inclusion of Julius Caesar, Joan of Arc, Voltaire, Victor Hugo, Nguyễn Bỉnh Khiêm (a 17th century Vietnamese poet and prophet), and Sun Yat-sen in the pantheon of saints along with Shakyamuni Buddha, Confucius, Jesus Christ, and Mohammed means that man holds an important place in the scheme of the universe. As Minh Thảo points out, Caodaism requires that loyalty to the family and service to society and the world be inseparable from the individual's spiritual practice.

The design and construction of the huge and beautiful cathedral was the work of a single person by the name of Ngô Văn Chiêu, a *fonctionnaire* (civil servant) in the French Protectorate. I learn from Minh Thảo that in 1926 after he had been instructed in a séance by the Supreme Being (represented by the Divine Eye) to found Cao Đài, Chiêu, who had no training in architecture and engineering, set out to build the cathedral himself. The gigantic construction with its tall towers, high dome, and high ceiling baffles me. I can't imagine how Chiêu could do it at a time when high-tech engineering didn't exist.

Though Caodaism is a relatively new religion in Vietnam, it's practiced in almost every household in Tây Ninh and other places in the Mekong Delta. Caodaists are serious worshippers of God; many men and women, I'm told, vowed to stay celibate to devote themselves all their life to their faith. The communist government had no success in imposing its rule on the worshippers, so it leaves them alone provided they confine their efforts to purely religious activities within the cathedral's premises as they're doing today.

In the afternoon, we go to the *Núi Bà Đen* (Black Lady's Mountain) for sightseeing. (*Núi Bà Đen*, the highest mountain in Tây Ninh, has a temple dedicated to the patron saint of the city. Emperor Thiệu Trị of the Nguyễn dynasty consecrated to her a large statue in black bronze on the mountain, hence the titular spirit's name.) We leave separately with Thảo escorting Nga and Hạnh accompanying me. We're met at the entrance by Tài, Mỹ Hạnh's brother, who puts us all in cable cars that take us right up to the Black Lady's

Temple. There is a huge crowd of pilgrims because it's New Year's Day. Monks in saffron robes (they must be government agents) do psychic readings for money while nuns conduct a Buddhist ceremony in the Taoist temple! In this market economy, holy places are turned into tourist and business centers. Mỹ Hạnh's father says a billion VN *đồng* ($800,000) were allocated for the construction of the road in front of his house, but half of the sum went to government officials' pockets.

At lunch, Mr. Nam, a guest of Minh Thảo's father, tells me that the takeover of the South in 1975 was like winning a big lottery for the communists, so big they didn't know how to handle it. He points out that the communist government is paying a price for eliminating from school curriculum subjects like civics and for rejecting the role of religion in the education of youth: the number of students and youngsters on drugs is increasing at an alarming rate.

The communists, who were atheists according to my observation in my past visits, have begun to realize the importance of spirituality. They start burning incense on the altar of Hồ Chí Minh and at *nghĩa trang liệt sĩ* (war martyrs' cemeteries).

***

February 6th

Minh Thảo makes me cry today when she stops a crowded shuttle for us to get a lift back to Saigon after our visit. She asks the driver to give enough room to "my elderly father." This is the first time I hear a girl refer to me in such affectionate terms. So, in her mind, I'm not only her teacher but also a father to her. Having missed being called "father" by my daughter Đoan Nghiêm since her death in 1995, I'm grateful for the opportunity provided by Minh Thảo today.

***

February 7th

After twenty-eight years of exile, this is the first time I'm back in my own country to participate in the Tết celebrations. We live in an apartment and are unable to celebrate this most important and beloved traditional holiday in the same way as when I lived with my father. We would stay up until past midnight to welcome the New Year and pay respects to our ancestors' spirits (the Vietnamese believe that their forebears live in a different world after their passing, and that they return to visit their descendants once a year on New Year's Day). In the following days, we would entertain visitors who came to wish us good health and good fortune all year round, and so forth. But watching my people here keep up that tradition and inhaling a whiff of the real Tết for the first time is such a delight! It's the same thrill, the same transports of joy, happiness, and excitement that I experienced on each return of Tết in the long, long past.

Students keep coming to visit us with flowers and gifts. They wish us happiness and good health, and we're deeply touched by their loyalty and devotion. What a beautiful custom!

Lan, whom Nga would like to have for our youngest son Kien (age 27 now), comes and takes us to dine with her group at Làng Nướng restaurant. She's a very sweet and pretty girl. I take several pictures of her and her group. Unfortunately, nothing comes out because I accidentally put the old roll of film in the camera!

***

February 14th (Valentine's Day)

Young Vietnamese celebrate Valentine's Day with great enthusiasm. According to the *Tuổi Trẻ*, around 3,000 couples gather at the *Hồ Con Rùa* (Turtle Pond) to sing and exchange vows of love. Kim's group joins us tonight at a restaurant in the suburbs to eat its specialty, *cháo vịt* (duck porridge). Kim, Vân, and Trâm (Lan, according to Kim, goes out with her boyfriend, to Nga's great disappointment!) are with us tonight rather than at the Turtle Pond because they have no boyfriends.

My students report that as usual Saigon streets are congested with motorbikes and walkers on this important occasion for youth. I can confirm it as we're heading to Thanh Đa restaurant to eat tonight. Our taxi can hardly move because of the incredible traffic jam.

Valentine's Day, according to a youth activities watcher here, was introduced to Vietnam a few years ago. It quickly becomes a big day for young Vietnamese. Valentine cards are sold like hotcakes on this day. Vietnamese youth are very enthusiastic about American customs almost ignored by young Americans in the States! This irony of cultural interaction is a common phenomenon in America. For example, Americans are big on the French Symbolists who were very devoted to Edgar Allen Poe, who was ironically ignored in America.

On our way home, we see something very sad but common in Saigon. In the endless flow of traffic on Hai Bà Trưng Street, we catch sight of a girl alone on the street corner. In the street neon light, her pretty face looks wan and tired but very alert. My hunch is that she isn't waiting for her date, but on the lookout for someone or something. On this Valentine's night when every young man and woman going out is accompanied by a date, you can guess what this youth is doing at this time in the street. She must stay alert because police may be around. Nga has a theory about her. She says she could be one of my students plying her trade for a living! Having seen young attractive women like this one at Tao Đàn Park, I feel terrible.

***

February 16th

The campus stays busy from sunrise to sunset, even on weekends. First classes start at 6:45 a.m., but a lively scene has already been seen at daybreak. Vietnamese students are perhaps the earliest risers in the world! Hordes of them come pouring through checkpoints while pushing along their bikes. But 6:00 a.m. is already late for Saigonese who are up in the wee hours every day. In the dusk of the day's early hours on Lê Thánh Tôn Street where we live, traffic gets heavier every minute. At the cross section of Lê Thánh Tôn and Tôn Đức Thắng (renamed from Cường Để Street after 1975), before dawn streams of bicycles and motorcycles scurry in the poorly lit street. We cross the street to get to the Botanical Gardens for our morning exercises by relying on the lamp light from a food stall on the pavement.

There is a tug at my heart when I see the tense, stoic faces of hurried people. They're my people, and they're so resigned to their sad fate. But they're honest citizens who're struggling to maintain their honor and dignity. To me, a typical unsung hero is a haggard but determined-looking motorcycle driver with his overload of woodpile the size of a small truck, or a barefoot child selling lottery tickets to support her family instead of going to school.

***

February 17th-18th

My endearing pastime since my return has been strolling along Lê Thánh Tôn on my way to bookstores on Đồng Khởi (formerly Tự Do), Lê Lợi, and Nguyễn Huệ avenues. I want not only to browse books, but to explore the beloved city I had little time to get to know when I lived and worked here almost four decades ago.

My search for the city of my imagination isn't rewarding. I'm trying to find "those people of years past," but they're no more. While things haven't changed much, people have. But for streams of motorcycles roaring as they pass street intersections and Western tourists haggling with vendors and gawking at everything, one would have thought Saigon is a deserted city.

There are fewer leisurely pedestrians now than in the past, most hurrying as though destination was the only thing on their mind, not leisure and pleasure.

I can't help reminiscing about my frequent visits here while I taught in Nha Trang in the early 1960s and about my subsequent appointment at Pétrus Ký (renamed Lê Hồng Phong) High School in Saigon in 1964. Probably because of my young age and probably because of the slow-paced, easy-going, affluent lifestyle that was accessible to most Vietnamese in the South, Saigon was a haven for people of my generation. When I was off teaching, I would spend my free afternoons leisurely sauntering on Lê Lợi and Nguyễn Huệ avenues for window shopping, browsing books, or just watching people. Everybody looked relaxed and happy. The girls just off from their afternoon classes chattering and giggling reminded me of Trang and her girlfriends who walked down my street in Đồng Hới when she returned home for summer from Hanoi.

My exploration pays off a little, as far I'm concerned. But strangely, while the people I see today are strangers, I feel I can relate to them. They're part of my emotional life. I feel a stab of nostalgia when I look at them and things around me, such as houses, buildings, streets. I seem to recognize my past or, as Ralph Ellison puts in his novel *Invisible Man*, "the early part of home."

A heartbreaking thing catches my eyes as I'm on my way to Xuân Thu Bookstore on Đồng Khởi Street tonight. On the dark pavement of the street, I bump into two or three kids huddling over something. When I get closer, I see them eating from a plate of rice, the tallest one, apparently the oldest brother, dispensing the meager meal he might have collected from a restaurant's garbage to his siblings. In the weak yellow light, they look thin and pale.

I feel the urge to give the kids some money but refrain from doing so, not wanting to break my 20,000 *đồng* ($2.00) bill! I walk away half a block, feel bad, and decide to come back. When I get back, they're already gone. I feel a twinge of sorrow, remorse, and shame.

***

February 20th-22nd

Now and then I see a saffron-clad man (a monk?) strolling in our neighborhood holding a brass bowl in front of him. He comes on weekends to our area, perhaps because there are many foreigners living here. Personally, just observing his demeanor, I doubt he's really a monk. The state-controlled Buddhist church here prohibits begging for food or money for any reason.

It's a common scene in Hồ Chí Minh City to see fake Buddhist monks and nuns stop foreigners to ask for money. I was embarrassed to see the other day a group of nuns stop a white man, the leader bowing to him and the unfortunate fellow, who apparently knew what the nuns wanted, took out his empty wallet and showed it to them while repeatedly bowing back to the nuns. I didn't know what happened later. Would they let him go or continue to harass him until he could satisfy their demand?

As we arrive at a temple near Bến Thành Market, some young kids stop us and ask for money. Clad in dark brown clothes with their heads shaved, they look like little monks. After they get our money and as soon as we turn around, they go back to their playing. I'm sure these kids are hired by a certain organization to work for them. The use of young children for this kind of business is very effective. We have a natural compassion for unfortunate children; besides, they're very persistent in practicing their trade. My informant tells me that the business is run by a ring of crooks who hire children from poor families and train them for the job. These little beggars can be seen at hotels where foreigners live, at tourist centers, or at major street intersections. During rush hours at a Hai Bà Trưng Street intersection, I see a small girl hovering a sleeping baby over extremely heavy traffic. By her side is a tin bowl with some change in it. Not far from the scene I spot two women placidly playing cards who, according to my informant, are the business owners. To enlighten me about this lucrative trade, he points to me a group of beggars, most of them teenage girls, marching in our direction with pale-looking sleeping babies on their backs. My informant says that these babies were borrowed from their poor parents and were drugged before they were assigned to "professional" beggars who would use sleeping babies to ply their trade.

Speaking of small children, I must confess that I can't walk away from little beggars. One afternoon, I saw a little girl stopping a foreign tourist to beg for money. She was around six or seven but was so small that she looked like a three-year-old. After she had received money from the tourist, she proudly turned it over to an older girl, apparently her sister, whose age I couldn't tell but she must be underage as she looked so young. I guess these kids don't have a mother.

I gave the little girl some money. The urchin immediately turned it over to her sister, proud and all smiles. Feeling a bit guilty because I wasn't that generous the first time, I came back for a second round and really felt happy this time. What was so funny about this little girl was she held out her hand to me again when I happened to go back to their place a little while later. She had been so busy and was so careless that she didn't seem to recognize me!

The little girl's demeanor shocks me a little. It's the same behavioral pattern I observed not long ago in a different little beggar near where we live. Kids tend to let go and act spontaneously with no premeditation nor affectation.

***

February 26th

Contingent upon the agreement between the English Department and the Fulbright Program, my teaching load is reduced to nine periods, but it turns out that I have more students to teach! A new class is added to the current three, and I end up teaching four classes in an upstairs auditorium with no AC and a steady temperature of 90 degrees! Ceiling fans run at full speed, but they only make our condition worsen because the auditorium is too small for 240 students. Before the start of the class, I already sweat profusely.

But this huge class is incredibly disciplined! It's so still you can hear the buzzing fans, and each time I tell the students to turn over a page of their textbook I can hear a rustling sound.

A very hilarious thing happens in this class when they take a test today. One of the students in this class, a young Buddhist monk, is caught cheating in his exam by the *lớp trưởng*. She reports the incident to me by using the Buddhist greeting gesture—pressing her palms together close to her heart with a slight bow to me—and pointing to the monk. That's her way of reporting that a Buddhist monk student, not a regular student, is cheating. I can't help laughing to myself when seeing my *lớp trưởng*'s clever way of alerting me to that monk student's irregular behavior in class.

Vietnamese students are generally too shy to participate in class discussions, let alone challenge their professors. Therefore, I allow them to submit written questions to me in class after my lecture. Their questions reveal that they tend to see literature as mirroring life *par excellence* and that art is to serve life. For this reason, they don't accept any literature that doesn't portray the rosy aspects of life. This has to do with socialist realism and Marxism they've been taught since high school, as well as die-hard Confucianism that Vietnamese are imbued with at home.

IN SEARCH OF LOST TIME (III)

It has been half a year since my arrival here. My appointment at Vietnam National University will end in May. My stay here so far has been very pleasant. I enjoy working with my students and come to love them better every day. The Phúc incident no longer bothers me, so I can concentrate better on my teaching. I also enjoy giving lectures at the Open University and Hồ Chí Minh City Faculty of Education, sharing my professional knowledge with my colleagues from other institutions, among other things. So, it turns out that I am useful to my people at home. This makes me feel good and proud.

Because of my hectic schedule, I am lax in keeping my writing. But I am not lax in observing, remembering, and recognizing things around me, those which remain of the distant past, and committing them to memory. Because I do not have much time left for my search for the past, everything here is important to me. I want to absorb everything and bring it back to America to relish it later. It is hard to pass up anything you happen to discover that was part of you in the past. Today, I pass by a kindergarten at playtime. I do not see the children behind the wall, but I hear their crystal-clear shouts and laughter and can visualize their lively activity. The sound of their voices resounds in me. I stand still, completely lost in a sea of remembrance. I *am* one of those children playing on the playground inside this school. I play to my heart's content with my friends. After school, *chị* Ngành, who is several classes ahead of me, comes and we walk home together. Suddenly, I feel a stab in my heart. I fall back into reality. The rare, delightful moment lingers on for a short while before it is completely gone, making me acutely conscious of the sense of loss, melancholy, and sorrow. I stand still, dazed, pained, and shocked by the happening. Perhaps finding my demeanor bizarre, a young woman approaches me and asks, "Are you all right, Uncle?"

***

March 1st

Nga and I leave for Đà Nẵng today as Saturday is the anniversary of my father's passing. This is the only time I can afford to visit my father's tomb as we'll be returning to the States at the end of this semester. Dean Hoàng has graciously granted me a three-day leave from teaching.

Our plane arrives at 7:30 a.m. We're met at the airport by Mỹ Hương and her children, Diễm and Xờm. It's cold in Đà Nẵng.

Immediately after our arrival, Nga and Hương head to Hội An to make arrangements with Long Tuyền Temple for the ceremony. When they return, they report some trouble. The abbot's assistant demanded a good sum of money, saying that the money we gave wasn't enough to cover the cost of burning incense for my father's spirit!

***

March 2nd

We leave early for Hội An. The in-laws of Danh, my brother's son, also join us. We stop by to pick up Dr. Quyền and his wife, my brother's friends, at their home in Đà Nẵng.

The city has changed dramatically since our last visit two years ago. There are large streets lined with green trees and beautiful houses and even mansions. Many Vietnamese are richer now than they were in the past. Hương says all credit goes to Đà Nẵng's Mayor Nguyễn Bá Thanh, a young Turk in the Communist Party.

The abbot greets us cordially. He seems happy when he sees me because I'm polite to him and willing to listen to his discussion of the Buddhist doctrine of the impermanence of existence, as well as his criticism of the regime.

***

March 3rd

On our way to Long Tuyền Temple, we pass by a grandiose *Nghĩa trang liệt sĩ* on the outskirts of the city. Apparently, the cemetery was built after the communist victory in 1975 to re-bury Vietcong soldiers killed at other places during the war. In our last trip, we saw similar cemeteries and monuments in every city and county across the south. In Đồng Hới, where fierce U.S. bombing occurred and heavy civilian casualties were reported, I saw no memorial for war victims. Living monuments and memorials, therefore, are strictly dedicated to those who died for what the government calls "the liberation of the South." By establishing and maintaining a haunting presence of the dead thus, the new regime means to remind South Vietnamese communists to always remember and appreciate those who lost their lives for the country's so-called liberation from *"đế quốc Mỹ và ngụy quyền Saigon"* (U.S. imperialists and their puppet Saigon regime). It also serves as a reminder to the U.S. of the "crimes" it committed against the Vietnamese people. Having suffered more than one million deaths in their war against "U.S. aggression," the Vietnamese communists are wary of their former foes despite the establishment of diplomatic relations between the two countries. These countless gravestones, the revisiting of the Vietnamese mass media of painful war-related issues such as the Mỹ Lai massacre and Agent Orange are meant to appeal to the American conscience and to hold the U.S. responsible for what it did to Vietnam during the war.

Since their 1975 victory, the communists have made a concerted effort to eradicate all the vestiges of the old regime. Most streets and schools are renamed; southern music, art, film, and literature are stigmatized as "decadent" and banned; commemoration of former South Vietnamese soldiers killed in the war is prohibited. I can't help thinking of the monuments and memorials commemorating the Confederates in U.S. southern states I happened to see in my previous trips. National reconciliation began immediately after the Civil War, starting with the North's withdrawing its troops from the South after its victory. Southerners were free to mourn their dead and participate in the Reconstruction. In short, the American South and its people weren't despised and humiliated because of their defeat.

***

March 4th-6th

After helping us get ready for our commemoration ceremony for my father, the abbot invites me to sit down and have tea with him. As a spiritual man, he candidly offers his criticism of the government's treatment of the war dead—those who died on the wrong side and those who are recognized by the government as war martyrs. Expounding the Buddhist view that all people, regardless of their political conviction, are equal after death, our monk argues that one million men and women who died for their South's independence and freedom should be properly recognized one way or another. As for the government's war martyrs, erecting monuments and memorials in their honor isn't enough. To find permanent rest for their souls and to help them pass into the Pure Land or Paradise, it's important that the government regularly have requiems held for them. Unfortunately, the old monk sadly observes, because the communist regime still holds an unfavorable stance vis-à-vis the defunct South, the dead aren't redeemed yet.

I wholeheartedly agree with the old abbot. Monuments, memorials, and mausoleums will be merely stones unless they inspire us to understand and appreciate the scribes written on these and provoke and sustain our loving memory of those who sacrificed for their noble cause. Because memorials are created for communal sharing, it's up to the present community and its successive generations to retrieve, interpret, and remember this discourse of the past. Would these monuments erected in the land of the defeated be able to gain proper communal sharing from a people who are still bitter about their loss of the war, whose fallen heroes are unrecognized and humiliated (the new regime calls them "soldiers of the puppet regime")? Because communal memory is a voluntary act, an activity that enables identical souls to remember their collective past, it can't be imposed on those who have nothing in common with the winner's culture or ideology. The war was so long and so brutal that it might take several generations in the South to recover. By that time the words, emblems, symbols carved on the monuments and memorials would have come off and nothing would remain but bricks and stones!

Nothing preserves history better than communal memory. The act of remembering isn't performed by one individual. It involves an entire community which not only commits itself to protecting the past but will pass the torch to the posterity. Rulers come and go, but history stays with the people because it *is* the destiny they've chosen for their country and because it represents the values and beliefs and principles that have inspired their struggle to protect their national identity. Those who usurp the country's history, take it into their own hands, and pursue their selfish purposes don't deserve a place in our memory. The monk at Long Tuyền Temple, a China scholar, cites Qin Shihuang as a notorious example of a tyrant whose folly and *hubris* kept him from realizing the universal law of impermanence. He thought he could conquer death with his might and vast resources. He couldn't find the elixir of immortality, his terra cotta army buried with him (a symbol of his attempt to continue taking history into his hands even after death) turned out to be mere stones!

***

As we follow the abbot to the temple's cemetery to participate in my father's commemoration ceremony, I am struck by an extraordinary scene: the small cemetery is abuzz with life. There is a family gathering at each of the burial sites. The monk tells me today is the *Thanh Minh* (Chinese *Qinming jié*, Tomb Sweeping Day, which can be roughly translated as Ancestors' Appreciation Day). People clear away weeds from their deceased relatives' tombs, touch up their tombstone inscriptions, burn incense, and make offerings of foods and libations to their spirits. It is a nice custom, a great way to remember the dead and keep family ties strong.

I am grateful to Nga for selecting this important date to commemorate the anniversary of my father's death, to "sweep" his tomb. Living in America for such a long time, I forget most of the cultural customs that are important to his memory. I feel bad about it because, as my father's heir, I was supposed to maintain this tradition. Had I not left Vietnam to pursue my study in the States, or had I returned home immediately after finishing my study, I would have by this time completed my term in a so-called "re-education" camp and could have been here at this moment with all my family—my wife, my children, my grandchildren—to pay tribute to my late father like everybody else today in this cemetery. To think that I am here by chance, not by choice, with no other relative but my wife, to sweep my father's tomb (do not count on my American offspring to do it after my death!), and that this could be my last time to honor his memory in this cemetery.

I envy native Vietnamese (not transplanted ones like me and other Vietnamese Americans) for their way of remembering their deceased loved ones. Each family I see today must have more than one generation participating in the *Thanh Minh* rites. The tradition continues year after year, generation after generation, with descendants exhibiting the same touching devotion to their forebears. The inscriptions on the tombstones will take on a lot of significant meanings after they are carved into the hearts of future generations. They may interpret their ancestors' stories differently, but they all will remember them permanently, respect them greatly, and love them dearly.

Speaking of monuments both as insignias of the past and stimuli and preservers of communal memory, I cannot help thinking again of the vision that briefly came up in my sleep as my bus was passing through Tennessee, the location of William Faulkner's legendary Yoknapatawpha County. Why did that vision occur? How could I, a foreign student who was not quite familiar with American history, "remember" that American past of slavery if it had not been because of the fiction of the Old South I had read in my graduate years? Monuments serve to help us understand, appreciate, and remember the past, but when the markings on the monuments come off and monuments become stones, it is literature that protects the past and makes it meaningful and important to future generations. In literature, the past is not merely remembered but *is* creatively remembered because the act of remembrance is performed through a polyphony of voices, each complementing the other by offering its community of tellers and listeners its own version of the past. Language—the literary text—thus transforms what would have been dead stones into living monuments testifying complex personal and social events that can live on forever in our hearts and minds. History cannot perpetuate without literature.

One of the functions of literature is to validate human experience and history. Through reading literature, we learn to be skeptical about false claims to glory by usurpers, to care more about the unfortunate, the victims of political greed and folly, to remember and be grateful to those who fought and died for their worthy cause but are insulted and humiliated by the victors. This bears upon our way of reading literature. When reading *The Iliad*, we do not rejoice over the victory of the Greeks, but we are saddened by the destruction of the Troy, by the slaying of Trojan men after their defeat and the forcing of their women into becoming sex slaves by the Greeks; in short, we remember the fallen heroes rather than the vanquishers. Thanks to Faulkner, not only is his defeated South redeemed, but its agrarian values shame the victorious money-driven North. With the increasing popularity of Faulkner's fiction and the emergence of southern modern literature. the Old South is getting more and more important in the American imagination. In brief, in memory, imagination (for lack of adequate historical information), and love, the vanquished warriors in the fiction of Homer and Faulkner are resurrected and assume their tragic but heroic dimensions. The best literature, as seen in the work of Homer, Tolstoy, and Faulkner, is the literature of sorrow and suffering, and no subject stimulates inspiration in writers better than wars. The horrors and ravages of Vietnam's latest war, especially specific tragic events such as the spring 1968 offensive, the April 1975 military debacle in the Central Highlands, the boat people exodus, which still bring pain and shock to many Vietnamese of the lost South at home and overseas, are a unique experience that should be represented and preserved in literature. Just as Faulkner and U.S. southern writers mourn their antebellum tradition destroyed by Yankee civilization, and Claude Simon evokes the tragic rout of France's army at the advance of Nazi troops, so Vietnamese writers, especially those originally from the South, should try to tell the blood-and-tears stories of their country's most grievous ordeal. Their concern should not be a literature of celebration and jubilation, but an enduring literature of grief and suffering that will occupy an important place in the memory and imagination of many Vietnamese generations to come.

During the three-day commemoration ceremony at my father's tomb site, I experience something extraordinary. There are moments when I drift to a region that is so serene, so peaceful that I forget all my anxiety, suffering, and weariness. There is a tug at my heart, but it is the spasm of boundless joy. I am back at my childhood home in Dalat, Vietnam is at peace, my family is intact, and I am an innocent happy-go-lucky little boy. Under the influence of the *Thanh Minh* (literally, pure brightness), it feels like experiencing a resurrection from a long winter of sorrow. The celebration of the ceremony in this small cemetery in the serene springtime, the monks' melodious chanting punctuated by the sounding of their gong and wooden bells, my joy at being at my father's tomb site at last, all resonate within me, purify my heart and my soul. This is my father's world. I do *not* fear death. Not at all! I have been wearied mentally and physically for too long. It would be nice to lie down and rest by my father's side. I am going to ask Nga when I die to bring my ashes home and scatter them over my father's tomb so I can be with him forever.

The ceremony ends at noon. The abbot invites us to have lunch with him. There is plenty of time for us to board the train to get to Huế in time to visit my parents-in-law's tombs. Tomorrow we will catch a Vietnam Airlines flight to return to Saigon early in the morning. My appointment at the University expires in May, and I am expected to resume my regular academic duties at my home institution in the States by late August. I am not sure I could be back for another visit.

My last three days at Long Tuyền Temple's cemetery left me exhausted. On the plane, no matter how hard I try to get some sleep to have enough strength for a long day at school tomorrow, I just cannot do it. Never did I feel such a great loss. When leaving my father and my family twenty-eight years ago, though weighed down with sorrow and worry, I cherished the hope of returning home and reuniting with them. Now that Father is dead and my home was taken, returning to a place that used to belong to me only intensifies my loneliness and sorrow. What I was experiencing during the last three days puts my Vietnam stay into perspective. While trying to fulfill my responsibilities as a Fulbright scholar, I see the sojourn as a quest for my lost past with the dead as my people. There is not enough room in my head for all of them. In addition to my loved ones and those I had known for a great part of my life who had loved me or had mistreated me, there are those who were my countrymen and countrywomen who had died for their country and for the ideological tenets they rightly or wrongly believed in. I have lived long enough to witness the indifferent passage of time and realize the futility of worldly glory and honor. As a great part of my memoir is autobiographical, I cannot help jotting down a line about those who had made my life miserable when they were living. They have long gone into emptiness, so there is no use in condemning them. Nor should I hold them responsible for what had happened to me and for my permanent exile. Those who made me suffer are lying somewhere. I am no longer their victim, nor do I bother about them. I would rather concentrate on those who loved me but whom I did not love enough when they were living. It was them who helped lessen my misfortune, strengthened me morally, enriched my experience, and made me who I am today.

Two weeks after my return from my visit to my father's tomb in Hội An, I am notified today (March 28th) by Dr. Tài that, at the request of the English Department and the College, the Fulbright Program has renewed my appointment for another term. After consulting with Nga, I will write my institution in the States and ask for an extension of my sabbatical until next January.

(As I am revising this section of my memoir, I learn with great sadness of Dr. Nguyễn Văn Tài's premature passing. He was an administrator and academician I greatly admired. Had he been living today, the American Studies program he was passionate about could have borne fruit.)

We both are ecstatic. One year's stay is not enough to make up for our agelong absence from home. There are many places to visit, many things to do before we return to the States permanently. Nga also wants me to continue helping my students, whom we both have come to love. The other reason is very important. One year of living here is long enough for me to learn about the new Vietnam. There is no need for me to keep a diary anymore. As I do not have much time left, I need to concentrate on the theme of my book, my search for the past. I need to continue searching for it in Dalat, my childhood hometown, where I first lost my paradise. I also want to explore places I might have set foot on in my long, long past. My past is here in this country and nowhere else. Every minute of my remaining stay counts. Everything, every being I come across, relates to my past or is suggestive of it. All *are* immensely valuable to me.

The other day while doing grocery shopping with Nga at an open market in the neighborhood, as I shared earlier, I saw a rooster whose leg was tied by a string to his owner's vending area. Because the bird stood immobile in a very resigned manner, in my journal entry I compared him to my people's desperate condition. Curiously, when that rooster's image resurges in my mind today, along with my excitement about the opportunity to stay longer and my overwhelming love of Vietnam, it takes on a positive meaning. It stimulates my memory of the same rooster we raised with other birds in our country house premises in Quảng Bình. I can now see him cocking his head, puffing out his plumed throat as he emits a cry of absolute vainglory. This rooster—and subsequently other ones I saw at home in my childhood and adulthood—awakened me in the wee hours when I traveled with my father in the countryside. Whatever sight I encounter here in my native land is filtered through the lens of my memory and imagination to become a metaphor for a paradise I once had.

The past can light on people and things that strike you as familiar as though you have seen them somewhere. I habitually buy newspapers in the morning—and occasionally magazines—not always to read (Vietnamese newspapers carry nothing "newsworthy," but only print stories that have been censored by the government), but to collect them as mementos of my stay here. As if to compensate for so many losses I have suffered due to my long exile, I am accumulating as much as I can of anything that is related to Vietnam, knowing nevertheless that I cannot take everything with me back to the States.

After dinner, I rush to my favorite newsstand on the corner of our street to get some newspapers that I forgot to buy in the morning. Nightfall. A light rain taps on my head and shoulders. In the streetlights and under the pressure of the heavy traffic, the air feels more congested than it does during the day. There is a twist in my heart. Things suddenly look painfully familiar, so close to me and inseparable from me that I feel they are part of me, belong to me though I am a stranger here. I do not feel threatened by this place at all. It has been almost forty years since I left Vietnam, but tonight I recognize it easily and my love of it has never diminished.

The newspaper vendor seems amazed by my odd demeanor. Rather than acting like a casual customer who pays for his stuff and then leaves, I stay and strike up a friendly conversation with her. I even gaze at her as I talk. She looks aghast, not realizing that the voice I hear tonight when she invites me to browse her magazines strikes me as poignantly familiar and dear, like the voice of a lost sister or a lost sweetheart. My desire to renew contact with my past and my native land through this woman and this city overpowers me, so much so that I can recognize them all in the person of this woman and this place. I talk with her with great ease, relishing hearing my own voice and her voice. I hear the same newspaper vendor whose voice I had heard, see the same rain and traffic on a Saigon street I had seen thirty-five years ago when I was a teacher at Pétrus Ký High School. The past at this *moment délicieux*, to borrow Proust's phrase, is back right before me and inside of me. It overwhelms the present and nullifies the debilitating inhibition that estranged me from this place upon my first arrival.

I walk home, relishing the taps of the light rain and the compressed buzz of the night traffic. The plangent din triggers an amalgam of things—sounds, images, impressions, feelings—coming en masse out of the air and from inside of me, nebulous, unorganized, robust, full, oppressive but ethereal and soothing. I flow with the buzz, forgetting my way to our residence. This is the past I thought I had lost before returning home, a past made up of sounds that I heard at this hour in a late evening in 1960 when I was leisurely sauntering on this same street after getting off an express train coming from Nha Trang. This is the same past that came upon me the other day when I saw the children merrily play on the school playground when I was going to the college campus to teach, or when I am wakened by the cry of a food peddler in the stillness of night every day in my neighborhood. In the still night, that same delightful noise which has been lying dormant in me for the last forty years comes back to life, carrying me on its wings to my faraway past and the forgotten time. My paradisiacal past relived, coalescing with the pleasurable present, blocks completely my consciousness of the traumatic years after the loss of South Vietnam. What fascinates—and confuses—me is the physical world I am inhabiting and the remembered/recreated one are fused into one, so much so that I cannot tell which is real and which is imagined. Could it be that my romantic father had instilled in me, his eight-year-old son, the mysterious meaning of Chuang-tse's butterfly dream parable? Does this virtual enduring present mean that I will soon capture my lost paradise during the remainder of my stay here?

In *Swann's Way*, Proust uses a vase as a metaphor for the hiddenness and retrievability of the past. "An hour is not merely an hour; it is a vase full of scents and sounds and projects and climates." Throughout *À la recherche*, one of Proust's recurrent themes is echoic memory—sounds retained for a long time, when remembered, can evoke emotionally charged memories. But our past is not resurrected only with its sounds. It is brought back to life simultaneously, as Proust would say, with its colors, shapes, and images. As transient as it can be, sound nevertheless is very important to an exile like me who lost everything at home and who can rely on nothing to search for his lost time except the distant echo of the past.

PARADISE REGAINED

Dalat

Dalat University through the Vietnam Fulbright program invites me to give a week-long workshop on U.S. literature to its English faculty. Though Nga and I have planned to travel around the country in the summer, I decide instead to accept the invitation. Visiting the place where I was born and spent my early childhood, the starting point and end point of my search for lost time, the genesis and completion of my book, is a golden opportunity for me. I cannot help waiting for my return to that dreamland.

Most passengers who travel with me in the bus are Western tourists (I hear their conversation in English, French, and some other languages I do not understand) who probably are going to Dalat for sightseeing. Judging by their look and dressing, they must belong to a colony of Westerners living in an inexpensive area on Phạm Ngũ Lão Street adjacent to Bến Thành Market. Vietnamese lump the group into a common appellation *"Tây Ba lô"* (Western backpackers), so called because of their modest belongings and living accommodations. They want to live as economically as they can to save money for traveling. Dalat is part of their exploration of Vietnam after the war.

I am going to Dalat not to do sightseeing, but to teach and take some time off to search for my past. I want to see if visiting my birthplace could help me regain my lost paradise, the early years of my childhood, to complete my book about the quest. Some forty years ago, after graduation from college, I visited Dalat to get a "feel" of my childhood city. Although being back at my birthplace brought back wondrous memories, I did not feel that the past and my remembrance of it was something I could live without. Like most college students in the late 1950s, I was infatuated for a while with the popular corrupt form of French existentialism, foolishly embracing its philosophy of *carpe diem*. After I got married, working hard for my future and my family took precedence over everything. Young, practical, optimistic, and busy, I did not care as much about the past as about my future. The past that I had cherished so much in my boyhood after my leaving Quảng Bình grew dimmer and dimmer in my memory.

My dream-building, as mentioned earlier, ended abruptly on March 26th, 1975, after news of the loss of Huế reached me in America. The comfortable life I had enjoyed as a graduating doctoral student immediately turned into an interminable nightmarish present after I lost contact with my family. This lasted a few years. Though later I was able to resume normal activities, I lost forever my ability to dream. I was involved in research and professional activities to improve my credentials to keep my job rather than to satisfy my desire to become a good scholar. I developed a tendency to shun human contact (except in the classroom, where I strove to be a friendly teacher) and a propensity for taking refuge in memories. The more I live with memories, the less I pay attention to the present and the better I remember the past.

March 1975 marked not only the end of my future but the coming full circle of a person's life, as far I am concerned. It did happen too early for a person like me, who was in his prime physically and intellectually. In America, it is not unusual for a senior citizen to talk about his dreams and to continue making plans for his future.

I wake up from a doze when the bus stops for a break at Bảo Lộc, about 110 kilometers from Dalat. Located at the foot of the Langbiang Highlands, this little town enjoys a year-round cool atmosphere and green landscape. We get off at a very busy shop which carries a wide selection of highland products like coffee and oolong tea. To aid our selection, we are invited to sample each of the brands on display. While Vietnamese customers busily go about their shopping, noisily haranguing with the sellers, my fellow passengers, the *Tây Ba lô*, quietly sip their tea or coffee, casting their curious looks at this interesting part of the world.

About an hour later, our bus begins climbing a route winding through a pine forest. The trees are tall, serene, and majestic in contrast with the dense, wet, awe-inspiring tropical rainforest of the lowlands below. In front of me is the blue Langbiang mountain range, half hidden in white clouds. It is a little after noon in early June, and yet it is so cool and pleasant. We must be at the outskirts of Dalat. *Before the Indochina war, the boy often traveled with his father all the way from Dalat to Quảng Bình by train, the only means of long-distance travel in the 1940s. Traveling from Dalat to the coast was very precarious. Because the slope was steep, a chain connected to the rail was used to reinforce the train's brake system. The train inched very slowly and cautiously, making everybody apprehensive but not the boy (living under his father's protection, he always felt safe, so the idea of fear never occurred to him), who enjoyed watching the scenery recede backward as the train moved forward. He was particularly thrilled when the locomotive started its winding course and gradually exposed all the carriages to view, making the entire train look like a giant boa squirming through the picturesque misty mountain landscape. As the train was chugging down the precipitous Langbiang Pass, it occasionally submerged in a sea of clouds. It felt like the train was floating in the air. Before the train arrived in Tháp Chàm, he had fallen sound asleep. He woke up when the carriage jerked forward. It meant that the train arrived at a major station and new carriages were being attached to it. The jerk was powerful, but the sound it produced was so soothing that he was rocked back to sleep. He vaguely heard his father's voice muttering "Ga Tháp Chàm" (Chàm Tower Railway Station). It is so called because it is located right at the foot of the only remaining Cham temple on the outskirts of Phan Rang City. Standing in a weed-grown area, the ancient tower in ruin evoked in the child the horrors of the nether world, the Chams' terrible curse on the Vietnamese for taking away their land. The boy opened his eyes and looked through the car's window. The tower's silhouette against the gray sky was moving slowly, and he knew that the train was rolling into the station. As soon as it stopped, an army of peddlers, most of them small children, scurried around, crying out their wares. They carried a small kerosene lamp which gave off just enough light for them to do a quick transaction with buyers from the train. The cacophonic commotion lasted less than ten minutes. As soon as the train whistled, signaling it was on the move again, the boisterous crowd fell into silence and rapidly disappeared into darkness like phantoms.*

These scenes of years past unfold in my mind like a silent film. I experienced them on all the train journeys I took with my father in my childhood. I enjoyed them but took them for granted, not knowing that these pleasurable moments were not to stay with me forever. Only when I grew older and understood the importance of memories did I realize that the past was inseparable from my identity. But no sooner did I begin to appreciate and value what I had taken for granted than the war broke out. Not only did my train journeys abruptly end because of the war, but as fighting raged and we had to flee for safety constantly, I lost my ability to dream about them. After I came of age and got married, work, family, and other practical matters left me no time to think about the lost world. When I came to America, the past became entirely irrelevant to me as my sole preoccupation was study. After March 26th, 1975, because I did not have a future to work for anymore, the past suddenly became alive and took over my conscious life. Not the past full of tender things like my train journeys, but the nightmare that began after the fall of Huế. It ended with our family reunion that occurred eight years after our separation, but its haunting presence will not go away until I catch sight of my birthplace today.

After twenty-eight years, the nightmare ended but only after I had lost my father and everything that was dear and important to me—my home, my country, my life dreams. As I sit on this bus taking me to my birthplace, images of my lost paradise, with which my train journeys are connected, surge in me. They rise like waves, one coming after the other, sending a tremor coursing through my body. The bus is slowly climbing the last steep road before arriving at its destination. Opening wide the window and closing my eyes, I inhale the scents of the Langbiang mountain and listen to its rustling pine trees. Images of my childhood hover before my eyes, getting clearer and clearer in my mind. I feel a tingle of joy and excitement mixed with stinging pain, and I know what it means. It is my body's initial contact with the reawakening past, like a harp that vibrates when its strings are plucked by a phantom artist. But I just perceive the sounds and scents of the past; I have not immersed myself in the real past. Granted, the sounds and scents I now perceive are the same ones I perceived as a child, but this is because nature is unchanging rather than because I have fully recovered from my past. The people whom I loved and who loved me are not here anymore. Instead of the sheer pleasure and excitement that came upon me when I returned to Dalat in 1960, a poignant feeling of unassuageable sorrow and loneliness pervades me. I feel like someone who is about to relish the joy of being home when he suddenly realizes that he does not have a home anymore, that he's lost everything save his memories. Can I regain my paradise when what remains is a sum of thin echoes and vague fragrances, not powerful enough to help me face the strange world in the days ahead in this city?

The bus pulls into the driveway of a beautiful villa, and we get off in the pretty chilly, crisp air of a limpid sky that I recognize right away. I am met by an attractive girl who says she is from the Office of International Relations. I learn from her nametag that her name is Trần Thu Huyền (strangely, I feel she is not a stranger, though we meet for the first time, probably because we have the same family name and I am back in my hometown). I am taken to the campus in a Toyota where Thu Huyền says I will be staying during the workshop.

I am put in a pleasant room of a building overlooking stretches of lush vegetation with scattered handsome red cottages. Thu Huyền says the building before us was a housing facility for Dalat University's faculty before 1975 and is now occupied by the administration. A couple of hours later, Dr. Long, a very nice gentleman from the administration, comes to take me to dinner at a restaurant down the hill. Partly hidden amid sun-gilded gladiolus vines, the place has the elegance and tranquility of a French residential villa rather than a restaurant. As soon as we take our seat, the owner, an elegant-looking lady, comes over and greets us warmly. Judging the way they speak, Dr. Long seems to be a frequent guest here or at least he knows the owner very well.

A pretty girl takes our order. She addresses Dr. Long as "*Bố*" (Daddy). As I listen to them further, I learn that it is her way of showing that they are close to each other. I learn further that Dr. Long has a doctoral degree from Moscow University, lives on campus by himself, and frequently eats here. He is a nice man, a little quiet, but very thoughtful.

***

June 11th

After giving me a quick tour of the campus (there isn't much for him to show me because the campus is very small), Dr. Long takes me to see Dr. Đông, the university's rector. Despite his overseas training, Dr. Đông strikes me as a bureaucrat who's serious about carrying out the government's policy to the letter. He asks me to adhere strictly to the topic of my workshop, which is methods of teaching U.S. literature, and avoid discussing "politics" and "sensitive issues" by all means. (To appease their interlocutor in the face of a controversial issue, Vietnamese—and Asians—prefer circumlocution rather than straightforwardness. We're supposed to guess at his or her intent and faithfully carry it out. Thus, "politics" means "criticism of the government"; "sensitive issues" refer to those considered "taboos" by the government, such as Hồ's private life and the 1979 border war with China. Though I've lived in the States for a very long time, I'm quick to understand Dr. Đông's message.) Perhaps seeing shock or displeasure on my face, Dr. Đông tries to placate me by saying that Dalat's People Committee, which controls the entire citizenry's thought, including the educational system, isn't as "easy-going and relaxed" as Hồ Chí Minh City's rulers. He says that he highly values academic freedom and wants his institution to be free of political interference, but he has no choice.

I spend the rest of the day exploring the campus. The university is seriously downgraded. Except for the entrance, most buildings, streets, and the landscape obviously lack upkeep. Some new-looking residences are at odds with the general campus housing architecture. Further down the campus are stretches of tilled land ready for new planting. These things, as I recall, didn't seem to exist in my summer 1960 visit. Before the fall of South Vietnam, the University of Dalat was a Catholic institution run by a Jesuit priest, Father Nguyễn Văn Lập, who in a short period of time turned it into a first-rate private university. Located in a beautiful vast hinterland on the outskirts of the city with a year-round mild climate, the campus was an ideal spot for me to meditate on the past (the idea of searching for my lost time, nevertheless, didn't occur to me at that time).

***

Evening of June 11th

Have dinner at Langbiang restaurant and Hằng waits upon me again. Since the restaurant isn't busy tonight, Hằng has some time to chat with me. She tells me she was born in 1973 and her dream is going to college to study to become an elementary teacher. Had my daughter Đoan Nghiêm been living now, she would have been Hằng's age and would have been a teacher, too. Suddenly, there is a strong twist in my heart. *The little girl's parents were notified of the arrival of a new heart this morning, and preparations are underway for their daughter to undergo a heart transplant at Texas Children's Hospital tonight. They're both excited about the girl's chance of living a normal life after her long illness. The man instantly cringes with fear. While waiting to be taken to the operating room, the girl, who has been watching the cartoon channel all afternoon, suddenly switches to a documentary of Bruce Lee. To the father's horror, the girl's eyes are glued to Lee's casket at his funeral. She won't let go of it until the nurse comes and her mother explains everything to her, kissing and comforting her. When her speechless father holds her in his arms and she sees his tearful face, she wouldn't release her grip on him. She seems to know she isn't going to see her father again.*

That was the last time I saw my adopted daughter Đoan Nghiêm before her death at age 10. I saw her again only when she never woke up after her heart transplant. She never opened her eyes again after the fateful operation that killed my precious little one, disfigured her, transformed her from a beautiful smiling little girl into a horrible-looking little thing.

I didn't have the courage to tell my father at home when he was living that his granddaughter was dead. Nor could I bring myself to talk about my little darling until now, that is, fifteen years later. It was too painful to think about her, let alone write at some length about her. She wouldn't have died had I taken better care of her, had I not consented to that fateful surgery. Because my daughter got sick and died in America, she wasn't as lucky as her little aunt Như Cẩm, who looked like an angel when she drew her last breath.

***

June 12th-14th

Meet this morning with Ms. Lê Thị Thi, Dean of the Foreign Languages Department, and her staff. Ms. Thi is a Vietnamese academic administrator I really like. She's friendly, polite, and humble. She seems to have a genuine interest in British and American literature, which is rather unusual for an educator trained in the Marxist-Leninist tradition. Though I know I'm still being watched, I feel I'm appreciated for coming here to help *my* people, and that's very important to me. Seeing that Ms. Thi's Foreign Languages Department needs U.S. literature textbooks, I offer to donate all my teaching materials before I return to the States.

Although it has been twenty-five years since their victory, the communists still have difficulties in running South Vietnam's higher education system. North Vietnamese educators who were trained in the former Soviet Union and with a strong dose of Marxism-Leninism are unequipped to manage a system that followed a Western liberal arts tradition before the regime change. A notable example is Dean Hoàng in Saigon who censored my lectures because, being a hardcore Marxist, she didn't accept what she thought was American writers' "subversive and decadent thinking." Although Dean Thi is an exception, I think she must have trouble adjusting to an environment predominantly Christian not long ago.

My U.S. literature workshop meets in the afternoon today. The university makes it "important" by hanging a banner with the headline "U.S. Literature Workshop" in the auditorium with my name and academic title underneath. The participants include the English faculty and graduating seniors. I'm surprised to see Dr. Long in the audience. What's he here for if not to "watch" me and report any "wrongdoing" to the administration?

After my lecture, we have a short break (Dr. Long has already left). I'm surrounded by such an enthusiastic audience with a lot of questions about America. They have a great interest in their country's former foe, a "sensitive issue" that Dr. Đông has asked me to avoid discussing with the workshop participants. It's amazing that while the authorities are anxious to keep themselves in line, my colleagues here maintain such a relaxed attitude in all these matters!

As the workshop progresses and as we get to know one another better, I discover that my Vietnamese audience is more enthusiastic about the subject I teach than about what I was doing in the U.S. We adhere to a tight schedule trying to cover as many topics as we can, ranging from major currents in American literature to techniques of teaching American literature to Vietnamese students. Some workshop members even express their willingness to "sign up" for teaching American literature in the very near future, should such an opportunity turn up. What I find moving is that during my visit they take me into their confidence and share with me their concerns and aspirations. They tell me they lack many things: books for their library, scholarships for advanced study in the States, professional assistance in designing course syllabi, teaching tips, etc. They make me feel as though *I* represent America and have authority in all these matters!

***

June 15th-18th

State TV today (June 15th) says that the two Koreas are meeting to discuss the possibility of reunification. If we can trust Kim Jun Il's willingness to reconcile with South Korea, then the peninsula's reunification could avoid the kind of tragedy that happened to Vietnam. I feel jealous of the Korean people's fortune. Had Vietnam been reunified peacefully, I would've been home by now and wouldn't feel like an outsider, a "Vietnamese foreigner," as a friend who just returned puts it. I feel attached to the Vietnamese people because they represent the past I lost and wish to recover through them. They seem to sympathize with my desire to be part of them. But I feel there is something that holds them back and prevents them from warmly reciprocating with me, and this, I'm sure, has to do with my American training and my long stay in the U.S. My desire and attempt to connect with them, or to be exact, my pathetic condition, may provoke in them pity and resentment. Yesterday, a woman in the workshop invited me to her temple when she learned that I'm a Buddhist and was born in Dalat. I was thrilled when she told me that its name is Linh Sơn, a memorable place of my childhood. But when I started pouring out my fond memories of the temple, she looked aghast, apparently thinking something was wrong with me. How could a normal person talk about a place commonly known to everyone here so excitedly? It's difficult for her to imagine why a stranger like me could be so warm to them and their country. She doesn't seem to know that things she takes for granted are extremely precious to me. I thought I had lost Dalat forever, so getting back here is like regaining my paradise. Because this woman doesn't know my real purpose of coming here, she's shocked and dismayed at my strange demeanor. Had I told her that yesterday after getting out of the workshop, I went to Dalat's Central Market and spent all afternoon gazing at people doing their business, she would have thought I was insane. Yes, I might be insane, but this was because I was so excited to find in these folks that things and people of ages past became alive and were reconnecting with me albeit momentarily.

Had the communist takeover of the South not taken place or had the country been reunified peacefully, I would still write this book but with a different approach. I wouldn't have conducted my quest via this indirect route. I wouldn't have titled chapters of my book "Via Dolorosa." I would have returned home permanently, would have connected with my past—my deceased loved ones, the old earth that had nurtured and sustained me before I went into exile—directly and at leisure, fully confident that, like Marcel Proust, I would find it ultimately because of my commitment to searching for it until death. Nothing hurts me more than feeling like an alien or being treated as such in his own country! This disheartening truth I'm facing now may cause me to end my quest and return to America sooner than I planned.

***

June 19th-20th

I am taking some time off, trying to find traces of time past lurking somewhere on this campus. I don't have much time left for my search as the workshop will end in a few days. Since my arrival here, this is the first time I have found myself in the mood to devote all my time to what's important to me, the reason for my coming here. My visit is very pleasant, but because of my time-consuming association with the living, the present doesn't benefit my search much. I want to relive my past, connect with the dead, the absentees, whom I knew or might not know but who made my birthplace then a true paradise.

As I want to spend as much time as I can to explore Dalat, I divide my time between eating out and dining at the campus restaurant to be able to see Hằng to whom I feel close because she reminds me of my late daughter Đoan Nghiêm. I closely watched people I saw outside the campus and in various restaurants. I couldn't relate to any of them because they were all strangers to me. But having listened to the tone of people's voices for a while and now being able to detect their Dalat accent, I gradually feel they have a close affinity with me. In his study of the use of memory in Proust, Georges Poulet says that owing to "the silent work of memory," Proust's narrator Marcel can recognize "the known in the unknown." Echoic memory, given time to work, plays a key role in recapturing the lost past in Proust's novel. In *The Captive,* when participating in a concert at Mme. Verdurin's house, at first Marcel didn't know what was going on. Suddenly, right in the middle of Vinteuil's sonata. he recognizes *the little phrase* "glittering with glittering effects of sound . . . *recognisable in this new guise*" (emphasis added). Likewise, the babel of noises at Dalat Central Market I heard the other day and the conversation between the restaurant's owner and her guests I hear today release in me a Dalat like the genii that just got out of the bottle, a Dalat which was never lost but which reappears with full colors, accents, nuances that I *can immediately recognize*. Proust uses "sealed jars" as symbols of hidden gone years that are waiting for his narrator to uncork the release of the past.

***

My search for the past in Dalat gets more urgent as I don't have much time left here. Two days ago, I experienced a rare "privileged moment" when, by hearing familiar sounds, I could recognize my lost Dalat in these strangers. Today, I encounter another *"moment bienheureux"* when I stumble upon some cobblestones in the alley on campus and drift into a delicious moment of the past. Invoking the dead who were dear to me, like Uncle and Aunt Gia, Aunt Hoa, and particularly Như Cầm (before I return to Saigon, I plan to visit again the cemetery where my sister is lying somewhere) becomes an effortless, quick process for me now. All it requires is to return to the old earth where we lived our lives together. Their resurrection will be powerful, their images vivid and compelling, and I will be reliving for a short while my happy past. How exciting for an old exile to be in touch with the old earth again! Though I'm not yet at *Cây Số Sáu* (where my former home was), I already hear the echo of the past from that section of Dalat, which is five kilometers away. Not only are the currents of the earth connected, but all the souls of the past—*chị* Ngành, Kim, Uncle and Aunt Gia, Aunt Hoa, my sister Như Cầm, and all the people dead and absent, known and unknown to me—gather here with me. Because my people are phantoms, not in the flesh, they appear and vanish quickly. Images of the past appear constantly but intermittently, as if my memory was having trouble catching up with lost time, with lost opportunities due to my long absence from home. Images of the past are as fragile as my health, my human condition. Not shielded anymore by youth and idealism, which had made me take for granted the pleasure of remembering my past in my 1960 visit, and still recovering from the bout of serious illness I contracted two years ago, I become aware of my mortality, feeling more than ever the urgency to dig up my forgotten past to relive it as much as possible during the remainder of my stay.

My last day at this campus is overwhelming. The Foreign Languages Department throws a farewell party for me today (June 23rd). I'm given a bouquet of flowers and gifts and invited to come back later to help the university and students. I'm moved by Dean Thi's expression of her appreciation on behalf of her faculty and staff that I find very sincere. I feel good to hear her praise my academic credentials (it is rare for a communist official to sing the praises of someone who was trained in the South Vietnamese and American systems) as well as my "patriotism" shown in my "willingness to come all the way from America to help Vietnam." I was greatly touched when, in her speech, the dean said that she hopes I will return to Dalat to live because I was born here, and it was my former hometown. (Dean Thi's mention of Dalat strikes a chord of wistfulness in me. It isn't easy to realize the dream, though it seems simple enough.)

In the evening I'm taken to a banquet given by my workshop participants in a luxurious restaurant. It's very kind of them to go out of their way to treat me that way, but it's also a Vietnamese custom, as I've seen in Hồ Chí Minh City, to honor foreign guests sumptuously despite the host's modest budget. Again, I'm showered with various gifts. I know it costs them a lot of money to put together this event for me, but since it's a social custom, declining it would hurt my hosts' feelings. It's their way of showing me their appreciation, helping me remember them, not an effort to seek any favor from me. If I was awkward enough to blurt out a crude remark like "Thank you so much, and I'll reciprocate someday," as is an American custom, I would hurt their feelings. Reciprocate their kindness I will have to, but I will do it in a more tactful manner. I'll give their Foreign Languages Department all my books I have in Saigon before I return to the States. I'm determined to do whatever I can to show them my gratitude for making me feel like I *am* a member of their large family rather than a suspicious *Việt kiều* who needs to be watched.

When Thu Huyền comes to take me on a tour of Dalat, I tell her that I want to move out to a hotel and stay a few more days to explore more of my birthplace and former hometown better. I want to be on my own, in my privacy, on this so-called pilgrimage to the land that used to be my paradise. At the same time, I want to see the attractions of the city that I heard much about but did not have a chance to see for myself because I left Dalat when I was so young, so I applaud Thu Huyền's recommendation that I stay in a small hotel in Cây Số Sáu.

Bảo Đại's summer palace, according to the local tourist agency, is one of the city's great attractions. Vietnam's last French-educated emperor spent most of his time in this famous resort city enjoying himself before going into exile. The palace enjoys a fantastic panoramic view, but royal objects inside are scarce, probably because of looting. An admission fee is charged for viewing the palace-turned-museum, though there is nothing worth seeing here.

After seeing the former royal palace, I don't want to explore the city anymore. It is hard to find anything here that can help me remember Dalat as the city of my childhood. Maybe like Huế and Saigon, Dalat has changed so much since the communist takeover, or maybe I didn't get to see much of Dalat during my last visit and therefore was not aware of the change. I can't help asking myself this question: if Dalat isn't the city of my childhood, my paradise, the purpose of my quest, then why did I fall into a quasi-trance when hearing the whispering pine forest upon my arrival in its suburbs? This so-called cataleptic phenomenon is the *moment bienheureux* Proust speaks about when his narrator tastes a madeleine dipped in tea and recalls Combray, his childhood hometown. Like Marcel's Combray, my Dalat is *not* dead; it just lies hidden inside me and waits for, as Jorge Luis Borges has observed about Proust's *The Captive*, "a proper, unsuspected stimulus" to revive.

Now that the workshop is over and I can put behind me all its constraints—lectures, contacts with the workshop's participants and the administration, Dr. Đông's request for observing political correctness—I want to be alone to reacquaint myself with my old paradise. I don't know how much I will be able to accomplish in this endeavor because I'm running out of time and my remembrance is haphazard and erratic. But this project is something I can't live without.

***

My hotel is on a hilltop. Thu Huyền points to an area with little red cottages interspersed with row after row of green beds of vegetation and says it is Cây Số Sáu. There are more houses now than in 1960 when I visited the Gia family, but these neat, unbroken, and lush green rows of vegetation strike me as achingly familiar. There is a sharp squeeze in my heart when, upon Thu Huyền's pointing, I glance at a white hill facing the hotel and glittering in the afternoon sun that she says is the city's cemetery. It's here that my sister Như Cẩm was buried but I couldn't find her grave during my last visit. The past must be lurking around here, and I will have to be confronted with it in no time.

The same sensation that overcame me when I first got off the bus and set foot on Dalat a week ago is returning to me, except that it's getting more intense. I feel and see and hear sounds and images of the past not only rising inside me but also pouring out on me from the air, the earth, the landscape, and objects around me, uninterruptedly and uncontrollably. They must have been accumulated and repressed for such a long time and are under pressure to burst out! A mild tremor flutters through me, perhaps in a combined attack of neuralgia and neurasthenia. Standing out in the mass of recovered images are the dead—Như Cẩm, *chị* Ngành, Uncle and Aunt Gia, Aunt Hoa. Even my parents and my little girl Đoan Nghiêm who were buried in separate places assemble here. It's like a family reunion to me. People, objects, things, events, landscapes also compete for emergence, though not as sharply—the *montagnards* with their sad faces silently, resignedly filing past my childhood home on their way to town, my coming out at night to chant a mantra I had memorized from a Chinese book written in the same vein as *Arabian Nights* in an attempt to summon the genii to my service, my family eating lunch with the old abbot of Linh Sơn Temple where I saw a giant tortoise that was said to return to pay its respects to the spirit of the temple's founder on his death anniversary. Compressed with many long years and months, the excavated past explodes into my consciousness, its attack seizing me, penetrating the core of my body and soul, making me feel dizzy, making me feel the loss of the sense of time. No sooner is an old scene about to vanish than a new one overtakes it, and the process continues *ad infinitum*. I feel its power, its weight pressing on me, but I can't articulate it. I close my eyes to feel, hear, listen to my beloved past—my beloved ones, my beloved land—coming back to life.

In my quest for the past, my beloved people are those who are long dead or absent. Finding them means finding my past. After so many years, I have now come to realize that the past is not lost but is at my fingertips, for the people whom I loved and who loved me are still around and can be invoked instantly. Just as the earth—Dalat and its landscapes—is, remains unchanged and cannot be destroyed, so are my people not subject to the law of mutability. The dead are not gone forever, but they lie dormant on this land, nurtured and sustained in their invigorating sleep by the earth until I return to excavate them for our reunion.

The dead, when invoked, bring back with them their world—my lost world—with its full colors, imagery, sounds, and scents. Remembering heals our traumatized mind by enabling us to dwell on our pleasurable moments and shut off those marked by suffering and sorrow. I vividly remember the time when my sister was living, not when she drew her last breath. The air raid alert that sent *chị* Ngành, me, and school children rushing to the shelter was a terror, but I only recall a sweet *chị* Ngành, my beloved sister-figure, who was holding my hand in hers as she led me to safety. When I remember her today, a most delightful sensation akin to the thrill of first love arises. The entire process of reliving the past involves involuntary memory, as I am making no mental effort to recall and dig up the past; it just comes out from the recesses of my soul spontaneously and unobtrusively. When that blissful state ceases because I am exhausted or consciousness interferes, then another past event immediately arises and plunges me into the next bout of reverie.

Being back in the country where the only people I knew are long dead or absent and which, especially the young generation, belongs to a regime we South Vietnamese fled twenty-five years ago, at first, I found myself a total stranger and a lost soul. Only now, when I am *here* in my birthplace, do I clearly understand the purpose of my quest. It's the past world and its people—the dead and the absentees—that I want to recover in this trip home. It's easy to find this world because its people are the dead, that is, those who are recognizable, familiar, precious, and important to me. I can relate to them and feel at home with them. Invoking them and their world means invoking my former self, my darling cohort. I see *me*, the little boy, as having his most pleasurable time in their company. In his pristine world, he knows only joy and merriment, entirely free from problems and worries, unaware of the passage of time that made him wiser but was the cause of his suffering and sorrow. By reconnecting with my people in the past, I can emulate their ability to conquer time. Because they no longer exist in the temporal world, cease to be mortals, and are free of sorrow and suffering, their world and mine remain intact. When my past is conjured up, my sister is a two-year-old baby, my family the happiest one in the world, and me an innocent, happy-go-lucky seven-year-old boy.

I decide not to visit the cemetery. Forty years ago, I couldn't find Như Cầm's grave, so it's useless to try again this time. Nor do I want to try to find where Uncle and Aunt Gia, Aunt Hoa, Kim, and Ngành last lived. They, all the landscapes of Dalat in the past, and my entire childhood *are* within me, not to be found anywhere.

Before returning to Saigon, I want to see instead the pine forest not far from my former childhood home. I used to get there to daydream after reading. I used to follow the scents of my favorite characters—fictional and yet so real and fascinating. After my sister's death, I also often went there to cry because I did not want anyone to know that I was mourning her. (Besides my father, it was me who was visibly affected by the tragedy.)

Things I experience today are not different from what has existed in my memory ever since my childhood—the sky-high shady trees rustling in the breeze, the sharp fragrance of the pine forest, the pleasant feeling of peace and security to be home. Halfway to the top of the hill, as I turn around and look down at the city far below, I am overcome by a sensation of dizziness, exhaustion, and fear. My head swims, my feet tremble. Do I have enough strength and time to make it up there in my remaining life? Can I successfully recover a happy past that did not last, is getting more and more distant and remote, and is beyond the reach of my flimsy memory? My quest is often frustrated by interfering memories of a different past that haunts me, will not let go of me although I try to not think about it. Can I call this past "past"; that is, when it began after the end of my happy childhood, spanned some thirty-odd years of my life, and though it ended with my family reunion in America, it still reverberates and rankles in my consciousness like a fresh wound? In my sleep, and sometimes when I am awake, the same old terror comes back and attacks me with the same force, though less frequently than it did in the nightmarish years after I lost contact with my family. Because this "past" is *not* over, but only a permanent painful present for me, it isn't the purpose of my quest. Although being back in my birthplace allows me to catch a glimpse of my lost home, will this vision last? Is it powerful enough to counteract the trauma that has haunted me since I lost all my life dreams and went into exile, the cause of my return to search for this lost paradise?

Fatigue already sets in before I try to reach my old favorite hilltop. Across from where I am, Dalat cemetery, where my sister is lying, is glittering in the last daylight. She and the other dead who were dear to me have left this world of sorrow for a long time and are resting in peace. But tomorrow, I will have to return to Saigon and prepare for our trip back to America. I must live out my destined life of exile. I fear that this could be my last effort to regain my true paradise. I do not think I can do it again because I will be too old for such a formidable endeavor and paradise can be recovered only once in a person's lifetime. Nevertheless, while my quest for paradise is not totally successful (no quest for paradise is totally successful!), it allows me to exhume my past and enjoy it for a short while, which is more than I could hope for before this trip. Now that I have found my past with its landscapes, things, and people, I will take them back to America. It is like taking your country and people into exile with you. This will increase my nostalgia as it is a constant reminder of our uprooting. But all things considered, it's better than pining away in sorrow and guilt because you can derive consolation and even strength from those that were—and still are—dear to you.

EPILOGUE

Why I Write

Human beings are capable of survival in the face of great calamity, and I am no exception. I lost the will to live when Hué fell to the communist forces on March 26th, 1975, and I did not get news from home for several months. Later, an occurrence changed the course of my life. It was my narrow escape from death on Guadalupe Street when I was dragged out of the heavy traffic while I was still in a daze. The kind lady who saved my life might have seen me jump across the street while the red light was on.

Since the failure of that apparent suicide attempt, I felt the necessity to get out of the dark, long winter to live for my family more than ever. Instead of living like a normal person, I abandoned myself to the past. But it was a different past. It did not consist of delightful moments of my childhood (which Proust called *moments bienheureux*) that I evoked as a youth in Dalat, my childhood hometown; nor was it the ideal period during which I had worked hard for my future and my loved ones until March 26th, 1975. This period, which I had seen as my extended joyful present with flashes of a promising future, suddenly became a past full of painful memories. I did not have to evoke it; it just evoked itself. An accidental remembrance would unlock a floodgate of hurtful memories and despairing thoughts. Despite my desire to live like a normal person for my family's sake, dark thoughts crept in. This phenomenon occurs when a person is at the border between life and death. In the maze of my unconscious thinking, I picked life over death.

That is the genesis of my book. At the apex of despair when everything became meaningless and suicidal thoughts cropped up in my head again, I turned to literature. My companions were Hawthorne's Arthur Dimmesdale, Faulkner's Quentin Compson, and my own dark thoughts. I turned to them for solace because of my affinity with them, because, like them, I was torn by sorrow, remorse, and suffering.

This nightmarish past and the sorrow of my ensuing exile would have been the topic of my very "dark" writing hadn't something happened and changed my writing interests. In 1995, after the normalized relations between the two countries, I returned to Vietnam to visit my ancestors' tombs. A soon as my plane landed on Tân Sơn Nhất Airport in Saigon, I experienced a powerful sense of déjà vu. Familiar images surged in me, wave after wave, like river tides, followed by a sensation of something I had very well known before, something so peaceful and pleasurable. I knew this was the *real* past I came home to search for. It had taken me twenty years to make an unconscious longing come true. Now that my quest began in earnest, I wanted to have a balanced view of my past. I wanted to resurrect *moments bienheureux* of my childhood like Marcel, Proust's narrator, in *À la recherche du temps perdu*. Great literature, particularly the writings of Faulkner and Proust, shaped my life and my thinking. Reading Faulkner aggravated my loneliness, sorrow, and depression, but at the same time, it provided me comfort during the difficult years after 1975 because there was a compatibility between me and his dark characters. Meditating on Proust's writing and trying to decipher the meaning of his discourses about lost time alleviated my deep sorrow of exile, even bringing me joy—the joy of sorrow. Had I not I read Proust's novel, I could not have the joy of briefly regaining my paradise. By engaging in the quest for the past, I could understand better the meaning and value of suffering in my present life, as well as the bliss of my early years I did not appreciate because of my childish immaturity.

Now that my quest is over and I am back in America, I want to write about it. Because my past lapses into a dark, unconscious world, writing about it is like groping around in a labyrinth with nothing to guide me but a feeble consciousness weighed down with sorrow and remorse. Because my lost world is important to me and writing is the only way to keep it alive, I must write about it. Through writing, rather than through other avenues, I can organize my aberrant thoughts and set a pattern for my newly recreated past. With the words laid out on the pages of my book, I can talk to my lost world, hear its echoes, see its features, feel its presence at my own pace and leisure.

The magic of the written word is shown in Proust's novel. For a long time, this novel has brought me comfort and peace of mind. When reading Proust, I hear in my remote consciousness—and in my imagination and night dreams—from a faraway land and time the light taps of raindrops at the window on a winter night in my Quảng Bình home; they speak to me, ache me, make me feel terribly homesick but also wiser. Reading Proust makes me understand why even insignificant things have a mystery and a soul of their own with a perfect design in structure, musicality, and emotionality. Listening to the rain, as Proust observes, is like listening to a symphony. Like the rain I heard in the past, the world that belonged to me has a meaning, a life, a purpose, so plentiful, so rich, so fascinating but so difficult to grasp.

I must write my own book about this lost world. I cannot help it. I must bring out what I have kept inside for such a long time—my frustrated dreams, sorrows, and regrets. Susan Sontag says that writing is an obsession, "a very driven thing," but I think it is more than that. I must write myself out because it is my salvation, because *my repressed anguish must be voiced and heard.* Writing will also prevent me from forgetting my people—those who are dead and absent—by reminding me that they still exist and matter to me. Writing protects these people from oblivion, from the tyranny of time that threatens to plunge them into nothingness, into perdition. Condemned to eternal silence by the public, the dead would not be remembered if we did not tell their stories. Like the stars on the firmament, disparate but linked together, our fate is intertwined. Just as Proust talks about temporal and spatial interconnectedness in his attempt to recover the past when he writes, "I can hear the echo of great spaces traversed," so I feel that my ancestors' lives and mine are interwoven here and now and that I can hear them speaking to me. It does not merely involve remembering my father's sad face on that gloomy, overcast day of late August 1972 as I said goodbye to him (and saw him for the last time) to come to the United States for graduate study. It entails a lot more than that, just like weaving a multilayered tale of his life—his struggle to raise me and my two brothers as a single parent, his untold suffering and sorrow revealed in the sad poems he recited to lull us to sleep in his lap, his terse but heartrending writing about his mother (our grandmother), a young widow whose untimely death left my father and his younger brother orphaned so early in life. My father's tale also affects deeply my childhood, adulthood, and old age. I heard his chant of T'ang verses in his lap, and still hear them now with inconsolable sorrow. Similarly, at my birthplace in Dalat after more than five decades since her death, Như Cầm becomes alive in me. *Time stops, and I* am *a seven-year-old boy playing with his two-year-old sister.* The temporal-spatial interconnectedness that Proust speaks of causes me to imperceptibly switch from the childhood scene in Dalat to Đồng Hới the moment my father takes me to Trang's home to see her. She casts at me a sidelong teasing glance. Her haunting image follows me all the way to Huế. Many other people from home dead and absent, whom I have been carrying with me in the depths of my unconscious since I became an exile and since when I do not remember, suddenly rise to the surface of my consciousness, get involved with me again, demand my attention. You cannot remember them by just talking about them. *You must write about them. You and they will not find peace until you explain in your written words how they lived, suffered, and died for your sake.*

With the above thoughts, I have found rationale for my search, peace for my soul, and a model for my book. It is simply exhuming the past to love and remember. Like Proust's narrator, I come to realize that the past or Paradise *is* within me. After more than four thousand pages in which he deals with his quest, Marcel discovers that "all the infinitely unrolling past… I had been carrying [is] within me" and "this distant moment [is] still clung to me and I could recapture it, go back to it, merely by *descending more deeply within myself*" (emphasis added). This is what I have experienced and tried to achieve in my search. A truth is dawning in my mind. Since my past continuously resides in me (Faulkner says that "the past is never dead. It's not even past"), it does not necessarily mean that it can be evoked only in Vietnam, but rather I can relive it even in the land of exile. As I remember, when living in the States, I felt a spasm of sorrow when I incidentally hit upon something commonplace but excruciatingly painful. A distant thunder rumbling through the sky would quickly send me back to my ancestral home in a village in Quảng Bình. Instinctively and instantly, I would relive the haunting terror of a flood that left my father's older brother dead and our village in ruin. The peal of the bells in a parish church that I heard on an evening in Fairfax, Virginia, on my way home from teaching a class at George Mason University, I had also heard in the distant past in Dalat, Đồng Hới, and elsewhere in Vietnam. In the States, what I enjoyed most was when I was waking up to the rain on a summer night. Though it came down from the sky, it seemed to arise from the deep recesses of my soul. Its sounds were much comforting to me as they had been in a long, long past. So, it can be said that I must have carried them along with images and sounds of my native country when I came to America. Thus, the pain of my so-called exile was caused by my failure to descend deeply into myself to hear these sounds and see these images again, and to find out why they were so familiar and struck, though briefly, a chord of recognition in my heart. Only at the end of this quest do I realize that the past is incarnate in the present, for if it does not exist in me, why does it appear so familiar and lively when it resurfaces in my consciousness?

There is no doubt that I have been carrying in me this past with its sounds and images and subtle nuances since the formation of my consciousness. Proust says that his narrator Marcel is "already in existence" when he hears again the tinkle of the little bell of his Combray home. To be in existence means to be in the past, to be in life again. This sort of time stays within me, progresses through various stages of my life, even reaches far back into my long-forgotten years in a certain previous life. The search for Paradise is exciting and never ends. With this newly found faith, I am willing—and ready—to live out the remainder of my existence in America, continuing my unfinished quest of the past.

WORKS CITED

Aciman, André. Interview. "Six Writers on the Genius of Marcel Proust." *Literary Hub* 11 July, 2016.

Bakhtin, Mikhail. *The Dialogic Imagination.* Ed. Michael Holquist. Trans. Caryl Emerson and Michael Holquist. Austin: University of Texas Press, 1981.

Bảo Ninh. *Nỗi buồn chiến tranh* [The Sorow of War]. Westminster, CA: Hồng Lĩnh, 1992.

Bergson, Henri. *Time and Free Will: An Essay on the Immediate Data of Consciousness.* Trans. F. L Pogson. New York: MacMillan, 2006.

Blanchot, Maurice. *The Space of Literature.* Trans. Ann Smock. Lincoln: University of Nebraska Press, 1989.

Bùi Bích Hà. *Buổi sáng một mình* [Alone in the Morning]. Westminster, CA: Người Việt, 1989.

Faulkner, William. *Light in August.* New York: Vintage Books, 1972.

------. *The Sound and the Fury.* New York: Random House, 1946.

Herr, Michael. *Dispatches.* Harcourt Brace Jovanovich, 1982.

Khái Hưng. *Hồn bướm mơ tiên* [A Butterfly's Fairy Dreams]. Saigon: Nam Cường, 1952.

Morrison, Toni. *Song of Solomon.* New York: Alfred Knopf, 1977.

Moss, Howard. *The Magic Lantern of Marcel Proust.* Boston: Nonpareil Books, 1963.

Nhã Ca. *Giãi khăn sô cho Huế* [Mourning Headband for Huế]. Fort Smith, AR: Sống Mới. No date of publication.

Nguyễn Du. *The Tale of Kiều.* Trans. Huỳnh Sanh Thông. New Haven: Yale University Press, 1983.

Pinat, Etienne. "La Question du temps chez Maurice Blanchot." https://www.academia.edu /3798512/Pouillon, Jean. *Temps et roman*. Paris: Gallimard, 1946.

Proust, Marcel, *Remembrance of Things Past*. 2 vols. Trans. C. K. Scott Moncrieff and Frederick A. Blossom. New York: Random House, 1932, 1934.

Rose, Phyllis. *The Year of Reading Proust*. New York: Scribner, 1997.

Simon, Claude. *The Flanders Road*. Trans. Richard Howard. New York: Riverrun Press, 1985.

Trần Hoài Thư, *Thơ miền Nam trong thời chiến* [South Vietnamese Poetry During Wartime]. 2 vols. Plainfield, NJ: Thư Ân Quán, 2021.

Tran, Qui-Phiet. "The Chronotope of Memory and Time in Bảo Ninh's *Nỗi buồn chiến tranh* (The Sorow of War)." *Journal of Vietnamese Studies* 14.4 (2019).

Trịnh Công Sơn, composer. "Bài hát trên những xác người" [Sing on the Corpses]. Khánh Ly, perf. June 1, 2014. Video.

United States. Dept. of Defense. *The Pentagon Papers*. Washington: GPO, 1969.

Walker, Alice. *The Color Purple*. New York: Harcourt Brace Jovanovich, 1982.